THE PRUNING OF

Trees, Shrubs and Conifers

THE PRUNING OF
Trees, Shrubs and Conifers

by GEORGE E. BROWN

Second edition,
revised and enlarged by

TONY KIRKHAM

with a new Foreword by Roy Lancaster

TIMBER PRESS
Portland • Cambridge

First published in 1972 by Faber and Faber Limited,
copyright © 1972 by the estate of George E. Brown.

*All photographs in this second edition are by Tony Kirkham; all diagrams are by
Miss Audrey Barton, with the exceptions of Fig. 3a and parts of Fig. 5, which were drawn
by Tony Kirkham, and Fig. 3b, which is reproduced with the kind permission of the Oregon
State University Extension Service.*

Frontispiece: *Platanus occidentalis*, The New York Botanical Garden.

Published in 2004 by

Timber Press, Inc.

Timber Press

The Haseltine Building

2 Station Road

133 S.W. Second Avenue, Suite 450

Swavesey

Portland, Oregon 97204, U.S.A

Cambridge CB4 5QJ, U.K.

Printed in Hong Kong

Library of Congress Cataloging-in-Publication Data
Brown, George Ernest.
    The pruning of trees, shrubs, and conifers / by George E. Brown ; with a new
foreword by Roy Lancaster.--2nd ed, rev. and enl. / by Tony Kirkham.
        p. cm.
    Includes index.
    ISBN 0-88192-613-2
    1. Pruning. I. Kirkham, Tony. II. Title.
    SB125.B76 2004
    635.9'77--dc21   2003053707

This book is dedicated to my Wife

—G. E. B.

To my Mum and Dad,

for encouraging me into the

wonderful world of arboriculture

—T. K.

Contents

Foreword

Like many others whose horticultural career began with a local parks department, I have had a lifelong interest in the welfare of amenity trees. Eighteen years with a major tree and shrub nursery and ten years as curator of the Hillier Arboretum in Hampshire, England, further added to my appreciation of woody plants, and my travels in the world's wild places have familiarised me with tree and shrubs growing where *they* choose to rather than where man would like them to.

Trees and shrubs, but trees especially, growing in the contrived landscape of a park or garden or on a roadside or housing or industrial estate are often stressed by variable and sometimes downright unsuitable growing conditions, requiring remedial action to help them cope and achieve their potential. The bewildering variety of situations in which trees are expected to grow and the demands placed upon them by practical considerations such as safety regulations and under-ground services, not to mention the problems of vandalism, accident, storm and neglect, make it imperative that the knowledge and practice of tree care, especially planting and pruning, be maintained at the highest level for the benefit of present and future generations as well as for the trees themselves. The importance of skilful and sympathetic pruning cannot be stressed too highly, whether the subject be a tree, shrub, conifer or climber. The basic rules, if followed, are simple, sensible and ultimately rewarding.

It was a moment of huge significance when George Brown's *The Pruning of Trees, Shrubs and Conifers* was first published in 1972. I knew the man and I recall the great sense of gratitude felt towards him by those whose lives revolved around trees and shrubs and their care. George, a thorough and respected professional with an unrivalled knowledge of his subject, had produced a guide for profes-sionals and amateurs alike, and for the first time we had a comprehensive, prac-tical and up-to-the-minute account of one of gardening's oldest arts and crafts. Over the years his book has been reprinted several times and has continued to educate and instruct, attaining almost biblical status as a result. Tampering with a book held in such esteem was never going to be easy, but the advances made during the last thirty years in our understanding of a tree's reaction to damage and pruning—and the changes in pruning techniques and aftercare as a consequence—made the present revision an overdue necessity.

In my early years with a parks department I was taught the then-current methods of pruning trees, which involved cutting a damaged or unwanted limb flush with the mother limb or trunk; I was then encouraged to seal the wound with a proprietary tree paint. I even passed an Arboricultural Exam on the basis of these techniques. How times have changed. Today, the target method of pruning, which involves cutting the limb back no further than the collar, and the abandonment of so-called tree paint to seal wounds have revolutionised our approach to the subject and, in doing so, have greatly improved a tree's ability to recover and flourish. Since the first edition, many new plant introductions have been made to Western cultivation, and readers will be pleased to find some of the most important of these, *Sinocalycanthus chinensis* and *Heptacodium miconioides* among them, included here. Updated information on the important aspects of pests and diseases and pruning for wildlife is to be welcomed, as are the new colour photographs replacing the black-and-white originals.

Tony Kirkham, who "grasped the nettle" in providing the present revision, is a professional in the same mould as George Brown and is currently enjoying the same experience in managing the Kew Arboretum and its internationally important collection. His experience covers woody plants and their care in cultivation and, just as importantly, their origins and behaviour in the wild. It is a valuable and refreshing experience he brings to this revision of the pruner's handbook, and I feel sure that were he alive today, George would have found in him a companionable soul mate.

—*Roy Lancaster*

Preface

The subject of this opus, the pruning and training of trees and shrubs, is a surprisingly wide one, and the methods which are used are so diverse that no attempt has been made to deal with these in detail. In many cases there is a considerable overlapping with cultural methods generally, but in a book of this nature it has been found necessary to define boundaries where in actual fact none really exist.

As an example, no attempt has been made to explain the advanced and skilled techniques that are involved with the profession and art which is widely known as tree surgery. This is more a subject for a companion book, wherein the various operations involving the use of specialized equipment and often work at considerable heights can be explained in detail. In the hands of the unskilled person there is a considerable element of danger in heavy tree work, and it is a subject which cannot be taken lightly.

Having thus defined the limit in this direction, it should be emphasized that the work does explain principles of tree pruning in detail, and the reader is taken to the point where he knows what is needed and why.

The same is true also of other related subjects, for example with pests and diseases. The reader will find a chapter that deals with the subject in a very practical way, but only in so far as their control relates to pruning. In order to be practical the metric measurements (in m. and mm.) are approximate only.

—*George E. Brown*

When George Brown first wrote this technical book in 1972 he based all his work on observations that he made during his daily work in the arboretum at the Royal Botanic Gardens, Kew. Having such a wide reference collection of woody material upon which to practice and perfect the skills of pruning was the only way that anyone could ever, at that time, write such a definitive work on such a wide subject. There are other written works on the subject now in print, but still none to rival the work that George Brown originally did with this book. Today at Kew I continue to observe and monitor tree and shrub growth in the collections where he left off. With the mountains of technical information from research and the approved standards in the specialized areas of pruning from both the United States and here in the United Kingdom, I have attempted to bring this reference work up-to-date, using *RHS Plant Finder 2001–2002* as my main reference and the *Hillier Manual of Trees and Shrubs*, 2002 edition.

A major advance in the science of arboriculture since 1972 that has changed the course of practical arboriculture is target pruning, the positioning of the final pruning cut in relation to the branch bark ridge and the branch collar. I hope that the reasons for this are now more clearly explained and help the pruner, whether professional or amateur, to put this technique into good practice.

A second major change, should good target pruning be followed, is the restriction in the use of wound sealants or tree paints as a means of speeding up the healing process, allowing the tree to use its own natural defence systems.

Good pruning is an art and a science, and it is important to set the parameters with the subject before attempting to deal with the pruning. If we first ask the questions 'Does it really need pruning?' and 'What do we want from this plant? why? and how best can we achieve that goal without further detriment to the plant?', then it may be possible to prevent further unnecessary mutilation to our treescape. Couple pruning with modern proactive approaches to growing woody plants—such as correct initial selection, good planting and establishment techniques, decompaction programmes, feeding, mulching and relieving stress from modern environmental factors—and there is no reason why we should not see more healthy trees growing with dignity in our surrounding gardens and beyond.

—Tony Kirkham

Acknowledgements

Anna Mumford at Timber Press U.K. for her help and encouragement through this project.

The following dedicated staff at the Royal Botanic Gardens, Kew: Roger Howard, Tony Hall, Andy McClure and Jon Hammerton, for their help with photographs and information; Steve Ruddy, for the IT support.

Penny Allanson-Bailey at A&F Warehouse for the provision of tools and equipment in Plates 49, 50 and 51.

And finally Sally, Jennifer and Robert for putting up with me through the many hours spent at the screen.

—*T. K.*

Chapter One

The General Principles of Pruning

INTRODUCTION

Pruning is an operation that regulates and controls growth, flowering and fruiting, and with its aid the form of a tree or shrub is determined, often in its early years while still in the nursery.

The Need for Pruning

It is often asked why pruning should be needed, as it does not occur in nature. Apart from this not being absolutely correct, for twig shedding is found under natural conditions, there are several answers to this question.

In nature, the tree or shrub that is produced is not always a good shape. Growth may be typical of the species, but under natural conditions plants are often found in ecological communities and in direct competition with other plants which may be larger. The larger plants frequently overpower the weaker, which will die unless they adapt to these conditions. This is not so in the garden, where the weaker ones may be protected by pruning the stronger subjects, be they trees or shrubs.

Trees and shrubs are commonly planted by paths or roads, as hedges or screens, on boundaries and against walls. If not pruned, they may well outgrow their positions or impede vehicular or pedestrian traffic.

Development often involves farmland, natural woodland and even gardens, large and small. The trees and shrubs that are preserved and allowed to remain are left under an entirely different set of conditions. They are also likely to come very much under the public eye and are often in enclosed positions. To help them to conform to their new environment it may be necessary to correct their shape and control their growth by pruning.

Many trees and shrubs, as they develop towards maturity, accumulate a number of dead twigs and branches, which should be removed as they are unsightly and may hinder development or harbour pests and diseases. Diseased wood should also be cut out.

Most plantings are made with a definite type of tree or shrub, which from experience is considered the most suitable form of the particular species or variety. Their training to these forms often involves the adoption of a pruning system that may take several years to complete. The need for these forms has been universally recognised for generations and British Standards publications lay down very definite sizes and types for the nursery stock of many common species and varieties.

A number of shrubs are grown for their displays of flowers and in many cases they are special varieties which have flowers larger than usual and which do not occur under natural conditions. Pruning is a necessary part of their cultivation if the required standards of growth and blossoming are to be maintained. Without it and a complementary feeding programme, growth may be weak and the flowers small, though in some cases all that is needed is the systematic removal of seed heads or fruits.

Only with good pruning and training can the grace and beauty of trees and shrubs in summer and winter be fully realized. Good training and growth in particular show up very plainly with deciduous subjects in winter. A well-balanced plant improves most surroundings and helps to provide a restful scene for mind and eye but a mutilated tree or shrub is depressing and, in a modern urban setting, may be seen by thousands.

Some Basic Principles and Preconditions

It must not be assumed, however, that constant pruning is a necessity. Good nursery techniques require the provision of the best growing conditions in addition to correct pruning. Once a good plant has been produced and has been planted correctly in its final position with due regard for its particular needs, good growth will follow, provided of course that there is freedom from diseases and pests. Pruning is then often reduced to a minimum once the initial head or framework has been formed.

There are, of course, exceptions to this. Many shrubs are pruned annually for a particular reason, such as improved flowering, better foliage, etc. As a general rule, however, ornamental trees and shrubs, left to develop naturally in a suitable locality and environment, flower and fruit without regular pruning. Only a small proportion require the sort of attention normally necessary for economic crops, such as the apple.

Most important, pruners should know exactly what they are pruning for. They must have a thorough knowledge of the growth and flowering habits of the subject they are pruning and of the effects likely to be produced by the operations. Good judgement, skill and care are always needed, and conscientiousness and a love for trees and shrubs are essential. The care of tall or mature trees in particular requires considerable experience as it may involve a large outlay on heavy equipment.

It is important that the general public should learn to love and appreciate trees and have a broad understanding of the work and problems connected with them. Good trees and public health and safety go hand in hand, and the latter should always be an overriding factor in any decision involving trees.

PRUNING CUTS AND HEALING

The Natural Response to a Cut or Wound

Any wound made on a woody stem that is growing actively and is healthy brings about a response in healing. This is the result of a reaction to the wounding by the meristematic cells, which then divide very rapidly, especially during the growing season. These cells, which form a tissue referred to as cambium, are in a continuous cylinder just beneath the bark. By rapid division they form a circle of raised tissue and by continuous growth and division on the inside of the circle the healing growth or callus moves over the bare face of the wound which, as a result, gradually becomes smaller. Thus healing is a gradual process, the rate being directly related to the growth and health of the tree or shrub. It will be seen at once that if this wound is untidy or jagged the cambium may not be in a continuous circle and healing will thus take longer, for the various sections must first of all join.

As healing continues, the outermost layer of cambium forms a protective tissue or cork, a change which is brought about by the accumulation of a fatty substance called suberin on the walls of these cells. This layer of cork functions in exactly the same way as the surrounding bark but the healing tissue will always remain distinct throughout the life of the tree or shrub. Sometimes when a branch is removed, a number of shoots proliferate from the cut surface. These may need thinning out or may be removed entirely as often as is necessary at a later stage. They are referred to as epicormic shoots.

Selecting the Position of the Cut

The position of the cut should be selected very carefully. It is important to ensure that the living tissue is maintained in the region of the cut by present and future

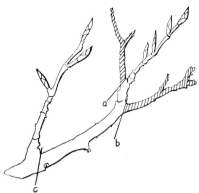

Fig. 1. A Beech twig showing the ideal positions of cuts to remove snags (at a and b). However it might be better, in view of the unhealthy condition of the growth, to make a cut at c. The lower growth appears to be healthier.

growth and that the general appearance of the tree or shrub is not spoilt by the pruning. The choice is governed by the following considerations.

(i) If dead wood is being pruned away the cut must be made back to sound living tissue. It is important that the final cut does not cut into the collar, if it has grown along the dead branch, as good callus formation and healing is only possible from sound wood behind the collar, see Figs. 1 and 2.

Plate 1. A poor finished formative pruning cut on a *Betula*. This snag will die back, causing infection and further decay in the branch system.

(ii) It is essential that the cut is made at a point close to a branch or bud. Careless pruning often results in a length of stem being left projecting beyond this point. This piece of stem, which is called a snag (see Plate 1, Fig. 3a), will in the course of a few months die back to the tissue in the region of the nearest bud or branch. Thus healing over the cut is at the best delayed, but more often it is never completed because of the length of the snag. In due course, air and moisture combine to bring about the decay of this snag, but by this time the process has extended into the heartwood and a cavity is formed which may shorten the life of the tree or shrub. The subject is dealt with in greater detail under the heading 'Cavities, Decay and Wounds' on page 29.

It is noticeable, however, that those shrubs that regenerate freely, often from the base, can safely be cut back to older wood despite the fact that no buds may be visible. Should a snag be evident at a later date after new growth has broken out, it can be removed before extensive rotting occurs. It may even break off. As a general rule, snags are more likely to lead to trouble if they occur on trees and

Plate 2. Coral Spot (*Nectria cinnabarina*) growing on a *Fagus sylvatica* snag left by poor pruning.

Fig. 2. Crown reduction, or heading back. This is necessary with stag-headed trees or where dieback needs to be corrected on a large or small scale.

Cut 1. A very bad cut and one that will leave a snag of dead wood.

Cut 2. Well positioned to a selected limb, but this is in poor health and has no future.

Cut 3. Well positioned to a branch which is in good health.

shrubs that have a permanent framework, rather than on those that grow quickly and regenerate freely. Often the latter, e.g. *Rubus*, produce canes from ground level which have a life of only two seasons, and the snags which are left after the old canes are cut off are not a real danger as they die off naturally.

Plate 3. Branch bark ridge and branch collar clearly shown on *Liriodendron tulipifera*.

Plate 5. Young callus (8 weeks) from fresh final cut.

Plate 4. *Quercus* sp. clearly showing the branch collar.

(iii) The removal of diseased wood calls for extra care, for the infection may have progressed well beyond the portion that is completely dead or shows some form of fungal fructification, see Plate 2. A good example of this is Fireblight (*Erwinia amylovora*), where infection often extends for several feet through the stem or branch beyond the first visible signs of dieback.

(iv) It is essential to relate the position of the cut to the branch system as a whole. The tree or bush should, after pruning is completed, have a balanced and natural appearance. The position of the cut should not only be just above a bud or branch, but the most suitable one should be selected. To do this properly, a full knowledge of the natural habit of growth of the tree or shrub is essential.

The Angle of the Cut

When a complete branch is being removed a cut that is close with the parent stem sheds water readily and there is less chance of its gaining access to the wood. This is known as target pruning. The final cut should be made just outside the branch

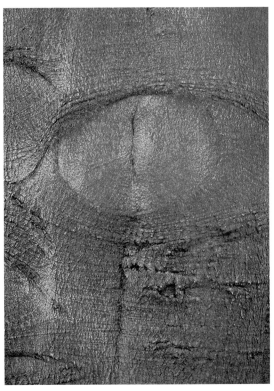

Plate 6. Full circle of callus around a well-positioned final cut.

Plate 7. Completely concealed wound on the trunk of *Fagus sylvatica* from good target pruning, showing branch bark ridge still intact.

collar, which is clearly identified by the branch bark ridge, see Plate 3. This raised area, the branch collar (see Plate 4), should not be damaged or removed by cutting operations, as it contains parent branch or trunk tissue. This reaction zone left on the tree has the ability to compartmentalize the wound created and produce tissue, known as callus, that will eventually cover the wound, see Plates 5, 6 and 7.

The angle of the cut also depends upon the nature, thickness and mechanics of the main stem. The point to remember is that while the general aim is to make the cut close to the stem, but beyond the branch collar, the need to keep the wound as small as possible is also important, see Plate 8. At the same time the position of the strengthening tissues or wood should be considered. A cut in line with the main trunk or branch may cut through some of the tissues supporting the wood that is to remain, with a weakening effect both structurally and physiologically; this is known as flush cutting, see Plate 9. This would be a mistake and should be avoided at all costs, see Fig. 3c.

Plate 8. Position of the saw beyond the branch bark ridge for final cut for good target pruning.

Plate 9. A poor position for final cut, demonstrating flush cutting.

Some of the points and considerations given above may prove to be mutually conflicting, but with actual practice and experience there should be little difficulty in deciding where and how to make the cut in each particular case.

Avoidance of Tearing

Just as it is important to cut at the best angle, beyond the branch collar, it is equally so to avoid tearing the bark on the trunk or part of the tree from which the branch is to be removed. The effects that follow from a bad tear as a result of removing a limb can be enumerated as follows.

(i) A larger area is exposed and therefore the danger of pests and other harmful organisms entering the wound is increased.

(ii) The circle of cambium that surrounds a clean wound is broken in the region of the tear. Therefore the healing process is slowed down.

Plate 10. First cut, the undercut on the 3-cut method.

Plate 11. Second cut, the top cut on the 3-cut method.

(iii) With a bad tear it is possible that a portion of the heartwood will also be torn out. This often leaves the base of the tear in a very untidy condition. Thus more work is involved in the task of cleaning the wound, for a pocket or sharply uneven surface should never be left where moisture can collect.

(iv) A bad tear as a result of a cut, even after cleaning, will be evidence of bad workmanship and this is undesirable. Pride in the work and in the finished appearance is important.

It is sometimes said that the surface of wounds should be pared smooth with a sharp pruning knife. This is true of the smaller cuts, where the outer tissue and the wood itself may be ragged and untidy; however, with the availability of good quality, sharp pruning tools today, there is less likelihood of a rough edge being left. With the larger wounds, however, only the edges and outer tissues need be pared. The large area of inner wood need not be touched as long as it is in a reasonably sound condition.

Method of Removing a Branch

With a light branch it is an easy matter to take the weight with the free hand as the cut is made, but this is not possible with heavier branches. Indeed, it might be unsafe even with lighter wood in high and difficult positions. It is possible, however, to cut off a very heavy branch by removing it gradually section by section. With large heavy branches this may involve several cuts and the use of slinging with ropes, in order that the pieces may be lowered gently. As each cut is made it is important to undercut at least $\frac{1}{6}$th of the diameter or until the cut closes, before cutting through the limb from above. This is made just beyond the undercut, see Plates 10 and 11, Fig. 3d and e.

Once the weight has been taken off, the final cut at the stub end should be from top to bottom in order to ensure that the surface of the wound is neat and on one plane. Also, by this method the cut may be directed to be on the correct side of the branch bark ridge and at the desired angle, see Plate 8. With a small limb, the free hand can be used to take the weight, but with a heavier limb, even though it has been reduced to a stump, it may be necessary to use a slinging rope before the cut is made in order to take the weight.

The Protective Dressing

When a cut is made, a considerable amount of heartwood is exposed which, in the case of the larger stems and branches, has become salignified or hardened to give mechanical strength. This remains healthy and perfectly preserved, provided the tree

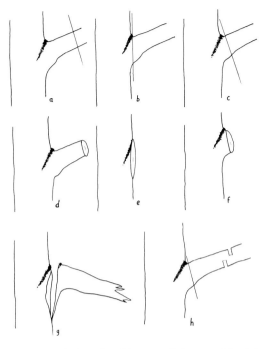

Fig. 3a. Diagrams that illustrate good and bad cuts.
(a) The final cut has been poorly positioned leaving a bad snag.
(b) A poor final cut which has been made too close to the trunk or parent branch (flush cutting).
(c) The correct final cut made just beyond the branch collar is sloping to allow for an increased girth of the trunk or parent branch, through and below the junction in this region.
(d) A bad method of removing a limb. The only cut has been made without lightening the limb in any way with the result that the weight, as the limb has fallen, has taken the bark and possibly some structural wood away for a considerable length down the trunk.
(e) The branch has been removed in sections using the 3-cut method, the sequence of the cuts being 1 and 2 to reduce end weight and 3 the final cut of the stub end, the fall of which can be controlled as it is cut off at the branch collar.

is in a healthy condition and is able to combat harmful pests and organisms. In the past, protective wound sealants or tree paints were applied to the exposed wound immediately after cutting, to protect it from air, water and spores of destructive fungi and accelerate wound closure. They were usually bitchumen-based, waterproof sealants of a pliable, non-crack nature, occasionally with fungicidal properties, but were often applied, sealing in the microorganisms behind the paint. The microclimate created behind the sealant encouraged faster decay and rarely prevented insect or disease infestations, often limiting the production of callus formed by the trees own defence barrier, by killing the non-harmful organisms. Decay often went unnoticed, sealed in behind the painted barrier, soon developing into serious cavities.

Research has shown that these dressings rarely worked and it is recommended that no dressing be used, allowing the tree to utilize its own natural defence system held in the trunk or parent branch tissue directly behind the branch collar, hence the need for accurate target pruning. The exception to this rule may be with the sealing of pruning wounds on the Red Oaks in the United States, as a possible preventative measure against the spread of Oak Wilt (see Quercus in Part II).

The Healing Power of the Cut

The healing power of the cut varies, for much depends upon the size of the wound,

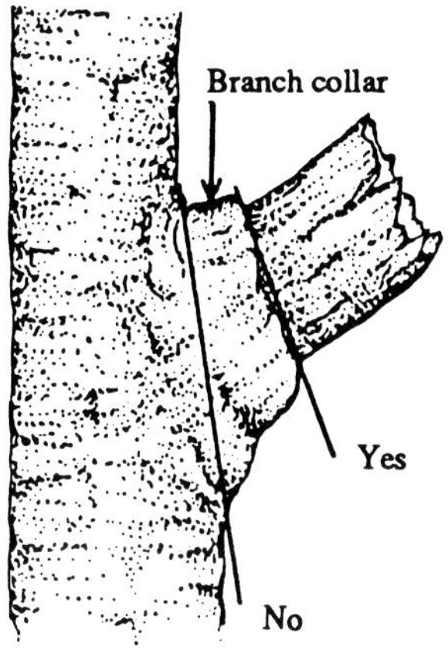

Fig. 3b. Correct and incorrect cuts (reprinted with permission from EM 8742, *Sustainable Gardening: The Oregon-Washington Master Gardener Handbook*, reprinted January 2003, page 87, courtesy of Oregon State University Extension Service).

upon the age, health and vigour of the shrub or tree and upon the actual species or type. Some wounds will be too large, or the tree too old to heal completely.

Dealing with size first, the small cuts, especially those on young trees, heal very quickly. Part of the reason for this is that the increase in girth is so rapid in a fast-growing tree that the area is soon engulfed by the developing tissue. Wounds of a similar size on older trees may take several years. The old, weak tree that is declining may never form more than a callus on the outer edge of the wound and even this may not be in a complete circle. The rule here should be to remove branches as young as possible, as small cuts do less damage to a tree than large cuts. Formative pruning on young trees in the nursery will reduce the need to prune when the tree reaches maturity.

When good pruning practices are carried out (i.e. the final cut is made just outside the branch collar), the result is that a good full circle of callus forms around the pruning wound very quickly. When flush cutting is carried out, a larger wound is created and the result is callus production along the sides of the wound with dead spots at the top and bottom. These dead spots begin to die back further, developing into cracks, cankers and decay, eventually leading to defect problems and branch failure, see Plate 12.

As stated earlier, the species or type needs to be taken into account. As an example, the English Oak (*Quercus robur*) will heal over much faster than the Californian Horse-chestnut (*Aesculus californica*), which is often slow and uncertain and whose wood may rot in the meantime. With shrubs that renew themselves readily from ground level and have a cane growth, for example the Ghost Bramble (*Rubus thibetanus*), healing above ground level where the wood has a pith centre does not take place. This is not important, however, for the natural habit of these plants is to lose their wood after it is a few years old. By that time the rootstock

Plate 12. An old flush cut showing dead spots at the top and bottom of the wound on a *Tilia* sp.

has either sealed over the point of connection with the old stem and has thus healed itself completely, or the root is a creeping one and has moved on to fresh ground, leaving the older parts of the plant to die.

Healing is very important with those shrubs that do not readily renew their wood with a cane habit of growth, but keep their framework throughout their life, for example the shrubby Magnolias.

BLEEDING FROM A WOUND OR CUT SURFACE

A number of subjects, particularly deciduous ones, bleed if wounds (or pruning cuts) occur in the late winter or early spring. This is caused by the flow of sap, which is commencing to 'rise' or become active during this period, in preparation for bud development and growth, which takes place in the early part of the year. Once bleeding has started from a wound, it is difficult, if not almost impossible, to stop until the subject breaks into leaf, when the flow which is being lost is taken by the developing growth. With this difficulty in mind, it is important to avoid

cutting live branches of deciduous trees during the weeks before bud break, especially in those subjects that bleed badly, e.g. the Birches. (The genera that are especially prone to bleeding, *Betula*, *Acer*, *Carya* and *Juglans*, are mentioned in Part II.)

It is unusual for a subject to be killed by excessive bleeding, but in severe cases
it may cause considerable dieback. The edible Vine is often quoted as an example
of a subject that bleeds badly if it is pruned too late in the dormant period. It is
a good choice, for the vine is spurred back annually to the main rod system and
early winter is the best time for this. Should bleeding occur through late pruning,
the loss may be reduced by lowering the vine to the horizontal, until the buds
break. Lowering the rods in the spring is accepted as standard practice to
encourage them to break evenly.

With a small wound it is possible to reduce the flow by a very tight binding.
First the surrounds and then the wound itself are cleansed and dried as thoroughly as possible; this is important, especially if adhesive tape is used, for it will
not adhere to a wet surface. It may be possible to hasten drying by the use of an
electric hair-dryer, or a compressed air unit, but this is a question of availability
at the point required. Hand bellows are of course useful and also absorbent paper.
Best practice is to prevent the need for corrective measures, by pruning at the
correct time of the year for the specific genera.

CAVITIES, DECAY AND WOUNDS

The reader would be excused for thinking that this subject is outside the scope of
this work and yet good pruning and attention to the correct position of the final
cut will reduce the chances of a cavity forming and some account must be given
of their development.

The core of salignified tissue that extends through the trunk and branch system
and most of the roots has already been mentioned and it is important to remember
that the strength of the entire branch system of a tree depends partly on the condition of this tissue. It readily breaks down under the influence of bacteria and other
organisms that, however, are only active when suitable conditions are present,
including sufficient air and moisture. It should also be remembered that in a perfectly
healthy tree this salignified tissue is protected from these agencies and from the associated diseases by the outer sleeve of living tissue. It will remain healthy provided this
protective coat is intact and in good condition. The latter point is important, for the
surface tissues on a tree that is in poor condition may not function properly and thus
leave the heartwood unprotected. At this stage it is necessary to differentiate between
a cavity and a surface wound.

Plate 13. The beginnings of decay and cavity formation by leaving large stumps to die back from poor final pruning on a *Salix* sp.

Cavities

These often penetrate deeply into the branch or trunk, anywhere in the tree. There is evidence to show that degenerative processes which are initiated on stubs or snags often spread quickly into the parent branch or trunk by the old conducting tissue. As the break-down continues the whole snag becomes rotten and may hold considerable amounts of moisture which encourages further spread. A lengthy snag prevents complete healing and the resultant callus forms a cup-shaped lip that collects moisture as the snag rots away completely. When this happens the moisture or standing water often remains permanently, and this encourages further decay into the centre of the trunk or branch, see Plate 13.

Surface Wounds

As implied, these are formed by injury to the bark, often leaving the salignified tissues intact. The old conducting strands are thus unaffected and do not have open ends for the destructive agencies to gain a ready access. It should not be inferred that a cavity never forms from this type of wound, but usually, if it happens at all, it is a slower process, especially in the earlier stages, and this gives a longer time for healing. Often too, such surface wounds remain dry, for unlike snags they do not present a receptive surface to rain. Such exposed areas of dry, undamaged heartwood are more likely to be broken down by woodworm attack.

Causes of Injury

It has been mentioned that an injury to a limb readily leads to the development of a cavity in the parent branch or trunk unless corrected. This injury can be caused in a variety of ways. Wind, for example, sometimes accompanied by driving rain, may either snap branches and leave snags, or by taking them off at the main junctions leave bad tears on the main trunk. Ice forming on the branch system during a glazed frost results in a considerable increase of weight and, with the wood in a brittle condition through the cold, a break or tear is likely. Snow has the same effect, conifers and evergreens suffering particularly, see Plate 45. Dieback through disease, ill health or lack of light will also cause snags as dead limbs break off at the weakest point. Only rarely, however, does a direct tear on the main trunk occur as a result of dieback. These are some of the main causes of snag-producing injuries and it should be noted that such damage is more likely to occur on a weak, badly shaped tree. A well-trained tree with a good central leader is better equipped to withstand unusual stresses than, for instance, a tree with multiple leaders. Such a tree tends to be weak because of the uneven distribution of weight and the narrowness of its crotches and is, consequently, more likely to suffer severe damage. Such weakness, however, does not always result in an obviously dangerous tear or break. The injury is sometimes only a small crack which may go undetected for years—a disastrous period when air and moisture with the accompanying decay are channeled into the very heartwood in the crown or head of the trunk, see Fig. 10.

Development of Cavities

It must be recognised that however small a cavity is, once it has formed it is serious and in time, if allowed to develop, may weaken the tree and shorten its life. This may even be making light of the situation, for the wood deteriorates far in advance of the actual cavity and decay is often more extensive below the opening than above, see Fig. 4. The decay is usually most rapid in the softer wooded trees such as *Populus*, *Salix* and *Aesculus*. The more extensive rotting below the cavity is of course natural, for water often collects in the hollow, either as a result of rain or because of the seepage of sap from neighbouring living tissues. Once moisture does collect, putrefaction sets in and the effect is a progressive increase in the activity of the organisms causing the breakdown. This takes place very rapidly if there are other snags nearby, for the areas of degenerated and diseased wood quickly join up with each other and eventually the inner core of an entire trunk or branch will decompose to leave a hollow shell. The danger at this stage is from any large branches that are adjacent to the area of decay, as their junctions are weakened. Eventually they are shed and the hollow trunk is left standing.

Thus the story is one of progressive decay which may lead to a drastic shortening of the life of a tree. The rate of decay will speed up as the condition and health of the tree deteriorates, large limbs are lost and the root system suffers. It is therefore important to regularly inspect known cavities, at least once a year, monitoring the progress of decay, leading to a hazard evaluation.

More recent research has shown that most healthy trees do have the ability to create reaction zones that are able to limit the spread of decay. This is known as

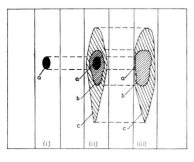

Fig. 4. A typical cavity in diagrammatic form.
(i) Opening to the cavity visible at (a).
(ii) A plan view from the same position as at (i) showing (a) the opening to the cavity, (b) the size of the cavity within the stem and (c) the area of degenerated tissue.
(iii) A sectional view of the stem taken from the side showing (a) the opening to the cavity, (b) the actual cavity within the stem and (c) the area of degenerated tissue.

Compartmentalization of Decay in Trees (CODIT). A signal is processed by the tree that causes the tree to put up barriers in both the active and the old non-conductive xylem cells, resisting the invasion of all but the more aggressive microorganisms. By invasive inspection or the removal of rotten wood from cavities by cleaning them out, the barrier may be broken down, allowing the decay organisms to spread laterally and vertically, greatly weakening the tree's natural defence system.

PRUNING AND THE ROOT SYSTEM

Work in the Neighbourhood of Roots

In this age of rapid change and development it frequently becomes necessary to work near or among the root systems of trees, especially in the urban environment. There is a constant need for the excavation around tree roots to repair or replace underground services and more recently the introduction of cable television has had detrimental effects on mature trees throughout our cities by the indiscriminate removal of major anchor and feeding roots in the path of a cable duct. The safety margin beyond which there is a risk to the well-being and perhaps life of the tree varies considerably and is dependent upon several factors, but it is outside the scope of this book to deal with these in detail. One of the more important factors, however, concerns the amount of care the operators are prepared to take both to avoid injury to the system and in making cuts properly. Again, this is not the place in which to deal with general methods of minimising damage to root systems, but an account of the sort of root pruning which is frequently necessary must obviously be included.

The Effects of Pruning Roots

A reduction of or injury to a root system affects growth to an extent that is directly proportional to the amount of damage incurred. Root pruning as a deliberate means of reducing growth is seldom used with ornamental subjects. Rightly, it is generally accepted that a careful selection should be made in the first place, when the ultimate size and habit are major factors to take into consideration.

In former days, root pruning was an established practice, with apple trees in particular, in order to bring over-vigorous trees into bearing. But nowadays, as a result of the wide range of selected rootstocks available, which provide an effective means of controlling size, vigour and fruiting, there is little need for such a drastic and expensive method and it has fallen into disuse. (But see 'The Pruning and Training of Semi-Mature Transplants' on page 54.)

Dealing with Damaged Roots

Roots should, if possible, be cut off cleanly in the first instance, but any torn and jagged wounds must be trimmed up, cutting them back to sound wood with clean, pared cuts. The root should be cleared of soil sufficiently for the cut to be made, wiping it clean to avoid damage to the cutting tools. With large roots, the cuts may be made with a saw and the surface pared smooth. Hatchet or axes were used for the severance, but the results were very poor indeed, with rough, ragged cuts and stress to the entire root from the striking of the axe. Today a chainsaw or handsaw are used, severing the root beyond the position of the intended cut, as in this way the final cut may be made without the surfaces closing to jam the saw. It is also easier to remove soil from beneath the stub end of the root before cutting. The final cut should be facing downwards so that soil does not sit on the surface of the cut allowing moisture to penetrate the wound, which will lead to the beginning of decay.

Sufficient time and resources should be allowed for this work as it is sometimes worthwhile to expose more root and to cut back cleanly to a branch root without leaving a stub end, even though it may be a minor one. The same rules and dangers apply to roots as to branches. Snags will die back, giving a means of entry for harmful diseases.

Great care should always be taken to avoid accidents, which are more likely when work is undertaken in cramped conditions.

Girdling Roots

This term is applied to roots which develop over the main buttress or surface roots in a partial circle near the base of the trunk, see Plate 14. The effect is to arrest or impede the development of the main roots, but the extent to which this is harmful depends upon several factors. There may be scope for growth and increase in thickness in the root system as a whole if only one or two are affected. Again, the girdling root itself may not be very strong and may either be forced out of position or give way

under increasing strain and pressure as the buttress roots swell. The first impulse is
to cut through the offending root, and this is the best course if it can be done cleanly,
but often the buttress or main roots have grown partly over the offending root and
this would be difficult. The fact, also, that there must necessarily be two cuts and that
the roots beyond the girdling position will die and rot, increases the risk of infection.

The matter must therefore be weighed very carefully. Obviously there is seldom
any justification in cutting through the offending root if it entails making an excavation and leaving a wound in a position where it is likely to be damp and moist for
a long period. It is generally more important to correct this condition on a growing
tree than on one which has reached maturity and is past the period of rapid growth.

With young trees, it is possible to reduce the chances of these roots forming by
careful training and planting. By cramming the roots into a small hole, either
when planting in the nursery or at the final planting, this is more likely to happen,
for the roots in part of the system may be twisted or looped together to bring
about trouble later. The correct method of planting involves a large enough hole
to allow the main roots to be straightened out.

There is also the same risk in planting trees and shrubs from pots or
containers, especially when the roots have developed, spiraling round the sides of
the ball through restriction. It is, of course, necessary to raise certain trees and

Plate 14. Girdling roots on a mature *Ulmus* sp.

shrubs in pots, but they should not be left in these too long, as the root system may become seriously pot-bound. The failure of *Eucalyptus* in later years is often due to spiraling roots in the first two years of the tree's life in the nursery.

PROPAGATION AND TRAINING

The good nurserymen and propagators take pride in their work and in the trees and shrubs under their charge. They must often wonder about the fate of the stock that they produce, but in present conditions of planting and development, a place will always be found for good, well-trained material, for which there is a very great demand.

Most nurserymen are ready to advise on the plants that they raise and, just as the planner and planter have much to learn from them, so they in turn should keep in touch with the conditions under which their young nursery stock has ultimately to be established. There must be a two-way flow of ideas and information.

Importance of Early Training

The future shape of a tree or shrub depends upon the nature of the training that is carried out in the early years after germination or rooting. A badly placed shoot or even a developing bud is quite easily removed when young, but if it is left until the specimen has reached maturity, not only does correction become a major operation but, even if this is possible, the effects may be seen for many years or may even be permanent. This is also true of the many shrubs that retain their branch system and build on this from year to year. As an example we may take *Magnolia ×soulangeana*, for with this subject much of the permanent branch system is formed in the first few years. *Forsythia ×intermedia* 'Spectabilis' has a stool-like habit, with the branches springing from ground level. In a healthy specimen, fresh growths will appear, to make up any gaps or to renew any of the older branches which often become weak and straggly with age. Such shrubs can make good a start from a poor one by the production of strong basal shoots which quickly outgrow the inferior ones, though in no way should this be used as an excuse for bad culture and methods of training.

Importance of Good Propagating Material

Poor seed or inferior propagating material often results in a bad start and a weakly, misshapen plant. The soundest policy, therefore, is to select the most suitable material for propagation and provide the best conditions possible for rooting and for subsequent growth during the training period. The following paragraphs give some of the factors that need to be taken into consideration.

Selection of material with conifers. Where the propagation of conifers is concerned it is sometimes necessary to use leading shoot material for propagation. The Monkey Puzzle (*Araucaria araucana*) is an example, for material propagated from lateral branches will not form shapely trees. Instead, they become no more than living branches with a unilateral habit. It is essential that the propagator should be acquainted with the growth and habits of the subject under their charge, so that they are able to adopt methods of training which are likely to give the best results.

The juvenile stage with some species. This may need to be taken into account, for the seedlings of some species pass through a juvenile stage when the growth may be entirely out of character with that of a mature plant. A well-known example of this is with the Ivy (*Hedera helix*). The juvenile stage is the creeping form, when the growth extends along the ground and up trees or other supports. It is at a later stage that the mature branching develops which produces flowers and fruit. If the mature form is propagated it will not revert extensively to the creeping habit.

The balance of growth and flowering. In the early years in the life of a tree or shrub there is a natural tendency for growth rather than flowering and subsequently fruiting. This is carried to the extreme with *Magnolia campbellii*, which may take up to 20 years to flower from seed, while *Sophora japonica* may take up to 40 years.

Vegetative reproduction favours earlier flowering. For example, *Magnolia campbellii* and *Wisteria sinensis* plants raised by grafting onto selected forms will flower within 10 to 15 years. *Cytisus scoparius* cuttings flower within a few months of rooting, while seedlings may take from 3 to 4 years. The general tendency of young stock toward growth rather than flower in the early years is to the propagator's advantage, but it also affects the gardener and tree grower when the tree is planted and is growing in its final position. There must, however, always be some growth, and a tree that fails to maintain the growing points usually dies, often after flowering and seeding profusely.

Early and premature flowering may seriously affect the symmetry of a young tree. A Sycamore (*Acer pseudoplatanus*), for example, in a poor position may flower prematurely even from the terminal buds. Thus forking occurs on the leading growths and the process is continued each year with the result that the crown too is produced prematurely thus affecting the ultimate dimensions and shape of the final tree. From this it will be seen that the flowering stage plays an important part in crown formation.

These are factors which must be considered both when propagating material is selected and throughout the period of training. It is important to produce growth in the nursery. Without this, pruning and training are impossible.

Chapter Two

The Pruning of Trees and Conifers

TREE TYPES AND TREE PRODUCTION

Classification: Tree or Shrub

The main difference between a tree and a shrub is that the former has a strong branch system that is built upon a trunk. This in turn strengthens to keep pace with the extending framework that develops as the tree grows. The shrub on the other hand forms a head of branches near ground level. The result is that with the former considerable height is often built up as, for example, with our larger trees that may extend up to a hundred feet or more. There is, however, considerable variation in the mode of growth among shrubs. A number adopt a suckerous habit, producing a crop of growths annually from ground level as the plant spreads. In some cases these growths extend and build up from year to year, as with the Black-thorn (*Prunus spinosa*), while with others the growths or canes die down after flow-ering in their second year, e.g. the Ghost Bramble (*Rubus thibetanus*). The suckerous habit, however, is not confined to shrubs, for some trees such as the Aspen (*Populus tremula*), the False Acacia (*Robinia pseudoacacia*) and the Tree of Heaven (*Ailanthus altissima*) will also spread by this means.

It is recognised that with many species the early training does affect the ulti-mate form and size. The retention and vigour of the leading growth will often be the deciding factor. By training, *Colutea arborescens* may be grown into a small standard tree, though normally it is a shrub. For general purposes, however, with comparatively few exceptions, woody plants may be broadly divided into trees and shrubs.

The problems of forming a stem that will develop into a trunk do not exist with shrubs, but it is important to train these on sound lines. Details are given in Chapter Three, and also in Six, which deals with the individual genera.

Types of Tree

Trees which are being grown in the nursery for final planting should have a sound framework, for when they are mature they will often carry considerable weight and may be exposed to gales and other strains. A tree is well equipped for this provided the framework is mechanically sound. A British Standards publication, 'Nursery Stock Specification for Trees and Shrubs' (B.S. 3936, Part 1:1992), deals with requirements for trees and shrubs. Broadly, so far as trees are concerned, the following types have been specified (the conversion to the metric system is approximate).

(i) Multi-stemmed Tree. A tree with two or more main stems, not necessarily uniform in height or girth originating at or near (above or below) ground level from one root system. Trees produced in this way are naturally found suckering at the base, or can be made to produce several stems by cutting back hard. They are usually measured by overall height from ground level. It is sometimes possible to provide stem girth measurements, to assist with the overall description, but the stems may be of varying sizes.

(ii) Standard Trees. They fall into 2 types, (1) Standard with branching head and (2) Standard with central leader, with various forms. They have a minimum circumference of 4 cm. at a height of 1 m. (3 ft.) from the ground and this is the criteria normally used for purchasing standard trees. The overall height of the tree and the length of leg or clear stem to the first branch varies, but some indication is given in the table facing.

There is an increasing demand for the Heavy or Extra Heavy Nursery Tree to fill the need for transplants which give immediate effect and as a means of overcoming the serious problem of vandalism which the smaller nursery trees are prone to suffer in some areas.

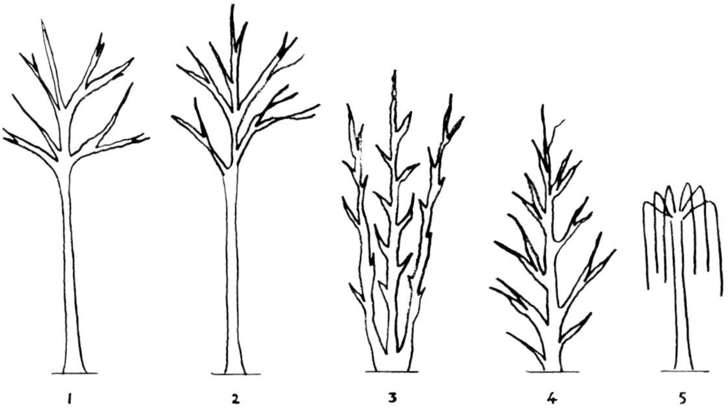

Fig. 5. Some of the types of tree described in the text.
(1) Standard with branching head.
(2) Standard with central leader.
(3) Multi-stemmed tree.
(4) Feathered tree.
(5) Weeping standard.

FORM	GIRTH (CIRCUMFERENCE) @ 1.0 M. FROM GROUND	OVERALL HEIGHT FROM THE GROUND	CLEAR STEM HEIGHT
Half Standard	4 to 6 cm.	1.75 to 2.5 m.	1.25 to 1.5 m.
Extra Light	4 to 6 cm.	2.0 to 2.5 m.	1.5 to 1.75 m.
Light	6 to 8 cm.	2.5 to 3.0 m.	1.5 to 1.75 m.
Standard	8 to 10 cm.	2.5 to 3.0 m.	1.75 to 2.0 m.
Selected	10 to 12 cm.	3.0 to 3.5 m.	1.75 to 2.0 m.
Heavy	12 to 14 cm.	3.5 m. minimum	1.75 to 2.0 m.
Extra Heavy	14 to 16 cm.	3.5 m. minimum	1.75 to 2.0 m.

(1) Standard with Branching Head. This is often referred to as a decurrent tree. These trees have a central main stem with an evenly balanced head with several main branches dividing in the lower crown, with no main branches crossing through. Standards with branching heads are grown for smaller trees such as *Malus* and *Prunus* species, for those that naturally form this type of crown, for example the English Oak (*Quercus robur*), or for trees that are susceptible to frost damage and lose their leading shoot in early life, for example the Foxglove Tree (*Paulownia tomentosa*).

(2) Standard with Central Leader. This is also referred to as an excurrent tree. These trees have a balanced head on a length of clear stem that is strong and reasonably straight. One of the main features with this type of tree is that there is a well-defined central leader running up through the centre of the tree.

(iii) Weeping Standard. A well-grown, straight stem and the same minimum diameter requirements, with a minimum height of 1.7 m. (5.5 ft.) from ground level to the lowest branch. The two types are naturally weeping, e.g. *Betula pendula* 'Tristis', and top-worked grafted specimen, e.g. the Kilmarnock Willow (*Salix caprea* 'Kilmarnock').

(iv) Feathered Tree. A good, well-defined prominent leader running straight up through the young tree, well furnished with evenly spread and balanced lateral growths along the complete length, except for the very bottom, according to the species, see Plates 15 and 16. The dimensions vary from 1.25 to 3.0 m. (4 to 10 ft.) and a stem circumference of between 6 and 12 cm. The overall height is the criteria used for purchasing feathered trees.

Where larger trees are concerned the single central leader gives a stronger tree which is more likely to be mechanically sound, for, as the large tree reaches maturity, the huge weight of the branching system is evenly spread over a large number of small branches. These also tend to come away from the central stem more or less at right angles and are therefore strongly attached, see Plates 17 and 18.

Plate 15. Nicely feathered *Liquidambar styraciflua* in the arboretum in summer.

Plate 16. A fine, young naturally feathered *Betula maximowicziana* in the arboretum.

Sometimes, through damage to the main shoot, two or more rival leaders develop, see Plate 19. Should there be just two, this is referred to as a forked or twin leader. Beech trees (*Fagus* spp.) and Pines (*Pinus* spp.), in particular, often split up into several rival leaders or codominant stems. These should be reduced to one at an early stage, for this condition should never be allowed to develop, see Plate 20. Rival leaders develop into very large main and ascending branches, see Plates 21 and 22 and Fig. 10. Thus the weight is carried by two or more codominant branches or stems that are comparable to tree trunks in size. Such a tree may well be furnished with the branches symmetrically placed, but they will only be on one side of each of the forked leaders. As codominant stems develop they trap included bark, especially in tight crotches forming a structural weakness at the point of attachment. Thus, as the branches extend, the leaders are pulled apart leaving the centre open. In addition, there will be a narrow crotch ('V' crotch) or angle between the central leaders that is a weak form of junction. This

Plate 17. Weak attachment of a lateral to the main stem.

Plate 18. Strong attachment of a lateral to the main stem.

is a serious condition when it is remembered that a large tree may be exposed to heavy gales. A major part of the tree may be lost by one clean split, which may also cause an irreparable tear down the main trunk, see Plate 23. Even a small crack in the crotch from the inner core to the outer bark will cause weakness that will become worse as air and water cause rot and decay.

It will be noticed that the Feathered tree may be formed into a Standard with a Central Leader merely by clearing the stem of branches up to the required height, a form of crown or skirt lifting, see Plates 24 and 25. The one important advantage with this type of tree is that it is easier to stake, not being as top heavy as the Standard with the Central Leader.

In no way should this section be regarded as a substitute for British Standards publication B.S. 3936, Part 1:1992. It is not complete in any way and the types have only been quoted to illustrate the progress towards standardization.

Plate 19. Twin leader or codominant stems on young nursery stock.

Plate 20. Removal of a twin leader on a young *Acer* in the nursery to prevent future problems.

Conditions for Tree Production

Trees of the desired specifications can only be produced under good conditions. It is hardly within the scope of this book to describe these in detail, but a brief account will show how they have a direct effect upon growth and the form of young trees even in the early years.

Shelter. Growth will not be good in an exposed position. Not only is there a danger of the leading shoots and main branches being broken in a very exposed site, but also they may not even develop properly or evenly. The prevailing winds in the United Kingdom are Westerly and South Westerly and shelter from the North and East is also desirable with the more tender subjects. This does not of course mean that the nursery site needs to be completely sheltered from all wind, for growth under such conditions might be too lush and the trees loosely formed, and this would be undesirable.

Plate 21. Codominant stems on young established tree. These are likely to split out and ruin a perfectly healthy young tree.

Plate 22. Codominant stems on a mature *Quercus rubra*. In time this will split out, destroying a fine specimen.

Frosts.   Severe frosts may affect the young growth of some evergreens and the unripened tips of deciduous subjects, in severe cases killing them completely. Certain genera and species are tender when young and, until they have developed substantial wood, are thus more likely to be affected than any others, for example *Paulownia* spp. It is, however, worth noting that even the young developing growths of the English Oak (*Quercus robur*) can be badly damaged by late spring frosts. It may be necessary to prune off frosted portions at a later stage when developing buds lower down indicate the nature and extent of the damage and when the most promising buds or young growths can be selected.

A reasonably fertile and well-drained soil.   A soil with these characteristics produces a balanced growth, which is neither too strong nor too weak and, in the case of deciduous subjects, one that ripens fully in the autumn and is thus less prone to winter damage. There is another factor in this connection. Such soils are easy to

Plate 23. Damage caused to *Prunus cerasifera* 'Pissardii' by a codominant stem tearing out late in life following a storm.

Plate 24. Removing unwanted feathers on *Acer davidii* in the nursery early, a form of crown lifting.

work by comparison with the heavier types and thus regular transplanting may be carried out under better conditions, while the root system itself is more likely to be lifted and transferred without breaking up. From a consideration of these factors it will be realized that the whole process of tree production must be treated as one and pruning and training are not just isolated operations in the nursery.

TRAINING IN THE NURSERY

Now that the forms of tree have been established and the main requirements for good growth have been considered, the methods of training required to produce the various types of tree may be described.

Plate 25. Crown lifting on a semi-mature oak to allow for ease of future grounds maintenance.

Plate 26. A well-planted and -staked tree in the arboretum.

Initial Training

From a seedling.   Development under good conditions is perfectly natural and straightforward and very little pruning is necessary during the early stages. With most subjects the terminal bud or growth extends from year to year, growths being stronger as the tree builds up in size. If the leading growth is considered to be weak it may be shortened, perhaps by two-thirds or more, during the winter to a strong bud which will take the lead under training during the following season. The lateral growths also increase in size and vigour, their production and development keeping pace with the leading shoot, so that often the young tree is broadly pyramidal. If desired the vigour may be directed into the leading growth by stopping the laterals to 5 or 6 leaves half-way through the growing season, see Fig. 6 (1, a and b). If the specimen is very weak, however, the loss of leaf surface that results from this might be harmful. It should be noted that the strongest growths

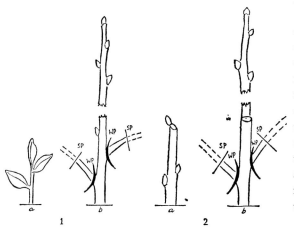

Fig. 6. Stages in training:

(1) Training from a seedling and from a softwood cutting. (a) At a stage when extensive growth can be expected. (b) After one season's growth, an extension of the terminal shoot has taken place. If it is desired to form a clean leg, the lateral growths may be removed, first stopping back at SP during the season of growth and pruning back hard to the main stem at WP during the dormant season.

(2) Training from a hardwood cutting. The procedure is the same, except that the topmost bud becomes and acts as a terminal (a). The side growths, originating from the buds in (a), are treated as shown at (b) in just the same way as with the seedlings or softwood cutting.

are often those that are produced when the young tree is 4 to 5 years old. The first few near ground level are usually small and do not develop extensively. This explains why even the feathered tree has a short leg, for these are removed during training in two stages, as described for a cutting.

From a cutting. A number of trees, most Poplars and Willows for example, can be propagated from hardwood cuttings. In the preparation of the cutting, the uppermost portion of the stem is often removed and the lower part is retained for propagating purposes. Thus the terminal bud is removed. However, the uppermost bud on the cutting normally assumes the lead as growth is produced and will grow the most strongly. The remaining buds usually grow out, in some cases rivaling the main one in vigour, but these should be stopped back to 100 to 150 mm. (4 to 6 in.) after approximately 230 to 300 mm. (9 to 12 in.) have been formed. This has the effect of channelling the vigour into the leading shoot, which should not be stopped. The stub ends of the laterals are not removed until the autumn or early winter as they have a strengthening effect upon the portion of the stem to which they are attached, and this is an advantage, see Fig. 6 (2, a and b).

From a root cutting. A few plants, for example *Ailanthus altissima*, may be propagated in this way. Often a number of adventitious shoots arise from the one cutting, but if a well-shaped tree is to be formed only one is needed for the main trunk and central leader. The most suitable one is therefore selected and the remainder are taken out.

From budding, see Fig. 7. As the bud grows out the stock is headed back, but often this is carried out in at least two stages, the first cut being 100 to 130 mm.

Fig. 7. Pruning and training from budding.
(1) The stock x budded at y.
(2) Growth being put on during the following season. The stock has been headed back, the stub end being used for support. The final cut, an operation referred to as 'snagging', is made toward the end of the season at (a). See Fig. 52.
(3) The subject after snagging has been completed.
(4) The growth at a later stage being trained to form a clean leg with a head. The growths on the stem below the selected branches are shortened, and are cut back to the stem during the winter.

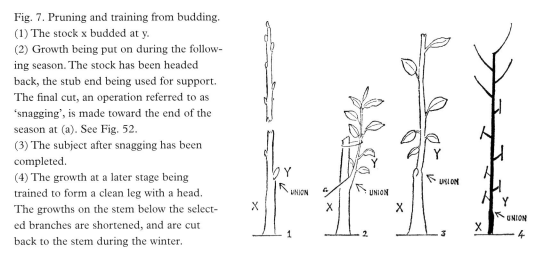

(4 to 5 in.) above the union. By this method the snag may be used with a tie for support to the young growth. Finally the stem is cut back cleanly above the scion which has by this time grown perhaps for one season and has become woody, see Fig. 52. When tree subjects are budded the growth may be clear of laterals and extend for 1 to 2 m. (3 to 6 ft.). Such a clean stem, developed in the one season from the bud on the scion, is referred to as a maiden. If the maiden growth itself has branched into laterals that have been produced also during the first season, it is referred to as a feathered maiden. Any growths produced by the stock are rubbed out or taken off at an early stage.

From grafting. The effect that is produced is very similar. The topmost bud on the scion develops into the maiden growth, see Fig. 8 (1, 2 and 3) at X's, while the lower ones also grow out and would, if they were left, form rival leaders, thus producing a low bush rather than a tree. When these reach a length of approximately 230 mm. (9 in.) they should be stopped back 80 to 100 mm. (3 to 4 in.) at Y's, see Fig. 8 (1, 2 and 3). In this way vigour is directed into the leading growth. These stub ends are cut back cleanly to the main stem during the winter, see Fig. 8 (4), at Y's. Any growths from the stock are taken off at an early stage as with budding, see Fig. 8 (2) at Z's.

The clean young growth produced in this way is also referred to as a maiden. If possible, maiden growths should be staked as a safeguard against wind damage, see Plate 26.

In all cases, if the growth is not considered to be sufficiently strong, the maiden shoot may be headed back to a lower bud. The effect of pruning growths

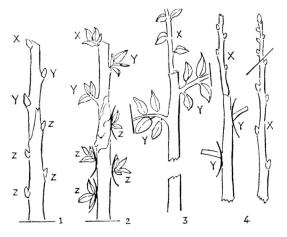

Fig. 8. Treatment during the first season after grafting.
(1) The graft as soon as it has been made and before waxing. Note topmost bud on scion at X, two other buds on scion at Y, four buds on stock at Z.
(2) A few weeks later when the graft has taken. The growths at Z on the stock are rubbed off.
(3) Again a few weeks later. The two growths at Y have been shortened.
(4) At the end of the season. The two growths at Y are removed close to the stem. The tip of the maiden growth is reduced to a promising bud if necessary.

of deciduous subjects hard during the dormant season is to reduce the number of buds, and the fewer growths thus produced are relatively stronger, provided the specimen is healthy. To respond properly, however, the root system and the tree as a whole must be encouraged, and care should be taken, for not all subjects will respond to cutting back. Many evergreens and conifers, for example, will not.

It is likely that in future years the use of special dwarfing rootstocks may increase among ornamental trees and shrubs. This development should take place with an increased knowledge of the existence of virus diseases. The responsibilities of the nurseryman may eventually include the propagation and distribution of a wide range of ornamental plants that conform to a guaranteed stock system.

Training to Produce Specific Tree Types

The training and pruning system that is followed depends entirely upon the type of tree to be produced.

Training of a feathered tree.   This is one of the most natural types and a strong and definite leader should be well furnished with lateral growths to near ground level. A natural growth, provided the central leader retains its dominance, ensures the desired effect. Occasionally some thinning of the laterals may be desirable.

It may be necessary to support the main stem in the early years to ensure a good straight trunk. The best method for this is the use of a stout cane and to attach the tree to it using the Max Tapener system, see Plate 26. The cane should be taller than the eventual height of the tree in the season to prevent abrasion of the leading shoot caused by rubbing against the sharp edge of the cane top.

Training of a standard with central leader.
The main difference between this type and the feathered tree is that the laterals are removed close to the main trunk, using the target pruning approach, up to a predetermined point to form a length of clear stem. The process of removal is carried out in two stages. As they form during the growing season they are stopped back to approximately 130 mm. (5 in.) when about 300 mm. (12 in.) long. They are not cut off close, because if left they have a strengthening effect upon the main stem. They are cut back cleanly to the branch collar during the dormant season.

The head that is formed may develop naturally without any pruning, but this depends entirely upon the extent and habit of growth and this varies considerably with the species. Crossing and crowded branches should be taken out. Even hard pruning back may be necessary to encourage stronger growth, either on the laterals or the leader. Sometimes this is necessary before the head is formed, but if the leader is pruned, care must be taken to train a replacement as the new growth breaks out.

Plate 27. Early training in the nursery using the Max Tapener system

It should be noted that a standard with a central leader might be formed from the feathered tree by cutting back the laterals up to the required height. This may be carried out gradually each autumn as the head is forming.

Training of a standard with branching head. The first essential is to run the leading growth up straight and clean until a sufficient height has been reached. Laterals that appear on this length of stem are stopped during the summer in the manner already described, the basal portions being cut off to the branch collar in the dormant season. As explained earlier, they are dealt with in this manner in order to strengthen the stem, see Fig. 7 (4). The single growth is then pruned back so that the laterals may form the head. It should be noted that the length of the leg is measured from the lowest branch to ground level. Allowance must be made for this when the position of the final cut is decided upon. The 60 mm. (2.5 in.) or so above the height allowed for the clean length of stem is the portion that produces

Plate 28. *Pinus thunbergii* grown and trained as cloud trees in Japan.

the branch system. It should be noted that the cut removes the leader, but during growth in the following season, the topmost shoot usually takes over. Should a completely open cup-shaped centre be required, this growth is removed with a portion of the older stem, otherwise a new leader will quickly form. Even after planting, this type of tree frequently throws up rival leaders and often they are allowed to develop without such a small tree suffering in any way. It is possible that the branching head will be less in demand in the future for a central leader is becoming more popular, even for smaller trees.

The production and training of large or heavy nursery trees.   The normal practice is to move trees from the nursery once the head has been formed, planting them in the permanent sites where they are to mature. However, where a high rate of vandalism is expected the larger transplant has become popular. This more mature stock with a stouter branch system is difficult to destroy and is thus a considerable advantage.

There is no vast difference in the training of this type of tree, for the need for a central leader is just as important. That this should be sturdy and substantial with a good, well-spaced supporting framework is essential. Growth, during the extra years that are spent in the nursery, should not be too vigorous, the laterals being healthy but short. The aim is to produce a tree that has every chance of growing out strongly once it has been planted in the permanent site. Sufficient transplanting to ensure that the root system is of a reasonably compact and fibrous nature is one of the most important operations in its production and it is a help in this respect if there is a high proportion of organic material in the soil. In this way growth is regulated without excessive pruning, but sufficient pruning is required to maintain a good form and to keep a clear stem up to a defined height. The total height may be from 4.6 to 6.0 m. (15 to 20 ft.). In some cases a more compact head is ensured by pruning back the main branches during the winter. Even in the nursery some form of supporting may be necessary, see Plate 27.

Training for group plantings. There is an impression that the beautifully symmetrical tree or shrub is the only one that should be

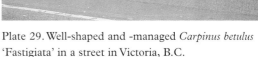

Plate 29. Well-shaped and -managed *Carpinus betulus* 'Fastigiata' in a street in Victoria, B.C.

grown. This is not correct, and one has only to take natural woodlands and groups of trees as examples. For landscape layouts and plantings in our parks, roadsides and gardens, group plantings are often desirable. Even so, it is generally true that the best results are from plantings that have been made from well-trained stock in the first instance. Trees in groups and woodlands must have a sound structure if the woodland is likely to be frequented by the public. It is noticeable that in 'natural' woodlands the trees are of various sizes, species and ages, and an attempt should be made to adopt this policy in plantings of this nature.

Training trees with character. There is sometimes a place for a twisted and gnarled tree, for example on the edge of a small coppice, or more so in Japanese gardens today, where specimens of *Pinus thunbergii* have been trained to suit the feeling of the garden, see Plate 28. Few would deny that such trees have character, but the raising and training of such stock must be on sound lines (see Plate 29), and the trees must not be allowed to grow too large for a framework which is not

Plate 30. *Pinus nigra* with a wide but strong branch junction at the base. Not a textbook-trained tree but one full of character.

structurally sound. There is only a limited demand for such trees and the vast majority of plantings should be made with well-managed and -selected trees and shrubs. Often too, trees develop their attractive character long after planting, see Plate 30. Suitable trees to grow on for this purpose may be selected at lifting time from nursery stock.

Natural Branch Formation

The impression may have been given that the formation of a branch system in a young tree is to a certain extent accidental. This is not so. The buds on a stem or twig are dominated by the terminal bud. This bud reduces the vigour of the remainder; in fact, those near the base often do not develop but remain dormant. They may remain in this condition for many years, perhaps throughout the life of the tree. However, should a break or a pruning cut be made in the upper portion, these lower buds may develop and grow out. It should be noted that dormant buds

Fig. 9. A diagrammatic illustration (side view and plan) of the natural branch formation which exists among many tree and shrub species. The lowest and oldest branch is No. 7, No. 6 being at right angles. No. 5 is at a completely different angle, and the opposite bud has only made a short growth. The two branches at No. 4 have been formed from opposite buds and have developed to fill in important compass points. So with No. 3 and No. 2, while the two growths at No. 1 are opposite to each other, one being over No. 5. It will be noticed, however, that there is a considerable distance amounting to several metres between the two. These diagrams were made from a young specimen of *Acer*. This mode of growth was already decided at the bud stage. The branches did not assume these positions during growth.

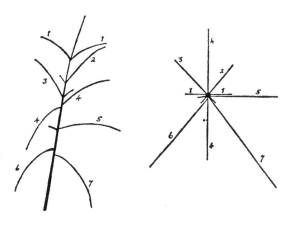

often keep pace with the developing stem over the years, ready to break out should the need arise.

Other instances of natural control exist and examples may be found in the Acers, see Fig. 9. The diagram is of the growth and formation of an actual young specimen of *Acer*. The leaf formation is opposite and decussate and one would expect the branches to be in tiers and opposite to each other, but in fact they are spaced out, often singly, along the length of the leader. The explanation lies in the fact that some growths are suppressed. Thus, for example, shoots 2 and 5 are strong but the opposite growth to each is short and has been suppressed. This is a natural habit and it does ensure that the main branches are evenly spaced along the length of main stem.

Twig shedding is another form of natural pruning, though often lack of light is the primary cause. Dead twigs on a rapidly expanding branch or trunk are quickly cut off by the thickening bark and callus, and thus they are unlikely to become a serious source of infection.

Notching and Nicking

These are established practices used in fruit-tree training. More particularly, they are used in the formation of the 'Delayed Open-Centre Tree'. In a well-formed tree of this type the branches are spaced evenly on a short central leader, which may be 0.6 to 1.2 m. (2 to 4 ft.) long. Nothing can be left to chance over such a short length of stem, and selected buds are encouraged to break and develop by notching. This is carried out during the dormant season, when a notch is cut about 10 to 15 mm. above the bud, completely removing a wedge-shaped piece.

This has the effect of stopping the flow of growth-inhibiting substances that are produced by the buds higher on the stem and as a result the selected bud breaks out into growth.

Nicking is carried out below selected buds in order to reduce their vigour. Again, this has been applied mostly to the production of fruit trees as a means of securing a more horizontal branching where the growths from the main stem tend to be erect. The ascending branch is cut back at one or two, or even three buds above the one which it is intended should grow out strongly to form the horizontal branch. Preferably, the bud selected for this should be a lower one. The remaining buds above this are prevented from growing out strongly by cutting a small nick just below each. The small amount of growth put on by a treated bud is sufficient to discourage an upward extension on the selected growth, thus forcing it into a more horizontal position.

THE PRUNING AND TRAINING OF
SEMI-MATURE TRANSPLANTS

The Semi-Mature Tree Nursery

There has been considerable debate upon the advisability of using the semi-mature tree for transplanting, owing to the high percentage of failures, which there has been in the past. There is, however, a growing awareness that adequate preparation has an important part to play in any ultimate success, and to prepare these trees for the stress that they will receive following transplanting, they are regularly moved in the nursery to develop a strong, healthy fibrous root system. Mainly, this concerns the production of a compact root system, a condition that is brought about by root pruning caused by the preparation of root balls for moving. A well-prepared specimen will survive in the root ball out of the ground for a full growing season provided it is well irrigated; and once planted, provided that adequate aftercare is given, successful establishment rates are high. Plantations are set up which are sometimes referred to as 'tree banks'. Good nursery stock is planted out and a few years later the trees are thinned and treated as large nursery transplants. Later still, the semi-mature trees are taken for planting into their permanent quarters.

This procedure is to be recommended, for both the shoot and root systems can be given adequate preparation. It is not proposed here to give full details of the various methods of preparing and transplanting semi-mature trees, this can be found in B.S. 4043:1989 'Recommendations for Transplanting Rootballed Trees'. But, whichever method is used, the main roots must be cut, preferably two seasons before the final move takes place, in order to encourage a compact easily moved system with lots of fibrous roots and root hairs between the trunk and root end. Undoubtedly this is better when carried out at intervals of 2 to 5 years while the trees are in the nursery, which is possible with row planting and by using specialist machinery.

The leading growth is just as important as the root system and it must be vigorous and healthy with the main branches well spaced. A compact branch system can, if necessary, be maintained by winter pruning while a clear trunk to 2.4 m. (8 ft.) helps the final move.

Semi-Mature Trees Taken from Woodland

The removal of trees from woodlands where they have been growing for many years is fraught with difficulties. Often, growth is strong and rank, indicative of a root system that will be difficult to move, as it will be large and extensive with the fibrous roots spread over a wide area, usually outside the prepared root ball. Preparation by root pruning, preferably two growing seasons before the intended move is important, the diameter of the root ball being at least ten times the diameter of the trunk measured at 1 m. (3 ft.) above ground level. The shoot system should also be reduced to compensate for root loss and at the same time improved in shape. It is an advantage to develop a clear leg to a height 2.4 m. (8 ft.) at least so that lower branches do not impede the use of machinery and moving equipment. Careful selection is important, for trees that are malformed, perhaps with forked leaders, are not suitable.

Prune roots with a good sharp saw or secateurs; see Chapter One, 'Dealing with Damaged Roots'.

CARE OF TREES AFTER PLANTING

Good nursery stock, adequately prepared is essential in the first place. But if strong, healthy growth is to be achieved in the years following planting the root system must be active and well fed. If the transplanting is into poor, dry soil there will be very little growth to train, and hard pruning to encourage it may be disastrous and wasteful of the growing years in the nursery. It is important to carry out good tree planting techniques if establishment is to be successful and not place further stress on the transplant. If good practices are carried out, then the newly planted tree will grow away unchecked, without any dieback of roots or loss of leading shoots and leaf production.

Plate 31. Poorly shaped *Ulmus villosa* due to lack of formative pruning. The removal of this scaffold would now seriously affect the health of this tree.

Young Nursery Stock

It is most important to establish a newly planted tree as soon as possible and it may be necessary to water to ensure a speedy establishment and the good growth that is required, especially during periods of drought. So far as pruning and formative training is concerned, it is important to continue the formative training process from the nursery through to the final establishment site; this will ensure that trees are structurally stronger and easier to maintain in the future, with less costs for mature tree care. Encourage longevity by removing potential structural defects that will lead to failure later in life, see Plates 13 and 31.

One of the most important points is to retain and encourage the leader for as long as possible (unless it is an open-centred branching head tree), see Fig. 10. Any dead, diseased or dying branches (the 3 Ds) should be removed beyond the point of damage to prevent further infection from pathogens. Remove any crossing, rubbing branches, or branches with included bark, which will lead to weak attachments in the future. Eliminating weaknesses early prevents wasteful, unnecessary repair work later.

It is important to identify as early as possible the first permanent scaffold branches, which will remain on the tree for its entire life. The height of these branches will be determined by the site and access requirements. A specimen in an urban setting will need to have the first branching relatively high, to allow for vehicular or pedestrian access, whereas a single specimen in a garden, lawn or bed can have them sweeping to the ground without interfering with anything. As the tree develops it may be need to have sub-branches removed from the main scaffold to maintain access; or, if the first permanent scaffold branches selected grow too large and low, the next ones up the main stem may have to substitute for them. If this can be determined early the need for large cuts will be reduced.

The desirability of pruning hard at the time of planting is often debated but the removal of branches and leaf should be kept to a minimum, as heavy pruning to compensate for root loss is extremely difficult to gauge. Too severe pruning can ruin the natural shape of the tree and heavy leaf loss will reduce the tree's ability to carry out photosynthesis, thus reducing food production that is essential if the tree is to establish. The trees also need the auxin produced in the shoot tips to establish new roots.

Adequate staking is also important until the tree grows away and is established. If the planting stock is relatively small and spindly, it may not need support or it may be possible to continue the nursery system of a stout cane and fastenings using the Max Tapener system. This will reduce the need for heavy-duty tree stakes, which are expensive and necessitate a more engineered approach to tree planting. Should poor staking techniques be carried out and good aftercare overlooked, irreparable damage can be caused to young trees by abrasion and girdling of the stem due to inappropriate tree ties, such as string or wire, and weakening of the stem by too much support.

Where stakes need to be used as a means of support, the short staking system should

Plate 32. A good example of basal flare from correct planting depth.

be used with tanalised round timber. The height of the stake should be a third of the overall height of the tree and secured by a single tie, not more than 25 mm. (1 in.) from the top of the stake. It is important to note that young trees require the process of seismomorphogenesis (the flexing and shaking of the stem by the wind) to increase the speed of incremental growth of stem diameter. The taller the stake, the less stem diameter and the weaker the trunk.

A sign of a developing well-pruned, -planted and -supported tree is the production of basal trunk flare, between the trunk and the root crown at soil level, see Plate 32.

Once the tree is established and growth is under way, increased vigour often results in the production of suckers and epicormic growths from the trunk and branch system. Any that break out should, if possible, be rubbed out as they develop; otherwise they should be cut out in the autumn. There may also be a

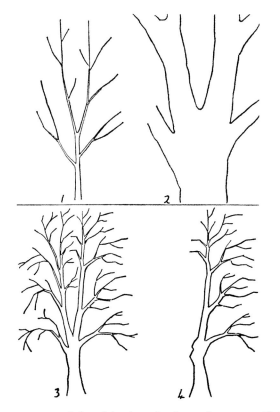

Fig. 10. The development of a tree with forked leader and the possible consequences. (1) A young tree in the early years after planting.

(2 and 3) The same specimen many years later at maturity, with a close-up view of the main crotch and an outline plan of the whole tree.

(4) The calamity that is likely to occur to such a tree. This may happen during high winds or bad weather and the tree is ruined.

need for thinning the branch system if this is at all crowded. Care must be taken to make the cuts cleanly to good parent branches, and without leaving snags.

Large Transplants

The same advice applies with these, and great care should be taken over the retention and development of the leader. Growth, to begin with, is often a little slower owing to the fibrous and restricted nature of the root system. As the tree develops, some thinning of the branch system may be desirable, for under nursery conditions the crown may be close and crowded. There should be no hurry to do this, for as growth develops freely, it will become more obvious where any cuts should be made.

Sometimes, through years of restriction in the nursery, growth is so slow that it does not break out readily even after two or three years of careful attention in the new site. This may be due to the bark and surface tissues of the stem being hardened, thus preventing expansion. There is a technique of deliberately slitting the bark of a young tree that is in this condition. A simple cut is made with the point of a sharp knife deep enough to penetrate the surface tissues to the wood.

The cut should be longitudinal and it may run the complete length of the trunk. This may be carried out after the first flush of growth is over in the spring, when callusing will be complete by the autumn. Stronger conducting tissues will be formed beneath this, and a better and more typical growth is speedily produced. This should only be carried out by a skilled person with experience of this practice.

The Development of a New and Stronger Head

The period of rapid growth following establishment is often very noticeable, especially with the faster growing subjects such as the Silver Birch (*Betula pendula*). A completely new head is often formed, and this is to the good, provided that it has developed from the original leader. If desired, the lower branches of the old head may be gradually removed, choosing the late summer period for this, and spreading it over three or four years if necessary.

It should be noted that this cutting off of the lower branches is required in the case of a feathered tree as the main head forms if a length of clear stem is desired.

Extra Heavy Standards and Semi-Mature Trees

A good tree will have a sound branch system and a prominent leader. When growths develop freely a few years after planting, a further selection and training may be desirable.

On the other hand, growth after planting may be slow, or there may even be some dieback. Cutting back may be desirable in order to restore the balance of shoot and root growth. This must be done carefully, choosing positions just above good growing points or back to main branches, avoiding snags that may die back to cause infection later. It is often desirable to carry out this pruning in two stages:

(1) during the summer, when the dead and weak portions are easily recognised. Any major cuts to be made back into the living wood should also be carried out at this time, for excessive bleeding, a risk with large spring cuts, would be disastrous to a tree fighting for its life.

(2) corrective pruning in later years as strong developing growth becomes established. This is carried out on the older growths that have, by reason of the move and check, become stunted.

Recovery from a Poor Start

The ability to grow away and make a good tree from a poor start varies. Some trees, such as *Picea*, seldom recover from a poor or broken leader. Again, young strong shoots do not break readily from weak wood and the hope of recovery may lie with the development of buds lower down, often near the base. Vigour, and the capability of growing and developing from dormant or adventitious buds are important if there is to be a recovery from a condition in which much of the former framework is poor or dead. Sometimes, freshly planted trees may die right down to ground level, breaking up strongly from there. Where more than one regenerating growth arises in this way and a single-stemmed tree is desired, the selection of the strongest and best-positioned one may be made at the end of the first season, when a general clean-up and pruning may be made, see Fig. 11 (2a and 2b).

The European Sycamore (*Acer pseudoplatanus*) is an example of a tree which will grow a strong leader and develop into a shapely specimen even after a poor start has been made. Secondary and annular thickening which follows the development of a new leader from a dormant bud or lateral gradually evens out any kinks in the stem of the young sapling and after a number of years there may be little evidence of the poor start. The damaged or broken leader should be cut back to a suitable growth or bud as soon as it is noticed, but the final cut may need to be adjusted later as a new leader develops, in order that healing and the formation of callus may take place with the development of the new stem, see Fig. 11 (1a and 1b). Even at a later stage, good pruning may help a tree to overcome the effects of the loss of the original leader. It is pointed out that a broken leader as well as a snag may become a source of infection.

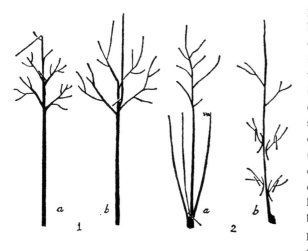

Fig. 11. Ways of overcoming a poor start.
(1a) A young tree with a broken leader, showing the position of a cut which could be made to a suitable bud or growth from which a new leader is likely to develop.
(1b) The position of the final cut is shown after the tree has responded by forming a new leader.
(2a) In this case the stem and branch system has either died or is very weak. However, suckerous growths are springing from the base. If it is desired to select just one of these the position of the pruning cut is shown.
(2b) The summer and winter pruning cuts carried out on the new stem, if a standard with a clean leg is desired. The laterals which have grown out below the level of the intended head are often so strong, that they branch in the first season, in which case the summer pruning should not be too severe, otherwise a considerable amount of secondary growth may appear.

To sum up and re-emphasize, the need for the early correction of any fault is important for the following reasons:

(i) the balance of the tree may be lost and a gap will occur which will often take several years to correct itself;

(ii) there is a reduction of the conductive tissues in the region of a wound until healing is under way. This will be more serious with the larger wound caused by delay, for this will take longer to heal;

(iii) the increased light which falls on the stem following the removal of a large limb may promote the production of epicormic growths in this portion of the branch system;

(iv) the loss of a large limb is a severe check to a young tree's root system. A portion of it may be killed and this will increase the risk of infection.

THE PRUNING AND MAINTENANCE OF MATURE TREES

Introduction

This section deals with the training of the tree as it reaches maturity and thus includes the removal of large limbs, and the various forms of crown work.

The term 'tree surgery' is often used collectively to cover these and other tasks connected with crown work on mature trees. In this context it is rather a loose term and is therefore a bad one and yet it conveys a sense of knowledge and skill. Both these qualities are needed, for often the work is undertaken at great heights using intricate climbing and safety equipment and involves the removal of a considerable weight of wood. In the hands of an incompetent arborist the risk of a serious accident is great, while a tree may be ruined by the faulty removal of a limb, perhaps causing considerable damage as it crashes to the ground. The health and safety implications are serious indeed.

Successful tree pruners or arborists must have a full appreciation of the growth and habit of the species or variety on which they are working, and a complete knowledge of the best way of achieving this object. They must be able to make the best of the material available, having in mind the safety of the tree after they have left it and the need for a natural effect when the work is completed. Thus something more is needed than just technical skill.

Many botanic gardens, local authorities and other public bodies, in addition to private establishments and commercial concerns, carry the arborist's craft to a very high standard. Yet there are far too many 'jobbing people' or 'cowboys' who go from door to door during the winter, offering to lop trees in order to let in the light, or

to prune, on the pretence that this is a task which should be carried out periodically. They work to gain profit from whatever they do at the time and also from the sale of logs for firewood afterwards. The trees that they work on are more often than not left in a mutilated state and beyond repair, an eyesore and eventually a liability. Those who engage in tree work should have a full knowledge of the recommendations set out on this subject by the British Standards Institution (B.S. 3998:1989 'Recommendations for Tree Work') or the American National Standards Institute (ANSI A300, Part 1:2001 'Pruning') and be able to work to these standards.

The leading arborist in an arboricultural team is the climber. He is supported by one or more as necessary, who work from the ground helping him to move equipment around the tree and in the removal and positioning of ladders. The groundsman will also clear the fallen branches, keeping the site generally safe and tidy and assisting the climber in his work. Often groundsmen are skilled climbers and share the role, as it is important that they

Plate 33. A highly professional, certified arborist at work in the Royal Botanic Gardens, Kew.

work together as a team and that they all understand and are fully conversant with the nature of the work to be carried out. A climber can only work effectively and safely when well supported from the ground. Never should climbing and ladder work be undertaken by one person on their own.

In addition to ability, the climber must have pride in his work, for many flaws and cavities can only be seen when viewed from above. Even the standard of the cuts that are made high in the tree cannot always be judged from the ground. An arboricultural manager should make sure that he has a climber and team who can be relied upon to carry out all types of tree work efficiently, safely and conscientiously.

As mentioned in the Preface, no attempt has been made in this book to deal with the subject of Tree Surgery in detail and the object of this short introduction is to stress the need for employing a specialized team on tasks of this nature, which involve work at heights from ropes, using sharp and dangerous tools, often with weighty limbs. They should be fully trained, certified arborists under a recognised educational study programme equivalent to that set by the International Society of Arboriculture with full and adequate insurance, see Plate 33.

Statutory Protection of Trees

Before carrying out any work on trees it is important to check whether the trees are protected by statute law under the planning and forestry acts.

The Forestry Act of 1967. If a live tree with a timber volume of 5 cubic metres is to be felled for saleable timber in the United Kingdom a Felling License will be necessary. This is controlled by the Forest Authority of England, Scotland, Wales or Northern Ireland and the application is sent to the Conservator of the Forests in the relevant country. Replanting of the land may be a requirement of the authority following the felling.

Tree preservation orders. The law on tree preservation orders is in Part 8 of the Town and Country Planning Act 1990 and in the Town and Country Planning (Trees) Regulations 1999. A tree preservation order, also known as a TPO, is an order made by a local planning authority (LPA) to protect trees or woodlands. The principle of a TPO is to make it an offence to cut down, uproot, lop or top, willfully damage or destroy a tree without the local planning authority's permission, to protect trees for the public's enjoyment, amenity and pleasure.

TPOs can cover all types of trees, including hedgerow trees (but not hedges or shrubs), and can cover anything from an individual tree to a woodland.

To find out if a tree on your property has a TPO you can contact the local planning authority's office, as details of orders are available for inspection. If there is a TPO on your tree, it does not make them responsible for the management of the tree, the owner remains responsible for the tree, their condition and any damage that they may cause. If the tree has a TPO, the planning authority's permission is required before any work is carried out on them, unless they are dead, dangerous or dying.

To get permission, an application to the local planning authority, detailing and justifying the pruning works or operations required, must be made in writing, sometimes on an LPA's own application form. If there are several trees on a property, a plan identifying the trees concerned may be required. Once the application has been lodged the LPA will consider permitting the work or permit it subject to conditions.

If work is carried out to a tree, without permission of the LPA, that deliberately destroys or damages it in a manner likely to destroy it, conviction in a magistrates court could see a fine of up to £20,000.

If an application to carry out work on a tree is refused an appeal to the Secretary of State for the Environment, Transport and the Regions can be made in writing within 28 days of the original decision. The Secretary of State may allow or dismiss the appeal.

Conservation areas. These are usually areas of special architectural or historical interest. Trees in conservation areas (CAs) can be subject to TPOs and are subject to normal TPO controls. However if they are not subject to a TPO, anyone wishing to work on or cut down a tree in a CA must give their local planning authority 6 weeks (42 days) notification of their intention to do so. No work must be carried out within that period. Upon receipt the LPA can decide either not to make a TPO (and inform the applicant that the work can go ahead) or to make a TPO, preventing the work's taking place. The same penalties occur should there be any contravention of this statute law.

If there are any doubts whatsoever, contact your local planning authority or arboricultural officer, who will give the necessary advice on particular trees.

Continuity of Formative Training

It may seem sufficient to say that training never ceases until a tree has reached maturity. This is true, but there is much more to the subject than just this. A watch must also be kept upon general condition, for without good healthy growth there cannot be effective pruning and training. It is, therefore, necessary to take account of all the factors that affect growth, and it is to help the reader to grasp this that the table at the end of this chapter showing the stages in the life of a tree has been produced.

Crown Cleaning out, or Deadwooding

This is the removal of dead, dying and diseased wood; stumps or broken branches to eliminate or reduce potential hazards; unwanted epicormic shoots and climbing plants like Ivy (*Hedera helix*). Any forms of unwanted rubbish accumulating in crotches such as squirrel drays and old notice boards can also be removed to tidy up the general appearance of the tree. This operation is often carried out in conjunction with the following forms of crown work.

Crown Lifting, or the Removal of the Lower Branch Systems

Sometimes referred to as 'raising the skirt'. The need to allow sufficient headroom for vehicles and machinery that may use certain service roads is dealt with in

Chapter Four. The removal of the main lower scaffold or lateral branches is also essential on roadside trees to allow head-room for vehicular traffic, which may include double-decker buses, pantechnican furniture vans, high-sided lorries, etc. In addition to a definite clearance being necessary, allowance should be made for the sway of the branches caused by wind and gales and the local turbulence that results from the speedy passage of large vehicles beneath the trees.

This operation may also be justified when the lower branches are close to a building and are thus liable to cut light off from certain windows, this may be considered an alternative to crown reduction. Again, there may be plants nearby whose well-being is important enough to warrant the removal of the lower branch system. By careful planning, however, and the selection of suitable subjects, it is often possible to overcome this latter problem without such drastic treatment. The cultivation of such shrubs as Rhododendrons, many of which require a light shade, is most successful when there is an overhead canopy, provided that it is not too heavy. But so much depends upon the planner. With branches cut-off at one level, the whole becomes unnatural, a scattering of bare-trunked, lollypop trees, in sharp contrast to a more natural planting, where branches are left, and encouraged in places to trail down to the ground, perhaps onto open patches and areas of grass, see Plate 30.

The best time for this work is during the late summer, for the branches are weighed down with foliage at this time, and this gives a better picture of the extent of the problem. Callus formation will also start before the winter sets in, when the rate of healing will be much slower. There is also little danger of bleeding at this period.

The removal of the branches at the main trunk is straightforward. It must be neatly finished, not only for the good of the tree, which is important enough, but,

Fig. 12. 'Lifting' a roadside tree to allow the free passage of tall vehicles or loads. The branch systems in broken outline should be removed. Although the lower branch which is over the bus is to remain, a careful watch would need to be kept on this, particularly during wet weather, and if necessary this will need to be adjusted by further pruning.

Plate 34. Young oak, lifted to the first permanent scaffold in its early years.

Plate 35. *Araucaria araucana* retaining the lower skirt to the ground to retain its natural appearance.

if by the roadside, it is a means of educating the public to appreciate good tree work. The crown and the tree as a whole must be left well balanced, both in appearance and weight. In other words, a branch moved on one side means that some balancing might be needed on the other, see Fig. 12. Such work on a large scale should, like any other tree operation, be carried out under strict supervision and with a good, well-trained and disciplined team, but with roadside work and with the safety of the public in mind, there is a need for special precautions. Often it is helpful to have some form of gauge made as a guide to the height and width of any vehicle which is likely to pass by.

It should be noted that the term 'lifting' is generally thought of as applying only to mature trees, but this operation may also be undertaken on younger specimens as part of their formative training. It may, for example, be desired to train a young feathered tree into a specimen with a clear stem or trunk. In this case, as the young tree becomes established in its permanent quarters the lower branches are removed, ideally spreading this over several seasons as the tree develops, see Plates 34 and 35.

Crown Thinning

This is the removal of branches and epicormic growth throughout the crown to reduce the overall density of foliage, including crossing, weak and dead branches, without affecting the overall shape of the crown, see Plate 36.

This operation should not be taken lightly, for it will affect the future shape and life of the tree. Obviously, that which is removed cannot be restored to its former growing position, but the full significance of this may not be realized until a piece has been taken off by mistake. It is of little use experimenting without any thought and far too many undertake thinning because it is something which they think should be done to trees, especially young ones, 'to assist in the formation of a shapely crown'. Thinning is not a means of beating time and of improving upon natural growth which includes branch shed. It is, however, a different matter if branches are removed which have started to decline in health and which are obviously dying. Crossing branches, especially on a younger tree, may be corrected by the removal of one or both of the offending

Plate 36. Crown thinning of a mature *Carya* sp.

pieces, but it should be remembered that a full branch system has a strengthening effect upon the framework as a whole, while a strong and vigorous root action is also encouraged.

The reasons for crown thinning may be outlined as follows:

(a) The operation allows light to penetrate the crown. This could be an advantage where there is heavy shading, for example near a building, to allow sunlight to reach windows, or over plants which are considered valuable and which should have more light.

(b) Wind resistance is reduced and this may be important to a tree that has a weak branch system. This also reduces the windsail effect on a tree.

(c) Weight is reduced and this may also help such a weak system. It should be remembered that the fall of heavy limbs may not only be dangerous to life, but often other branches on the trunk itself may be split or injured. This may ruin one entire side of a branch system, see Plate 23.

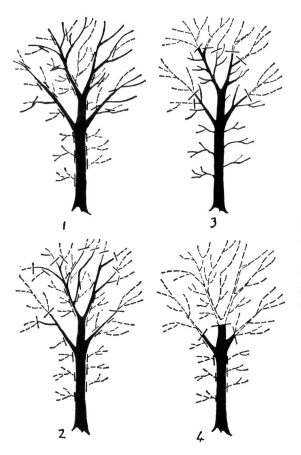

Fig. 13. Good and bad methods of dealing with a mature tree that is unsafe and is in need of attention. It should be borne in mind that only the main branches have been shown. The broken lines indicate branches that are to be cut out.

(1) This is correct. Those branches that are to remain have been left at full length with very little if any shortening.

(2) The branch systems that are to remain have been shortened. This may lead to cavities in the region of these cuts at a later stage and such shortening should not be carried out. (3) This form of lopping is definitely wrong.

(4) Lopped and topped to this extent it would make a suitable support for a climber, but the strong shoots resulting from the cuts would need to be cut out occasionally.

(d) It may be necessary as a means of restoring balance. It must be emphasized, however, that experience is needed to decide whether or not thinning is really necessary and, if it is, how extensive it should be.

Once it is decided upon, the procedure should be carried out in the following order:

(i) Remove any dead limbs and also those that show definite signs of dying through lack of light. It is to be expected that many of these will be found on the inside of the tree.

(ii) Remove badly shaped limbs, those with a narrow crotch angle and also any other dangerous limbs. Crossing and rubbing branches should be attended to.

(iii) The remainder of the branch system should be thinned evenly to the required amount, see Fig. 13. The arborist must take care not to over-thin, as the removal of too much leaf area will reduce the tree's ability to photosynthesize; not more than 25% of the tree's foliage should be removed.

Lateral branches from the scaffolds must be removed during the thinning exercise evenly from the main trunk out to the edge of the canopy in order not to create an effect known as 'Lion's Tailing'. Poor thinning operations remove all the laterals from the main scaffolds, leaving a bulk of material on the ends of branches. This then places too much end weight on the tips of the limbs, which will result in a weakened structure and eventually branch failure.

(iv) Before leaving the tree, the climber should check for and remove any 'hangers' left in the crown.

It should be noted that the work to be carried out in stages (i) and (ii) is really obvious, but while it is being undertaken the operator will naturally become more acquainted with the nature of the branch system and a decision upon the remainder of the work will thus be easier. As experience is gained it is possible to complete all the stages in one area before removing the climbing rope and equipment. Often it is better to start thinning in the top of the crown and then to work down, but the actual method of working will vary with the type of tree. The cuts should be made beyond the branch collar on the parent stem or branch, taking care not to weaken the remaining framework, see Fig. 14.

A decision upon the best time of year at which to undertake the operation is sometimes difficult. It is generally easier to gain an impression of shading, leaf formation and shoot density when the foliage is full and mature, but on the other hand, with deciduous subjects, the work will often be easier when it is carried out in the dormant season. Timing will therefore be a matter of judgement and convenience. The late winter or spring should be avoided with subjects which bleed, for example birch, maple, hornbeam and many of the leguminous species.

Crown thinning, which may result in the removal of a quarter of the branch system, is generally confined to deciduous trees. It is seldom necessary or desirable to treat hardy evergreens or conifers in this manner.

Crown Reduction, or Drop Crotching

Thinning in the normal way does not result in a reduction of the overall size of the crown. With crown reduction, however, the branches are shortened, the cuts being carefully positioned just above a substantial limb growing in the right direction, see Fig. 2. It is carried out over the entire main branch system if need be with the result that the overall height and shape is reduced and selected laterals form the new outline to the crown. It is important to maintain a balanced shape, appearance and condition. As with thinning, no more than 25% of the foliage should be removed from a branch that is to be reduced. If more is necessary then it may be more suitable to remove the entire branch.

Fig. 14. Part of a branch system under consideration for thinning. The broken lines indicate two branches that would be removed under a moderate thinning, the cuts being made at (a). Whole lengths are removed, making the cut as close to the parent branch as possible. Under a severe thinning policy, three additional branches are suggested for removal by making cuts indicated by (b).

Where the cut-back is extensive, this is obviously a drastic treatment, but it is justified where the branch system is considered to be inadequate for the full height and weight to be carried, or where the tree as a whole is failing in health and has, as a result, become 'stag-headed'. The branch dieback (stag-head appearance) is purely the symptom of a tree's poor health, and the removal of this dead wood should not be the basis of a control for a possible problem connected to the root system underground. Good husbandry should always form the basis of programmes connected with the management of trees, but a more definite decompaction and watering programme is necessary as a means of overcoming the condition of poor health.

Severe crown reduction will cause considerable stress to a tree, since heavy leaf loss and lots of large pruning wounds will lower its natural defence system and open the tree up to invasion from disease and decay. New growths from these pruning cuts are likely to be weakly attached and unsafe, so regular inspection of these wounds will be necessary as part of a tree management programme. Unfortunately following an exercise of heavy reduction, such regular follow-ups rarely occur.

Crown reduction may also be carried out to clear overhead power or telephone lines. Certain genera, for example *Fagus* and *Betula*, do not respond to crown reduction and may be killed by this type of pruning operation, see Plate 37.

Epicormic Shoots

These are strong shoots that spring directly from the main branches or the trunk when a tree is placed under stress. A number may spring from adventitious buds but they often originate from dormant buds that keep pace with secondary thickening. Normally they remain dormant unless activated by an extra supply of food as a result of an injury higher in the branch system. Thus the removal of a limb, even though the cut is made close to the main stem, may result in a flush of

Plate 37. Bad crown reduction to *Betula pendula* (this tree will probably die).

Plate 38. Dense epicormic growth resulting from severe topping of *Aesculus hippocastanum*.

epicormic shoots round the wound. As these are cut back, more appear and there seems to be no effective and permanent cure. All that can be done is to cut them back year after year during the dormant season. If left, they extend and take vigour from the crown itself and may cause this to die back, particularly in a dry season. An annual flush of these growths may also appear on the trunk, even down to the base and they should likewise be pruned back as hard as possible, see Plates 38 and 39. However it must be remembered that the tree is signaling a sign of stress and further diagnosis should be carried out and respective controls put in place as quickly as possible.

Sucker Growths

These spring from below ground level, either from or in the region of the root system, see Plate 40 and Fig. 45. They should be taken off cleanly as close as

Plate 39. Poor crown reduction to *Platanus ×hispanica* street trees.

Plate 40. Basal suckers growing from the base of a mature *Tilia ×europaea*.

possible to the point of origin on the stem. It may be necessary to scrape the soil away to reach the bases of the sucker shoots. The exposed piece should be wiped free of soil with a cloth, so that the secateurs or knife do not come into contact with grit that may spoil the cutting edge. Under no circumstances must a translocated herbicide ever be used to control these, as this will quickly lead to the death of the tree.

Crown Renovation, or Crown Renewal

Following the reduction of the major scaffolds, the tree is forced into the production of vigorous epicormic shoots from dormant buds along and at the end of the stubs. Following several years' regrowth, they will begin to make substantial-sized branches. A new crown can be made by selective thinning of these branches by retaining the stronger ones that will over time, provided the tree is healthy and able to form strong attachments at the pruning wounds, form a new crown. This practice is usually carried out on trees that have been badly pruned or topped in the past by incompetent people.

Lopping and Topping

Lopping is the practice of cutting back the main lateral scaffold branches of a tree to a stub or lateral branch not large enough to take over as the terminal growing point. Topping is taking the head out of a tree, often severely, either to leave it in a safe condition or in sympathy with a belief that it is something that should be carried out on trees periodically. These two operations are usually carried out together and are often referred to as purely 'Topping', see Plates 38 and 39. There is certainly no case at all for this operation, and too many of our present-day problems with trees are the direct result of this practice, which generally is a bad one, usually done by unskilled staff or people who don't care!! Not only does a tree that is treated in this way lose its natural shape and dignity for the rest of its

Plate 41. Death of *Populus* sp. due to too severe topping.

life, or at least for many years, but also it is such a short-term policy. A later paragraph explains how a tree that has been topped can eventually become dangerous, and the practice can only be justified in very rare circumstances. As an example of such a case, a tree that was already in a dangerous condition might be kept, after lopping, to form an effective screen and help to baffle the noise of traffic. Every effort, however, must be made to overcome the problem in other ways that will be more satisfactory, provided they leave the tree in a safe condition. For example, the branch system may be thinned to reduce the density and weight of the crown. An alternative method is to carefully reduce the size of the crown, while still retaining its natural outline. On the other hand, bracing may be the answer, thus leaving the framework in a safe condition. Sometimes it is possible to remove the target by fencing in a dangerous tree, but the barriers used must be effective against the public, including children.

If topping is undertaken, a planting scheme should be put in hand at the same time, so that the topped trees can be removed as soon as possible when the young ones are becoming established and are gaining height. With a small area, where space is not sufficient for the establishment of a young tree near an old one, the short-term policy of topping would not be justifiable, for eventually it would become necessary to take the tree out and valuable time would be lost in growing and training a young and perhaps more suitable one.

Factors to consider when deciding upon the future of a topped tree

(i) Age, vigour and general health. Provided there has been a vigorous response in growth, the stubs will be partly hidden. It may also be possible to thin these and improve the otherwise unsightly appearance, which is especially apparent during the winter. A tree that is very vigorous may, however, even after topping develop vigorous new epicormic shoots, which will grow and produce heavy wood that quickly becomes dangerous. It is important that any growth that has taken place after topping shall be safe and securely attached to the branch or trunk from which it originates. It should be remembered that the growths that are produced after lopping originate from dormant buds that are maintained and developed by the tree in the tissues just beneath the bark. They often grow very rapidly, and for many years at least are only held and supported by the surface layers of the branches from which they originated and are weakly attached. These soon become top heavy and fail at the stubs where they originate. Sometimes the new shoots can grow so quickly that they soon become taller than the tree before pruning and defeat the objective of the exercise, often producing a denser canopy.

The general health of the tree should also be considered, taking into account the rate of growth and the condition of the foliage. It can be taken for granted that topping has caused some setback in health, for the serious reduction of top growth, often between 50 and 100%, reduces the tree's ability to produce food and affects the root system. This may kill the tree if energy reserves are already low, especially on *Populus* spp., see Plate 41.

(ii) Condition of the wood. This must also be taken into consideration, for rot may set in with a large limb once it has been cut due to secondary disease infestation. The ideal pruning cut is just beyond the branch bark ridge and preferably to a sound growing point. Most topping cuts are made along a limb between lateral branches, creating stubs with large wounds. These trees, especially *Aesculus* spp., will not be able to close these wounds and the exposed tissue will begin to decay quickly. Deterioration may already be in progress at the time of making the cut, and this will be speeded up afterwards. Soon a cavity will develop on the top of the branch or trunk, breaking up the cut surface. In time, the trunk will become completely hollow, leaving just a shell to support the branch system that may have grown to considerable heights. Thus the tree will become very dangerous.

(iii) Size of branches which are cut back. Small branches that throw regenerating shoots after they have been topped usually increase in girth with this development. Thus the scar may eventually heal over completely, making a direct continuity of wood between the old and new stems. In such cases there is no weakness and the actual topping line may disappear completely. It should, however, be noted that callusing across the top of a branch is rather slow and even a small wound may take several years to heal.

Most of the cuts, however, which are made on topped trees are large ones. Complete healing is therefore very unlikely indeed and any attempt to restore shape and balance must necessarily be short-term. It is even possible that the process of thinning the young growths that is often connected with restoration work on topped trees will hasten the time when the same drastic process has to be repeated, for the selected growths will develop faster and their length and weight will render them dangerous. Subsequent toppings to make the tree safe must often be more severe in order to take the cuts below the areas of rot. It may also be necessary to cut back severely in order to correct an unsightly appearance, as topping makes trees look ugly and destroys the natural shape of the trees, especially during winter when the trees are without leaves.

There is another point to consider. One of the main principles in good training and formation is that narrow angles between main branches should be avoided to prevent the production of included bark. Yet this often results after topping, for two or more upright growths may originate from one point and the angle between them is most likely to be a small one. This, with the additional hazard of exposed and rotting heartwood in the narrow 'V' crotch, causes a serious weakness at the junction of the new growths.

(iv) It is also worthwhile to give some thought to the reason for the topping. As stated earlier, most topping has in the past been carried out needlessly or perhaps to let in extra light to a building and it should not be taken for granted that the specimen was unsafe, even though it was perhaps thought to be.

Method of inspection of a topped tree. Topping is an expensive short-term measure and if the tree is to respond to the operation, it will need to be continually monitored and have crown restoration work (crown renovation) carried out regularly. After the above factors have been considered, the following procedure should be adopted.

(i) Inspect the old cut surfaces, paying particular attention to the condition of the wood.

(ii) Inspect the junction of the new growth and the old wood with the aim of deciding upon the strength of the union. It should also be decided whether any thinning of these growths (crown thinning) is desirable, remembering that while a more natural habit is obtained in this way, even more vigour will be thrown into the remaining shoots. More wounds will be made and any weaknesses will thus be increased.

(iii) Inspect the remainder of the trunk, looking in particular for any cavities and make test borings (invasive inspection) if necessary to discover the condition of the heartwood.

(iv) In addition to looking at the topmost branches that originate from near the cuts, the remainder should also be inspected. Topping often results in the production of a large number of epicormic growths over the whole of the framework and it must be decided whether they can be thinned and trained to form future branches or be cleaned off as surplus.

Action after inspection of a topped tree.   When inspection has been completed, one of the following courses of action must then be decided on.

(i) *When the tree is unsafe.* Prune again, back close to the old cuts, but only if all the wood that will remain is completely sound;

or prune more severely, and as far back as is necessary to reach the sound wood (this is merely repeating the earlier mistake);

or head the stump back to a height of 3.0 to 4.5 m. (10 to 15 ft.) and use this as a support for a climber;

or remove the wretched specimen altogether and replace with a suitable young tree.

(ii) *When the tree is safe, with the wood at the original cut undamaged.* Leave the bushy head intact;

or thin out the overcrowded branches in an effort to balance the crown and thus produce a more natural growth (crown renovation).

In the latter case, the larger branches may be reduced in length in order to lessen wind resistance, making the cut just above a suitable point so that the development from this point may be according to the good principles laid down in other sections of this book, see 'Crown Reduction, or Drop Crotching', page 69. In all cases, arrangements should be made for the future inspection of the tree at regular intervals.

Other terminology.   Various other terms are applied to the practice of topping, for example 'heading' or beheading, 'tipping' and 'hat racking'. De-horning is a practice that is carried out with fruit trees, particularly apples, when they have become too tall and out of reach for harvesting.

Pollarding

This is an old form of labour-intensive pruning, usually carried out as a means of managing a tree from an early age to maintain a small manageable crown and produce small stems for ornamental effect. It should not be confused with topping mature trees, though the first crown reduction to form the permanent framework is a form of topping. Regular pruning of the young growths with secateurs or modern sharp saws is followed, often on an annual basis, back to 'knuckles' or 'knobs' formed at the ends of the scaffolds.

HEDGEROW TREES IN DEVELOPMENT SITES

When the pruning and training of hedgerow trees in a developed area is considered it must be realized that the environment as a whole has probably been changed. This may mean drastic changes in the soil, which will affect the root systems. Extra drainage means less moisture in the soil and the water table as a whole may be considerably lower. The conditions are often adverse to the well-being of the roots, which no longer have a comfortable existence, often being enclosed and covered by unkindly masses of tarmac and concrete. The changes can include an alteration in the soil level which stifles the feeding roots, or the laying of nearby mains and cables may, unless care is taken, involve the cutting of the main arteries of the system.

On the credit side, however, the hedgerow tree in the developed area, properly cared for and maintained, often has a more settled and even happier existence than before, for there are no grazing cattle sheltering beneath to compact the soil, to rub off the bark or to eat the lower branches, while there is little chance of damage from hormone sprays or close cultivation.

It is important, however, if this happy state is to be realized that the knowledge and experience of the arboriculturist is enlisted at a very early stage, preferably before the site for development has been planned. He should certainly be consulted before the work starts, so that he will know exactly what has happened in the vicinity which is likely to affect the trees and their growth when they are finally in his care. Even the removal of a nearby hedge, if this is to be carried out, needs to be done carefully and under strict and knowledgeable supervision, as otherwise the roots of a tree to be preserved may suffer unnecessary damage.

In contrast to such an early and timely consultation, the arboriculturist who is brought in at a late stage to advise upon a tree or planting is placed at a great disadvantage. He may have to advise upon the fate of a tree which has been saved at considerable expense and is a vital part of the planned effect, but which has been ruined by ignorance and a complete disregard of the laws of nature. The reader may well question the relationship of this to pruning, but the answer is that every new condition will finally affect growth and this in turn affects the arboriculturist and his pruning. This pruning should be carried out, not as a routine task which needs to be done, such as the final surfacing of a road, but as a means of correcting or improving conditions where necessary and possible. The pruning of a tree depends upon age and maturity and much of the advice that has been given in the previous section is applicable. However, there are certain factors that need special consideration.

Young Trees up to 20 Years Old

It is obviously necessary to train a lead, and encouragement and selection are usually necessary in the first instance. This may not be possible until good new growth is evident and is strong enough, and feeding, mulching and irrigation may be needed to encourage this. Some form of staking is necessary if the selected tree is very young and is likely, for instance, to miss the support of a hedge. When growth is very long and straggly, perhaps as a result of development through a tall, sheltering hedge, some cutting back may be advisable. This can only be carried out when there is a fair certainty that the tree will break out to enable a lead to be selected. As much care and skill is necessary with the selection and training of young trees from the hedgerow as with nursery stock. Trimming to form the desired length of clear trunk may also be required, remembering that it is better to cut at this stage than later when the wounds would be larger and the fault more difficult to correct.

There should be no hesitation in deciding to destroy poor and unsuitable specimens, especially if there is some injury or malformation that will be a continual and increasingly serious weakness as the tree grows older. Always bear in mind that fast growth is put on by good nursery stock after establishment and that replacement may be the better policy.

Semi-Mature Trees 20 to 60 Years Old

At this stage there will be some indication of the ultimate form and size of the tree. It may be too late to select a leader if the branching has split to form a head, but the first opportunity should be taken if this is possible and can be carried out without damage. Trimming to clear the trunk is often required, but there may also be such wounds as bark grazes etc. to clean up. Trees are frequently used as a means of supporting fences with nails or staples driven into the trunk. The policy must be to remove them if they can be pulled out without further damage, but otherwise it is better to cut them short leaving the remainder to be buried. If wires encircle the trunk these should be cut. Epicormic growths on the trunk and branches should be cleaned up.

Mature Trees over 60 Years Old

It is necessary first to look over such trees for dead wood. Branches die back inside the tree as it develops and these need to be removed. Considerable work is involved if the dieback extends over the branch system as a whole, and it is possible that a tree in this condition is dying rapidly and is not worth retaining. Expert opinion should, if necessary, be consulted at this stage. In addition to pruning back, the aim must be to improve the condition of the tree as a whole by feeding, aeration etc. Dead snags, the cleaning up of epicormic shoots on the trunk and the treatment of scars and cavities will naturally be dealt with at the same time.

With these older trees the soil is often compacted by cattle round the base with the main roots bare and damaged by constant wear and erosion. This is a condition that needs correction. Another effect due to cattle may concern the lower part of the branch system, for they will greedily eat the growing shoots. This leads to a stunted and congested shoot system at a definite level, referred to as the 'grazing line'. Growth is often reluctant to break out freely, even when this is possible after grazing has ceased, and the only solution is to thin as a means of relieving this congestion. The work may have to be spread over several years, choosing the dormant season.

TABLE OF TREE CARE AND MAINTENANCE

	NURSERY TREE	DEVELOPING TREE
Central leader or balanced head types	Train according to type. Maintain good growth and a fibrous root system.	Maintain principles of early training and correct faults as soon as possible.
Narrow V crotches through rival leaders	The best stage at which a tendency for these to form can be corrected. Pruning should be carried out with care.	As the tree becomes established, vigour increases and the rival leaders that tend to develop as a result of this often form a narrow angle with the main stem. Take care to avoid damage with ladder.
Branch pruning	Correct any harmful tendencies or potential weak attachments by careful pruning.	Watch for small snags and dead branches that may continue unhealed and are thus a danger. Gain the ultimate length of clear trunk desirable.
Wound healing	Provided that the cuts are made carefully, healing is usually rapid.	Wounds from pruning must be properly made to the branch collar, and callus formation will be vigorous around the areas that will be smaller than flush cutting.
Cavities	These are not likely at this stage, but snags are a potential danger and may lead to trouble later.	With rapid growth they are less likely. Watch, however, for possible sources, and dangers that may develop later.
Support	Staking and tying is often necessary to avoid damage and assist in the formation of a strong, straight leg with a balanced branch system.	At this stage strong anchorage and stout stem and branch system makes staking unnecessary provided that growth has been balanced and ripened.
Cultivation	Ground kept clean and weed-free to encourage good growth.	Planting circle kept free of weeds, to 1.5 m., to prevent competition and allow watering is necessary until establishment is secured. On a large scale systemic herbicides, such as Glyphosate, may be used.
Pest and disease control	A young nursery tree is likely to be swallowed up or permanently spoilt in cases of severe attack. In these formative years effective control is vital.	In the early stages control is still vital but later, as the tree reaches semi-maturity control becomes more difficult and expensive. Unless the attack is serious, control measures may be unnecessary.

	MATURE TREE	DECLINING TREE
Central leader or balanced head types	If a central leader has been formed it should have opened out at the top as part of the crown. Maintain a balanced head.	Check and correct weaknesses in the main branching system.
Narrow V crotches through rival leaders	It is too late to correct this fault in a major branch, although the removal of an offending limb may still be possible. The wound will be a large one. Bracing and/or thinning may be necessary.	An extended area of degenerated and weakened wood with included bark can be expected, and this would make the specimen with this weakness dangerous. Bracing often advisable. Thinning may also be required.
Branch pruning	Dead branches may appear from time to time as the crown extends and thickens, causing shading to a number of the branches. Corrective shaping may be necessary to meet the needs of a changing environment.	Some careful crown reduction and cleaning out may be necessary if dead branches appear. Dying back is likely from the extremities downwards.
Wound healing	It must be recognised that a large cut or wound made at this stage may never heal completely.	Large cuts or wounds will not heal completely and even callusing, if active, may be very weak. It is important to inspect old wounds regularly.
Cavities	A cavity that forms at this stage often remains for the life of the tree, although development may be naturally arrested and the harmful effects reduced.	Cavity development is likely at this stage, for the heartwood may naturally deteriorate beyond control.
Support	When a mature tree needs staking, or a support of any kind, it is normally considered to be an unsatisfactory state of affairs. A tree should be at its strongest at this stage.	Propping of the main lower branches may be necessary, especially with very old specimens. Bracing is also a means of support which may be necessary. Safety is always the first consideration.
Cultivation	Maintain healthy growth by regular mulches and good husbandry.	Correct any poor conditions, e.g. impoverishment or lack of aeration. A follow up programme of mulching can be considered.
Pest and disease control	As youthful vigour is left behind and more heartwood is formed, the danger is from the wood-penetrating saprophytic or parasitic fungi.	Control may be needed as a means of maintaining vigour. Weakness and pest or disease attack may hasten the end at this stage. The danger from wood-penetrating fungi increases. A decision must eventually be made as to whether the specimen is worth keeping.

Chapter Three

The Pruning of Shrubs and Climbers

GENERAL PRINCIPLES

Shrub pruning may be necessary for a variety of reasons and the method and timing vary considerably with the species or variety and with the age and condition of the subject. Regular pruning is only necessary with comparatively few shrubs, while for many it is not necessary or desirable at all.

Reasons for Pruning

The main reasons for pruning are given below, but it should be remembered that they are often inter-related. When a shrub is pruned there may be one or more objectives in mind. The main ones are as follows:

(i) to cut out dead or diseased wood and sometimes to free the subject of pest- or disease-ridden material;

(ii) to correct or improve shape; for example, a branch may be considered to spoil the general outline. It may also be necessary to prevent a shrub from overgrowing a weaker neighbour or a path, etc., see Figs. 17 and 18. A crossing branch may shut out light and air from the centre of the bush, or may be bearing down on others to spoil the general shape. It must always be borne in mind that certain shrubs such as *Poncirus trifoliata* have a tangled growth, and it would spoil them to train them too severely. This cannot be over-emphasized. A further example is provided by many of the Ericas and Callunas. They need an annual pruning, for otherwise they become tall and out of character in the garden where they grow under comparatively sheltered conditions compared to those which prevail in their natural habitat. Also the soil tends to be rich by comparison with that of moorland or heath and this again leads to rank unnatural growth.

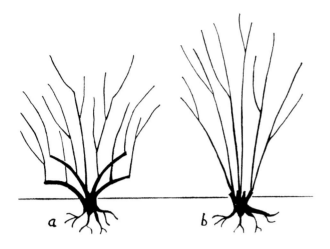

Fig. 15. The wrong and right methods of pruning a shrub which is to be encouraged to produce a quantity of new wood each year from near to the base—e.g. *Forsythia*. (a) This shrub has not been cut sufficiently hard. Too much of the old wood, which has arched over, as it has become heavy with flower and fruit, has been left. The result is an ugly bush and weakened growth. (b) The correct pruning of this type of shrub. There is no really old wood above ground level.

(iii) to maintain or improve flower display. For this to be fully effective, correct timing is very important, for the growth and flowering habits of shrubs in particular must be taken into account when deciding when to prune. This will be found to vary with position and locality and with such general conditions as soil type, rainfall, exposure to wind and sunshine, etc.

Habits of Flowering

Shrubs may be grouped according to their flowering habits.

Group 1. Those which flower on the current season's wood or growths

Generally, these subjects flower in the middle or towards the end of the growing season, the earlier part being spent in growth from buds which have rested during the winter on the previous year's shoots or on older wood, see Figs. 48 and 50. It will be noted that by drastic pruning, the number of buds or growths that can develop will be reduced and as a result extra vigour will be thrown into the remainder. An example of this is *Buddleja davidii*, for if this subject is left unpruned, the result is a large number of smaller flower trusses, whereas, if pruned hard, the reduced number of growths which develop produce much larger trusses. The pruning is in this sense a form of thinning. The timing for this hard pruning is important, for if it is left too late growth will have developed only to be wasted when subsequently cut off. With subjects which are treated in this way and which are not fully hardy it is important to wait until the severe weather ends, when the overwintering buds begin to break out in the spring from the living wood. In this way the top growth is left for protection during the winter, and it can easily be decided just where to make the cuts in the spring. If it is necessary to cut evergreen shrubs during the winter period the collections should be light and as scattered as possible.

Group 2. Those which flower from the previous year's wood

Many of the hardy deciduous shrubs are in this group. They can be divided into two main classes based upon their period of flowering:

(i) those which blossom really early, often before leaf or growth is produced, the flower buds opening directly upon the older wood, e.g. *Forsythia* spp.;

(ii) those which blossom later, producing short laterals during the spring and lowering from these in the early summer, e.g. *Philadelphus* spp.

Many shrubs in these two classes benefit from annual pruning, when wood may be cut out immediately after flowering, allowing the maximum period for the young growths to develop in the extra light and air, but the extent of this varies with the subject and the season. With Forsythias for example, or similar subjects which respond vigorously, some form of annual pruning after flowering is beneficial, while no pruning at all is needed with *Daphne mezereum*. This cutting out of the older wood with subjects like Forsythia can be looked on as a means of retaining vigour. Another example is the *Cytisus* hybrids, which may be cut back as the flowers fade and by this method spared the effort of producing heavy crops of seeds. Instead, this energy is put into developing growth, see Fig. 29. There are many other examples to be found in Part II of this book.

Group 3. Those which produce flowering spurs on the older wood

These spurs normally develop from year to year and are thus found even on the really old wood of the main branches. This habit is found, for example, among Rosaceous trees and shrubs, *Malus*, *Pyrus* and *Prunus* spp. to quote only three. Flowering may not be confined to the spur systems, for it sometimes occurs on the previous year's wood as well, e.g. *Chaenomeles* spp. Normally, a free-growing shrub of this group needs little if any pruning. Instead, shoot production in the early years followed by spur formation results in the achievement of a balance between growth and fruiting. In confined spaces, where some form of training is necessary, stopping rather than pruning may give better results. Stopping during the growing season provides a check to growth and in this way encourages spur formation and flowering.

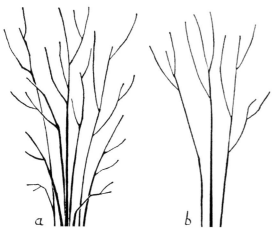

Fig. 16. A well-furnished shrub that is pruned hard fairly regularly compared to one that has been over-pruned—e.g. *Forsythia*.
(a) A well-maintained shrub with lower twiggy growths that provide a furnishing down to ground level. No really old wood remains.
(b) An example of over-pruning. Only the youngest growths have been left and there is no lower furnishing. Such over-pruning, carried out year after year, would eventually weaken the shrub.

Extent and Regularity of Pruning

This depends upon the subject, its vigour and general condition. Furthermore, pruning is not necessarily required as an annual operation and the only guide that can be given is to consider the extent of flowering and growth before a decision is made. Why for example prune a young *Forsythia* which is growing and flowering well? The same specimen may on the other hand need some pruning a year or so later when the proportion of old wood may be too high. In a sense, the pruner endeavors to regulate and adjust the balance between growth and flowering, but a poor or very good growing season can upset this.

It has already been mentioned that no pruning is necessary on *Daphne mezereum* and many other shrubs are in this category. It is difficult for the beginner to have a clear picture and to decide which subjects will benefit from pruning and which will not. It can, however, be stated that the response to pruning for invigoration and better flowering should be growth. Before a cut is made the pruner must be sure that the specimen will respond to such treatment by producing suitable growths, unless of course some form of thinning is being carried out, when it is important to leave a good spacing of the right type of wood. Experience and reference to Part II will help the reader to decide.

The main framework requires special consideration, for it must only be cut out if it can be readily renewed, unless of course it is diseased or dead. Many shrubs such as *Hamamelis mollis* have a permanent framework and this cannot easily be replaced, see Fig. 18. The stool habit, with its free production of young growths at or below ground level, obviously lends itself to quite severe pruning, when some of the older wood may be cut down completely to the base. Failure to cut this type of shrub sufficiently hard when the occasion demands will often spoil its appearance, as a considerable buildup of old wood results which will in time become ugly and support only weak growth, see Fig. 15.

Although there are exceptions, as a general rule the slower growing shrubs do not need much pruning. They are not likely to encroach but in addition they often retain their main framework, e.g. *Magnolia stellata*.

The Natural Effect

It is important to retain a natural appearance when pruning for an informal effect. This is emphasized again and again in Part II of this book, which deals with the individual requirements of the genera and species. Some shrubs, again to mention *Daphne mezereum* as an example, have a close, almost dome-shaped outline which is their natural habit and is not the result of pruning. Indeed, as stated earlier, pruning is undesirable with this subject. The majority of shrubs, however, have a more open habit, often with arching branches, and when they are pruned this can only be kept by cutting growths out individually. This will often mean making the cut well back into the bush where it is hidden by the growths which remain and which are left at full length. In addition, for a fully furnished and natural effect, the branching should be left to develop down to ground level. This is also emphasized frequently in Part II. It is often helpful to leave the lower twig growth in order to gain this fully furnished effect. The lower branching near ground level also helps to check weed growth and keep the soil moist through shading. The complete removal of these small growths creates a vase-shaped outline that is undesirable, see Fig. 16.

Special care is necessary when pruning prostrate or dwarf compact shrubs to an edge. An unnatural surface will be built up very quickly by merely cutting all growths indiscriminately to this line. Some should be cut off, back into the shrub, well away from the edge. In this way an irregular effect is obtained, possibly with small patches of bare soil here and there along the edge, see Fig. 17. With a border planting of Ericas, a wall effect may be avoided by lifting some of the younger and

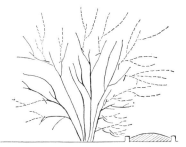

Fig. 17. When it is necessary to restrict the size of a subject that responds well to pruning, the task is a relatively simple one. The subject of the diagram is overgrowing a path (shown in section) and the suggested pruning cuts with the pieces to be removed are shown in broken line. By this method an informal and natural surface effect is maintained.

topmost growths and by cutting the older and dead ones away from beneath, taking them back close to the centre of the plant.

The same care to avoid a straight and hedge-like appearance should also be observed when pruning a larger shrub as a means of restricting growth, for instance, across a path. Such attempts are not successful with subjects that do not readily throw out new shoots and regenerate. In fact, some adjustment to the layout in these cases may be advisable if the specimen is to remain and develop properly, see Fig. 18. It would be wrong, for example, to cut back *Hamamelis* in this way, but a Yew (*Taxus*) or Box (*Buxus*) would respond very well indeed. To achieve an irregular and informal surface, the cutting back should be done at various levels on the framework of the bush instead of to one hard and definite outline. It should be carried out in three stages as follows.

(i) The large cuts are made on the older wood, often at points right in near the centre of the bush. They should be made very carefully and an impression of the effect that the removal will have upon the appearance of the bush as a whole should be gained before the cut is finally made. It is of little use being sorry afterwards. Often, only two or three such cuts are necessary, the object being to shorten the longest growths into the bush where they will break out again. They should be taken from the parts of the bush which are most crowded and where their loss will not be noticed.

(ii) The medium cuts are made, often on wood that is perhaps in the region of 5 to 10 years old. They should be made after the larger cuts, exercising the same care to avoid drastic cutting and to position each cut with accuracy. The overall effect should be taken into account as the operation continues, removing pieces over the entire surface one by one, carefully and cautiously.

(iii) The final stage involves the removal of a number of the tip growths which may be no more than 150 to 300 mm. (6 to 12 in.) long.

All this obviously controls growth, but the process may need to be a gradual one spread over a number of years. The fact that more light and air is let into the bush, results in the development of growths from the older wood, and by repeating the process on other branches in the following year or two if necessary, the shrub can be reduced still further.

The best period for this type of pruning depends upon the subject, but generally the spring is the best for evergreens. Deciduous subjects may be dealt with at any time during the dormant season, but the few weeks from late summer to the fall is also a very good time, for the effect on the existing foliage may then be seen.

When engaged on work of this nature it is often necessary to scramble and work inside the bushes, and it is advisable, therefore, to wear old clothing. It is a dirty job, particularly with large evergreens which are growing in the vicinity of industrial

Fig. 18. This specimen, overgrowing a path (shown in section), might well be a bush of the Witch Hazel *(Hamamelis mollis)*, one of the shrubs which retains a permanent framework of branches and which does not respond well to regular pruning. Under these conditions, the only real alternative to pruning would be to replan the surrounding area so that the path is re-routed or removed completely. The drawing was taken from an actual specimen growing in such a situation, with a background of trees on the side opposite to the path, and this has led to an unbalanced habit, with the specimen drawn towards the light across the lawn. Some would prefer to balance the bush by making a cut at (a), but in this setting, this mode of growth is quite in keeping. The background of trees and bushes would also need to be held in check.

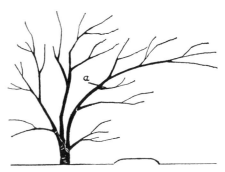

cities, and hosing down with a forcible jet a day or so before the work is to be undertaken will wash away most of the dust and dead material which has accumulated.

Variation of Habit

This has to some extent been touched upon in the previous section, but consideration must be given to those forms of growth found among shrubs that do not conform to the normal bushy habit. The prostrate habit of, for example, *Cotoneaster dammeri* as compared to the upright rigid growth of *C. simonsii*, must be taken into account. The former will seldom require pruning, except perhaps to halt the advance of the mat of creeping growths. There are many other examples of contrasting habits, even among closely related plants. For example, two *Viburnum* species provide another illustration where common sense and a full use of the powers of observation are absolutely necessary, if the varying habits are to be taken fully into account. *V. plicatum* has an upright stem which bears horizontal branches, whereas in close and crowded conditions, *V. opulus* is often a thin grower with long shoots which may develop through neighbouring shrubs if they are taller thereby gaining support in their search for extra light. Under these conditions it would be wrong to cut these long growths back in order to gain a bushy habit. Constant pruning would deprive the subject of sufficient light to the detriment of the shrub.

Hard Pruning

It will be apparent from the principles which have already been outlined that there is an advantage to be gained in cutting some shrubs hard back annually, but the position may be made clearer by the following summary.

(i) Half-hardy subjects cut back annually. As indicated earlier, these are not cut back in the spring until after the danger of severe frosts has passed and as new growths break out from the older wood. Much of the young growth may be killed during the winter, e.g. *Fuchsia magellanica*.

(ii) Those subjects which respond to annual pruning with an improvement of flowers, foliage or stems, e.g. *Cornus alba* 'Sibirica' (stem effect). With the majority this is carried out in the early spring, see Fig. 28.

(iii) Those subjects which respond to hard pruning by the production of adventitious buds or the development of dormant buds from the older wood. Such treatment is often followed by an improvement in shape that may be a good reason for doing this.

It will have been noticed earlier in this chapter that pruning is mentioned as a means of correcting shape. The nature and severity of the pruning will depend upon the necessity, and the ability of the subject to react favourably. Subjects which do respond readily and are completely out of shape may be cut right back, almost down to ground level as an alternative to the gradual shortening described earlier in this section. Many evergreens such as Yew (*Taxus*) and Box (*Buxus*), for example, will do this. The period for this drastic cutback varies, but with most deciduous subjects which respond the work may be carried out during the dormant season although if there is a danger of bleeding it should be completed before Christmas. Evergreens, on the other hand, should not be cut back during the winter. The work is best done in the late spring after the danger of severe frosts is past, otherwise the young growths may be damaged and the root systems checked when there is no foliage to feed them. Conifers in particular suffer from winter pruning. Hard pruning often seriously checks the root system, and any form of feeding, mulching and if need be irrigation, is helpful. The fresh rooting which develops with the new shoot system is encouraged by this treatment. There is the point too that hard pruning, carried out annually, drains the soil of nutrients and that it is necessary to make good this loss.

Heavy cutting back on occasion, when there is a favourable response, helps to correct any poor pruning which has been carried out in the past, perhaps through the use of unskilled labour.

The new growth that follows pruning may not be sufficient even to hide the large, ugly cuts that have been left behind on the old wood or stumps. In such cases it may be advisable to propagate from any growths which break out, and start again. Such growths breaking from the old wood often root quite readily.

The Need for Constant Vigilance and Records

With a specimen in a poor condition, perhaps continually showing dead twig and branch growth, some improvement in the culture is required, that is, of course, if the plant is to be retained and not destroyed. The danger is that one piece after another may be cut off by the conscientious worker in his efforts to keep the place tidy, without the plant's condition coming to the notice of the person in charge. This is only likely in a very large department, but there is much to be said in favour of a recording system that will prevent this happening.

It is also very important for the pruner or gardener to report any serious and widespread dieback which may occur over the collection, not just to cut it off and say nothing, otherwise a serious trouble may be present unidentified, e.g. Fireblight (*Erwinia amylovora*).

Due care must be taken with labels which are attached to a shrub for they can easily be cut off and destroyed with the arisings.

Care is also needed with tools, for if they are left lying about they are quite easily picked up with the arisings and perhaps lost. Brightly coloured tools are an advantage as they can be readily spotted if accidentally dropped, e.g. the bright red handles of the Felco No. 2 secateurs.

THE PRUNING AND TRAINING OF WALL SHRUBS

Many shrubs are grown against or within the shelter of walls. Not only do they provide a pleasant and interesting contrast and relief to the structure, but the warmer and more sheltered conditions, particularly with a warm, sunny wall, provide a means of increasing the range of subjects which can be grown in the garden as a whole. There is a great variety of form and habit among plants which are normally grown in this situation and this must be taken into account when deciding upon their management and pruning. It is emphasized that large and vigorous growers are not successful when restricted in height and size, e.g. *Celastrus orbiculatus* is better planted where it has ample scope for development.

The following examples show how pruning can be related to the variable habits of growth and flowering found among these plants, and it is only by having regard to these that the best results can be obtained. The account is by no means complete, and the reader is advised to consult Part II of this book for more details of any particular species.

True Climbers

Subjects which cling hard against the wall or support

Hedera helix, Ivy. The adventitious roots freely produced by the stems that are

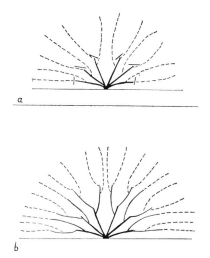

Fig. 19. Two diagrammatic illustrations of fan training in the early stages.

(a) A young specimen that has been trained from an early stage in the nursery is planted in position against the wall. The side growths are tied out on canes that are attached securely to the horizontal wires. All the growths must radiate from the centre like the spokes of a wheel; indeed, throughout the life of the specimen this principle should be followed. The actual centre must not be filled by a growth, another rule to adopt throughout the life of the bush. The growths are pruned back by approximately one third to an equal length. The subsequent growths, which may be tied in during their development, are shown in broken lines.

(b) The process is repeated as growth develops, but the use of canes may be dispensed with after the original branches are secured by the growths above them

tightly pressed against the wall hold the plant up securely. The mature growths, which branch freely, are produced at a later stage. There are two methods of treating this subject:

(i) The whole surface may be clipped over once or twice, e.g. before and during the growing season. This keeps the wall surface furnished without allowing the mature branching to develop, see Plate 44 and Fig. 35.

(ii) No pruning in order to allow the mature branches to develop, perhaps partially cutting them back at a later stage if they are considered too large.

Hydrangea anomala subsp. *petiolaris*. From the creeping mat of growths, lightly held by adventitious roots against the surface, mature branches short and spur-like are produced. These are the flowering shoots and they are therefore retained, perhaps being pruned back a little at a later stage if they become too long, see Fig. 37.

Subjects which are trained hard against a wall

This is often effected by tying them to a support system. They are in fact natural climbers and may be used to develop over an old tree or pergola system. By a suitable arrangement of wires or stakes, many of these subjects may be encouraged to cover the available wall space. They can be grouped for pruning purposes into four main categories.

(i) Those which are pruned back to a permanent framework and spur system. An example is the Wisteria, which has a spur system of flowering. A few permanent branches are trained fanwise against the wall as a supporting framework. As the space is covered and throughout the life of the plant, the extension growths that develop and are not required for framework purposes, are pruned back by stopping to 150 mm. (6 in.) during the growing season, cutting these back in the winter to the lowest one or two buds. They are not cut back hard during the summer, as the secondary growths that are often produced would not ripen properly. Any that do develop from the lighter summer pruning will naturally be cut off by this shortening back during the winter. In this way, growths that are not needed for extension are taken off and the energies of the plant directed into the production of flower buds. Such pruning also confines the plant, for the long growths would prove to be a nuisance to free passage, for example, by a path. In addition, shoot pruning during the summer provides a check to vegetative growth and thus promotes flowering, see Fig. 51.

(ii) Those which are pruned annually after flowering by taking out the old wood. This is done to encourage the production of young wood that flowers the following year, e.g. *Lonicera ×americana* responds in this way. This policy may result in much of the older wood being cut out each year, although it is usually necessary to leave the oldest stem wood. Also it is difficult to carry out this replacement pruning cleanly with many climbers, for the growths naturally twine round each other and it must be done carefully, without injury to those which are to remain. The subjects treated in this way usually flower along the length of the previous year's wood, see Fig. 38.

(iii) Those which are pruned back hard each year, often to near ground level. Clematis in the Jackmanii and Viticella groups are examples. They grow rapidly and flower on these growths during the same season. The pruning, carried out in the spring as the new growth buds swell, takes away the old growth, much of which has been killed during the winter, and thus prevents a hopeless tangle between new and dead wood.

(iv) Shrubs which have a scandent habit, gaining height by this means. Many of these subjects, if grown on a wall in a restricted space, become thick and untidy if left completely unpruned. *Forsythia suspensa* provides a good example. It is by nature a scandent shrub, producing large growths that clamber, but such extensive growths must be checked when grown on a restricted space such as a wall. This subject produces young growths from the old wood very freely and these can be used for the replacement of parts of the main framework, as this becomes necessary. In the same way, a proportion of the trailing growths that furnish the surface of a mature bush can be pruned away each year on a replacement system. Normally, as this subject flowers from the previous year's wood, pruning is carried out immediately after flowering, see Fig. 31.

With *Forsythia suspensa*, this may with advantage be carried out annually, but with many others, only a light and less frequent pruning is necessary. This pruning is often most effective when whole lengths are taken out, rather than short pieces (which is merely a form of formal clipping). When an annual pruning is required much of the framework is only semi-permanent.

NON-CLIMBING SHRUBS WHICH ARE PLANTED AGAINST A WALL

The following classification is based upon habit of growth and training.

Those with a permanent framework trained fanwise hard against the wall. Subjects that produce a crop of growths freely after pruning may be cut back annually to near the main framework, the period being adjusted with the flowering. For example, *Vitex agnus-castus* flowers on the current season's growths at the end of the season. Thus, these are pruned off in the early spring, being left for protection during the winter, see Fig. 50. On the other hand, *Prunus triloba* 'Multiplex' flowers in the spring on the previous year's wood. It is therefore cut back after the flowers fade and the new growths which develop bloom in the following year.

Chaenomeles speciosa and the various hybrids flower on a spur system as well as from the previous year's wood. They are typical of those subjects which respond to hard pruning close to the main framework, and this is often most effective when it takes the form of summer pruning, which promotes spur formation. In its simplest form, the summer growths are pruned back to approximately one-third of their length as the basal portion commences to harden. These are later taken back to two or three buds during the winter. A more intensive form of pruning consists of a periodic stopping, taking the young growths back to 50 to 80 mm. (2 to 3 in.), or even less as they develop, repeating this with any sub-laterals which arise a few weeks later. It is often necessary to start with this system of pruning as early as late spring, but the leading growths for the main branches are left to grow freely while there is wall space to cover. This frequent stopping during the growing season results in a reduction of leaf surface. This inhibits free and rank growth in both the shoot and root systems and thus encourages spur and flower formation. In addition to *Chaenomeles speciosa*, a number of other shrubs in the family Rosaceae such as the Cotoneasters and Pyracanthas respond to this treatment. It is really a type of Lorette pruning, which consists of frequently stopping back the growing shoots during the summer months, as sometimes used with apples when grown on cordon, fan and espalier systems.

It is emphasized that under this system the effect of the close growth and flowering from the main branches is a formal one. The original main branches should be carefully laid out to produce a near perfect design, whatever is decided upon.

Usually the layout is fan-shaped. Pruning and training is therefore necessary so that as the original branches grow and become more widely spaced, suitable laterals, usually two on each, must be retained to fill the gaps. Therefore, before any stopping is carried out, the required growths should be selected and secured to canes or wires laid in the right directions, see Fig. 19.

Weaker-stemmed shrubs which need support when grown against a wall. Generally, these are the more tender shrubs that need a wall for shelter. The provision of a support, while not absolutely necessary, enables such shrubs to reach a greater height than otherwise possible and thus achieve the desired coverage. Many of the Escallonias, such as *E.* 'Langleyensis', provide examples. Pruning is often necessary in order to keep the shrub within bounds, and this may be carried out after flowering, when lengths of the older wood should be cut back to younger growths nearer the centre of the bush. Also, in this way the shrub is saved from expending energy needlessly on a crop of fruits, see Fig. 30.

Strong-growing, self-supporting shrubs grown in the vicinity of a wall. Again it is usually the tender shrubs that are planted in such a position, for shelter. Often, branches are held back nearer to the wall, but no actual support is necessary. *Garrya elliptica* provides an example, for it can stand entirely without any support. Lengths of the older wood are taken out if any pruning is required in order to restrict size, see Fig. 32.

SHRUBS GROWING WITH OTHER PLANTS

Shrubs are sometimes grown among plants of a bulbous or herbaceous nature. In the wild or woodland garden, for example, it is common to find Primulas, *Meconopsis* and Lilies thriving with woodland-type shrubs including Rhododendrons. It is important to plant with a good spacing in the first place, otherwise the smaller subjects may be overgrown. Many of the woodland shrubs such as the Large-leaved Rhododendrons, *R. falconeri* for example, are loose-growing and are not commonly pruned nor do they take kindly to it.

Shrubs in sunny positions among herbaceous and bulbous plants are often used for background or framework purposes in order to provide sufficient height for smaller herbaceous plants that do not require staking. They must be sun-lovers, suitable for an open position and must have a reasonably compact growth. The latter is by no means the least important, for by making a suitable selection pruning is reduced to a minimum. With a large-growing subject in the wrong position, for example, in a small narrow border, the pruning may need to be severe. Not only is extra work involved, but also it is difficult to mask the cuts and avoid a mutilated or hedge-like and formal appearance that would be completely out of place. To be fully effective, the selection should provide shelter, background and height, with the minimum of restrictive pruning. It is a great advantage if they provide a display, either of flowers, berries or foliage. As an example, the larger Cotoneasters such as *C. ×watereri* would have few flowers and be difficult to control in a small herbaceous border, *C. conspicuus* being more suitable in every respect. It is also important that the herbaceous plants should not be allowed to swamp the shrub, for if these suffer the effect will be very tattered during the winter when the herbaceous tops have been cut down.

Any pruning that is necessary must be done carefully in order to keep a neat and attractive surface, at the same time retaining the natural habit. This is particularly important when the border is in display during the summer months. Shrubs suitable for the mixed herbaceous border may be placed in one of the following groups.

(i) Shrubs which respond to early spring pruning. These are very easy to maintain, for when the pruning is due the herbaceous plants are either just above or below ground level and thus do not impede the work. When the selection is made, height must be taken into account, for some are taller than others by reason of the amount of annual growth which they make; for example, *Hypericum inodorum* 'Elstead' grows taller than *Caryopteris ×clandonensis* even when they are both cut to ground level. *Spiraea douglasii* is much taller than either, for not only is the annual growth more extensive but extra height is gained as some of the previous year's wood is left after each annual pruning.

In addition to those which have been mentioned, there are many other suitable subjects which may be pruned in the spring. These include Callunas and many of the Ericas. They may be planted near the front of the herbaceous border and, although their inclusion is a departure from normal practice, it is not wrong, being purely a matter of taste.

(ii) Shrubs that respond to summer pruning after flowering. Obviously, pruning at this time restricts growth, but only to a limited extent. Many of the medium or large growers are in this group. However, this type of pruning often results in the removal of arching growths which interfere with the development of the herbaceous plants and in this way it is an advantage, for the younger growths which are left are more upright.

(iii) Shrubs which form a close matt surface and that respond to pruning. There are many shrubs that qualify, but again natural height and size must be considered, so that the need for pruning is reduced to a minimum. Such a compact grower as *Berberis verruculosa* needs very little attention in this respect. When pruning is needed, it may be timed so that any pruning cuts are speedily covered by developing young growths. Many of the suitable subjects in this group are the smaller-leaved evergreens.

(iv) Dwarf conifers. Many of the dwarf conifers can be used in this mixed planting, but it is important to ensure that these slow-growing subjects are sufficiently isolated so that they receive full all-round light, as otherwise their surface will be spoilt, becoming bare and unsightly. It may therefore be necessary to check the herbaceous subjects or perhaps to plant more suitable ones.

COLOUR BORDERS OR SPECIAL FEATURES

There can be no definite set of rules, for the pruning policy will vary according to the soil and growing conditions and of course with the species of tree or shrub being used. The purpose of the pruning, particularly if carried out annually, is to produce the best foliage effect, and the main object of this section is to give some general guidance on the pruning policy for a colour shrub effect, be the feature a large one or only a small corner in a shrub border. For full details of the pruning of individual species or varieties the reader is referred to Part II. Before pruning is considered, the planting distances need special consideration. As a general rule, the larger subjects should be in the background and be planted at such a distance that pruning is reduced to a minimum. A wide feature is needed for the larger subjects. Not only does the use of large growers in a small feature mean extra work, but also frequent pruning throws them out of character. *Acer negundo* varieties often lose their variegation on the growths that arise after pruning. Therefore, such large-growing subjects as these should be planted at least 8 to 9 m. (25 to 30 ft.) away from others which are likely to be permanent and fillers may be used for immediate effect. Also, an adequate spacing allows the blocks of colour to develop a bold and well-defined outline.

Pruning

The pruning falls into two categories:

(i) *Occasional pruning* carried out to correct size and formation. Normally, this is done during early to mid summer when the full effect of the growth and foliage can be seen and the adjustments made accordingly. The watch upon growth and effect should, however, be a constant one, so that it may be appreciated much earlier than midsummer that some attention is necessary. Often too, some thinning may be necessary as a particular colour or specimen becomes too dominant. If possible, this should be carried out at the same time, when the effect can be fully appreciated.

This type of summer pruning may only involve the removal of a few growths. For example, assume a Yew and a Variegated Holly are growing at 6 m. (20 ft.) apart. The Holly is 1.8 m. (6 ft.) from the front of the border and the Yew is farther back. The Yew is naturally the stronger grower and the long arching growths tend to smother the Holly and the whole effect becomes untidy. The offending growths need to be pruned in midsummer, taking them back in such a manner that an informal and natural surface is left. There may be an underplanting of *Mahonia aquifolium* beneath and between the two subjects. This will need to be cut back, often annually, otherwise the natural development of the lower branches of the Holly and the Yew will be quickly spoilt. In time, of course, these will smother the underplanting, presenting a surface on the edge of the border down to ground level. Very skilled pruning will be needed when the edge is reached, in order to avoid a hedge-like effect, especially with the Yew.

(ii) *Annual pruning*

(a) early spring. On many subjects this is carried out before the new growth commences, e.g. *Cotinus coggygria* and *Cornus alba* 'Spaethii'. Often the pruning is severe, taking the previous year's wood back to a common line near the older wood, see Fig. 28.

(b) after flowering in the early summer. A few subjects are dealt with at this period, for example *Weigela* 'Florida Variegata' and *Philadelphus coronarius* 'Aureus'. The old flowering wood is then cut out, leaving the new growths which have the strongest and best foliage.

Culture

It is emphasized that the best possible growing conditions should be given to trees and shrubs grown for foliage effect. They must not suffer from lack of moisture, organic material or nutrients, otherwise growth will be poor.

SUPPORTS FOR CLIMBERS AND SHRUBS IN RELATION TO THEIR PRUNING

It is not proposed to go into details on the structure of the various supports that can be used. However, the type of structure has an important bearing upon the pruning and it is not just a case of choosing the support and the climber and relying upon nature to do the rest.

The subject has to some extent been mentioned in the previous section, but it is hoped that by describing the type of support in relation to the pruning, understanding will be more complete.

Essentially, the structure should provide a means of support that is well adapted for climbing. This is important for the true climbers which gain support by twining stems or by tendrils, but not for most of the scandent or clambering subjects such as Rambler Roses and the weakened-stemmed shrubs e.g. *Forsythia suspensa*, for most of these need only be tied in position.

Some climbers are more adaptable than others; for example, many of the Clematis are weak-stemmed and rely upon leaf-tendrils for support. The straight metal pole with no laterals and a smooth hard surface is not suitable for these unless some help is given. Once the top of a support is reached, there is usually no difficulty, for the growths bend over this, thus securing a hold which is increased as branches are produced to form a bushy head. Support for the main vines or stems is, however, desirable even when the head is well supported, as if they are loose and hang freely they are liable to be broken and the climber ruined. Judged from the planning and layout point of view, the type of structure and species of climber should be in keeping with the surroundings. Whatever structure is used, it is important for the support and ties to be strong, and well able to withstand the strains of gales under the full weight of summer foliage and growths.

Free-standing Supports

Living trees and shrubs.   This type of support is often a very successful one and as the combination of climber and support plant is a natural one, it is used to full effect in informal plantings. Shrubs, or even the smaller trees, are not suitable for the larger climbers, as they may be speedily swamped and broken down by the heavy growths. The right selection is therefore important. The trailing growths of *Tropaeolum speciosum* are not of sufficient weight to damage medium-sized shrubs, whereas the stronger and more rampant growers, *Rosa filipes* 'Kiftsgate' and *Fallopia baldschuanica*, will quickly smother all but the larger trees.

Pruning is not normally carried out on a climber growing under natural conditions, although at times it would undoubtedly be of benefit; for example, some of the older wood could with advantage be removed from the Honeysuckle after flowering, provided of course that this could be done without damage to the younger shoots or the main vine. Again, it would be often advantageous to cut out dead wood, but this must be done very carefully, otherwise a vital piece may be removed which is acting as a support, even though it has long since ceased to function as living tissue. The scope for pruning a climber in such a position is very limited and must, therefore, usually be confined to the pendulous and free branches. It may also be necessary to prune away growths that have extended the climber beyond reasonable bounds and, if this is necessary, it should be carried out carefully in order to provide a good finish and not leave a ragged appearance.

It is often difficult to establish a climber to grow successfully upon a vigorous and extending subject, such as a medium-sized or mature tree in a full state of health. Much depends upon the soil and its moisture-retaining capacity, for a deficiency of the latter may prove to be a limiting factor. It is possible to control the support plant, but the advisability of doing this should be carefully weighed up before any cuts are made. Few would agree that the deliberate spoliation of a shapely tree in order to encourage a climber is a sound or justifiable policy. An old apple tree is ideal, for the canopy of foliage is not too thick, and sufficient light is let into the centre of the tree to enable the climber to become established. A tree that is declining in health can be cut back to act as a support; indeed, this is one of the policies that can be recommended for dangerous trees, provided that the setting is a suitable one and that there are no immediate dangers to people, should it subsequently fail. Trees used for this purpose must be left in a safe condition and should be inspected from time to time afterwards, see Fig. 20 (4). A tree may be deliberately planted and grown for the

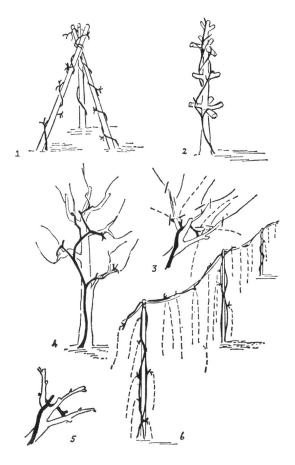

Fig. 20. Support for climber.
(1) The tripod system of support. Obviously a rigid method.
(2) The larch pole with the stub ends of the laterals left on for additional support.
(3) Part of a medium-sized living tree which is used as a support for a climber, in this case a *Wisteria* over a *Laburnum*. The position of the pruning cuts on both subjects are indicated. Both subjects are pruned, but the growths of the Wisteria that are to be removed are shown in a broken line as a means of distinguishing them.
(4) The overall effect after pruning.
(5) A close-up of the branch shown in (3). Note that both subjects will respond to this type of spur pruning.
(6) A vine trained to a pergola system. The broken lines indicate the growths which are pruned back to the main vine each December.

Plate 42. *Wisteria sinensis* grown in a bed as opposed to growing on a wall.

purpose of supporting a climber. The tree is pruned, perhaps on an annual or biennial basis, in order to reduce vigour, thus giving the climber a fair chance. An interesting combination is *Laburnum* as the supporting tree for *Wisteria*, but in this case
the latter is more likely to require a regular cut back as it is such a large grower, see
Fig. 20 (3, 4 and 5). By contrast, the stronger trees such as *Acer platanoides* 'Schwedleri' or *A. p.* 'Crimson King' may need annual attention.

Poles.   These are successful for the stronger-stemmed and scandent climbers such
as many of the *Rubus* spp. and Roses, see Fig. 41 (1 and 3), where the support gained
by tying the subject to the pole is sufficient. Climbers, for example *Wisteria sinensis*
may also be grown on such a support, see Plate 42 and Fig. 38 (1 and 2), although
control with such a limited scope for climbing is difficult with the larger growers
such as *Celastrus*. Subjects that climb by means of leaf tendrils may find it difficult
or impossible to find sufficient support on a straight and unbranched pole. This is
especially true of the metal poles or piping that are often used. In this case, and also
with wooden poles, a sleeve of wire netting, loosely wrapped to cover the entire
length, will overcome the difficulty. It is important to preserve the lower end of a pole
for as long as possible, whether it be of wood or metal. A preservative should be used

Plate 43. *Rosa laevigata* trained to grow on a strong tripod support system.

for the former, while the base of the metal pole, set in concrete which is carried just above the surface, will ensure a longer life.

Tripod of poles.   This support, see Plate 43 and Fig. 20 (1), has much to commend it from the point of view of stability, and if the poles are secured together 300 mm. (12 in.) or so from the top end, it provides additional support when the climber forms a head. Usually one plant is placed at the foot of each leg of the tripod. As the head develops pruning may be difficult, but it can be carried out with some subjects such as *Akebia quinata* and the Climbing Roses by lifting the head and cutting out the weaker wood beneath. Ideally the tripod of poles made from the longer tanalised tree stakes should be supported from the ground by three shorter stakes driven into the ground, by three bolts. This allows the supporting stakes to be renewed when decayed, without having to dismantle the whole supporting system and plant, by removing the bolts and stakes and replacing it with the new one.

Conifer poles with side branches.   With the side branches cut back to approximately 0.3 m. (1 ft.), these supports can be used for a variety of climbers. Those with tendrils or sensitive petioles in particular are well suited, for the stub ends of the branches, being radially placed and in tiers, are well positioned for their attachment. This type of support is much favoured, for example, for Clematis, see Fig. 20 (2). The ideal post should be a larch pole, as it is the most durable of softwood timbers. If there are insufficient side branches, the pole can be drilled alternately and extra rods inserted that will act as side branches.

Hazel or Birch brushwood.   This does not last in condition for very long—usually for a period of only a few months. However, it sometimes proves useful when placed against the main support in order to help a climber on to this. It may also be used for such climbers as *Eccremocarpus scaber* and *Codonopsis* spp., which are often killed down to ground level each year.

Old tree stumps or roots. These form a suitable support for subjects that are to be allowed to grow naturally like *Celastrus orbiculatus*, perhaps in the more informal parts of the garden. Neat pruning to give a formal effect would be out of place and must be avoided, especially along the edges where the subject meets the grass or the path. Many climbers in this position spread extensively and it may become necessary to cut away weed growths or saplings if they appear from beneath the canopy of these spreading growths. It may also help if a few growths are pegged down or tied in position, especially during the early years. This serves to emphasize the point that even in a wild setting, some work is occasionally of benefit if the best results are to be obtained.

Pergola and arbor systems. These take various forms but the subject chosen should be a strong grower so that it is able to cover the horizontal bar systems adequately, see

Plate 44. *Parthenocissus tricuspidata* growing on a brick wall without any artificial support.

Fig. 20 (6). Thus, the stronger Honeysuckles, the Vines, Wisteria and many of the Ramblers or Climbing Roses may be used. Such structures are found in the more formal settings and thus the climber that can be pruned hard annually either to the main vines or on a replacement system is likely to be easier to manage, and the effect will be a tidier one.

Wall Supports

Horizontal strained wire system. This is one of the most satisfactory methods of giving support to those subjects that need it. The main essentials are that the wires should be good and stout, galvanized, stainless steel or green plastic coated and held securely 50 to 80 mm. (2 to 3 in.) from the wall. They should be stretched tight by means of strainers at the ends. The wires, set at about 230 mm. (9 in.) apart, are threaded through 'vine eyes' that are driven in between the brick courses. From the gardener's point of view, one of the drawbacks to this system is that in the early years after planting, when the subject is being trained to cover the available space, there is a tendency for the growths of such subjects as Honey-suckles, which clasp their support by twining round them, to travel horizontally along the wires. This may be overcome by tying in bamboo canes, and using these as a support and encouragement for the growths to develop in the right directions. Alternatively, wires may be stretched vertically between the horizontal strands.

Trellis systems. These are quite popular and give good support for a wide variety of climbers. It is preferable that they should be well made and preserved, but it is also important that they are secured about 80 mm. (3 in.) from the wall to allow for the development of the vines or stems which have grown behind the trellis. Other-wise, as these swell and enlarge, the trellis may be wrenched from the wall or broken.

Wire fencing. The stronger forms may be used, but obviously there is a danger that these will be pulled out of place by the heavier climbers such as *Wisteria*, as their size and weight increases. The chain-link fencing is much stronger than chicken wire and is therefore more suitable. The plastic-covered material is long lasting and more preferable.

Wall nails or vine eyes. These may be used on brick and mortar walls, provided of course that they are driven in between the bricks. Their use should, however, be limited, perhaps to a few main branches. They are not suitable for the shrub or climber that needs a large number of ties.

Self-clinging Climbers

Included in this class are such subjects as Common Ivy, *Hedera helix*, and *Hydrangea anomala* subsp. *petiolaris*, which adhere to the surface by means of adventitious roots produced in quantity beneath the creeping stems as they develop, see Fig. 36. *Parthenocissus tricuspidata* is representative of a number of other species in this genus which produce tendrils that flatten upon contact with a solid object. Thus discs or pads are formed which cling very tightly to the surface, giving support to the whole climber, see Plate 44.

These self-clinging climbers may cause damage to buildings by way of loose tiles, blocked gutters and deteriorating wall surfaces. It is advisable to keep the growths of all climbers away from the eaves of a building so that there is no chance of the roof or drainage system being damaged or rendered ineffective. Even such climbers as *Clematis armandii* have been known to grow so vigorously that on reaching the eaves and the roof the tiles have been in danger of being loosened.

Self-clinging vines are detrimental to walls that have a rough coating such as pebbledash. A tiled wall is unsuitable for most climbers.

Chapter Four

Pruning in Special Circumstances

THE PLANNED EFFECT

The success of a planting finally depends upon the skill and judgement of the horticulturist or arboriculturist. Not only have the selected trees and shrubs to be planted properly, but they must be established and trained and finally pruned correctly if need be, to achieve the planned effect. It is emphasized, however, that good culture and pruning cannot overcome the effects of a bad selection. All the various factors including hardiness, soil preference, habit and ultimate size should be taken into account before a selection is made. It is important that the landscape architect or planner should provide a permanent record of the final desired effect for reference as the plan is established and put into being. Clumps of trees and shrubs may quite easily spread extensively and well beyond the boundaries that were first intended for them and, as a result, open spaces may be restricted or views completely spoilt. Even the removal of a few low branches to facilitate maintenance may change the character entirely, perhaps spoiling individual trees and the effect as a whole, see Plate 46.

Here are a number of policies that need to be laid down and properly recorded so that those who carry out the plan shall know exactly what is expected of them.

(i) The intended limits in size of trees or shrubs either singly or in clumps.

(ii) The extent, width or dimensions of any views and open spaces that should be retained.

(iii) The extent and depth of shade that is required, for example in paved squares or forecourts.

(iv) The extent to which a natural low branching is desired, bearing in mind that the natural and desirable habit of most trees is to produce branchlets which sweep down to or hang near ground level when mature.

(v) The size and outline of trees planted to hide or to frame buildings.

(vi) The extent of branching which is to overhang water. This should be based upon a proportion of the total surface area of water, but the areas in which shading is desirable should also be indicated. It is not healthy to have an entire water surface shaded.

(vii) The extent of the grass stretches that are to be kept open, in particular the sweeps down to the water's edge. In this connection it should be borne in mind that willows and alders, for example, grow and spread very rapidly and the whole edge can be quickly overgrown and hidden.

These are a few of the points that need to be considered in the formulation of a long-term policy. Some flexibility may be necessary on certain points such as the time and extent of any thinning. Where this applies it may be laid down when the policy is formulated and agreed upon. Of course, it must be recognised that it is possible to improve upon the intended plan, perhaps by pruning and thinning.

ISOLATED SPECIMENS AND GROUPS

Some trees and shrubs growing under natural conditions maintain a perfect symmetry, but there are many factors that often combine to make this impossible for the majority. Competition is often a cause of unsymmetrical growth, for it is impossible to maintain a perfect all-round form if the plant is subjected to one-sided light; indeed it would be wrong to expect it and unnatural to achieve it. Trees on the edge of a clump of shrubs in a mature border will often, when viewed, as individuals appear poorly shaped. Such a planting must be viewed as a whole, for it is only by this means that a perfectly natural and balanced effect is appreciated.

This must not be taken as an excuse for a crowded planting. Our gardens are made up of a heterogeneous collection, resulting from a desire to grow as many species as possible. Such large mixtures do not occur in nature where the trees and shrubs may be crowded but fewer species are represented in a given area. Bushes or trees in groups of one species often grow well together and a close planting is not such a serious matter. Each individual in these cases is able to fight for light, moisture and nutrients on equal terms with its neighbours. This is not so in a close mixed planting where the weaker species often need protection from the stronger by pruning invasive growths in addition to giving any extra attention which the weaker ones may need.

Balance

When it is intended to grow trees or shrubs as specimens they should be given equal light on all sides, thus obtaining the good symmetrical growth which is essential. Two interesting points are connected with this. Firstly, even the shaded side of an isolated specimen often grows and flowers at the same rate and manner as the remainder of the tree. An equal exposure to light and air often seems to be the critical factor rather than the influence of direct sunlight. Secondly, a tree—or shrub for that matter—balances growth as a means of maintaining stability. This stability and balance is obtained either by an equal distribution of the production of branches over and on all sides of the crown if possible, or by increasing the strengthening tissues in the root system, in order to counteract any unilateral development or strain. Examples of balancing have been observed where a large tree with a perfectly shaped crown remains standing even during gales with many of the main roots in an advanced state of decay. A tree in this condition is dangerous even to fell, for unless care is taken the balancing nature of the crown may be lost, the tree suddenly crashing to the ground. In the same way, once the balancing weight has been removed with the crown, even a light pull on the winch may bring the trunk down very quickly. Examples of strong anchorage on one side of the root system are quite common when the distribution of the weight in the crown is unequal, or in cases of a very strong prevailing wind. The strengthened rooting, with the thickened and extensive development of buttress roots and trunk on the sides where it is likely to be the most effective, can be very apparent.

Some of these points are also dealt with under 'Minimising Wind Damage' on page 108, which goes to prove that many of the factors connected with growth and practice are closely related and cannot be considered separately.

Planting Distances

The success of specimens will depend a great deal upon the planting distances, but the ideal spacing varies both with the habit and rate of growth of the species concerned and with the soil and conditions generally. Close plantings are often made deliberately for the production of a quick effect, or as a means of encouragement to the desired specimen in the early years. In the latter case, such a close planting acts as a nurse crop, giving shelter and forcing the development of a good stem and leader. It is important that removal of the unwanted plants be timed so that the specimen does not suffer in any way. When fillers or nurse plants are used, the planting plan should indicate which individual trees or shrubs are to be finally retained either as specimens or in groups. The person in charge can then arrange for those not required to be removed at the right time before they outgrow and spoil the remainder.

The specimen tree need not be completely isolated; in fact, one or more smaller shrubs may be planted in the vicinity to form a group. The choice of subjects for a group of this nature should be very carefully made, as it is most likely to succeed when the associated subjects contrast completely with the dominant tree. Sometimes they need to be planted many years later than the main specimens as they are often shorter lived. As an example of a combined planting for effect, *Cedrus atlantica* may be grown in association with *Parrotia persica*. The latter may need to be planted 50 to 80 years later than the Cedar, but once established, one or two branches of the *Parrotia* may even develop beneath the shade of the larger and evergreen subject.

What connection has this with pruning? Such an effect is not produced by accident and the pruner must keep a close watch to ensure that growth by the larger specimen does not harm the smaller in any way. At the same time, however, he must not spoil the overall grace and beauty of the Cedar. But even the pruner cannot be expected to do his work properly if the planting distances in the first place were poor and insufficient.

MINIMISING WIND DAMAGE

Wind is the one element that is likely to give the arboriculturist the most concern. It is, however, important to differentiate between plantings in inland areas at the lower elevations and those in coastal situations or on high ground. In the former positions the devastating effects of a strong gale-force wind are seldom taken into account when the selection and plantings are made. This is not intended as a criticism, for our gardens and arboreta would be considerably poorer without the enterprising and adventurous spirit, which has prompted past generations to plant up exotic and ornamental species. The point to remember is that should high winds of gale force penetrate such plantings, the results can indeed be devastating, and the aim must be to maintain shelters on the edge against the prevailing winds. If the impression is given that only exotic trees suffer from gale damage, this is wrong, for mature stands of native trees may also suffer severely. It is noticeable that the heaviest damage often occurs during the summer or early autumn when trees are in full leaf, perhaps laden with flowers or fruits, and the ground is at field capacity due to heavy late summer and autumn rains. The latter reduces the friction between the roots and the soil around the roots, acting as a lubricant, leaving the roots in the root plate to slide out of the ground when under pressure from strong winds. A heavy gale with driving rain can be disastrous at such a time.

Trees and shrubs that are growing in an exposed position will, of course, suffer from exceptional hurricane-force winds which are usually at their strongest in such areas, but at least some comfort may be derived from the fact that growth is inured to such conditions, while a suitable selection has been probably made in the first instance. There is also a natural selection which takes place over the years as a result of these conditions, the unsuitable subjects being blown about so much that they either do not grow, or are killed completely. Many of the exposed positions in the United Kingdom are in coastal areas where the full effects of salt spray must also be taken into account, and this proves to be another limiting factor.

Trees and Shrubs under Normal Conditions

Admittedly it is difficult to define exactly what is meant by the term 'normal conditions'. Broadly, those sites that are not unduly exposed come within this category. However, each site varies considerably in this respect, and indeed this is true of one part of a site when compared with another. Again, a site may be sheltered from the prevailing winds and yet be badly exposed to those blowing from the opposite direction. Sometimes winds blow at gale force from unusual directions and do considerable damage.

Mechanics of a Well-formed Tree

The healthy tree with a good central leader is mechanically sound and is therefore better able to withstand the buffeting and swaying caused by a full-force gale. If there is damage on such a well-formed specimen, the loss of a branch or two may not seriously affect the tree as a whole. Also a well-grown nursery tree with a well-tapered trunk and a number of strong and well-spaced branches is better able to develop into a wind-resistant form and habit than a poorly shaped one. At this stage it must be emphasized that the small feathered tree is better suited for such a development than a larger standard.

Pruning Hard to Increase Stability

A trained tree cannot be pruned hard back to near ground level for stability, but subjects which generate freely after such hard treatment, for example *Paulownia* spp. or *Eucalyptus* spp., may be dealt with in this way. Such a tree or shrub may thus be stabilized and this is often better than correcting the position by staking or by the use of guys, and good planting techniques with the suitable-sized nursery stock in the first place will overcome this potential problem. On occasions, it may be advisable to encourage stability and improve the shape of a leaning tree or shrub by the careful removal of weight on one side. It must be remembered, however, that trees and shrubs that retain a permanent framework and do not throw out freely after being cut back should not be pruned in this manner.

Pruning to Balance the Head

Quite often limbs grow out well beyond the general outline for the tree. While it would be undesirable to train and prune to a symmetrical outline it would be equally wrong to allow one or more branches to grow so extensively that the tree was out of balance and perhaps dangerous. A large limb jutting out beyond the general line may be caught by an unfavorable wind and be broken off at a point that spoils the appearance of the tree. In addition, the large, lower limbs of the Horse-chestnut (*Aesculus hippocastanum*), for example, often produce strong upright branches, forming a large surface exposed to the wind, and with the increased weight a break is likely under stress. It is of course desirable to correct such tendencies at an early stage rather than to leave it until the removal of a large limb is involved, as this inevitably means a shock to the tree and a wound which may never heal completely.

Maintaining a Balanced Branch System

The influence of balance in a well-shaped tree, particularly with one that is symmetrical, should not be underrated. A large, shapely specimen, often with the lower branches pendulous and reaching the ground, has a low centre of gravity which adds to stability. This is why a balancing for weight in addition to appearance is necessary after the removal of a main scaffold limb.

Maintaining Balance in a Clump or Group of Trees

A balanced and unbroken outline is desirable with a clump or group of trees as a whole. It is for this reason that there should be a reluctance to remove any one that will leave a gap in the outer 'skin' of foliage and branches. This would let the wind into specimens which as separate individuals may lack balance to such an extent that they would not be capable of standing up even in a moderate wind. A community of trees with a given area has grown up under a certain set of conditions, with the growth and shape conforming to the general pattern of the forces which normally prevail. The removal of one or more of the trees or a building, or, alternatively, the erection of any form of structure, particularly a large and solid one, may seriously alter these conditions.

The importance of this may be more easily appreciated by considering the effect on the waterweed of the current in a rapidly flowing stream. Under normal

Fig. 21. Showing the effect of a shelterbelt under exposed conditions.

(a) The effect of a single line of sheltering shrubs. The specimen shrub growing in the lee of this screen can be expected to reach the height of this shelter and to be of reasonable shape. However, this will depend upon several factors including the nature of both the screen and sheltered plants.

(b) A screen planting in depth. This is very necessary if height is to be built up under exposed conditions.

It is not claimed that shapely specimens can always be grown behind such screens. The position is not always clear cut, as there are so many local factors to consider. For example, sloping ground may make it impossible to build up any height with the screen plants

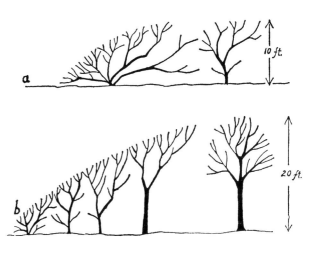

conditions, the clumps of weed are compact and moulded to definite shapes. But the removal of a large stone will so alter the flow that its effect on the weed can be detected over a considerable area.

It is also common knowledge that the water rushes with increased speed between large stones or in narrow places and this has a direct analogy in the effect on airflow of the large blocks of flats or offices which are often erected near plantings of trees and shrubs. As with the stream, the increased speed is in the narrower reaches but the effects are felt both above and below these points, and the strong eddies and turbulence stretch over a wide area.

Branch thinning, crown thinning. Individual trees or groups of trees which are suddenly isolated and left in an exposed position as the result of an alteration or development, or faced with strong winds from a different direction to the prevailing winds, may not be strong enough to have a form and habit which is capable of withstanding high gales. The sudden exposure of strong winds to the dense crown may act like the sail effect of a sail on a yacht, placing considerable stress on the main scaffolds, trunk or root crown, which could lead to failure. There may, in these circumstances, be justification for a careful crown thinning of the branch systems to allow a freer passage for strong winds through the crowns. Again, trees that are suspected of being weak, perhaps through overgrowth or old age may, after careful consideration, be dealt with in this way. The reader is referred to the section dealing with this operation in Chapter Two, but it is emphasized that the crown must be left in a balanced condition. There is evidence that once the wind is let into the crown, the branches on the lee side may be subject to extra strains and stresses.

Pruning and maintenance in exposed positions.   A careful selection is important when the planting up of an exposed site is considered. A windbreak of commoner subjects that tolerate and grow under such conditions is usually a necessity and, if one is not already growing, it should be one of the first considerations. Coastal areas are subject to high winds which, blowing directly off the sea, are laden with salt spray driven in the form of a drenching mist. Trees or shrubs in order to withstand such rigorous conditions must either have a tough, resistant foliage or be capable of rapid regeneration as one set of growths is cut away prematurely, even during the height of the growing season, by adverse conditions.

It may be advisable first to construct a fence and to plant up hedging material behind this. For this purpose such shrubs as *Prunus cerasifera*, the Myrobalan Plum, are ideal. *Euonymus japonicus* and *Griselinia littoralis* are examples of evergreens that will thrive well in exposed positions on the south coast. The object of this is to build up height gradually. The windward side of such a screen will need very little, if any, pruning; in fact the wind will do this and it is advisable to leave the close, stunted growths which form under these conditions completely alone. Even dead branches and twig growth give some shelter and should be left, for the training of any plant in such a position is almost impossible. With the subjects that are in the lee of this it is a different matter. Training and shaping is possible but only until they grow past the shelter of the hedge, when growths will become windswept and stunted, see Fig. 21. If extra height is required, taller, wind-resistant subjects such as *Acer pseudoplatanus* and *Fraxinus excelsior* may be planted behind the first planting. These should be

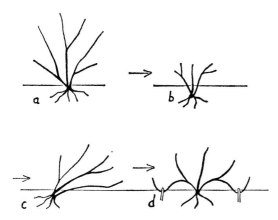

Fig. 22. Methods of planting on a very windswept site, e.g. privet for use as a shelter. This is a subject which throws up strongly from the base and thus with encouragement will produce a thicket of cane-like, almost suckerous growths.

(a) The shrub planted under normal conditions. Alternative methods in exposed positions are shown in b, c and d.

(b) A deeper planting with hard pruning.

(c) Planted at a low angle away from the wind.

(d) A normal planting with the outer and lower branches being held in position by pegs, thus adding to the stability and encouraging rooting.

planted out when small as whips so that they may establish quickly. Gradually in this way height may be built up sufficiently for well-trained trees to be grown in the lee.

The leggy shrub that requires a stake is not suitable for planting in this situation for the top growth will have a levering action and even the slightest rocking will delay or even prevent establishment. The low, bushy plant that has been formed by stopping or pruning is more suitable, for it can be planted to rest close to ground level where the surface area will be small and where there will be little resistance to the wind until further growth is put on after rooting and establishment. This treat-ment is only successful with those shrubs that generate readily, see Fig. 22 (b).

Shrubs may be set out with a slightly deeper planting as an aid to extra rigidity and firmness and with many subjects extra rooting will be promoted from the buried positions. Great care must be taken to ensure that the subject treated in this way is able to respond naturally and freely to the new conditions. Often, it is possible to plant so that the shrub leans away from the prevailing wind. Another alternative is to layer the longer growths securely and thus give extra stability. Again, this is only possible with subjects which are likely to respond readily, see Fig. 22 (c).

LIGHTNING DAMAGE

The extent of the damage to a tree struck by lightning may vary enormously. In extreme cases trees may be completely ruined, with the crown broken up, the trunk spoilt by the entire stripping of bark or even the whole tree blown completely apart. Occasionally a thin strip of bark is blown off from where the lightning strike hit the tree in a spiraling effect to the earth. When repair is out of the question removal is the only course to take, but if only a few branches are affected, it is possible to retain a tree, provided that it is left in a safe condition. Any branches badly damaged beyond natural repair should be removed and the crown balanced accordingly. Often, however, the loss of a crown or a proportion of the main branch system proves to be such a check that there is a gradual decline in condition and eventually the tree may die prematurely.

With the harder-wooded trees such as the Oak and Ash, a continuous groove may be taken out running the complete length of the trunk. Quite often this is not deep with only a narrow strip of the bark and a V-shaped portion of the wood affected. Such a wound should be cleaned up, the surface being left smooth and free of splin-ters. The edges of the bark should be cut back cleanly where it has been left in a rough state. Conifers will naturally ooze resin to seal the wound and should the tree be in good health, callusing will soon begin. See 'Surface Wounds' in Chapter One.

In areas where lightning strikes are commonplace, lightning protection systems such as lightning conductors may be installed as a preventative measure, especially in heritage trees or the tallest conifers such as *Sequoiadendron giganteum*, *Sequoia sempervirens* and the taller *Abies* spp.

COUNTERACTING THE EFFECTS OF SHADE

The effects of shade are well known on sun-loving subjects, for with the longer internodes which result, the growths are weak and far from typical, there being little or no flowering. Often too, a tree or shrub in a position where light strikes on one side only is drawn out of shape toward the sun and away from the shaded quarter, see Fig. 18. This is known as phototropism.

Shrubs which are poorly shaped as a result of too much shade can be improved by hard pruning, but only if they are capable of breaking into growth from hard wood after they have been cut down. The growth that follows will also be quickly drawn up unless the condition causing the shade is corrected. If overhanging trees

Plate 45. The upper crown of *Cedrus libani* badly damaged from snow. This could possibly have been avoided with some proactive, careful thinning of end weight.

tion of Holly (*Ilex aquifolium*) at the Christmas period. It is therefore necessary to deal with the varied and often conflicting requirements in detail.

Material for Decoration or Shows

The need for great care has been emphasized and therefore it is important to allow sufficient time so that the cuts may be accurately positioned and treated afterwards if necessary. It must also be emphasized that in many cases it is a pity to have to remove anything, but there are exceptions. Forsythias, for example, are pruned, if necessary, after flowering and therefore there may even be some advantage in an earlier pruning, for the young wood may have an even better chance to develop freely and to ripen fully. Shrubs such as *Hamamelis*, on the other hand, which have a permanent framework that is not readily renewed, should not be cut for this purpose. The removal of one small piece does no harm, particularly if it is a side branch, but the loss of larger whole branches would be serious.

The collection of show material without harm to the tree or shrub is more difficult, for there is an understandable temptation to put in the finest sprays or blooms that are usually on the best growths. The advisability of taking such wood from the specimen in question should be carefully considered, and it is really a matter for the owner to decide. With sufficient care, the dangers of permanent damage will be reduced, and this may mean ladder and secateurs work rather than the use of standard pruners from the ground. The temptation to cut too much should also be avoided. It is easy to be so keen on providing enough that eventually there is a large surplus. It is also better to distribute the collecting over the entire specimen rather than to cut in one place only, which may leave it ragged and unbalanced. If a growth is essential to the good of the specimen it should not be taken.

Christmas decorating material often poses a particular problem, for it means cutting such evergreens as Hollies, Yews and other subjects at the wrong time of year completely. It is worth noting such a requirement several months in advance and, if it is possible, delaying any cutting back which may be needed until the material can be used. This, however, is only advisable with a light cutback. The severe pruning of evergreens should not be carried out until late spring.

Propagation Material

Material for propagation is gathered as scions or cuttings. Usually, small pieces are involved and there will be a natural tendency to avoid strong leading shoots, as these will not be suitable for propagation purposes. Apart from this, however, care is needed to avoid both snags and tears as the material is removed. In many cases where semi-ripe cuttings are removed they are taken directly and singly from the bushes. With these it is possible to cut the material cleanly and close to the stem taking the very thin slice of the older wood which will facilitate rooting. The pieces should not be torn off if the parent branch is to remain on the shrub. It is a mistake to remove all the growths from one branch; rather, a suitable selection should be made over the entire bush.

With a limited number of subjects which are mainly coniferous, such as *Araucaria* and *Cephalotaxus*, the leading growth may be pruned back to provide a number of upright growths for use as cuttings, owing to the inability of the laterals to glow into shapely specimens after rooting. This would only be carried out on surplus stock or on specimens which are considered to be unsuitable for growing on, as the loss of the leading growth usually spoils the shape, perhaps permanently.

In the case of specialized propagation departments or with larger establishments, the practice of growing special stock plants to provide cutting or scion material is a good one. Such stock plants should be selected as being true to type and free from virus and other diseases. The Myrobalan Plum (*Prunus cerasifera*), for example, grown in a hedge and hard pruned each year during the winter, will provide good material for rooting as hardwood cuttings. A tree or shrub grown purely as an ornamental specimen should not be used extensively for providing propagating material.

Where scion material is needed from a parent plant that has failed to provide good extension growth over the previous few years, hard reduction of some of the branches may encourage epicormic growth from the wound that will be suitable for budding or grafting. An example of this could be *Aesculus indica* 'Sidney Pearce', which puts all of its energy into flowering at the expense of vegetative extension growth.

PRUNING IN RELATION TO MAINTENANCE OPERATIONS

The Use of Machinery

The growing use of machinery must be taken into account and it is becoming more than ever necessary to co-ordinate tree and shrub pruning with the needs of administration and maintenance. Many of the routine tasks such as leaf collection, fertilizer and top dressing applications, grass cutting and other turf operations have been extensively mechanized and the tendency is to use larger machinery and equipment which require more headroom, see Plate 46. The temptation to cut off the lower limbs to allow free and effective use of such machinery is very real, and it may in certain situations be justified, but usually the more natural effect of low branches and twig growth reaching the ground is preferable.

Plate 46. Problems with using modern machinery and grounds maintenance access due to low skirt.

Service roads to key points should have sufficient headroom for large vehicles, and it often pays to clearly mark these routes in order to avoid mistakes and damage in other parts. Mowers and leaf- or flail-collectors are, however, now in production which need a reduced amount of headroom and these are ideal for use in tree plantings where a natural effect is considered desirable. On big establishments the use of the larger machinery is justified but its use should be confined to the wide-open areas, using suitable machinery for the confined spaces and under low branches. Extensive damage can be caused by ride-on mowers working close to a branch system. The little extra care which is necessary in order to conserve the lower branches is well worthwhile when the increased beauty which results from this is taken into account. In some situations the sward may be killed off by low scalping with an old pedestrian rotary mower or by an application of Glyphosate and the surface area mulched with composted wood chips or some other organic mulch material. These can be topped up annually and the leaf fall in the autumn can be left for the tree to recycle in situ on top of the mulch, improving the fertility of the soil. The lower scaffold and branches can be left to

Plate 47. Mature tree mulching on *Cedrus atlantica* 'Glauca' to retain lower skirt and remove access requirements.

grace the skirt naturally and the need for mowing and potential tip damage removed. Under the canopies of mature trees where it is not possible to mulch, it may be possible to naturalize bulbs between the dripline and the trunk, thus reducing the need for regular mowing, see Plate 47.

The Conservation of Organic Material

Low branches also reduce the wind force at ground level and thus the stabilization of the annual leaf-fall is encouraged with obviously beneficial results to the tree, see Figs. 23, 24 and 25. Litter, all too commonplace, can also be held or grounded in the same way so that it can be collected more easily. There is a great need, therefore, for the landscape architect, the horticulturist and the arboriculturist to work together when the creation and maintenance of a planting is considered. Shrubs have a part to play in this field but planting distances must be carefully considered. Sun-loving shrubs should not be overshadowed by the trees,

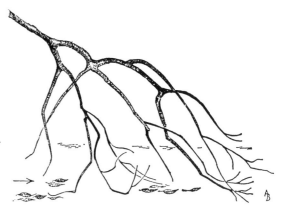

Fig. 23. The effect of low branching is that it retains leaf fall. The finer branch systems of some subjects such as *Crataegus* have an almost 'spring-like action' which tends to hold them to the surface. It may be necessary to run a ring of herbicide around the dripline to prevent herbage such as bramble, thistle and grass from growing through this lower furnishing.

remembering that it is only to a limited extent that such ill effects can be over-come by pruning, see Fig. 26. If planted very close it may even be necessary to cut half the trees away to prevent overshadowing. Shrubs that are used in this way should be encouraged to furnish right down to the soil surface. Care is therefore necessary to avoid removing this growth during pruning.

Irrigation

Automatic irrigation is now used to an increasing extent with a permanent network of sprinklers and irrigators. When deciding upon their location, the sizes and forms of any existing shrubs should be taken into account in order to ensure a wide and even distribution of water. Severe pruning is often a bad way out of difficulties resulting from a bad placement, but the careful removal of one or two branches may be sufficient to ensure a better distribution, and provided that care is taken to retain a natural habit, this is often advisable. Trickle irrigation by

Fig. 24. A carefully planned and maintained planting of smaller trees and bushes on part of the perimeter of a group of large-growing species provide a means of retaining a portion of the leaf fall. Careful pruning may be necessary in order to maintain such a planting.

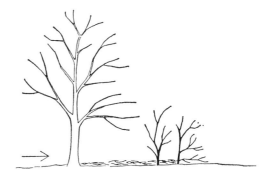

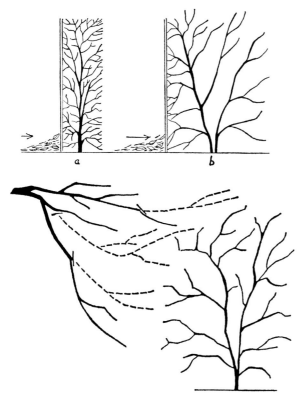

Fig. 25. A method of retaining leaves or litter by a hedge, with a wire netting fence against the formal edge. It is possible to allow an informal growth on one side as shown in (b), but the planting should be a greater distance from the fence to encourage a more balanced growth.

Fig. 26. A background of trees or large shrubs may be essential to neighbouring subjects, either for effect or shelter (or both). The encroaching branch systems may spoil the selected subjects unless they are pruned and kept in check occasionally. This needs to be carried out very carefully, otherwise a hedge-like effect will result. The broken lines indicate the branches to be removed.

means of leaky pipes through shrub borders is another way of irrigating shrubs without the need for any pruning. However it is important that regular checks are made and not forgotten and the irrigation not left on indefinitely otherwise root rot and diseases like phytophthora may cause permanent damage. With trees, it may be possible to remove the lower branches that impede the course of the irrigator without destroying their beauty, but careful consideration is necessary before doing this.

Planned Accessibility

It is a great help toward good pruning and maintenance if the pathways and main rides are kept regularly mown and are thus free from long grass. Where branches are left to sweep the ground a regularly mown area round the trees gives good clearance to coarser grass-flail cutting machines if there is any long grass left to cut. Other essential work, such as regular inspections or repair work after gales, is made easier and is carried out more efficiently. Young trees may also suffer by neglect in long and rough grass, and accessibility by means of mown paths is always worthwhile enabling the trees to be checked, pruned and trained in a more satisfying manner. Most arborists respond to work being carried out properly by such an improvement in standards.

Weed Control

Weed control is one of the major tasks in a collection of trees and shrubs, especially during the early years after planting. Tree pits kept clean and free of weeds for a minimum of 1.5 m. (5 ft.) diameter will ensure successful establishment and continued optimum growth. Training in some form is often required, but this cannot be carried out properly without good healthy growth to work on. Rank weed growth may prove to be such a check that the young tree is ruined, the lower branches often suffering the most. Very large groups of such thorny subjects as *Berberis* are difficult to keep weed-free and for this reason single or restricted plantings are often to be preferred. The control of seedling trees and bramble is often difficult with large and close plantings. Most *Berberis* regenerate freely if cut down to ground level and this can be used as an effective control. It should be carried out in the spring.

WILDLIFE CONSERVATION

Tree lovers are also nature lovers. They like to think of trees and woodlands as providing a home for the many kinds of birds and associated forms of life which are part of our heritage. The sounds of bird life contribute towards a full appreciation of trees and woodlands; for example, the call of the Yaffle, the Green Woodpecker, is part of the atmosphere and background for a scene that would seem empty without it. However, it must be faced that good arboricultural practices, extended over large areas, would bring about a vast reduction in the numbers of some species; in fact, this is actually happening as man takes over ever larger stretches of the countryside.

It is easily possible to be too tidy in the informal garden, perhaps edging and mowing to standards which are more in keeping with neat and formal layouts. A parallel may be drawn with trees that are growing in nature reserves. The natural nesting place for the Little Owl is in a cavity, often quite high up. The Woodpecker or Flicker feeds on grubs that are found in the wood of branches and stem systems, and often such trees are declining in health. Thus the requirements of nature seem to clash completely with the standards required of good arboriculture. This is true to some extent in areas that are open or accessible to the public, for example, where the trees are in public parks and woods, or by the roadside. Cavities, rotten branches or dead trees are dangerous, and the safety of the public in these situations must be given the first consideration. There is a great need for more restricted reserves which have centralized areas, properly enclosed by secure child-proof fencing, in order that dangerous trees can be left to provide natural homes and feeding grounds for the birds and animals. The provision of nest boxes or the creation of artificial cavities for bat roosts, by the removal of hollow wedges in the trunks of sacrificial trees is of course helpful to those species that normally nest in cavities.

In these restricted areas or zones in the garden that are less formal, the role of the arboriculturist changes, and safety may no longer be the first consideration, provided that the area is secure and free from public entry. Cavities and decaying wood may be left. In the United Kingdom under the Wildlife and Countryside Act (Schedule 5) 1981, all bats and their roosts are protected and if bats are found in a cavity or following inspection a roost is suspected, the relevant nature conservation organization must be contacted before any further work is carried out on the tree. The removal of dead wood or the cleaning out process can be kept to a minimum that satisfies safety requirements. 'Conservation dead wooding' may be adopted, where large loose pieces are kicked off by the arborist and the peg that is retained by the parent branch is presumed safe and unlikely to pose a hazard. This leaves a piece of dead wood, essential for saproxylic organisms.

The creation of 'monolith' trees when living trees have reached the end of their life is an alternative to complete removal. The major scaffolds are cut back to a safe manageable framework and the tree is allowed to break down naturally and become standing dead wood. Some would say that broadleaf species are better for greater biodiversity, however in an area where conifers predominate, the dead conifer would be the better option. In order to make the topped tree look more natural, the large scaffold cuts can be finished with a 'coronet' cut, which emulates the snapping off of a major limb and speeds the breakdown process by encouraging invasion of fungi, insects and birds. The root plate will provide a haven for the many different species of fungi and insects like the Stag Beetle (*Lucanus cervus*), which is becoming a threatened species due to habitat loss.

It is important to realize that these pruning and management methods are alternatives to those explained in Chapters One and Two and must only be used where it is safe and there is a need to encourage greater biodiversity at the expense of a healthy tree. Monitoring is extremely important for safety reasons and the health and safety of public and visitors must come first in any situation.

Even in such protected areas nature must never be left to run completely wild, e.g. alien trees such as the Sycamore (*Acer pseudoplatanus*) may soon predominate and perhaps spoil a natural woodland. This would be wrong and some control is necessary in such circumstances. Regular inspection and control is therefore necessary. Again, various species of ground cover plants, providing an ideal shelter and home for many birds and mammals can become too dense and extensive. Hazel coppice, also valuable as shelter, becomes leggy and loses the lower branches unless it is cut down once every 5 to 7 years. A rotational system of cutting in blocks is advisable in order to avoid the whole area being cut in any one year. These ideas may seem to some to be taking the matter beyond all reason, but it must be remembered that many of our rarer species will only thrive in a balanced community.

Chapter Five

Pest and Disease Control

Pruning may be regarded as one of the weapons of defence in the fight to prevent the spread of a number of pests and diseases, but the effectiveness of this means will obviously be influenced by many factors. This account should only be taken as a guide, and no attempt has been made to include a detailed account of each pest or disease and its control. It is limited to a number which may be controlled by pruning, and this section has been included with the intention of showing how some troubles at least can be checked or even controlled by this means.

Hygiene plays an important part in pest and disease control, and dead or diseased branches should be cleared from the trees and ground and, if possible, destroyed by burning. Normally this clearance should not take place in the type of conservation area referred to in Chapter Four. With the bacterial diseases and some others it is important to disinfect any tools which are used, after each cut is made through diseased wood.

Plate 48. Coryneum canker (*Seiridium cardinale*) spreading through a Leyland Cypress hedge, possibly speeded up with regular pruning.

127

DISEASES	TREATMENT
Oak Wilt (*Ceratocystis fagacearum*) This fungal disease, not yet found outside the United States, affects the vascular system of Live Oaks and several of the Red Oaks, including *Quercus shumardii*, *Q. marilandica* and *Q. nigra*, causing death in a few weeks or months. The disease is spread above ground by sap-feeding beetles and below ground by root grafts.	Prevention of the spread of the disease is the most appropriate method of control. Beetles carry the fungus to fresh wounds, including pruning cuts. Timing of pruning operations is essential: prune when the beetle is less active, during the winter between late autumn and early spring, never between mid spring and midsummer. The use of wound sealants is now being recommended on Red Oaks to prevent the attraction of sap-feeding and disease-carrying beetles. The sterilization of pruning tools with alcohol between trees will reduce the possibilities of arborists spreading the fungus between infected and non-infected trees. Root pruning to remove root grafts will prevent the spread to neighbouring trees.
Black Spot of Roses (*Diplocarpon rosae*)	The prunings should be gathered up and burnt.
Grey Mould causing dieback of Roses and other woody subjects (*Botrytis cinerea*) Spores may enter through pruning cuts particularly where snags are left. The blackened, diseased areas spread down the stem.	It is important to make good pruning cuts and to avoid leaving snags. Prune back dying shoots when observed to the first healthy node and burn arisings.
Bacterial Blight of Lilac (*Pseudomonas syringae*) This is the most serious disease of Lilacs, linked to wet, cold humid conditions and frosty nights. The symptoms are similar to those of Fireblight.	Prune out stems to provide better circulation of air and the sterilization of tools with alcohol or bleach between pruning cuts. Avoid pruning on wet, humid days to prevent the spread of the bacterial ooze to other plants.
Bacterial Canker of Cherry (*Pseudomonas syringae morsprunorum*) This may occur on a variety of Ornamental Prunus. The most serious infection is through wounds, including leaf scars in the autumn.	Winter pruning is advisable since overwintering cankers infect the leaves to produce shot holes in some spp., and the leaves carry the infection through to the summer, the bacterium passing from the leaves into fresh wounds in the autumn.
Bacterial Canker of Poplars (*Xanthomonas populi*) Susceptible subjects include *Populus ×jackii*, *P. tremula*, *P. alba* 'Pyramid'.	Dead wood should be cut out and cankered branches should be removed, although it may be difficult to do this without spoiling the tree. Some species and varieties are more susceptible than others and if a tree is badly affected it should be taken down and replaced.
Nectria Canker (*Nectria galligena*) Ornamental Malus, *Pyrus*, *Prunus*, *Sorbus aucuparia*, *Fagus sylvatica* and *Acer* spp. are attacked.	All small branches and shoots which are infected and cankers on branches should be removed during the winter. A watch should be kept for new developing cankers during June, July and August; these should be cut out as soon as possible. Old and badly diseased trees should be destroyed.
Dieback of Poplar (*Discosporium populea*) Affected patches are often found around wounds. Found in the upper crown of *Populus nigra* 'Italica'.	Nursery stock should be pruned during the summer when healing is rapid. The upper crowns of the Lombardy Poplar can be reduced back to a healthy crown to make safe, or remove if dieback is too severe.

DISEASES	TREATMENT
Coral Spot (*Nectria cinnabarina*) The dead and dying wood of a wide range of trees and shrubs are affected, but the fungus may become parasitic, especially on specimens which are in poor health with unripened wood and after a very long wet period, particularly Plums, *Acer*, *Carpinus*, *Tilia* and *Juglans* spp. See Plate 2.	Cut out and burn infected wood as soon as the pustules are noticed to healthy wood. Also cut off dead wood whether infected or not. Improve growing conditions.
Blossom Wilt, **Spur Blight** and **Wither Tip** of Plums, Apples, Flowering Cherries etc. (*Monilinia laxa*) A variety of Ornamental Cherries, Plums, Peaches and Apricots may be attacked. It is usually associated with the fruits, but the infection may pass on to the spurs and supporting wood.	Cut out dead branches, twigs or spurs during the summer months when they may be evident among the foliage. Never leave until the following spring when the infection will pass on to the new buds.
Dutch Elm Disease (*Ophiostoma novo-ulmi*) This fungus, spread by the Elm Bark Beetle (*Scolytus* spp.) is the most serious disease of *Ulmus* spp. Most susceptible are *U. procera*, *U. ×hollandica* and *U. minor* subsp. *sarniensis*. It also affects *Zelkova* spp., although these usually recover.	Prevention is the best means of control and any trees showing symptoms of the disease should be removed and destroyed as soon as possible, especially in disease-free areas. Badly affected trees should be removed and arisings burnt on site to eliminate potential breeding material for the beetle.
Canker Stain of Plane (*Ceratocystis fimbriata* f.sp. *platani*) This disease is not yet present in the U.K. but is in Europe affecting *Platanus* spp.	This disease is associated with bark and pruning wounds, so care must be taken to avoid the spread of the disease by sterilizing tools and equipment between pruning operations on individual trees. The reduction of pruning operations in known areas of infection will also limit the chance of further spread.
Fireblight (*Erwinia amylovora*) Many Rosaceous trees and shrubs are liable to attack. Infection is most likely during and immediately after flowering. Plants most susceptible include *Pyracantha* and *Cotoneaster*.	The diseased portion should be cut well back beyond the visible zone of infection. No wood with a foxy brown stain should be left. Destroy badly infected specimens. A daily inspection during and immediately after the flowering period is essential. The disinfecting of tools after each cut is particularly important with this disease.
Powdery Mildews (*Microsphaera*, *Podosphaera*, *Sawadaea* and *Phyllactinia* spp.) These are found on many broad-leaved trees such as *Quercus*, *Malus*, *Crataegus*, *Acer* and *Corylus*. Infected growths are covered with a white powdery mildew.	Avoidance of pollarding, hedge trimming etc. will reduce the incidence of these diseases by limiting the amount of susceptible soft tissues available during the summer period. Diseased growths should be cut off, carefully collected and burnt as soon as they are noticed, particularly primary infections in the spring.
Silver Leaf (*Chondrostereum purpureum*) This attacks a wide range including Plums, Apples, Peaches, Morello Cherries, Rhododendrons and Poplars.	Cut back any branches that are affected and are dying, well beyond the brown stain that may be seen in the wood. It is useless just to cut off silvered parts. The fungus is not usually present in them, but below. Pruning should be done where possible shortly before midsummer and fresh wounds painted with an effective fungicidal paint.

DISEASES	TREATMENT
Rhododendron Bud Blast (*Pycnostysaralls araleae*)	Infected buds that become apparent during the winter should be removed by hand and burnt.
Witches' Brooms (*Taphrina* spp. on broad-leaved trees, *Melampsorella caryophyllacearum* on Abies) A fungus which invades the branch systems causing malformed growths. Mites, insects or 'bud-sport' may also cause this type of growth.	All branches or brooms should be cut out cleanly and to the standards of good pruning.
Coryneum Canker (*Seiridium cardinale*) A slow-spreading, disfiguring and fatal disease of Cupressaceae including *Cupressus macrocarpa*, *C. sempervirens* and *×Cupressocyparis leylandii*. See Plate 48.	The removal of affected branches below dead bark will slow the spread down, but ultimately the tree will die and need to be removed.
Cytospora Dieback of Cherry Laurel (*Cytospora laurocerasi*) A disfiguring disease of *Prunus laurocerasus* that can sometimes kill.	Trimming hedges by shearing one-year-old shoots reduces the chances of infection. If older wood is to be cut, this is best done in summer; treat fresh cuts with a wound paint suitable for silver leaf.

PESTS	TREATMENT
Aphids and **Adelges** The heaviest concentrations of this vast tribe of sap-feeders often occur near the tips and growing points of the current season's shoots.	With trees and shrubs which are summer pruned, this provides a partial control. The prunings should be collected and destroyed.
Ash-bud Moth (*Prays fraxinella*) The terminal buds of Fraxinus excelsior may be destroyed.	Infected shoots should be cut out. Reduce rival leaders resulting from the loss of terminal buds to one.
Goat Moth (*Cossus cossus*) The larvae tunnel into the main trunk and branches which may cause them to fail in strong winds or physical pressures.	Cut down badly attacked trees. Dying branches may be cut beyond the tunnel. It is sometimes possible to kill the larvae with a piece of wire pushed down to the full length of the holes.
Leopard Moth (*Zeuzera pyrina*)	As for Goat Moth
Asian Longhorn Beetle (*Anoplophora glabripennis*) Present in China, Asia and North America; affects *Populus, Acer, Aesculus, Quercus, Prunus, Ulmus* and *Alnus*.	Branches, crowns and whole trees may be killed or severely affected. Remove affected parts or the whole tree and dispose of arisings by burning to eliminate potential beetle populations.
Lilac Borer (*Podosesia syringae*) Affects most Lilac cultivars.	Encourage multi-stemmed shrubs by growing cultivars on their own roots and allowing plants to freely sucker. By removing affected stems, other healthy shoots can be trained to form a new plant by good pruning.
Pine Shoot Moth (*Rhyacionia buoliana*) Pines, and in particular the Scots Pine, are attacked. Often, the leading shoots are affected, the tunnelling larvae causing distortion and perhaps their death.	Provided that the tree is vigorous and there is a replacement growth suitably placed to form a leader, affected shoots may be cut out.

Chapter Six

The Specific Pruning Needs of the Genera

INTRODUCTION

In the following list I have described the pruning of nearly 450 genera of trees, shrubs and conifers. The emphasis is on hardy subjects, but many species classed as half-hardy or tender in the United Kingdom have been included. It was not possible in a book of this size and scope to include every species, still less all the garden cultivars and hybrids. The habits of growth and flowering have, however, been described for many species and in the larger genera the species have been grouped, where possible, according to these habits and to their pruning needs. If, therefore, readers find that a particular species or cultivar is not mentioned they can, in the vast majority of cases, apply the treatment recommended for a species with similar growth and flowering.

The botanical names of the genera and species have been used throughout, but I have included, in Appendix I, a list of common English names with their botanical equivalents.

ABELIA

These shrubs love a sunny, rather sheltered position where they will flower well in summer and later again in the season, producing fresh growths freely from the base. Thus, sufficient growth is produced to allow some of the older wood to be cut out completely and by this means the development of the younger shoots is encouraged.

A. chinensis is usually grown as a bush in sheltered borders in the South and West, but, even so, some dieback can be expected after a severe winter. The final pruning should therefore be left until the spring when the exact extent of the winter's damage can be ascertained. If it is desired, one or two of the very oldest branches may be cut out in the late autumn but there seems to be little point in this as they do form extra protection for the plant as a whole. With *A. serrata*, another deciduous species, treatment may be similar, but often there is more dead and twiggy growth to be cut out. *A. triflora* produces a thick mass of erect growths, but this is a natural habit and there should be no attempt to thin these out extensively, cutting out just the dead and oldest shoots. *A. schumannii* is slightly tender and may die right back in a severe winter. Should the wood survive for several years, the oldest growths may be cut out in the spring, but small furnishing shoots should be left at the base and the natural arching habit of the growths must be retained to preserve the typical habit of this species. *A. umbellata* is a large shrub with spreading habit and it may be necessary to prune the longer branches back to more upright growths in order to retain a specimen within a given space. The larger wood has an ornamental bark effect and size and girth is worth developing for this. *A. spathulata*, an upright grower, requires little beyond the thinning of the oldest wood in the spring.

The evergreen species and hybrids are typified to some extent by *A. ×grandiflora* (*A. chinensis* × *A. uniflora*). This usually needs wall protection when the growths are tied up to the supporting wires. The development of free growth may be encouraged by leaving the laterals unpruned, but new growths, which are strong and fast-growing, must be tied in as they develop, otherwise once they have arched over, the laterals that are produced will be upright. Then, when the growth is finally tied up, these vital shoots which are to produce next season's flowers will be turned in to the wall and thus spoilt. The strong growths are well worth saving and they can be used to replace the oldest branches that may be cut out after flowering. As a rule this subject flowers on laterals from the previous year's wood but the season is extended by the production of blossoms on the earliest of the young growths. *A. floribunda* has a similar habit and the same general principles apply.

To renovate all the species above, all the stems can be cut back to the base in early spring to produce strong new shoots from the ground.

ABELIOPHYLLUM

The only species is *A. distichum*, which is hardy. This shrub should be encouraged to grow vigorously for it flowers early in the spring on growths made during the previous season and the stronger these are the better will be the flower display. Good culture and feeding are therefore important.

Worn and twiggy wood should be cut back to strong growths in the centre of the shrub after flowering. The general shape and natural lax, open habit should be taken into account.

This subject is often grown against a sunny wall for the protection of the early flowers. In this position strong shoots develop which are 2.4 to 3.0 m. (8 to 10 ft.) in height. The best policy is to tie in the framework and then to allow the laterals to develop, cutting back a proportion of these each year in order to maintain vigorous growth. This should be carried out after flowering, but in addition some tidying up may be done during the growing season. The very pendulous lower branches often root freely on touching the ground and quickly develop into young plants. These must be removed at an early stage as otherwise they will compete with the parent and a bare patch will be left at the base. Free standing shrubs should be pruned as for *Forsythia*, which see.

ABIES

It is essential that these trees have a strong leader at planting time, a characteristic that develops at an early stage in the nursery provided that the stock is kept healthy. The task, after planting into the final quarters, is to encourage establishment as quickly as possible, in order that the rate of growth and development of the leader is maintained without check. An essential feature of these trees is the long, straight trunk that is formed from this leader. Under ideal conditions the lower branch systems are often retained and this greatly adds to their beauty. When the lower branches are lost, sometimes even to half the height, their beauty is to a large extent spoilt. It should be remembered that they are difficult to grow well on dry soils and many species thrive best on a deep, moist soil, with shelter, a fairly high rainfall and no atmospheric pollution. Generally, any branches that are seriously dying back should be taken off at the trunk. No other pruning is normally necessary. In the event that the leader is lost in the early years, usually from severe weather conditions or from bird damage, certain species such as *A. pinsapo* and *A. koreana* have the ability to re-produce a new leader, if left alone.

ABUTILON

The hardiest species is *A. vitifolium* but it is only possible to grow this evergreen shrub or small tree in the open without protection in the milder parts of the country. It is usually grown with wall protection, but even so, it is likely to be severely damaged or killed during very hard weather.

As wall culture is more common this will be described. The plants should go into their final position directly from pots, planting in the spring when the growth is about 0.3 m. (1 ft.) high. The leading shoot should be retained and it is therefore advisable to stake this with a strong bamboo cane, making further ties as it extends. The central leader is continued for almost the complete height of the plant. No support is needed other than ties on to the main stem to prevent the plant from blowing out or coming away from the wall during gales. It is fully capable of supporting its own weight, for it is a single-stemmed shrub, not a climber. Should the leading growth be broken when the plant is young it will often form quite a broad-based bush with rival leads. Thus if it goes unattended without the selection of one of these, there is often considerably more lateral development away from the wall. As it is, the laterals from a mature plant will often grow out from 1.2 to 2.4 m. (4 to 8 ft.).

Little pruning is needed other than the cutting off of the old flower heads, but this is very necessary in order to avoid wasted energy in the production of a heavy crop of seed. This, together with a watering if this is necessary, will often prolong the life of this shrub for many years, for it is often short-lived, dying suddenly usually just after flowering.

There is no difference in culture if grown in the open, either with a single leader or as a multi-stemmed shrub. A sunny position is needed.

A. megapotamicum is an attractive shrub to grow in a warm, sheltered corner against a wall. A small plant set out in the spring soon establishes itself, and the growths are tied fanlike against bamboo canes which are themselves secured to the wires. Each year, provided the plant survives the winter, further growths are produced from the base and over the shrub. These should be tied in to gain the utmost protection from the wall, cutting out some of the older wood each spring when the extent of the winter's damage can be seen and taken into account. There should be no cutting out of old wood in the autumn as this is more likely to survive the winter. Young vigorous plants can be cut back hard in early spring to rejuvenate them.

ACACIA

These trees or large shrubs are not totally hardy and they will only succeed in the mildest parts of the British Isles or where they are grown in the shelter of a warm sunny wall. *A. dealbata* and *A. baileyana* are the two most commonly planted outdoors, producing fragrant yellow flowers in late winter to early spring. They may be planted 0.3 m. (1 ft.) or so away from the base of the wall and staking may be necessary as they are vigorous. Sometimes in a favorable position they will assume almost tree-like proportions even away from a wall and often fail in the ground due to circling roots that have been left following the planting of container-grown plants. Most Acacias will respond to pruning if they become too large for their position, provided that this is carried out in the late spring. At this period living wood is apparent and frosted and dead growths can be removed.

ACCA

A. sellowiana normally requires the protection of a warm, sunny wall. It is difficult to train hard against a wall, and it is better when grown as a bush planted about 0.6 m. (2 ft.) from the base. It will then be self-supporting, branching from ground level and forming a rigid, bushy shrub. It will have a spread of several feet from the wall, but it may be restricted by careful and gradual pruning back into the main branch system, on an annual basis after flowering in summer.

ACER

Acers vary considerably in their form, habit and size and in their soil requirements and uses in the garden. This complex genus is divided botanically into groups or sections and this is a convenient form in which to account for the pruning. Only those sections that are commonly grown are dealt with here. It may, however, be stated that with good, healthy and free growth very little pruning is necessary or desirable beyond that which is required for training purposes and for the retention of a leader with the larger growers. The liability to bleed, especially if cut in the spring, is a weakness which is common to most, less with *A. campestre*. It is important, therefore, to carry out any pruning which is necessary in the late summer or early autumn. It is often difficult to prune larger specimens back to a natural shape, due to the opposite buds which make it difficult to find natural, single growing points.

Section *Platanoidea*

A. platanoides, the Norway Maple, has a close head with heavy branching and often with a free production of dwarf shoots along the length of the framework. These should not be removed nor should the branches be thinned for this is the natural habit of growth. In addition to the well-established varieties, a number of selected clones have appeared, particularly in North America, which have a more compact form making them suitable as street trees. These are often termed 'tailored trees'. Examples are 'Crimson Sentry', 'Cleveland Two', 'Summer Shade' and 'Columnare'.

A. platanoides 'Schwedleri', the Purple Norway Maple, is sometimes grown as a support for climbers, e.g. *Clematis tangutica*, the growths being pruned back hard to a main framework each winter or, if preferred, at longer intervals. The maple provides support and also acts as a foliage contrast, see Fig. 20.

Most of the remaining species in this group are also of tree size and thus a 1.8 to 2.4 m. (6 to 8 ft.) standard is normally planted. *A. cappadocicum* var. *sinicum* in particular should be encouraged to spread and sweep down with low branches, as the foliage, flowers and fruits are most attractive.

A. campestre, the Common Field Maple, may be grown as a 1.8 m. (6 ft.) standard and be trained well in the early years to retain a leader and have well-spaced branches. The natural growth however, is to produce a very close branching and this should be left to develop and no attempt be made at thinning. Occasionally, a strong growth is produced which extends up through the centre of the tree. Should such a growth originate in a mature tree close to the central axis it may be left, for usually it is a sign of renewed vigour. An upright growth on the extremities of the branch system will eventually throw the tree out of balance, in addition to the danger of the extra weight breaking the branches. It should, therefore, be carefully reduced, keeping a watch for any subsequent growths which may break out.

An attractive trunk and branch system may be formed by planting two or three young trees of this species together, allowing them to grow with their heads interlocked as one.

This subject forms a very good hedge plant where, to gain full benefit of the attractive foliage, it may be clipped during the winter. It is also ideal for training over a framework to form an arbor. The annual shoots from this framework should be pruned back hard each winter.

Section *Acer*

A. monspessulanum is similar to *A. campestre* in form but *A. sempervirens* is usually much slower in growth and needs encouragement, with a good deep soil.

A. opalus. Although this is a strong grower there is often considerable difficulty in retaining a leader as the vigour is thrown into the lower branching. A system of stopping may check this at an early stage but the habit, although variable, is to open out to form a head very quickly with a dense crown. Should the branches be clothed with dwarf shoots these are best left. *A. hyrcanum*, very similar in appearance, is a slower and smaller grower but tends to retain its leader more readily.

A. saccharum, the Sugar Maple, should not be confused with *A. saccharinum*, the Silver Maple, which in the United Kingdom is a much larger tree. *A. saccharum* often produces a short branching head in the U.K. and tends to be compact. Training and pruning should be as for *A. saccharinum*.

A. pseudoplatanus, the Sycamore. This species, although not a true native, is found throughout the British Isles even in the most exposed areas. The main reason for its success in the exposed positions is that it is a strong, quick grower and is capable of a speedy reaction to damage to growth by development from the remaining axillary or dormant buds. In the nursery it is a strong grower and responds well to training; thus, with care, perfect standards with a good central leader can quite easily be produced.

This species seeds profusely and is distributed far and wide in a most efficient manner; in fact, the resultant seedlings will grow so rapidly that the general effect of an ornamental or amenity planting is quickly ruined. The saplings growing on the edge of a clump of trees where there is more light will in a matter of a few years increase the size of the wooded area thus changing its whole character and in many cases spoiling the lower furnishings of the mature trees. In addition, therefore, to carrying out the required maintenance on mature trees, it is important to eradicate surplus Sycamore seedlings at an early stage. There are a number of varieties that differ from the type in growth. For example, *A. pseudoplatanus* 'Brilliantissimum' is slow-growing and compact, and it is difficult to maintain a central leader.

Section *Lithocarpa*

A. macrophyllum develops into a large tree with fairly upright main branches. The outer and lower branches develop a semi-pendulous habit as the tree matures. This form should be encouraged as it brings the yellow racemes down to eye level where their beauty and scent can be appreciated.

A. franchetii is usually very slow to establish as a young tree, but once happy in position it will begin to make strong growth through a central leader.

Section *Palmata*

A. palmatum. Considerable variation exists among the many varieties and forms of this species. The type plant ultimately forms a large bush or small tree, but it is slow-growing and takes many years to reach full size. The typical habit that should be encouraged is one in which the branches, originating from low down, almost at ground level, grow up at a sharp angle supporting a twig and leaf pattern of great beauty, many of the lower and outer branches sweeping down almost to ground level where they can be seen to best effect. Often, the only pruning necessary is on neighbouring trees in order to encourage the free branching and unrestricted development of this species, see Fig. 26. This advice may also be applied to the many varieties and the most common mistake is to crowd specimens, thus spoiling growth. These plants require shelter from cold winds, while they are prone to damage from late frosts and subsequently coral spot. *A. japonicum* and other species in this section have similar habits and the general advice above applies to these also.

Section *Macrantha*

This important group, the Snake Bark Maples, is made up of species with a smooth bark that is striped white. *A. davidii* as an example has a typical habit of growth. The branches originating at the termination of a short trunk sub-divide to a very limited extent but instead produce many dwarf shoots along their lengths creating a graceful 'fox-tail' effect. A leader should be retained for as long as possible allowing branching on a leg of 0.9 m. (3 ft.). The early training consists of the removal of crossing branches that originate at the base of the head. At a later stage any small branches which tend to hide the bark effect should also be removed. For the best effect, the long branches must not be restricted through lack of light or pruning. Once established, trees need minimum pruning and do not respond to hard pruning or renovation. Unfortunately this group is susceptible to coral spot. In most respects the remainder of the species in this group are similar in habit. Among these are *A. crataegifolium*, *A. pensylvanicum*, *A. grosseri* var. *hersii*, *A. capillipes* and *A. rufinerve*.

Section *Rubra*

Two large-growing species are in this group, *A. rubrum*, the Red Maple, and *A. saccharinum*, the Silver Maple. The latter is a most distinctive tree and as it is a large grower it should have a 1.8 to 2.4 m. (6 to 8 ft.) leg with a strong leader. As the tree develops, the length of the leg may be increased even to 3.0 to 4.6 m. (10 to 15 ft.) in order to display the shaggy bark to best effect. The lower branches become pendulous at a later stage, but this habit is seen at its best with *A. saccharinum* f. *laciniatum*, which has deeply cut foliage. This species has a high rate of scaffold and branch failure due to poor branch attachments and is susceptible to *Ganoderma applenatum*, which causes serious internal decay in the trunk.

Section *Trifoliata*

A. griseum, the Paper Bark Maple. In addition to the general effect, the great beauty of this tree is in the bark. This may be seen at its best when there is a definite short trunk 0.9 to 1.2 m. (3 to 4 ft.) with a well-shaped head. The leader should be kept for as long as possible until the head is formed. The branches, if allowed to grow freely without crowding or lack of

light, produce an almost tiered effect. The outer branch tips sweep down to ground level, but with care the mower can work beneath them as they are not stiff.

A. maximowiczianum is normally trained on a 0.6 m. (2 ft.) leg and the head quickly splits up into several ascending branches.

A. mandschuricum is a small deciduous tree, sometimes a shrub, and is best trained to be multi-stemmed.

Section *Negundo*

A. negundo, the Box Elder. This and the variegated forms are fast-growing but the type plant is the largest and will form a sizeable tree. However, once the clear stem is formed and the crown is developing, the vigour in the leader is reduced and finally fades completely as more and more growth and weight is put into the branches. In time these become heavy and spread out to open the crown, causing epicormic shoots to break out as a result of the extra light. Also, strong upright shoots are often produced in the region of any cuts that have been made on horizontal branches. This extra weight should be reduced and it is often advisable to brace really old specimens as the wood is brittle.

The form 'Variegatum' is often planted in a colour border to add to the general effect. It will, however, quickly outgrow the slower ones such as *A. palmatum* and should not be planted too close. A distance of 6 m. (20 ft.) is suggested. This variegated form must be allowed to grow freely without pruning for most of the buds that break out near a cut will revert to green foliage and the general effect of the tree will be spoilt.

ACRADENIA

A. frankliniae. This evergreen shrub of dense growth is tender and needs a sheltered position in the warmer parts of the country. No pruning is required apart from the removal of dead growths but it must have sufficient space to develop. It may grow up to 3 m. (10 ft.) high and be 1 to 2 m. (3 to 6 ft.) in spread.

ACTINIDIA

These vigorous climbers require an extensive support if they are to be allowed to grow freely, for they produce long growths which twine round each other if there is no other means of attachment. Thus, in a confined space, unless they are pruned, they form an untidy and hopeless thicket.

Grown on a wall, the best method is to train the growths to cover the space which is allocated. Afterwards, growths that extend beyond these bounds are stopped back to 150 mm. (6 in.) when about 0.6 m. (2 ft.) in length. Thus it is necessary to look over the shrubs several times during the growing season. These shortened growths are then cut back hard to one or two buds during the winter. Some species, such as *A. deliciosa*, produce shorter growths or spurs on their older wood and this system of pruning encourages their development. Young growths springing from low down and in the centre form ideal replacements for the older and worn growths. They should be tied in as they develop. This replacement pruning should be carried out during the winter.

Another method is to use a tall pole or a tripod of poles for a support, see Plate 43 and Fig. 20 (1). The growths are left to arch down once the height for the shrub has been reached, but again stopping is necessary to prevent a chaotic tangle. Some of the older branches may be cut out each year during the winter, tying in the younger ones as replacements.

When the larger growers are used to climb over trees the added weight often becomes a problem. However, it is often possible to reduce this by breaking off the dead growths of the climber. This may be carried out during the summer. Pruning should be carried out with care as living wood can easily be severed.

A. kolomikta is a less vigorous species which if trained on a sunny wall will produce large leaves splashed with creamy pink and white. Pruning should be carried out in late winter by removing weak growth, retaining 5 to 7 strong growths and reducing the laterals on these by two-thirds. The same pruning technique can be applied to *A. polygama*.

ADENOCARPUS

These are deciduous or partly evergreen shrubs or small trees and are half-hardy. *A. foliolosus* is a semi-evergreen which needs the protection of a sunny wall. It should be planted approximately one foot from the base and if trained to a single stem it may reach a height of 1.8 m. (6 ft.) before the head opens out. The horizontal branches are in tiers. Staking may be necessary when the plant is young. Pruning back is necessary where single growths are overlapping the edge or interfering with neighbouring plants. They may be cut back after flowering to leave a furnished effect. *A. decorticans* is a deciduous shrub sending out long horizontal branches and also needs shelter. Pruning is much the same, making careful cuts to remove offending growths after flowering, in such a way that the cuts are hidden.

AESCULUS

The most common species is *A. hippocastanum*, the Horse-chestnut. At maturity it often forms a very large tree with heavy branching. In addition, the mature scaffolds have a heavy downward sweep, some even becoming long and pendulous. To allow for this habit and to produce a good, safe, long-living tree, nursery stock should consist of standards with a good central leader. It is important to retain this leader for as long as possible so that the weight may be evenly spread over a number of well-positioned branches.

Large trees sometimes show a tendency to produce upright branches and to grow vigorously from these, even though they may originate from near the extremity of a lower limb. Such growths are best cut back, at an early stage if possible, for not only is the outline of the tree thrown out of balance, but also the extra weight which builds up on the branch may cause it to break off leaving a tear on the trunk. It is difficult at times to account for this, but extra light on one side of the tree or a succession of wet summers and good growing years are frequent causes.

Sometimes the main branches exhibit longitudinal cracks on the bark and these should be examined carefully from time to time. Should they not extend beyond the bark they have probably been caused by the rapidly swelling stem and there is no danger, for they heal rapidly, leaving just the scar for the remainder of the life of the tree. Deeper cracks or splitting caused by gale or storm damage occur frequently on trees in exposed sites and these need attention. Often when a wound is made, a large number of growths are produced in the following spring from the cambium on the outer edge of the cut. This is one of the reasons why unnecessary pruning of established trees should be avoided, for these growths, even after selection by thinning, are seldom strong enough to replace any branches which have been lost. Their attachment to the tree is weak as they have originated from surface tissues and are never directly connected to the heartwood of the parent branch or trunk. It is sometimes possible to thin to one or two growths on the lower edge of a wound and to leave these to hide the full view of this from the ground, thus improving the general effect. The other danger, in common with most trees, is that of the heartwood rotting before healing takes place, but although the rate of healing is often rapid the heartwood of this species quickly deteriorates.

A considerable variation in growth and form occurs among seedlings, and there are a number of varieties that display this to an even greater extent. *A. hippocastanum* 'Memmingeri' often has dense branching with dwarf or epicormic growths over the entire system. These should not be removed, as even more will develop in their place that will involve further cutting. It is important to recognise these habits and to prune and train accordingly.

A. turbinata, the Japanese Horse-chestnut, and *A. hippocastanum* var. *pyramidalis* both tend to produce their branches from one point, the head opening out as soon as branching occurs. It is difficult to form a leader with these.

A. ×carnea, the Red Horse-chestnut, produces a dense canopy and with free, unrestricted growth and full light the branching will develop closely down to ground level. This is the best form in which to grow this tree and there should be an open foreground to allow this. There seems to be a tendency for this hybrid to form cavities and it is therefore important to retain the leader and to avoid narrow forking, at the

same time keeping a close watch on old specimens in particular for any trouble that may be developing.

Another characteristic of this particular hybrid is the formation of large burrs that occur on the trunk and main branches. These appear as cankerous, corky eruptions, but healing and callusing may keep pace with their increase in size as the trunk or branch itself enlarges. In such cases, apart from the unsightliness, there is little to worry about. There should be no attempt to cut or gouge out this mass of corky tissue for it will often go back deeply to the centre of the limb or trunk and there will be no hard surface on the face of the wound with very little healing taking place from the edges. Should rot have set in, however, without any visible callusing, it may be taken as a sign that the tree itself is beginning to decline in health An attempt should be made to improve the health of the tree and to consider complete removal of the affected branch, as they are prone to failure where they join the main trunk, leaving a nasty tear.

With *A. ×carnea* 'Plantierensis' the lower branches not only reach the ground but they will actually grow along it for a short distance afterwards. This produces a very good effect and great care must be taken with the mower when it is used in the vicinity of these growths. It is better to use the rotary type beneath the branches with an assistant to lift these as the cutting proceeds, or provide a mulched area around the dripline of the canopy to eliminate the need to mow.

A. californica is not a large grower, branching low and wide with the outer branches becoming almost pendulous. A 0.9 m. (3 ft.) leg or a multi-stemmed specimen from ground level is sufficient. Growth is better in a sheltered position. Any wounds must be watched continuously, for the soft heartwood rots very readily before callusing is complete. The tree normally produces plenty of shoot growth from the region of any cuts.

A. indica, the Indian Horse-chestnut, produces a very shapely tree with clean growth; the cultivar 'Sidney Pearce' is grafted, the main essentials being to start with a good standard tree and to retain the leader afterwards. The same is true of *A. flava*, the Yellow Buckeye, although the habit of growth is completely different.

A careful study of the ultimate size of each species must be made before a site is selected, for some, e.g. *A. pavia*, the Red Buckeye, make only small trees. However, it is important to retain a short leader through the crown, for the branches on a poorly shaped tree are prone to damage from summer gales. The smaller growers suffer very quickly if denied light by invasive overhanging limbs, the affected portions dying back perhaps to spoil the shape of the tree.

A. parviflora rarely forms a single trunk and spreads by means of sucker growths at the base expanding into a clump which, although only 2.4 to 3.0 m. (8 to 10 ft.) in height, may be quite extensive. There is no pruning, apart from limiting the spread if it becomes necessary. This should be carried out with great care in order to preserve unpruned, flowering growth on the outer edge with furnishing down to ground level.

AGERATINA

A. ligustrina. This shrub is tender and can only be grown in milder districts. It flowers on strong shoots of the current season springing from a woody branch system that is often short and limited in extent. Pruning should be carried out annually in the spring, and consists of cutting back the growths produced during the past season to within 50 to 100 mm. (2 to 4 in.) of their base. This should be carried out before the new growth commences.

AILANTHUS

A genus of large, strong-growing, suckering trees of which one is commonly grown in the open, *A. altissima*, the Tree of Heaven. In its early years is it very fast growing but competition after planting is desirable for this helps to draw the leader up. Often, the branches develop horizontally, but turn to grow vertically for a considerable height, even to the level of the leading growth. This is a habit of growth that is difficult to check and old specimens with heavy branching may need bracing or a prop beneath a large horizontal branch. The tree heals very well but new growths appear near old cuts and these must be

removed. Rival sucker growths formed on the root system should also be taken out. *A. vilmoriniana* is similar in growth but the branches are more upright. Both species are fast-growing when young.

A. altissima can be grown for the tropical foliage effect which it produces if annual or biennial coppicing to ground level is carried out. By planting in a group or bed at 0.6 to 0.9 m. (2 to 3 ft.) apart, and by feeding and watering if necessary, strong growths 1 to 2 m. (3 to 6 ft.) in height are sent up annually.

AKEBIA

A. quinata and *A. trifoliata* climb by means of slender, twining stems which are freely produced from a few short, stout branches at the base. They may be used for covering old stumps where little training is needed. The whole will eventually become an untidy mass of dead and living stems, but this matters little in the wilder, more natural parts of the garden. Posts and pergolas are also used for training, but some tying is often necessary, otherwise the whole climber may easily slip down and form a mass of growths at the base of the support. It is also an advantage to allow the growths to grow over the top of the arch or stake, as extra support is gained in this way. A few

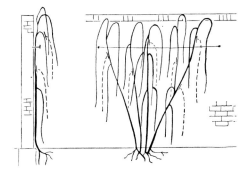

Fig. 27. An *Akebia* sp. trained to a wall. The pendulous growths are trained behind the horizontal wires for support. The dead and weak growths that would be cut out are shown in broken line. With a large established plant a greater proportion would need to be cut out each year.

short stub ends of branches may also be left on the stakes in order that growths may coil round these and thus help to hold the mass of twining branches in position, see Fig. 20 (2). A tripod system of poles is also useful, see Fig. 20 (1). It is possible to reduce the weight and general untidiness by carefully removing dead wood, doing this in the winter or early spring.

When grown against a wall the stems should be trained behind one to three strands of horizontal wire. These wires should be stretched at approximately two inches from the wall face. The upper strand may be at 0.3 to 0.46 m. (1 to 1.5 ft.) below the height of the wall as the growths are capable of a limited amount of self support, see Fig. 27. In addition, they arch over and the long pendulous growths are attractive. Often, a few of the growths twine together but this does not matter a great deal. Pruning consists of cutting out the weaker and dead growths during the winter. Sometimes also there are dead tips which need to be cut back, especially after a severe winter.

ALANGIUM

A. platanifolium and *A. chinense* are half-hardy shrubs with an interesting stem formation and leaf pattern. Even when grown in a sheltered position the young growths are often killed back into the older wood. However, the plant will break out from living tissue and even from the base at soil level, thus making good its appearance and the only pruning necessary is the removal of dead wood in the spring. They can also be grown successfully against a warm wall in more exposed areas.

ALBIZIA

A. julibrissin is the hardiest semi-deciduous species but even in the warmer parts wall protection is usually necessary. Without the warm summers, ripening of the wood fails to happen and the plant succumbs to frost damage and fails to flower. However, owing to the fast rate of growth and the fact that it is capable of developing into a tree 9 to 12 m. (30 to 40 ft.) high when grown under good conditions, a high wall and some pruning will be necessary. It needs no support beyond

a strong stake. The pruning to restrict this subject should be carried out in the spring, taking the previous year's growth back if necessary to 5 or 6 buds. It is wise to encourage as much furnishing on the lower part of the plant as possible for the main stem quickly becomes bare as growth is concentrated more and more at the top of the plant.

ALNUS

The strongest species are good growers, naturally producing a definite leader and so developing straight trunks with well-spaced, small branches. They tend to be pyramidal in outline and, as they develop, the trunk may be cleaned to a height of 1.5 to 1.8 m. (5 to 6 ft.) when the lower branches may be left to sweep own to the ground as they extend. The following species and hybrids are in this group: *A. ×aschersoniana, A. cordata, A. glutinosa, A. matsumurae, A. rubra* and *A. hirsuta*. Also *A. nitida* and *A. subcordata* retain their leaders well.

A. japonica has a definite tendency to branch from ground level and may become a large shrub. This is even more marked with *A. maritima* and *A. viridis,* which are definitely shrubby, and no attempt should be made to form a leader. The latter species may not be more than 0.9 m. (3 ft.) in height.

A. incana may develop into a shrub or small tree. It shows a tendency to form rival leaders, especially in exposed positions and is therefore not the best alder for height. The golden form, *A. incana* 'Aurea', also shows this tendency while *A. glutinosa* 'Aurea' has a better colour and gives height quite readily.

The following also show interesting variations in growth. *A. firma* retains a leader well with long, graceful branches but the shade cast is very light. *A. glutinosa* 'Imperialis' is a thin grower with delicate branching and should have a sheltered position. *A. maximowiczii* is a small tree but the leader slows down as heavy thickening goes into the lower branches. *A. tenuifolia* is a dense grower and it is difficult to retain the central leader beyond 2.4 m. (8 ft.), so this tends be grown more as a multi-stemmed specimen *A. ×spaethii* is often difficult to grow to any height and occasionally, after a very severe winter, considerable dead wood is produced.

To produce an informal effect by the waterside, an even spacing should be avoided and a number may even be planted in threes allowing them to grow together to form clumps.

ALOYSIA

A. triphylla. In nature, this species forms a small tree, but it is not perfectly hardy and thus does not reach these proportions in regions with hard winters. In the mildest climates it may be grown as a bush in the open, but wall protection is usually necessary, and even with this it may be killed outright during a severe winter. A proportion of the young growths are killed each winter, and these should be pruned back to living wood in the spring just as the buds break. Frequently this means going right back to the older wood. The inflorescences, which terminate the current season's growth, are larger and more effective as a result of hard pruning, provided it is accompanied by feeding and mulching. In addition to growing this subject as a bush at the foot of a wall, the growths may be trained to the surface, when much of the wood will be retained from year to year. The pruning is much the same, the previous year's growths being taken back to the main framework in the spring.

In colder districts a loose bracken protection round the basal branches may be necessary to save the shrub during the winter.

AMELANCHIER

It is most important for the nurseryman and the arboriculturist to be aware of the two distinct forms of growth which are found in this genus—suckerous and non-suckerous.

Suckerous or stoloniferous species. Generally these form a thicket of stems and branches that vary in height according to the species and require no routine pruning. Thinning the crowded stems can be done in winter to renovate neglected specimens. The following species are examples: *A. humilis, A. canadensis, A. spicata* and *A. stolonifera.*

Non-suckerous or non-stoloniferous species. These may be single- or multi-stemmed and to some extent this is dependent upon the initial nursery training. A 1.8 m. (6 ft.) length of clear stem may be formed, although some delightful old trees have a much shorter length of clear trunk. With a shorter, feathered young tree it is possible to start with a lower branching at 0.9 m. (3 ft.), and to maintain the leader for 1 to 2 m. (3 to 6 ft.). Although the branching under this system may not be regularly spaced, some quite attractive forms are developed and it is a pleasant breakaway from the stereotyped standard. The species only develop into small trees or large shrubs and once a head is formed the leader breaks up very quickly. It should, however, be borne in mind that most of the small tree species readily throw strong shoots from the lower stem system as they become established in their permanent quarters. These must be rubbed out as they appear if it is desired to retain a clear stem; alternatively, the required number may be trained to alter the shape of the tree, provided there is sufficient space and light for the additional branches in the head system. Normally, this can only be carried out when the head is in the early stages of development. *A. laevis* and *A. lamarckii* will form small, multi-stemmed trees. *A. sanguinea* and *A. ×grandiflora* are shrubby and form one or several stems. The same is true of *A. asiatica* and *A. alnifolia* and its variety *semi-integrifolia.*

×AMELASORBUS

×*A. jackii* (*Amelanchier alnifolia* × *Sorbus scopulina*). This unusual bigeneric hybrid is a strong-growing shrub and requires very little pruning beyond the removal of dead wood. It is seen at its best with an open foreground and with furnishing down to ground level.

AMORPHA

These are deciduous shrubs or subshrubs, either retaining a permanent branch system or dying down to a woody stock near soil level. *A. canescens* usually dies back each winter to a woody stock. Thus all the previous year's wood should be cut back, dead or alive, in the spring, just before the new growths break out and these will flower the same year. *A. fruticosa* forms branches which remain and thicken year by year. Again, flowers are produced on the current season's growth. Left to develop freely, the branches spread and become ungainly. Occasionally, therefore, some pruning is necessary, either to shorten these back to a suitable growth or to cut them out entirely. The shrub freely produces young growths which will act as replacements. Never should pruning be carried at one level year after year, otherwise mopheads of growth will be produced which are unsightly. For foliage effect, this species may be cut right down to near ground level in the spring but the growths will not flower. The remaining species are similar in general habit to *A. fruticosa*.

AMPELOPSIS

Ampelopsis climbs by means of coiling stem tendrils and is therefore distinct from *Parthenocissus*, which produces flattened discs that adhere strongly to their support. The strongest species, for example, *A. glandulosa* var. *brevipedunculata* and *A. megalophylla*, are suitable for growing over trees, in addition to such structures as sheds, walls or fences. They are often better in the wilder parts of the garden where they can ramble at will. Training and pruning under these conditions is difficult, unnecessary and undesirable, unless growth goes beyond the intended bounds. When they are trained to single poles and left to develop freely, growth becomes tangled and unmanageable in such a restricted space. A method of control is to prune back annually to two or three permanent rods, which are tied to the support. Under this system, spurs build up which are twisted and knotty and have great character. The young growths are taken back to the lowest bud in early winter after leaf fall, when there is least likelihood of bleeding. When trained along horizontal pergola systems the young growths, which are long and slender, hang down to form a curtain. Annual pruning back to the permanent rod is carried out in just the same manner, see Fig. 20 (6). *A. arborea* is better suited to wall culture. Supporting wires are needed and annual pruning may take the young growths back to a permanent rod system.

ANTHYLLIS

The most commonly grown species is *A. hermanniae*, which has a compact habit in the earlier stages of development. As maturity or old age is reached, bushes often become heavy, with a loose habit which is caused by the crowded condition of the growths on the ends of the branches. A limited amount of careful cutting back after flowering will correct this, but this may need to be spread out over 2 to 3 years before this is corrected. The shrub benefits from the protection of a sunny wall or corner in the rock garden. *A. barba-jovis*, Jupiter's Beard, is a subject for wall culture, the main branches being tied and trained as the shrub develops. No pruning is normally required in the nursery.

APHANANTHE

A. aspera. This rare tree in the elm family forms a rounded head with pendulous branchlets. It should be given a sheltered position but it must have full sun as it is important for the wood to ripen properly. It is a difficult tree to grow well in regions with hard winters, as any wood which is only partially ripened is often killed back during the winter. It should be trained with a clear trunk of 1.8 m. (6 ft.) and allowed to form a natural head.

ARALIA

These are plants for a light, well-drained soil, for, while growth may be stronger in a moist, rich medium, the wood which is produced is inclined to be pithy and unripened and in this condition may not winter well especially in cold districts. On a stiff clay, growth may be very poor indeed and it is usually impossible to develop these shrubs beyond the bush size.

A. elata is usually the largest woody grower and under ideal conditions extends its branch system to become a very large shrub. It requires plenty of space and should be allowed to branch freely. Pruning that involves cutting back large branches can easily spoil the curiously crooked and twisted framework, which is quite attractive in the winter. In a position where the shrub is against a dark background, the growths often sprawl out towards the light and as the branches grow older, longer and heavier, some of the lower ones may need neatly propping. The inflorescence terminates the current season's growth, but the short, woody shoot tip which supports this remains attached, extension for the following season being taken over by the topmost bud beneath this. Thus, in time, a number of old, dead shoot tips remain attached to the branches. These should not be mistaken for dieback, which is usually extensive with specimens on a wet heavy soil after a severe winter. This species is often suckerous but unless an enlargement of the clump is needed, the suckers should be removed. The variegated forms should not be allowed to sucker as they are propagated by grafting onto stocks of the ordinary type. Any suckers that are produced are, therefore, stronger reversions and will soon outgrow the required form.

A. spinosa is similar to *A. elata* in many respects but it does not grow as large and will not branch as freely, consisting more of upright stems and branches but suckering extensively. *A. chinensis* is also similar, but is a smaller grower.

ARAUCARIA

A. araucana, the Monkey Puzzle, is a tree which must be grown as an isolated, symmetrical specimen if it is to be seen at its best. With a clear surround, for example on a lawn, the branch systems can reach down to ground level with a graceful and natural sweep. The tree should retain the leader until the ultimate height has been reached; however, should the central growth be killed or removed for some reason, a number of adventitious buds may be produced on the central stem and near the original growing point. Often they arise at the point of origin of the highest, and of course youngest, tier of branches. When these have developed sufficiently the strongest may be selected to extend the central trunk. The branches

retain their character as such and will not assume the role and character of leading shoots, even if the adventitious buds fail to appear or a lateral is actually rooted as a cutting, see page 36. This tree will appear very ragged if dead branches and dead wood are apparent, and any work carried out to remove these is very rewarding despite the difficulties and unpleasantness of the task. The dieback of a branch is usually progressive and it is advisable to remove the whole branch back to the main trunk.

ARBUTUS

Normally, this group of evergreen shrubs requires little pruning. It is important in the nursery stage to give them shelter but to allow them to grow freely. Normally they are grown in plunged pots to avoid a check in growth at planting time and staking will be necessary at an early stage. After planting they should be left to grow freely and no attempt must be made to form a trunk. As the leading shoots extend, the smaller branches inside the bush are deprived of light and die. They should be cleaned out as growth extends, for the bark is attractive. Most species form spreading trees when mature, the lower branches assuming a low angle of growth as they are weighed down by extensive development. This is a fortunate habit, for with a clear foreground of grass running up to the perimeter of the tree, a close and rewarding inspection may be made of the flowers and fruits during the autumn and winter. One feature that is common to all *Arbutus* is that they regenerate freely if cut back quite hard, provided that the root system and the plant as a whole are in good condition. It may be necessary to be drastic in this manner following storm damage, or after a very severe and long spell of cold weather when the foliage and small twig growth may have been killed. In the latter case no pruning should be carried out until new growth breaks out.

The above introductory notes serve for *A. andrachne*, *A.* ×*andrachnoides*, *A. unedo* and *A. unedo* f. *rubra*. A larger-growing species, *A. menziesii*, the Pacific Madrone, should if possible be trained with a definite trunk. Shelter will be needed for this in the more exposed gardens which may be obtained by planting in a very small clearing, surrounded by fairly large Rhododendrons. Both genera have similar soil requirements and the young Arbutus is encouraged to grow for the light with a good clean stem. The site may be carefully and gradually opened out at a later stage.

ARCTOSTAPHYLOS

Quite a common prostrate plant, particularly in alpine collections, is *A. uva-ursi*. It forms a mass of growth and foliage and is thus ideal as a ground cover plant. If the plant grows to the edge of the border and needs cutting back to restrict the spread, an informal and pleasing effect is obtained by continually cutting out growths individually with the secateurs in summer after flowering. The shears, used to clip along the edge, will result in a hard line that will not be in keeping with an informal effect. Occasionally it may be necessary to dig the rooted pieces out along the edge to check spread.

A. manzanita is a rare species which usually grows to a height of 1.2 to 2.4 m. (4 to 8 ft.). It needs a sunny position with some shelter. It requires no pruning and should be allowed to grow freely, when it will usually form a short leg and branch rather stiffly from this. Good growth should be encouraged, for if this subject becomes unhealthy it often dies off very quickly.

ARISTOLOCHIA

A few woody species may be grown in the open. They are vigorous climbers with foul-smelling siphon-like flowers, twining in an anti-clockwise direction round supports such as arches, branched stakes and other supports. *A. macrophylla* and *A. tomentosa* are among the most reliable species. Pruning consists of cutting out any dead and weak, straggly growths as the buds commence to break in the spring, but it is not possible to retain a tidy habit and hard pruning to encourage new shoots which can be retrained may be necessary.

ARISTOTELIA

A. chilensis. This evergreen Chilean shrub normally needs wall protection, but it may be grown in the open in milder areas. The main branches are strong and upright, the laterals spreading. The shrub is grown as a bush and is thus planted 0.3 m. (1 ft.) or so from the base of the wall. Pruning to restrict size, if necessary is carried out in the spring and again in the late summer if further shortening is required. The cuts are made into the bush to keep an informal surface. Sometimes long, strong shoots are produced in the crown of the shrub and these may become top-heavy with growth after a year or so. This tendency, which is more likely to occur as a result of the shrub being cut back by frost, should be corrected at an early stage.

ARONIA

The two species and one hybrid of deciduous shrubs have a stool-like habit and when healthy a good supply of strong young wood is thrown up from the base. This allows for good replacement branches as the older ones need to be cut out. These shrubs, *A. arbutifolia* and *A. melanocarpa*, have a spreading and arching habit and this is part of their natural beauty. Pruning, if it is necessary, should be carried out after the autumn foliage and fruiting displays are over. This is often in mid winter and the cuts should be made as close to the base as possible, provided that there are the required number of replacement shoots.

ARTEMISIA

This is a genus of herbs, subshrubs and shrubs. Their foliage is the most attractive feature and for this reason it is preferable to keep the growth strong and healthy by fairly hard pruning to prevent them from becoming old and woody.

A. abrotanum is the most common. Without pruning, this subject becomes very straggly and unsightly with bare stems that become prominent as the branches are weighed down. It should be cut back quite hard in the spring just as growth commences, to prevent this happening. Sometimes mice will eat away the surface bark on the stems at ground level and a watch should be kept for this, especially during the winter.

A. arborescens should be cut back hard to the older wood at the base of the shrub in the spring. It appreciates the shelter of a sunny wall. The remainder of the woody subjects of this genus respond to hard cutting back in the same way, although many may be killed back by hard weather during the winter, especially in exposed conditions.

ARUNDINARIA. *See* Bamboos

ASTER

A. albescens is a semi-woody shrub which flowers on the ends of the current season's wood. However, growths that are produced from the previous year's wood are more likely to flower than those that spring up directly from the base. It should therefore be planted near the base of a warm, sunny wall where there will be more likelihood of the young growth surviving the winter. Pruning consists of cutting out the old growths in the spring to ground level. The strong, young growths that spring up from the base should be retained at full level if living. However, if dieback has occurred, they may be cut back to breaking buds, which are often found at ground level. The entire removal of top growth often reduces any chance of flowers being produced the same season.

ASTERANTHERA

A. ovata is a small climber but it may, under ideal conditions, reach a height of 1 to 2 m. (3 to 6 ft.) when grown against a wall. When it is growing freely it produces comparatively long growths which give the shrub height. It is necessary to tie these in position, although the shrub will clamber into neighbouring plants on its own account. Sometimes the long thin shoots will run along the surface of the soil as a form of ground cover. If required these may be tied up against the wall to thicken and improve the effect as a whole. This subject will withstand cutting and it is beneficial to cut out the weaker wood. This should be carried out in the spring.

ATRAPHAXIS

This small genus of deciduous shrubs have, even in a sunny position, a rather untidy and sprawling habit which, however, may be improved by cutting out some of the older wood in the spring. This may mean taking back quite large shoot systems as with *A. muschketowii* or small ends as with *A. frutescens.*

ATRIPLEX

A. halimus is very good near the coast, although it can also be grown inland. The branching is stiff to begin with, but as the bushes reach maturity they open out and become loose. However, annual pruning in the spring, as the new growth commences, corrects this tendency. In addition, the growth tips damaged by frost may be cut back to living wood at this period, but a formal outline should be avoided. This subject also forms an excellent hedge plant near the coast when trimming should take place in the spring as the new growths appear.

The treatment for *A. canescens* is similar.

AUCUBA

The species most commonly grown is *A. japonica*. It is a strong-growing shrub and will thrive in poor, dry positions, often in quite dense shade beneath trees. Sometimes after very dry periods there is some dieback which needs to be attended to for appearance's sake. As this subject is often grown to provide a background to a border or to fill an awkward gap, it is desirable to have it as large and free-growing as possible and thus it is very seldom that it needs any pruning. The minor branches keep extending year by year and even mature bushes throw up strong cane-like growths each year, which reach almost the height of the plant before they branch out. An annual mulch of composted leaves and a discontinuation of the annual forking through the odd corners every spring to 'tidy them up' is more effective in getting good growth than the pruning knife. Any pruning to shape should be carried out so as to leave an informal effect, cutting out whole growths near to ground level rather than snipping off small branches.

There are many varieties but they all have the same habit of growth. The narrower-leaved forms, such as 'Salicifolia' form a bush that is lighter in foliage effect than the broad-leaved types such as 'Hillieri'.

This is not a good subject for formal hedging for, if it is clipped, portions of the large leaves are left on the plants, and the whole effect is very unsightly. Also, it is difficult to keep the base of the hedge well furnished unless a sufficient width is allowed, leaving the lower branches at almost full length.

AZARA

The various species are similar in many respects in that they are bushy and will form a strong framework of branches. Also that they will respond to careful pruning if this is needed to restrict them, while maintaining a surface which is pleasantly evergreen.

A. microphylla may be grown in the open in the milder localities, but it should have shelter. It will then form a large shrub or small tree 6 to 9 m. (20 to 30 ft.) in height. Usually it is left to branch naturally from the base. It may also be grown on a south-facing wall, when the main branches should be trained fanwise, six to eight being selected. From these the laterals are used as furnishing and, if it is necessary to restrict it in any way, the pruning of a few growths every May taken well back into the framework will still leave the plant adequately furnished. Another method of growing this subject in the shelter of a wall is to plant it a foot or so from the base and allow it to grow naturally as a bush. *A. lanceolata* produces slender branches from the base of the bush but it is tender and needs protection. The other species may also be grown as self-supporting bushes with a wall for protection, *A. petiolaris* being one of the largest, often developing into a very dense bush or small tree.

BACCHARIS

Two species are commonly grown, *B. halimifolia*, deciduous, and *B. patagonica*, evergreen. Grown in the open in a sunny and windswept position these subjects need very little pruning, as the shrubs keep compact and rounded. In the shade, growth is weakly and effective staking difficult. Rarely do they flower in a shady position. Both species respond to hard pruning in late winter.

BAMBOOS

There are three groups of bamboos that require three different methods of pruning—tall open running, clump forming and herbaceous.

Tall open running bamboos, which include *Pleioblastus linearis*, *P. simonii*, *Phyllostachys nuda*, *P. viridi-glaucescens* and *Semiarundinaria fastuosa*, can be thinned out: the rigid wind-resistant canes make them less likely to fall over after being thinned. Thinning of bamboo canes on large established stands of bamboo can be done to increase the diameter and height of individual canes (depending upon climate and temperatures), to increase the amount of rainfall and sunshine the new shoots and canes receive and to expose the attractive canes. It is important to make sure each cane is given enough space. The best time to thin the canes is in the early spring, when the season for snowfall is coming to an end and the spring sunshine is starting to warm the soils.

Remove dead and damaged canes from old stands that have become overcrowded to encourage new growth. Thin out up to 40% of the total number of canes to allow light and space for the new shoots to develop and not become overcrowded and compete with the established canes. When completely removing canes ensure they are cut back as near to soil level as possible, as this will help create more space for the new shoots to develop and keep the stand looking clean and tidy. This will also discourage pest and diseases from living at the base of the bamboo and, in time, possible fungal infection of the stand.

Clump-forming bamboos, which include *Fargesia murielae*, *F. nitida*, *Thamnocalamus spathiflorus* and *Yushania anceps*. Thinning of this group of bamboos should not be undertaken unless it is the removal of a few canes on the edge of the clump. They have a rhizome that produces canes that are close together in a clump and can easily be distinguished from the open running bamboos.

If you were to remove too many canes from a clump-forming bamboo, the remaining canes would soon collapse and fall to the ground, as the canes are not rigid enough to stand alone. In nearly all situations, it would be unwise to thin out any canes from this group of bamboos.

Herbaceous bamboos, which include *Pleioblastus auricomus*, *P. variegatus* and *Sasa* spp., can be cut to ground level every year or every other year with a pair of shears, to encourage the new coloured growths.

BERBERIDOPSIS

B. corallina climbs by means of twining stems and is normally a subject for a cool, shady wall. It should be trained up vertical wires, or bamboo canes tied to the horizontal wiring system and will usually climb up these quite readily, but an occasional tie may also be necessary.

It is seldom necessary to prune this subject, especially on the main branch systems. On occasion, the minor branches benefit from thinning if it is felt that they are too thickly placed. In this case the older and weaker ones should be removed but this must be carried out very carefully in the spring.

BERBERIS

Many of the species and varieties have a growth and a habit that is quite distinct and any pruning that is carried out should be aimed at retaining this. Great care should be taken in the selection of species and position so that there is no need to restrict growth and size by pruning.

The more vigorous species are really large growths; for example *B. chitria* or *B. aristata* may reach a height of 3.7 to 4.6 m. (12 to 15 ft.). In addition, they have an arching and wide-spreading growth and should be left to do this naturally. Where there is sufficient space, groups may be made up of several bushes in proximity to form a complete tangle. A thorough weeding of such clumps may be impossible

and eventually sizeable saplings of such trees as Ash and Sycamore appear and must be eradicated. One method of overcoming this problem is to cut the whole clump down drastically to within 300 mm. (12 in.) of ground level during the winter. This will allow the site to be thoroughly cleaned over a period of three or four years before the plants grow together again.

With an arching species it is sometimes difficult to keep the lower growths. The pruning of deciduous bushes such as *B. thunbergii*, if it becomes necessary, should be carried out during the growing season when any dead branches will be evident and the living ones can be retained. It is important to retain these with the large growers as otherwise bare stems will be exposed which may not readily furnish up again. Any cuts that are made should be back to a suitable growth, the tendency being to cut out lengths of branches, rather than small pieces. The branches are often close together and it is not always possible to cut cleanly without snags. *B. manipurana* among others is very heavily branched and if there are smaller plants beneath the spread they are likely to be smothered, particularly after heavy rains or snowfalls. The most difficult species to restrict without spoiling are the dense and very compact growers such as *B. candidula*. Any cutting back must be carefully carried out in order to retain the natural surface.

B. dictyophylla is attractive, especially during the autumn and winter, when the young stems, covered with white 'bloom' are very prominent and there are often brilliantly coloured leaves on the older branch systems. The production of strong young wood may be encouraged by pruning out some of the older wood as occasion demands, accompanying this with mulching and feeding. *B. virescens* also has young stems which are attractive, these being light brown in colour. Careful and selective pruning with general feeding and mulching may also encourage their production.

B. ×stenophylla is often used as a flowering and informal hedge plant. The arching growths are cut back after flowering to suitable developing shoots and by this method the general outline and proportions of the feature are retained. The quickest and easiest way is to clip over the surface, but a better method is to prune each growth individually with the secateurs, choosing a suitable point just beyond a replacement shoot. Feeding and mulching and, if necessary, watering should be carried out after the operation is completed. *B.* ×*stenophylla*, like a number of other *Berberis*, develops creeping stolons, a characteristic which in the case of this hybrid is inherited from one of the parents, *B. darwinii*.

BERCHEMIA

These are twining shrubs, but the strongest growths that extend for 1 to 2 m. (3 to 6 ft.) in one season are often scandent and arch over onto nearby shrubs and even small trees. One of the strongest growers is *B. racemosa* and this free habit is more in keeping with the wild garden. *B. flavescens*, which appears to have a more definite twining habit, will throw strong scandent growths which twine later, or even produces laterals which have this habit. When grown in a natural setting little pruning is required, although it may be necessary to restrict size by cutting back any long arching branches which exceed the bounds. This may be carried out during the winter. Under a more restricted system of culture, for example against a wall, the ordinary horizontal wiring system will support the growths in the early stages. As the shrub matures the many growths may be held in position by extra horizontal wires tied over the branches and original strands. Thus the branches are held between two wires. Lateral growths are left to branch freely from the main stems. Pruning consists of cutting out the weaker branches and even some of the main stems if these are crowded, as otherwise the shrub soon becomes a mass of congested growths.

BETULA

Birches require very little pruning but it is desirable to maintain a central leader among the tree-producing species such as *B. pendula*, *B. platyphylla*, *B. maximowicziana* and *B. luminifera*. It is important therefore to recognise that there are small bush forms such as *B. nana*, the Dwarf Birch, *B. ovalifolia* and

B. apoiensis. While these species may only be 0.6 to 1.2 m. (2 to 4 ft.) in height, *B. occidentalis* is still a shrub at 4.6 to 6.0 m. (15 to 20 ft.) high. The tree species will mostly develop height whether or not they develop rival leaders, but two species, *B. nigra* and *B. davurica* will sometimes divide at ground level to develop into large bushes with rounded heads. Should a single leader be retained they may develop into large trees.

It is important when Birches are to be taken from the nursery that they should be young and well shaped with a good leader and that they are planted up in well-prepared positions and well irrigated. Strong and rapid growth should be maintained by careful treatment thus reducing the shock to a minimum. It is often noticeable that the strong lateral growths which ultimately form the main branch system are produced when the young tree is growing fast in its final position at 1.5 to 1.8 m. (5 to 6 ft.) in height. A feathered standard should be produced in the nursery and there should be no attempt to train a clear stem. The small lower branches may be trimmed up gradually when the trees are growing rapidly in their final positions. This should be carried out in late summer and the whole operation spread over 2 to 3 years, leaving the desired clear trunk. This allows the coloured bark to be seen to best effect, particularly on species such as *B. albosinensis*, *B. ermanii* and *B. utilis* var. *jacquemontii* and its many cultivars. Some of the lower branches can be left on a few outside trees of a group planting as this produces a more natural furnishing. Multi-stemmed specimens are also now grown by the nurseryman to get the maximum effect from the bark on the trunks.

Sometimes when a leader breaks, the strongest growths develop, not immediately below the broken portion but lower down in the branch system. In such cases the new leader should be selected from these stronger growths. Such pruning must be carried out in the late summer or autumn, never in the spring when wounds bleed very badly.

Birches develop better in full all-round light. In a position that is shaded on one side by a large tree the main stem will be weak, and later as growth extends the top may arch over, especially when it is heavily laden with fruit.

BIGNONIA

B. capreolata is the species which is normally grown against a wall in warmer parts of England. It is a climber and will in nature reach heights of 12 to 15 m. (40 to 50 ft.), using even large trees as a support. On a wall, although the tendrils that it produces are an aid to climbing, the growths or main stems must be spaced out and tied to supporting wires. In the spring the laterals that are produced from these should be pruned quite hard, by at least a third or more. The weaker growths should be cut out entirely during the summer, as new shoots are produced. In this way, the air and all the available sunlight is let into the wood to encourage flowering the following year. The aim is to maintain the vigour of the shrub by encouraging young and strong wood, at the same time cutting out the weaker shoots which shade them and prevent good ripening.

BILLARDIERA

B. longiflora is not really hardy and needs a sheltered position in a mild locality. It climbs by means of slender twining stems and thus a vertical wiring system is needed. If wall culture is attempted the vertical strands can be secured to the horizontal wires. With a pergola system wires may also be necessary.

Little pruning is required, but dead stems may be cut out in the spring. Weak growths may also be treated in the same way, but great care is necessary to avoid damage to the remaining growths.

BRACHYGLOTTIS

A group of mostly evergreen shrubs from New Zealand and Tasmania, bearing clusters of daisy-like flowers on the previous season's growth in summer. These are sun-loving shrubs which are not completely hardy and thus prove more difficult in the colder districts. In many parts of England the shelter of a sunny wall is desirable. They are very happy in coastal districts where the growth tends to be more compact and typical.

Most of the species are better for an occasional hard pruning, for example, once every four or five years, in the spring just as the new growth is about to commence. The shrubs, if healthy and vigorous, break out freely. This will also occur if a hard pruning is given by cutting away wood that has been severely damaged during the winter, provided of course that healthy wood remains. Left unpruned, these shrubs often present an untidy appearance, as the older branches become heavy with extensive shoot development and thus grow over edges and other plants. Heavy falls of snow also weigh the branches down and they may never return to their former position. However, it must be stressed that by a little careful, corrective pruning each spring the need for this periodic drastic pruning may never arise. These observations apply, among other species, to *B. greyi*, *B. laxifolia* and *B. monroi*, the latter tending to have thinner growths which are weighed down more readily. *B. rotundifolia* has a stiff habit and does not need pruning unless it is necessary to cut out dead wood.

B. 'Sunshine' (Dunedin Group) should be pruned hard back to old wood to renovate old plants in spring when the threat of frosts has disappeared and clipped to shape after flowering in summer to maintain a healthy free-flowering plant. When shrubs go beyond renovation they should be removed and replaced with new plants.

BROUSSONETIA

B. papyrifera forms a small spreading tree, the main branching starting low, often near ground level. This is the natural habit and it should be allowed for in the nursery. It is fast-growing when young, but is liable to late frost damage at this stage. Due to the soft nature of the wood, it is liable to decay quickly when it is exposed. Any necessary pruning should be carried out in autumn to early winter to avoid the white sap's bleeding. The same principles apply to *B. kazinoki*.

BRUCKENTHALIA. *See* Erica

BRUNNICHIA

B. cirrhosa, grown for its unusual winged fruit, is the only hardy species in this genus but it may be killed down to ground level in a severe winter. It produces slender stems and climbs by means of tendrils. A stake is necessary, but the stub ends of the branches should be left on this as further support, see Fig. 20 (2). Pruning consists of cutting out any dead wood from time to time.

BUDDLEJA

The growth and flowering habits of the plants in this genus may be classified into three types:

(i) those which flower terminally on the current season's wood;

(ii) those which flower from the previous season's wood;

(iii) those growing out in the spring to flower from large terminal buds or growths which develop on strong wood made in the previous year.

Those which flower terminally on the current season's wood

With these, the habit of growth and flowering is such that the late spring and early summer are devoted to the formation of shoots that are often 1 to 2 m. (3 to 6 ft.) in length. These are eventually terminated by the inflorescence, which opens and sets seed all in the same season, as that in which the growth is made. *B. davidii* and the various cultivars of this species all have this habit. Left unpruned, they develop into large spreading bushes full of dead wood and small branches that blossom very poorly. Hard pruned annually in the spring, taking each shoot back to the lowest growths, the vigour is channelled into fewer shoots which as a result are strong with correspondingly large panicles of blossom. The pruning may either be carried down to ground level or to a main framework of a few branches about 0.9 to 1.2 m. (3 to 4 ft.) in height according to vigour. The need for a larger framework is indicated when the growths are excessively vigorous, especially at the top of the bush, and in order to achieve it, selected, well-positioned growths should only be pruned to half their length for the first two or three years after planting.

The plant which has this framework is large and needs a suitable setting and position, while that which is hard pruned to ground level is more suitable for the front of the border. However, for the first few years the hard-pruned plant may be so vigorous that the growths may have to be stopped when 0.6 to 0.9 m. (2 to 3 ft.) in height to encourage a shorter and bushier habit. This species comes into growth early in the spring, but as pruning encourages more active growth it should be delayed until there is no danger of really cold weather returning. It should, however, be carried out before the open growths extend otherwise some vigour will be lost.

Among the other species which also flower on the current season's wood are *B. crispa*, best grown on a small framework, *B. forrestii* and *B. nivea*.

Those which flower from the previous season's wood

B. alternifolia, a popular garden plant, is in this group. It produces long arching growths that become pendulous under the weight of flowers and growth. On a healthy specimen, new growth, if freely produced and left unattended, causes the older growths to die through lack of light as the others are formed above them. To prevent this happening and to maintain the balance in favour of young growth, the old, flowered shoots are cut out in midsummer, as soon as the blossoms drop, back to promising growths that are developing at this time. In the early years much of the older wood is supporting extension and must be left, but as the shrub reaches a mature size the pruning can be more severe. At all times dead wood should be cut out.

This plant is sometimes grown as a standard on a 0.9 to 1.2 m. (3 to 4 ft.) leg. It is trained in the nursery by staking a selected strong growth once the plant has become established and removing all superfluous shoots that develop beneath the head as it is formed by hard pruning at the required height.

Those which grow out in the spring to flower from large terminal buds or growths which develop on strong wood made in the previous year

B. globosa may be taken as an example of this group. The pruning is based on a policy that retains the larger terminal buds that remain leafy throughout the winter. During late winter to early spring the weaker and dead wood is cut back to suitable points leaving the flowering wood. If the shrub becomes too large, however, it may be cut back quite hard but flower will be lost for one season at least depending upon the severity of the pruning. *B. colvilei* is also in this group although, unlike *B. globosa*, it is completely deciduous. The large terminal buds must be retained and, as the annual growth is quite extensive, this shrub will reach heights of 6 m. (20 ft.) or more. Except in the milder regions a high wall is needed as the plant is not fully hardy. Pruning consists of cutting out the weaker shoots in the spring.

Buddlejas are sometimes grown as wall shrubs and for this purpose the more tender species may be selected. *B. colvilei* has already been mentioned. It is an upright grower which is almost self-supporting and ties are not required to support weight but only to keep it in to the wall. *B. fallowiana* is a tender species and is not considered hardy throughout England. It flowers on the current season's wood and these growths are pruned back to the lowest pair of buds early the following spring to a main framework which is trained fanwise to the wall. An ample supply of growths is produced from the base and these should be thinned at an early stage. They may be used for the renewal of some of the old and worn out branches if this is required. *B. madagascariensis* and *B. auriculata* will also benefit from wall training. All Buddlejas are sun lovers. The soil should be well drained but they are strong growers and require feeding and mulching. This is especially true of those that are pruned hard each year. They all respond well by growing from really old wood if the shrub is cut back hard.

BUMELIA

B. lycioides is grown as a small tree from 3.0 to 3.7 m. (10 to 12 ft.) high. It should be trained with a single leader and as the lower branches are removed a 1.2 m. (4 ft.) leg can be formed. The growths and branches are distorted in an interesting way. This species, which is the hardiest of this genus, may lose wood during the winter and the specimen should be looked over for this as the buds break in the spring.

BUPLEURUM

B. fruticosum is not really hardy but it may be grown in favoured spots or in the shelter of walls in the regions with hard winters. As the shrub reaches maturity at a height of 1.5 m. (5 ft.) or more it often becomes untidy with thick, twiggy wood which weighs the branches down and eventually they may trail on the ground. When the shrub has reached this condition it may be cut hard back to within a few inches of soil level in mid to late spring when it will regenerate strongly forming a good shapely bush by the autumn. The curious flower display will, however, be lost for one season. Apart from this, there are no special pruning needs.

This shrub is very good in exposed positions by the sea and it may be used for hedging purposes. If grown for this purpose it should be clipped annually in the late spring.

BUXUS (BOX)

When grown informally as a bush very little pruning is necessary unless it is required to keep bushes down to a definite size. Size may be controlled by carefully cutting back the longer growths as they extend beyond the desired limits. These should be taken out individually making the cut with a pair of secateurs or saw at a suitable point well inside the bush. Thus, an informal matt surface remains. This type of pruning may be carried out at any time during the summer months as for Yew. Very old and large specimens which have completely outgrown their position may be cut back really hard to within 150 to 300 mm. (6 to 12 in.) of ground level. Often when this is carried out the lower branches will be found to have layered and thus the area of the stool is a large one. It is often better in the long run if these are taken out, restricting the remains of the shrub to the very centre. Provided that the shrub is healthy there will be a rapid response, but feeding and mulching will help this. The best time for this drastic cutting back is during late spring when the resultant growths will have a long period before them for development and ripening before the winter sets in.

Overgrown and straggly specimens that have grown in shade may be dealt with in the same way, but it may be desirable to thin neighbouring trees to encourage better growth. However, there should be a wide consideration of the whole planting before this is done for the surrounding specimens may be more valuable.

B. sempervirens, the Common Box, is a variable shrub and has given rise to many named varieties some of which are very old indeed. As examples that illustrate this variation 'Handsworthensis' is a strong-growing erect form while 'Prostrata' develops into a large, spreading bush with a horizontal branch system. It is important to recognise any particular habit before pruning is undertaken. It is difficult and sometimes impossible to correct and adjust the habit of growth of some varieties by pruning, hence the desirability of selecting the one most suited to the situation in the first instance.

B. balearica will develop into a small tree 6 to 9 m. (20 to 30 ft.) in height, especially if a leader is selected and retained in the early years during and after the period of nursery treatment. None of the remaining species require any special training or pruning.

Some of the stronger-growing forms have been used for many centuries for formal hedging and topiary work. Clipping should be undertaken during mid to late summer. With constant clipping it is important to keep the bushes in good condition by feeding when necessary as otherwise bare patches occur.

CAESALPINIA

C. japonica may be grown against a sunny wall in the warmer localities. The foliage effect and the tracery

of branches are quite pleasing but it does not often flower. In the nursery it should be encouraged to branch from the base, if necessary by stopping. It is difficult to train this species hard against a wall and it is better grown as a bush, being planted one foot from the base. Reaching a height of approximately 1.5 m. (5 ft.), the branches have a horizontal habit. Where restrictive pruning is necessary, and it often is, for this shrub is most formidably armed with recurved prickles even on the leaf stalks, it should be carried out in the spring, taking last season's growths back hard to the basal 50 to 80 mm. (2 to 3 in.). Staking or tying may be necessary to keep the shrub in to the wall.

CALCEOLARIA

C. integrifolia is commonly grown in the shelter of a wall as it is definitely tender. It may be grown in the open in the milder southwestern parts of England. When healthy the growth is very bushy. Protection should be given during very severe weather by using bracken, straw or sacking, but even so there is often damage during the winter and severe cutting back may be necessary in the spring. However, the wood, if living, will break out freely and the shrub will soon recover.

CALLICARPA

These shrubs have a bushy habit and throw shoots from the base very freely. When young they have an erect and almost crowded growth, but often at maturity the branching is spreading and even horizontal. This is partly due to the weight of the extending growths and the heavy crops of fruits they often carry. Any branches which have grown out of shape, old and woody, may be cut back in the spring just as growth commences. It is better left until this period as the younger growths may be damaged in a severe winter. The above advice applies particularly to *C. americana*, *C. japonica*, *C. japonica* var. *angustata* and *C. bodinieri* var. *giraldii* although allowance must be made for the fact that the latter is taller growing. *C. mollis* is tender and needs wall protection. *C. dichotoma* is compact and every effort should be made to retain a well-balanced but informal effect as the foliage is quite attractive. It will also need a sheltered and warm position.

CALLISTEMON

These must have the protection of a sunny wall and even in this position they are best suited to the milder localities. Training hard up to the wall is difficult and they are better when planted 0.3 m. (1 ft.) or so away from the base. By stopping at an early stage a bushy plant is encouraged. Finally, as the plant grows it may need staking. Pruning is not desirable as the characteristic spikes of flower are produced along the upper lengths of the stronger growths. *C. citrinus* 'Splendens', *C. linearis*, *C. subulatus* and *C. salignus* may be grown in this manner.

C. sieberi forms a compact bush of upright growths branching from ground level. It also should be given wall protection and be planted at approximately 0.3 m. (1 ft.) from the base. The spread is at least 1.2 m. (4 ft.) and owing to the type of growth only a limited amount of pruning is possible. It is therefore important to allow sufficient space for development.

CALLUNA

C. vulgaris. Although there are many different forms and varieties of this popular shrub they all look neatest and at their best when they are thick and well furnished with young growths of good length which completely hide the bare woody stem system as it builds up over the years. Often after a number of years, if they are left unattended, growth becomes poor and the plants present a thin and worn appearance. They may even die off in patches to become woody and straggly with the result that bare soil is exposed and weeds spring up to choke the remaining growth. Long before this stage is reached the old plants should be replaced with younger stock.

However, by annual pruning of the young growths in the spring the branch system is kept more compact and the plants will have a longer useful life. The need for this arises from the fact that growing conditions are artificial for these plants in the average garden for the soil is rich and the area sheltered, and thus in the initial years growth is stronger. On the moorlands where this plant is frequently found the almost constant winds, the sun and the poorer soil encourage a more compact growth. It should, however, be remembered that a proportion of old and woody plants do occur even in their natural habitat.

The pruning should be carried out annually just as the new growths appear in mid spring. This consists of cutting back at least half of the previous year's growth. The new growths that are along the length of the old flowered shoots are thus cut off and a more compact framework results as the lower tips are encouraged into activity and take the lead. The cut should not be made into the old wood for often this does not break freely and generally about one half of the previous year's growth is removed. Pruning should not be attempted if the growth is very short and poor. Replacement is then a better proposition. A variety of tools should be used in order to avoid a completely uniform or domed effect. This is most likely to occur when the shears alone are used and so the pruning knife and secateurs must also be considered if a varied and more natural effect is required. Care must be taken, however, when using a knife on plants that are very old and woody, for at this stage they are brittle and are likely to break easily. Electric hedge-trimmers may also be used although the tendency to prune too hard with these should be guarded against.

Young nursery stock should be tipped soon after being planted out from the cutting frames in order to keep growth short and stocky. Left unpruned, the few shoots on each plant will be long and straggly. It is important throughout to take the character and habit of growth of the variety into account when a pruning policy is decided upon. Thus, such dwarf forms as 'Foxii Nana', 'Mullion' and 'Hypnoides' need not be pruned in the normal way, although the latter occasionally throws strong reverted growths that should be cut out as soon as they appear. 'Ruth Sparkes' has bright yellow foliage but green reversions frequently appear and these must also be cut out. 'Elegantissima' is an upright grower with long flowering shoots and care is necessary in selecting the point at which the pruning cut is made to ensure that sufficient young growth is left.

Finally, seedling forms frequently occur among established plants and these should be searched out at flowering time because they normally revert to the colour of the type species.

CALOCEDRUS

C. decurrens is the species most commonly grown. It is columnar and should be grown as a single specimen, when, with an adequate amount of light, the foliage will be retained in a good condition down to near ground level. The natural habit, in the early years at least, is to form a single leader, but rivals often appear as the tree gets older and gains height. There is no need to worry about this, as it does allow the tree to gain an increase in width proportional to its height.

Old specimens, particularly those in industrial areas or exposed to the pollution of large cities, often lose a considerable amount of foliage, leaving exposed to view a mass of dead stems and branch systems. This, in addition to spoiling the appearance, is a danger sign and, if left unattended, such specimens deteriorate further until recovery is out of the question. The dead wood should be cut out and a programme of feeding and watering and, if necessary, aeration by spiking, should be adopted in order to encourage recovery and a better appearance.

With old specimens, the upright scaffolds do begin to break apart, due to strong winds, snow and heavy end weight and it may be necessary to position some support cables to prevent the canopy collapsing.

CALYCANTHUS

These have a stool-like habit of growth, freely producing young shoots from the base. Thus quite a dense canopy is produced, the lower branches even spreading on the surface of the soil, producing good ground cover and keeping weed growth to a minimum. These should be encouraged.

The habit of growth is such that old branches that are cut out are quickly replaced and this pruning is carried out, if necessary, in the spring. *C. floridus* var.

glaucus is the neatest grower while *C. occidentalis* spreads out extensively with horizontal branches and thus has a more open habit. The flowers are produced terminally on the young wood during the summer.

CAMELLIA

These popular evergreen shrubs require very little pruning. It is, however, advisable to prune the young growths in the spring before the new buds break, if a young plant shows a tendency to be leggy. A thick bushy habit is desirable. *C. japonica* is grown in many varieties which vary considerably in habit and form and the typical habit of each variety should be taken into account if it is found necessary to prune any growths which appear to spoil the general shape of the bushes. In an exposed position it may be necessary to remove any growths which appear to be too tall or heavy or affect the stability of the shrub in any way. Normally, staking should not be required but it may be used for the correction of a poor shape. For general effect branching should be allowed to develop right down to the base of the plant.

Some young plants flower so freely that it may be advisable to disbud them before the flowers open in the spring in order to encourage growth. On the other hand, old plants which have become weak may be cut back quite hard, removing as much as one third of the shoot system. This should be carried out just as growth is about to begin in early spring, making the cuts at the most suitable point. Mulching and feeding help to ensure a good response. The resultant shoots may be thinned if necessary.

The young growths in the spring are sometimes damaged by frost. If so, these should be left until it can be seen just where the new breaks are going to be produced. The removal of faded flowers by careful pruning will give the bushes a tidier appearance.

Often Camellias are grown in sheltered areas against a background of screening trees and shrubs and it may be necessary to prune these carefully from time to time in order to retain a shapely bush, see Fig. 26.

·   *C. cuspidata* has a graceful habit with an upright twiggy growth. *C. sasanqua* has a comparatively loose habit. It may be grown as a bush but it also responds to wall culture. The branches are tied fanwise to the wire support system and laterals are encouraged to grow out from these. Overgrown shoots are shortened by a system of selective pruning after flowering. Occasionally, an old worn branch may be cut out completely to be replaced by the promising new growths that are freely produced.

CAMPSIS

This is a genus of strong climbing shrubs. *C. radicans* produces aerial roots which are of some assistance, even in the garden when it is grown under natural conditions over old tree trunks etc. Usually, however, both *C. radicans* and *C. grandiflora* are grown against a sunny wall for protection and support. Under these conditions ties are made to the wiring system. Often, growths develop against the wall beneath the wires and this provides support. When a site is selected it should be remembered that these species, their varieties and hybrids are vigorous and are only at their best when able to develop to considerable heights, for example 6 to 12 m. (20 to 40 ft.).

With a young plant, the early training consists of covering the available wall space with the main branches. When the pruning of a mature plant is considered it should be remembered that they flower from mid to late summer on the current season's wood. The young growths produced during the previous season are cut back in the early spring close to the main stems leaving only one or two of the lowest buds. Each spring and summer the growths produced may flower in the late summer. However, in the following spring they are cut back hard, unless required for replacement. If needed for this purpose they should be shortened by approximately one third, back to the stouter wood.

CARAGANA

These are rather sparsely branched shrubs although *C. arborescens* can be trained to form a small tree. They require very little pruning. Raised from seed, like so many other shrubs, they gradually build up a strong branch system. In the first instance the growths are short and very twiggy, but stronger ones develop from the base of the plant over two or three years as it becomes established. The natural growth of many of the species is almost suckerous but centralised at the base of the shrub. This natural development is emphasized, for shrubs that are raised from cuttings do not pass through the successive stages of this progressive buildup. Instead, one or two strong growths are often thrown up which, unchecked, will produce a very leggy plant which may not have the necessary stability without staking. A bushy plant should be encouraged by stopping in the nursery after one season's growth. This not only encourages the production of laterals but will also promote suckering from the base of the plant. When pruned back in this way good breaks are more likely on the young wood. Caraganas build up a spur system on the older wood and the buds in this region do not break as freely.

In training the tree form of *C. arborescens*, a leading shoot is selected and all suckerous and lower branches are removed. Standards of the other species can also be raised but by grafting onto 0.9 m. (3 ft.) stems of the above species. Grafted plants often sucker badly and a constant watch should be kept for these during the growing season.

Dead wood should be removed in the spring for the new growths will then show this up very plainly.

CARMICHAELIA

One or two species are grown in the open in the warmer localities but normally they need the shelter of a sunny wall and should be planted 300 mm. (12 in.) or so away from the base. Staking will probably be necessary, while any of the growths that have been frosted during the winter should be patiently cut back as soon as the shrub is active in the spring.

CARPENTERIA

C. californica, when it is healthy and vigorous, forms a well-furnished shrub with many growths originating from the base while the older branches are attractive with flaky bark. However, the older wood thins out at the top over the years through exhaustion from flowering and as a result of damage during the winter. These may be periodically cut out at the base, to be replaced by the young growths that spring from this region. The natural habit of the more vigorous branches is an upright one but lower furnishing branches should be left to improve the shrub's appearance. One interesting characteristic is that whatever the angle of the branch the growing parts usually assume an upright position.

This shrub requires the shelter of a warm, sunny wall but it should be planted well away from it and allowed to grow as a bush. It is difficult to train hard up against the wiring system.

CARPINUS

C. betulus, the British native hornbeam, is one of the most handsome trees in this genus. It is advisable to train a young tree as a feathered standard or a 1.8 to 2.4 m. (6 to 8 ft.) standard with a clear stem, for the bark effect on a mature tree is very attractive. This also allows plenty of headroom for standing beneath the tree to study the fine tracery of branches during the winter and the leaf canopy and shade effects in the spring, summer and autumn. Apart from the retention of the leader through the crown in the early stages very little pruning is necessary. As the wood in the centre of the crown dies it should be thinned out, but it is not necessary or wise to attempt a premature thinning of a dense crown of living wood. A beautiful effect is gained by allowing a mature tree to produce outer branches that grow right down to near ground level. The fruits hanging down like small lanterns remain on for several weeks after the leaves have fallen and thus increase the effect.

This species is also an effective one to plant by the waterside. Sometimes, as the branches extending over the water become heavier, they may be weighed down beneath the surface for part of their length. Provided that the growing tips of the branches are not submerged this does not seem to harm them in any way.

Often this species bleeds rather badly in the early spring both from old wounds and rotted snags and although this seems to do no permanent harm it does emphasize the need to effect a complete healing as speedily as possible after making a cut. Due to the smooth, hard bark and plentiful supply of rising sap, grey squirrels are attracted to this tree in the spring and can cause considerable damage by stripping the bark. Should the trunk or any of the main scaffolds be girdled, failure is inevitable and the tree can die.

C. b. 'Fastigiata' has a close-branching habit forming a pyramidal head.

The Common Hornbeam is a good hedge plant. It should be planted 0.3 to 0.5 m. (1 to 1.5 ft.) apart, and if it is to be a tall hedge over 1.2 m. (4 ft.), it should be allowed to go unpruned for two or three years after planting in order that strong growths may be produced which will carry the height better. If the hedge is to be over 1.8 m. (6 ft.) in height a much wider spacing is required. Planting depth is critical and should the final soil or mulch level be slightly above the nursery line, establishment will be unsuccessful.

C. caroliniana forms a fine network of twiggy growth. It is a small and slow-growing tree and should be given sufficient light and air on one side at least to allow the branches to come down to eye level. *C. japonica* should be treated in the same way, for it is a small tree but has a very delicate and beautiful leaf effect. *C. orientalis* and *C. coreana* are trees or large shrubs which need very careful training in the nursery if they are to reach any size. *C. orientalis* has a close branch system which is often coated with dwarf shoots. These should never be cut off, as with this species they do no harm and add greatly to the character of the tree.

As *C. turczaninowii* grows, the leader appears to divide and bend over. This should be ignored, as the leader straightens itself as it grows and naturally finds the dominant leader to take over. *C. fangiana* should be allowed to develop a broad crown which will display the long catkins to the best effect.

CARYA

This is a very distinctive genus with species, such as *C. ovata* and *C. cordiformis*, that are fast-growing and normally form good straight leaders ultimately developing into fine, shapely trees. It is important that they grow away without check even from the seedling stage. They should be sown in long pots after a stratification period and be planted out into their permanent positions from them as young as possible, in order not to damage the tap root. Alternatively the seed can be sown directly into its permanent site, with some protection, which will ensure there is no check at transplant stage. As the leader and upper branching extends, a clear trunk of at least 1.8 to 2.4 m. (6 to 8 ft.) should be formed, choosing mid to late summer as the pruning period. Usually, with a straight trunk and leader the lateral branching is not extensive. The lower and outer branches should be left to grow down to eye level and with a dark background to the autumn colouring the effect is very pleasing.

C. illinoinensis does grow in the United Kingdom, but it needs sufficient sun to ripen the wood properly. It is thus prone to attacks by Coral Spot (*Nectria cinnabarina*), and other destructive organisms.

CARYOPTERIS

The species grown in the open are semi-woody and may be cut back to near ground level during the winter. Even during a normal winter much of the top growth is lost as a large portion dies back after flowering.

C. ×clandonensis is the most widely grown. The growths that spring from the short, woody branches at the base produce a terminal inflorescence in the late summer and autumn. These growths are pruned back hard to near their base in the spring just as the buds are breaking. The pruning is left until this period in order that the cuts may be made into the living wood without leaving any dead. By pruning back hard to within approximately 25 mm. (1 in.) of the older wood height is only slowly built up but the number of growths is reduced and thus the heads of flowers are larger. Also, by pruning hard the wood is kept close to the soil and is thus more protected.

C. incana and C. mongholica are very similar in their pruning requirements but they are taller and need not be cut back so hard; in fact it is only necessary to cut back the dead tips of the shoots as the buds break in the spring.

CASSIA. *See* Senna

CASSINIA

This genus consists of evergreen shrubs that are heath-like, and all the four species that may be grown outside will withstand hard pruning, an operation that is necessary to correct an untidy habit. This cutting back hard into the old wood, perhaps only 300 mm. (12 in.) or so from soil level, should be carried out in the spring. Thus, the basal portion of the branch system may be retained. C. leptophylla subsp. *fulvida* is the hardiest and can sometimes be grown in the open border in the South. For the remainder, some form of wall protection is advisable, where, with staking, a height of 1.8 m. (6 ft.) or more is sometimes reached. Generally, however, if staking is necessary it is because the shrub has become untidy or weak-stemmed, and some form of pruning is therefore desirable to correct this. In the nursery young plants should be stopped to encourage a bushy habit.

CASSIOPE

There is no need to prune these apart from the removal of any dead pieces that make the plants unsightly. The upright-growing species such as C. tetragona may blow over and their shape be spoilt unless they are closely planted, staked or sheltered.

CASTANEA

C. sativa, Sweet Chestnut, is the most widely known species in this genus. It will form a heavy branching system but provided the tree is in good health, it is structurally strong and safe. However, when a specimen dies back, especially in the crown, it should be held suspect and be carefully inspected. Declining health with heavy branching can be dangerous, as they are liable to drop limbs suddenly through the wood becoming very dry. Often, by a careful reduction of the branch system the life of such a tree may be extended for many years. Establishment after the final transplanting often takes two or three years but growth is then very rapid with the tree forming a good straight leader quite readily. A 1.8 m. (6 ft.) clear length of stem may be formed in the nursery or when the tree is growing away in its final position. The spiralling bark effect is an attractive feature of this tree. Suckerous growths are freely produced even from the base and trunk of mature specimens and these should be removed annually. This ability to sucker freely is made use of when it is grown under a coppice system for large stools are formed which are very long lived. In addition to the numerous fruiting varieties there are several variegated and dissected forms. The former in particular reverts very readily and an inspection should be made during the summer to cut out any offending growths. No attempt should be made to control reversion in a large tree that has lost a considerable portion of its variegation.

Of the remaining species, although a tree form can be trained with *C. dentata*, they do not seem to be as adaptable to our climate as *C. sativa*. *C. henryi* forms a stunted tree with rather graceful growth while *C. mollissima* is often a very slender grower and may split up into two or three stems at a very early stage. *C. seguinii* and *C. pumila* should be left to grow as large bushy shrubs or trees. The former is ideal on the edge of a clump of trees and its foliage retains a green colour for longer than many other trees.

CASTANOPSIS

C. cuspidata is a large evergreen shrub or small bushy tree and should be left to grow naturally from the nursery. It requires a warmer climate and occasionally is damaged from late spring frosts or cold winds. Should this happen, the damaged area should be pruned out to live undamaged growth.

CATALPA

The most commonly grown species is *C. bignonioides*. When mature it forms a spreading head with a strong branch system. In the nursery stage it should be trained with a leader up to 1.8 to 2.4 m. (6 to 8 ft.) so that when the head is formed there is a good length of clean trunk. Once branching is established it is difficult to maintain a leader and the crown quickly forms

and opens out. The lower branches sweep down to ground level on a mature tree but there appear to be two forms. With one, the branches actually touch the ground and develop close to the surface from this point, while the other form has branches which sweep down at the same angle until within 0.3 to 0.6 m. (1 to 2 ft.) of the surface when the ends turn upwards again. The effect is more natural where the branches reach the ground but grass cutting is difficult and damage easily occurs. They should be carefully lifted, with assistance, when mowing is attempted beneath them or the sward should be killed beneath the dripline to eliminate the need for mowing.

Large old trees that are considered unsafe can have their branches shortened and bracing or propping may also be necessary. Even old trees will regenerate very freely from cuts and a branch that has been shortened to reduce weight may be even heavier after a few years as a result of the new growth that have been put on. Growths often develop near wounds even though these may be large and on the main trunk.

C. speciosa is a pyramidal tree and naturally develops a leader through the tree although this may need to be trained during the transplanting period and immediately afterwards for these disturbances often have a retarding effect. When training, if a young tree has opened its head too early, the rival leaders may be stopped to encourage growth in the selected shoot. This is better than cutting out the offending branches. At planting time there should be a clear stem of 1.8 to 2.4 m. (6 to 8 ft.) for this allows the main branches to develop a natural and almost pendulous habit after growing out a good distance from the trunk. Thus the lowest branches will, from a height of 2.4 m. (8 ft.), almost reach to ground level.

All Catalpas like a sunny, sheltered position with a well-drained soil, these being the conditions which produce ripe, sound wood. In wet and cold districts dieback and cavities frequently occur. The growths on young plants are also susceptible to frost damage in the late spring.

Of the remaining species, some difficulty may be experienced in growing and training *C. fargesii* and the variety *duclouxii*. The strong upright growths in particular do not seem to ripen properly unless the situation and soil are perfect.

CEANOTHUS

There are two distinct types of growth in this genus. Firstly, those that are mainly evergreen, flowering in the spring on growths made during the previous year. Many of these are not hardy and are grown against a wall for protection. Secondly, there are the smaller deciduous species that flower in the late summer or autumn on the current season's growths. These are often grown in open beds.

Evergreen species and hybrids—wall training

Generally, these are too weak to be grown near a wall without any support whatsoever, for the bushes grow out towards the light and thus become top heavy, to be finally torn down by gales or heavy snowfalls. It is better to plant them hard up against the wall and to tie the branches out fanwise to the main support system. By this method there is ultimately a greater latitude in training than if a single stem were first trained up to the height of the wall, and laterals trained out from it. With the fan system the replacement of old branches by selected young growths is more straightforward. It is necessary, however, to start off with a bushy plant and this habit must, if necessary, be encouraged in the nursery. Many will naturally branch low and extensively but a few such as 'Dignity' often tend to be single-stemmed. Thus, until the allotted wall space is covered the leading growths are tied in. The laterals are pruned reasonably hard after flowering, but never into the older wood that is devoid of foliage. It is desirable to carry out this pruning carefully so that an informal effect is retained with the cuts hidden. In the early stages a large quantity of young growths often appear near the base of the shrub and these need to be thinned out before they develop into main branches. Growths that are needed for replacement must be kept tied in, for if allowed to grow away from the wall at an angle, the laterals from them will become upright. Once such a unilateral development has taken place it is difficult to tie in such growths effectively. Much

depends on the adoption of a good replacement system over the years, for the best flowering is from the younger wood and continued cutting back, using the old branch system in its entirety, does not give such good results. Examples of evergreen species are *C. dentatus*, *C. rigidus* and *C. thyrsiflorus*. *C. velutinus* is a larger grower than many, reaching a considerable height and forming quite a stout trunk. It therefore needs a large wall and, if trained to a single stem, apart from one or two ties to the wall, it needs no support. *C. thyrsiflorus* var. *repens* may be grown against a low wall for the shoots are held up by their springy nature against the surface.

The hybrid between the deciduous and evergreen groups, *C.* 'Burkwoodii', may be wall-trained but the pruning back is carried out in mid spring and the young growths that are produced flower in the following summer and autumn months.

It must be emphasized that the evergreen species may be grown out in the open, given some shelter and a suitable climate. Hybrids such as 'Edinburgh' are almost hardy. Sun and full all-round light are important for if there is a heavy background screen on one side the shrubs have a drawn and leggy appearance that even staking does not fully overcome. Some pruning helps to control this untidy habit.

Deciduous species and hybrids

Such species as *C. americanus* and *C. coeruleus* are deciduous and produce growths during the spring and summer which flower in the autumn. They have, however, been hybridised extensively and such cultivars as *C.* ×*delileanus* 'Gloire de Versailles' and *C.* ×*pallidus* 'Perle Rose' are quite popular. This group, which is grown in the open border, is first pruned lightly to encourage the formation of a rigid framework up to a height of 0.6 to 1.2 m. (2 to 4 ft.). The previous season's growths are then cut back hard to two pairs of buds just as they become active in mid spring. If this intensive pruning is to be successful it is important to maintain good growth by feeding and mulching.

CEDRELA. *See* Toona

CEDRUS

C. libani, the Cedar of Lebanon, is seen at its best in a lawn setting where, with sufficient space, the branch systems can develop and spread out to show the full beauty of this tree. In habit, the tree when young is pyramidal and it is only at a later stage when maturity is reached that the branches spread out extensively. A central leader should be retained for as long as possible although, at a later stage, often when the tree is 12 to 15 m. (40 to 50 ft.) high and growing vigorously, rival leaders may develop. It is almost impossible to keep a constant check on a tree at this height and some specimens are more liable to develop rival leaders in the upper crowns than others. However, it is often these more upright branches which tear out from the main trunk during gales when the tree is mature, especially if they occur at a time when the tree is laden with snow. This may be looked upon as a natural habit that cannot be corrected but which may ultimately prove to be a weakness.

It is important to cut out as much dead wood as possible for the health of the tree, and also to reduce the end weight on the branch systems. These dead pieces are most likely to develop on the undersides of the branches as they are weighed down with extending growth. Sometimes the smaller and lower branches may need to be cut out as they become overshadowed or hidden by larger and higher systems. It is better to anticipate this rather than allow the branches to die back before they are removed for the wounds will callus much better with earlier removal. Another tendency that needs correcting if it occurs is that of weaker branches lying on the stronger ones beneath them. The offending limbs should be cut off neatly, the position of the cut being selected with great care, otherwise the appearance of the tree will be spoilt. Old or even mature cedars seldom produce sufficient new growth to cover up the ugly effects of poor pruning, especially if the cuts are large ones on old wood.

Large wounds, especially if they are on older specimens, may be slow to heal and callus over but the exposed heartwood, if it is sound at the time, will remain in good condition, often for the life of the tree. Normally, pruning cuts should be made as close to the parent branch or trunk as possible but often the latter in particular may be deeply furrowed. A furrow may even be positioned immediately beneath a limb that is to be removed. In such cases the position of the cut should be adjusted for there must be adequate supporting tissue round the wound if the callus is to be complete. We must now consider the tips of spreading branches. Two kinds of growths are produced, the long extension shoot with scattered leaves and the short spurlike shoots with tufts of leaves round each growing point. A specimen in full health produces a balanced proportion of extension growths during each growing season. A lack of these accompanied by thin and poorly coloured needle growth on the dwarf shoot system is a sure sign that all is not well and that the root system and culture generally should receive more attention. From this it may be gathered that the leading growths even on the branch systems are important.

If these are able to spread out and develop with plenty of space and light the branches will grow out horizontally and the lower ones will eventually sweep gracefully to the ground. When these vigorously growing branch systems are pruned, perhaps to prevent a spread over a path or border, there is often a buildup of arching growths, which is out of character and spoils the appearance of the tree. One should try if possible to avoid the need to restrict the natural spread by re-planning the nearby features.

In common with many other trees the cedar will often develop extensively in one direction in response to a one-sided light condition. When placed hard up against other trees, if the light is sufficient on one side, it will furnish up completely on this surface. The fault with this type of planting is that the cedar is a long-lived tree and the chances are that the neighbouring trees will eventually need to be taken down, leaving it lopsided and with no chance of acquiring the balance necessary for it to stand as an isolated specimen. Specimens sometimes lose their needles completely during the winter months. Such a condition should be watched very carefully, for while it is recognised that some trees are more likely to do this than others, it may also be due to impoverishment. Some trees of *C. atlantica* also have this habit.

C. atlantica. Much of the advice given for *C. libani* also applies to this species. Growth is variable, apart from the fact that in most cases a central leader is naturally and readily formed. In addition to great variation in colour, some forms have a heavily laden appearance with pendulous subbranches that will even grow along the surface of the ground if encouraged and protected. Other forms exist where the branching is completely horizontal and a few even have a system where the extremities of the branchlets turn up. Such trees of the latter form often have a thin appearance.

C. deodara. The pruning and training of this species are similar in many respects. It is not as hardy as the two species already mentioned and appreciates a sheltered position, especially when it is in the earlier stages of development. The leading shoot, especially when the tree is young, has a natural arching or pendulous habit. There should be no attempt to straighten this out by ties to the stake which must be used to establish all trees of any size in their final quarters. *C. libani* var. *brevifolia* is a stunted grower with no particular pruning or training requirements. It is desirable to encourage and retain a central leader for as long as possible, however it will soon want to become multistemmed and the central leader will soon be lost.

CELASTRUS

These are vigorous climbers producing long growths that in one season extend for 1 to 2 m. (3 to 6 ft.). These shoots either twine round or loop over neighbouring branches or supports, with an arching habit. Laterals and compound branch systems build on these.

With such a vigorous habit these are difficult shrubs to contain in a small area. All that can be done is to cut back the long growths that arch out too far in such a manner that the natural habit is retained. Usually this means cutting back a few complete lengths rather than cutting every growth to a given line, when the outline would be too formal and artificial.

Allowed freedom in the wilder parts of the garden, the long arching growths can spread over old stumps at will. These shrubs can also be planted to climb over trees which have been lopped back, perhaps to a

height of 6 to 9 m. (20 to 30 ft.), because they were unsafe, see Fig. 13 (4). Old trunks of *Robinia pseudoacacia* are ideal for this purpose as the wood is so durable. Such a position is an ideal one for the climber, for after it has gained the top of the support it produces long branches that hang down and fruit freely. Little pruning is necessary under these conditions apart from cutting out dead wood. This should be carried out during the summer for it is difficult to distinguish living from dead unless the subject is in active growth. Actually, there is little need even for this and it is really a refinement which few can afford to keep up.

CELTIS

The Hackberries must have good growing conditions and they require careful culture even in the nursery stage. A check causes stunted growth and it may take several years for a tree to grow normally once this has occurred. In the meantime the leader may be lost and this may add to difficulties later when free growth is resumed. The tree species are trained as feathered standards, but a number of them often develop into shrubs rather than trees. Among these are *C. glabrata*, *C. pumila* and *C. tournefortii*. These may fail to respond to attempts to produce a trunk.

The largest grower is *C. occidentalis*, from North America, whose general habit allows a leader to be retained up to 11 m. (35 ft.). The lower branches tend to be horizontal and often become pendulous and heavy. In addition, upright growths may be produced on the ends of these lower branches, and their development should be watched for as this can quickly be the cause of excessive weight. This is more likely to happen where thinning of neighbouring trees has in the past been undertaken and the trees are exposed to more light and to better growing conditions.

C. australis, from S. Europe, N. Africa and W. Asia, does not display the same degree of hardiness as many of the deciduous species coming from China, Korea and Japan such as *C. jessoensis* and *C. choisiana*. The growths of a young tree in particular, being strong and perhaps not fully ripened, are prone to frosting during the winter. To some extent this is also true of a related species, *C. caucasica* and, although it is reputed to be hardier, wood which is exposed in wounds tends to rot quickly and produce cavities. *C. sinensis* displays extensive powers of regeneration and produces a crop of vigorous young growths from the region of wounds, which need to be carefully thinned. Sufficient shelter is an essential part of the successful culture of all the species.

CEPHALANTHUS

C. occidentalis. This deciduous shrub is very bushy with branches that spring from ground level. The terminal flower heads are produced on the current season's wood. Little pruning is needed other than the cutting out of old branches in the spring, thus encouraging the long lengths of young cane which will produce good flowering growths later in the season. The tips of the shoots that have supported flowering growths die back and these may be cut to living wood as the new growths break out. This shrub is very late in breaking into leaf. Bushy plants should be encouraged in the nursery by pruning.

CEPHALOTAXUS

These are similar in many respects to yews and they will respond to pruning in the same way, for they will form new growths very readily even from the oldest wood. *Cephalotaxus harringtonii* var. *drupacea*, the Cow's Tail Pine, forms a spreading bush and the habit is very desirable as this species develops sub-branches which sweep gracefully to ground level to form lower furnishing. Too frequently they are crowded in densely shaded places where little can be expected to grow properly. These shrubs appreciate a little light shade but if it is too dense they become weak and leggy, the branches being bent down and untidy. Shrubs in this condition should be cut back, if necessary to within 100 mm. (4 in.) or so of ground level, choosing mid to late spring for this operation. At the same time it may be possible to lighten the overhead shade by careful pruning.

The species mentioned freely produces branches directly from ground level, but *C. fortunei*, the Chinese Plum Yew, tends to produce only two or three erect stems and in time may be 4.6 to 6.0 m. (15 to 20 ft.) high with tiers of branches.

The cultivar *C. harringtonii* 'Fastigiata' is quite distinctive, having an erect fastigiate habit similar to that of the 'Irish Yew', but older specimens often present an untidy appearance as their branches become heavy and pull the bush out of shape. Careful tying-in can improve this habit, although a specimen which is badly out of shape may need to be cut hard back to the base in the spring, when it will break out readily although it is slow-growing.

CERATOSTIGMA

C. willmottianum is the most outstanding shrubby species. Normally, it needs the shelter of a sunny wall where a woody branch system will build up to a height of 300 mm. (12 in.) or more. From this, growths break out in the late spring and after growing through the summer the flowers are produced in terminal clusters in the autumn. A young plant produces growth shoots that have very few if any flowers in their first year. Pruning is carried out in late April as the buds commence to break and consists of cutting back the old flowered growths to the living wood, generally at their base. The extent of dieback depends largely upon the severity of the winter and occasionally even the old wood is killed entirely. Should a plant become very old and woody at the base it should be replaced by a young plant. *C. griffithii* is even more tender but the same pruning treatment may be applied.

CERCIDIPHYLLUM

C. japonicum, developing into a tree often 9 m. (30 ft.) or more in height, has a natural habit of forming several rival leaders from low down, often at ground level. Thus a mature specimen may have three or more trunks but the growths are ascending and a close crown is formed. The lower laterals have a horizontal habit. This tree is best grown in a sheltered position as it appears to dislike strong winds. The young growths are readily frosted in the early spring, while the tree also appears to dislike a very hot and sunny position, especially on a well-drained soil. A woodland environment on a moisture retentive loam suits it best, while a background of trees and a grass foreground provide an ideal setting. A natural growth should be encouraged in and after the nursery stage and no attempt should be made to retain a single leader. *C. j.* var. *sinense*, however, often develops a single trunk.

There are several good forms of *C. japonicum* now in cultivation, including *C. j.* f. *pendulum*, *C. j.* 'Marioka Weeping' and *C. j.* 'Amazing Grace'. These should be treated as the species, but allowing the pendulous habit to grow naturally.

C. magnificum is generally a tree of medium height and is often the most suitable one to grow.

CERCIS

These shrubs or small trees thrive on a well-drained soil and many good specimens are in areas in which the underlying subsoil is chalk. This is mentioned because it is very difficult indeed to grow good specimens in areas overlying a badly drained clay. In such areas the wood often dies back badly after wet seasons and is also prone to attacks by the Coral Spot fungus (*Nectria cinnabarina*). Dead or diseased branches should always be attended to immediately. Cercis seem to thrive better in the southern part of the country and is a sun lover.

C. siliquastrum, the Judas Tree, is the most common species. The natural habit is to branch low at ground level into two or more stems which grow upwards almost vertically. Often too, additional growths are thrown up from the base or from the lower parts of the branches. Sometimes this low-branching habit proves a weakness at maturity, for a break may occur during summer gales affecting a large portion of a tree and it may be wise to provide support by bracing if this is considered a danger. During a very severe winter this species is sometimes killed down to ground level but it may break vigorously from the base in the spring. *C. canadensis*, the North American Redbud, and *C. racemosa* are more likely to form small trees and can be trained to a single stem. *C. chinensis* is more shrubby and often requires the protection of a wall. *C. occidentalis* should also be left to branch naturally and become shrubby in the nursery.

They should be transplanted at an early age as they resent disturbance, while the young growths are sometimes prone to frost damage.

CERCOCARPUS

In many ways these uncommon Rosaceous plants have the mode of growth which is typical of this family. *C. ledifolius* from western North America produces dwarf and spur-like growths on the older, hard, heavy wood as distinct from the young extension shoots. No definite pruning policy is needed, although should it become necessary to restrict the shrub in any way, it is usually possible to take the pruning cuts back to promising extension growths thus keeping a good informal effect. This may be carried out during the dormant season.

CHAENOMELES

In many respects these shrubs are very similar to the Malus and thus to the ordinary apple in their flowering and fruiting habits. When young they build up and concentrate upon growth and at this stage very little flower is produced. Two or three years later spurs form on the older wood and flowering commences. Growth slows down over the years as a bush becomes larger and vigour is spread over a large number of growing points. At this stage flower buds are also produced on the young shoots at the end of their season's growth.

C. speciosa, which is the parent of many of the popular varieties, has a spreading habit and forms a tangled bush which may be 3 m. (10 ft.) high and as much in width. It is best grown on the edge of a lawn, or in the less formal parts of the garden, where it can be left to develop freely right down to ground level without any pruning whatsoever. It is even permissible to allow crossing branches, indeed, such wild growth is the habit of this shrub.

This shrub is also very popular for growing against a wall where it is valued for its early display. The first object is to cover the wall space by training the strong young growths fanwise. In this position the shrub must be restricted and the growths coming away from the wall at right angles must be dealt with, as otherwise they will extend even fuller the following year. Also, if they are left too long they will sway in the wind and it may be difficult to secure the main branch properly.

One method of pruning and training is to stop all growths coming away from the wall during the growing season at five leaves, unless they are required for the extension or replacement of the branch system. The sub-laterals which develop from these are stopped at two leaves, and this is repeated if further growth is put on. The original laterals which were stopped at five leaves may be pruned back to two or three buds in the winter, alternatively the subsequent policy can be to thin out the branch systems with a view to repeating the stopping on the remaining ones the following year. If treated in this way the shrub has a less formal appearance. Later, this thinning process may need to be more severe in order to keep the shrub within bounds.

There are several variations of these methods but basically they are forms of summer pruning. By restricting growth the leaf surface is reduced, which in turn curbs the activities of the root system and the vigour of the shrub as a whole. In its simplest form the treatment consists of cutting back all the young wood to two or three basal buds during the dormant season, but without the additional summer pruning, the shrub may be longer in coming into full flowering. Summer pruning also helps to control Aphis.

C. cathayensis is also a good shrub to grow as a wall specimen. It shows a tendency to throw up a few strong shoots rather than to branch extensively. These growths may be spaced out fanwise. After the early vigour has been controlled by pruning and stopping this species will settle down to regular flowering and cropping. Occasionally the long growths can be replaced by young shoots springing from the base.

C. japonica is a dwarf shrub approximately 0.9 m. (3 ft.) in height which is suitable for growing at the base of a south-facing wall. With the forms of *C. ×superba*, which are hybrids between the above two species, vigour must be taken into account when the type of training is decided upon.

With all the species and hybrids, stopping is a form of pest control, for aphis in particular feed among the undeveloped leaves, and are thus inaccessible as far as contact insecticides are concerned.

CHAMAECYPARIS

This genus includes some very fine species and cultivars which if planted and trained properly will give great satisfaction. One of the most important factors upon which ultimate effect is dependent is the position in relation to the general environment and surrounding plantings. Some shelter is preferable, but it is also important to allow sufficient space and light for the development both of the laterals down to ground level and of the leader itself. These trees are at their best when furnished down to ground level and with a clear foreground, so that this effect can be seen to the best advantage. Too close a planting is a major fault and when planted in a group they should be not less than 4.6 to 6.0 m. (15 to 20 ft.) apart.

C. lawsoniana is a variable species and there are many varieties. This variation is apparent among seedlings and with some the lower branch systems loop down onto the ground and root freely giving rise to new leaders and a clump-like growth. Generally it is better to train this species to one definite leader in the early years, but later, as the size increases, rival leaders may form, even along the length of the trunk. This appears to be no disadvantage to a mature tree.

The forms and varieties with a naturally spreading foliage tend to be tidier and easier to look after than a number of the fastigiate or columnar cultivars which may become untidy and bare at the base. *C. lawsoniana* 'Erecta Viridis' is an example and some tying-in of stray branches is often needed after gales or snow.

C. nootkatensis, the Nootka Cypress, has very similar growth to the former species but the branchlets have a distinct drooping habit. Mature specimens are often seen which have a cluster of rigid branches at the base and on one side. This is a natural habit, a type of juvenile foliage and branching which is left behind as extensive and mature growth develops. It has nothing to do with stock growth from grafting, a common but mistaken belief.

Similar conditions and training are required for the remaining species and cultivars that reach tree-like proportions. Special mention should be made of *C. pisifera* 'Squarrosa', for the branch systems are so densely packed with juvenile foliage that they may be weighed down and spoilt by the buildup of dead material within the tree or shrub. Although the task of removing this is a difficult one it lightens the branch system and improves the general appearance.

C. lawsoniana, the Lawson Cypress, is often used for hedging purposes. The young plants should be set out approximately 0.9 m. (3 ft.) apart, each being staked with a cane tied to a horizontal wire. The leaders are retained until they reach from 150 to 300 mm. (6 to 12 in.) beyond the desired height. The tops are then cut to a lateral approximately 150 mm. (6 in.) below this height. The upper laterals then grow up to form the top surface. Undoubtedly the best effect is obtained when the secateurs are used in trimming, when complete and individual sections of the branch systems are removed, leaving a matt surface.

CHAMAEDAPHNE

C. calyculata, the only species, forms a clump-like growth with a mass of thin arching stems originating from ground level on which the small white flowers are borne. To keep the plant tidy it is occasionally necessary to cut out individual dead branches.

CHIMONANTHUS

C. praecox. This subject from China is valued for the fragrant flowers that a mature bush produces during the winter months. A young bush in the early stages of branch formation blossoms very sparsely if at all, and it is not until the rate of annual growth slows down that the shorter, flowering wood is formed. Almost invariably these flowering growths are part of a mature branch system. The flower buds are produced in the axils of the leaves on the current, or youngest, wood and are fully formed before the fall. The shorter growths may produce a bud in almost every axil but more often a number of growth buds remain to extend into wood in the next season.

Undoubtedly this subject flowers most freely if a branch system is left to mature without any pruning. Grown as a bush in the border or in the shelter of a wall it may quite easily be left to develop naturally. Plenty of vigorous renewal wood is thrown up from the base and the older branches may be cut out if they become weak. The same applies when it is actually tied to a wire or support system on a wall. Free growth can be allowed within reason provided that there is sufficient space. Some restriction of growth away from the wall is possible by a reduction of the branch system, taking away whole sections consisting of both old and young wood, and by cutting a whole branch out occasionally using a new shoot springing from the base as a replacement.

It may be necessary to exercise an even more rigid control by annually cutting away all wood growing at right angles to the wall. This must be carried out in late winter in order to allow a full season's growth for the new wood. The cut is made on the previous season's wood hard back to the buds at the base. The success of this system will depend upon the vigour of the shrub but the type of season and the amount of sun must also be considered. In conclusion, as a general rule, the less the pruning the more the flower.

CHIONANTHUS

The two species of Fringe Tree in this genus must have good soil and plenty of sun both in the nursery and in their permanent positions, otherwise growth will be poor and stunted. *C. virginicus* from eastern North America is the larger grower and will form a small standard tree under ideal conditions. If growing freely in the early stages a 0.9 m. (3 ft.) leg may be formed when tree-like proportions develop, though it is often difficult to produce a shapely tree as the branches develop an upright habit. If this occurs it should be taken as a characteristic which is difficult to correct, and provided that the overall development is satisfactory it need cause no concern. The branch extremities should be left to develop naturally and at maturity they will become pendulous. Often this subject will break freely from cuts on old wood.

C. retusus from China and Korea is more often shrubby, producing branches which originate at or near soil level. The latter can be cut hard back to the base to regenerate a new plant with renewed vigour.

CHOISYA

C. ternata has a very dense and bushy habit and it will break very freely if pruned back hard to the old wood. It may be necessary to do this after damage from very severe winters or if the shrub has become badly overgrown.

It is a shrub that loves shelter and the sun and is frequently grown against a south wall. There should be no attempt to train it hard against the surface, for a free-growing bush flowers better and gives a more natural foliage effect. The flowering period is during April and May, but occasionally flowers are produced later. However, a second display is certain if the flowered growths are pruned back by about 250 to 300 mm. (10 to 12 in.) as soon as the first blossoming is finished.

CHRYSOLEPIS

C. chrysophylla is the hardy species of the two in the genus. It is a low-branching shrub or small tree that forms a very dense growth. It should be allowed to grow unpruned and thus to form a complete canopy down to ground level. Sometimes a random branch dies back leaving a gap when it is cut out. However, regeneration often takes place strongly, especially with mulching. This will occur even though the top is almost entirely killed by severe weather. Young plants should be left to branch naturally in the nursery.

CISTUS

These are hard-wooded shrubs and most of the species do not respond well to cutting back, as they will not break freely from stems and branches once mature bark has formed. Thus, after being cut back

by frost the whole plant is often killed. There are exceptions, however, for example *C. monspeliensis* shows a great potential for regeneration from the old wood and this allows any sprawling branches to be cut back. *C. parviflorus* also shows this characteristic.

In some instances, winter damage is confined to the tips and cutting back provides a good solution, provided that the cuts are not taken back into the ripened wood. This should be carried out in the spring just as growth commences. In fact, all forms of pruning, even the removal of dead wood, should be left until this period so that the extent of any winter damage can first be ascertained.

In the nursery, compact and bushy plants should be encouraged by stopping during their first and second seasons of growth, doing this in the spring and never going back into the ripened branches. Straggly plants often blow over in the wind, and this leads to root disturbance while the exposed lower branches are more likely to suffer damage during the winter.

CLADOTHAMNUS. *See* Elliottia

CLADRASTIS

Grown properly, these form delightful trees. Preferably they should be on the edge of a grass area or as a lawn specimen so that the growths can develop right down to eye level. In the nursery and as a young tree after planting the young shoots sometimes suffer from late frosts. They are best when transplanted into their permanent positions at an early stage and this should be done as soon as a good leader has been developed. The one important point is to retain the leader and to keep the tree growing without check. The reason for this, in addition to the pleasant effect of a well-shaped tree, is that the wood is brittle. An early formation of the crown may result in excessive weight being thrown on two or three branches, with the danger of these splitting at the crotch especially during high summer gales when the tree is mature and in full leaf. Bracing may avert this disaster with an old tree that has branched low. Should any corrective pruning be necessary it must be carried out in the late summer owing to the danger of bleeding at other times.

C. *kentukea*, Yellow-wood, is the largest grower of the four species, reaching a height of 12 m. (40 ft.) or more. It shows a tendency, when a large limb is lost, to throw young growths on the stems of the remaining branch system. These should be thinned, and a watch kept as their extension will produce extra weight. *C. sinensis* is often smaller and more beautiful and the head may open out early when about 6 m. (20 ft.) in height. The top branches, when the tree is mature, develop in one plane, giving a flat-topped effect. *C. platycarpa* and *C. wilsonii* have similar requirements.

CLEMATIS

Clematis are mainly climbers, raising themselves by means of their leaf stalks which coil round any support. The type of support will vary according to taste and position but the larger growers which retain a permanent and extensive branch system, e.g. *C. montana*, are well suited to the larger spaces on walls, fences, pergolas or even trees. If the support is smooth, it may be augmented by a trellis or wire system, provided that this is strongly secured. It may be necessary to tie-in some of the main growths whichever type of support is used, see Fig. 20.

The ultimate size to which a Clematis will grow must be taken into account when deciding on the position and variety. Excessive pruning to restrict size, especially with the larger growers, often spoils their effect and display. The extent and type of pruning is directly related to the habits of growth and flowering, and clematis may be classified for this purpose in the following groups.

Group 1. Species and hybrids which flower on the previous year's wood

These are mainly the larger growers, often flowering in the spring, and include *C. alpina*, *C. cirrhosa*, including var. *balearica*, *C. chrysocoma*, *C. macropetala* and *C. montana*. They require very little, if any, pruning except to cut out the dead wood or perhaps to attempt a reduction of a hopeless tangle. If these varieties are grown in a small or restricted space they may well appear untidy and, if a clean-up is needed, hard cutting-back may be resorted to in the early summer as the flowers fade.

Hybrids in the Florida, Patens and Lanuginosa groups have similar habits of growth and flowering. The main crop of flowers in the Florida group, which include hybrids like *C.* 'Proteus', *C.* 'Duchess of Edinburgh' and *C.* 'Belle of Woking', is produced directly from the old wood in the spring, but smaller flowers are often formed on the young growths in the autumn. Little regular pruning is needed but it may be necessary to tie in a number of the growths.

The Patens group include *C.* 'Barbara Jackman', *C.* 'Bees' Jubilee' and *C.* 'Elsa Späth' and should not be pruned unless some tidying-up is needed and this is best done after flowering. Sometimes there is a second flowering in the autumn on the young growths.

The Lanuginosa group, which include *C.* 'Nelly Moser', *C.* 'John Warren' and *C.* 'W. E. Gladstone', flower on the previous year's wood during summer followed by a display on the young growths in late summer and early autumn. Normally, very little or no pruning is necessary but should the plants become a hopeless tangle and affect neighbouring plants some cutting-out may have to be done in late winter. In extreme cases this pruning may be taken down almost to the base.

The evergreen species *C. armandii*, *C. aristata* and *C. marata* are also included in Group 1. If grown in a sheltered site they may produce trailing growths which flower profusely and may be thinned out annually after flowering. The cuts should be made back to suitable young shoots which should be apparent at this stage.

Group 2. Species and hybrids which grow extensively and flower from the young wood during the summer and autumn

These produce long vigorous growths that break from the older and stouter wood, and the flowers are produced on these growths during the same season. They often develop into a heavy, tangled mass that builds up year after year and looks very untidy. In addition, this mass of growth may become top-heavy and hang down to deprive the lower parts of sufficient light and air to support foliage and growth. In a restricted space this cannot be tolerated and the answer is to cut the last year's growths back in the spring to the stouter wood. Where there is plenty of room, perhaps in the wilder parts of the garden, pruning is to a large extent unnecessary.

Species in this group which may be pruned hard, as strong growths break out within 0.3 m. (1 ft.) of ground level, are *C. campaniflora*, *C. potaninii*, *C. texensis* and *C. viticella*.

A number of the species need only be cut back to about 1 m. (3 ft.) but the position of the cut depends on where the stronger growths break out from the old wood. These include *C. flammula*, *C. florida*, *C. orientalis*, *C. paniculata*, *C. rehderiana* and *C. tangutica*.

Hybrids in the Jackmanii, Viticella and Texensis groups have similar habits of growth and flowering. The Jackmanii group include *C.* 'Jackmanii Rubra', *C.* 'Gillian Blades', *C.* 'Perle d'Azur' and *C.* 'Gipsy Queen'. Their natural habits lead to most of the blossoms being produced on the upper parts of the plant. The best policy is to prune back hard to within 0.3 m. (1 ft.) of ground level and this should be done annually in late winter before growth commences. As a result, the new shoots start low down on the plant each year and thus it is kept tidier.

The Viticella group include *C.* 'Etoile Violette', *C.* 'Ville de Lyon' and *C.* 'Lady Betty Balfour'. With this group also, growth commences from the living wood below those portions which carried the flowers during the previous year. Hard pruning prevents a straggly habit.

The Texensis group include *C.* 'Duchess of Albany', *C.* 'Gravetye Beauty' and *C.* 'Princess Diana'. These are in many ways similar and also respond to hard pruning.

It must be emphasized that the hard pruning advised for these three groups of hybrids is not essential for flower production. In fact, the flowering season may be extended by missing out the pruning altogether. As with the particular species having these habits of growth and flowering, they may be left unpruned if they are growing in natural situations.

Pruning and Training after Planting

Some of the early flowering, large-flowered cultivars are susceptible to Clematis Wilt (*Phoma clematidina*), and the pruning out of affected growth back into unaffected tissue is the only means of effective control.

It is important to distinguish between the two types of growth and flowering outlined above, for some pruning and training is needed soon after planting.

Group 1.   The growths should be tied in on a fan system if against a wall, fence or similar structure; otherwise they may be tied up to the support. The weak ends should be pruned away in the early spring as growth begins. Good early training will help with any corrective pruning required later.

Group 2.   As growth begins after planting pruning should be hard, taking the top shoots back to the lowest breaks.

CLERODENDRUM

In this large genus of shrubs and climbers there are three species which are grown in the open. Two that are strong growing and will reach a height of 3 m. (10 ft.) or more are *C. trichotomum* and *C. trichotomum* var. *fargesii*. In training, the head of branches is often formed on a short leg. As this head develops to maturity the standard of flowering may be improved by shortening the wood made during the previous year back to the last pair of buds in the early spring. Thus a restricted number of new growths is produced which are terminated by the inflorescences later in the season. The process should be repeated year after year, but it may be necessary to maintain vigour by feeding and mulching.

Injury to the root system by hoeing or digging will promote the production of suckers and this should be avoided. If they do occur they may be used for propagation.

C. bungei is a semi-woody suckering shrub, but even in a sheltered corner it is often killed down to ground level each year. The growths should be cut down in the spring, leaving them during the winter for protection.

CLETHRA

Both *C. alnifolia* and *C. tomentosa* develop a mass of growths that spring from soil level. As clumps become established the thicket spreads by means of suckerous growths. This habit may be more pronounced in *C. tomentosa*. The frequent production of new wood from the base allows the older branches in a clump to be thinned out at ground level and some of the weaker suckers may also be cut out with advantage. This should be carried out during the winter. When a clump extends beyond the intended limits and becomes too thick and weedy the whole mass is best dug up and selected pieces replanted after the soil has been reconditioned.

C. acuminata, *C. barbinervis*, *C. monostachya* and other more tender species form larger shrubs or even small trees. They may be allowed to branch from ground level and renewal growths will be thrown up from time to time. This allows a limited pruning during the winter if growth is weak. *C. barbinervis* has attractive flaking bark on the mature branches and with a specimen near to the edge of a border this may be seen to full effect.

CLEYERA

C. japonica forms a dense shrub with close bushy growths. Most of the growth and foliage is on the extremities of the branch system, leaving the supporting branches and main stem bare. This shrub requires very little pruning. It often develops a single main trunk, and branches from this and does not renew the main branch system.

The subject normally requires wall protection, where it is grown as a bush near the foot.

CLIANTHUS

C. puniceus. The only successful method of growing this subject is by training it closely to a sunny wall for protection. Even so, this is only possible in the most favoured districts. After one stopping, if necessary, in the spring in order to encourage a bushy habit long growths are produced which are tied in for the winter.

Finally the wall space is filled, when a policy of thinning out the old lengths of wood to make room for the young growths is carried out in the spring just as growth commences. It is advisable to delay this pruning until the spring as the older wood is more likely to survive a severe winter, after which there may, in addition, be a considerable amount of dead growth to be cut away.

COCCULUS

C. orbiculatus climbs by means of slender twining stems and is suitable for growing up pillars, pergolas or a tripod of stakes. A mass of twining stems is formed and pruning, even of the dead wood, is difficult and must be carried out very carefully as otherwise there may be a loss of support. Normally, however, little pruning is required apart from the removal of growths that have trespassed onto neighbouring shrubs.

COLLETIA

C. hystrix is the hardiest species. One feature of this shrub is that it will respond to cutting back at almost every stage, breaking out with one or two strong laterals beneath each cut. The main branching is sparse, and bushy plants should be encouraged in the nursery by at least one pruning in the spring. After the initial pruning, and provided the permanent position is open and sunny, the shrub should be shapely and no regular cutting back will be needed. Later, however, the old branches may become heavy and bent down with age, and it is then that the offending branches can be shortened to a suitable point with good effect. Occasionally a young growth springs straight from the old wood at the base of the plant, extending for 1 to 2 m. (3 to 6 ft.) in one season. These should be encouraged as replacements for old branches. In a position that is shaded on one side the shrub often needs a stake as the growths lean heavily toward the light.

C. paradoxa needs the shelter of a wall in a warm, sunny position.

COLQUHOUNIA

C. coccinea. This shrub, which sometimes grows up to 2.4 to 3.0 m. (8 to 10 ft.) high, has a loose habit with wood which is like that of the Buddleja in appearance except that the branching is not as rigid. It may be killed back into the old wood during a severe winter, in which case it should be pruned back to living wood as the growths break in the spring. It flowers on the current season's wood.

In the nursery and afterwards a bushy framework should be encouraged by pruning, as this will provide a stouter and more rigid branching.

COLUTEA

These leguminous shrubs flower freely for a long period during the summer on the current season's wood. One of the chief aims, therefore, is to keep them growing strongly so that a good quantity of young growth is produced each year, on the principle that the more growth the more flower. One pruning policy which is quite popular is to cut away the annual growth in late winter, making the cut back to a permanent framework, leaving only the two lowest buds of the young wood. If this method is to be carried out, the framework must be encouraged to branch freely from ground level and the shrub left to develop up to a suitable height before hard pruning starts. This height will vary according to vigour; for example, *C. arborescens* is much stronger than *C. orientalis.*

A variation of this is to train a single stem up to a height of 0.6 to 1.2 m. (2 to 4 ft.) and to prune back to this each year, gradually forming a head of multiple spurs. Specimens treated in this manner may have a certain attraction, but they lack the natural beauty of a free-growing specimen. Even the hard-pruned bush lacks natural beauty after a number of years and the response may become weak.

A limited amount of pruning may be carried out with a free-growing bush. This consists of cutting out some of the oldest and weakest growths, or even branches, in late winter. The cuts are made carefully

to a suitable growth making certain that the natural shape is retained.

It is necessary to stake these shrubs when they are planted in windswept sites. Hard cutting back after planting also ensures a firmer hold for the shrub when it is planted under these conditions. *C. istria* requires a sheltered position and should be planted in the vicinity of a wall.

COMPTONIA

C. peregrina, the Sweet Fern, is a sun-loving shrub in a monotypic genus in the family Myricaceae. Grown in a suitable position, little pruning is required.

CONVOLVULUS

C. cneorum. This shrub is often planted at the base of a well-drained sunny wall. The short growths are freely produced from a woody rootstock that develops just above the ground. Normally, no pruning is necessary but occasionally old growths become long and woody, ending up in a heavy mop-head of leafy shoots which give the shrub an untidy appearance. Such growths may be removed down to the base or crown of the plant in the spring.

CORDYLINE

Cordyline australis, the Cabbage Tree, from New Zealand requires very little pruning, apart from the removal of dead leaves and old faded flower stems. When planted at the limits of their hardiness they may suffer from frost damage. When the new growth follows in the spring, the stem can be cut back to just above the new shoots. They will respond to cutting hard back to the ground or new basal side shoots in order to form a multi-branched specimen.

CORIARIA

In this small genus of herbaceous plants and shrubs are three or four species that are sufficiently hardy to be grown in the warmer parts of England. *C. napalensis* is perhaps the most distinctive and it will keep its wood in a normal winter. It has a stool-like habit with strong, arching branches that spring up from a woody root-stock at ground level. New growths, in addition to arising directly from the base, are also produced along the lower halves of the arching branches in a similar manner to many of the *Sambucus*. This and the other woody species are so strong-growing that considerable height may be put on in one season. Staking for the first year or so after planting may be necessary especially with a pot-grown specimen where the roots are coiled round and lack anchorage.

The main pruning should be carried out in the spring and consists of tipping back any growths that have been frosted during the winter. In addition, any of the older growths, which are considered to be crowding out better growths, may be removed, taking the cuts back to a suitable growth. Thus, the balance may be kept in favour of the young wood, which gives the better effect.

C. sinica is similar in many respects and needs the same treatment. *C. myrtifolia*, being less hardy, is killed down to ground level in most winters. *C. japonica* and *C. terminalis* are semi-woody and die down each year to a woody base, which is at or just below ground level. The pithy wood is often dead by the late autumn. Pruning consists of cutting these dead growths back in the spring.

CORNUS

There are two main types of growth form and habit so far as the arboriculturist and gardener are concerned: the larger growers which will develop a definite trunk under training such as *C. controversa* and the shrubby species such as *C. alba*, many of which have coloured stems and will respond to annual pruning. It is important for the propagator and nurseryman to recognise these two habits as there are great differences in their training.

The tree-forming species

C. mas is in the Section *Macrocarpium* and will form either a very large shrub, or a small tree. Much depends upon the nursery training, and unless a

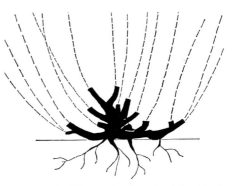

Fig. 28. A stool of *Cornus* that is cut back hard in the spring, just as the new growth is about to begin. It is grown by this method for stem effect.

leader is selected it will usually branch low down near ground level. The branch system is very spreading and the lowest growths will grow along the surface. Little will thrive beneath the canopy of foliage, as it is very dense. If a leader is selected in the nursery stage a clear stem 0.6, 1.2 or even 1.8 m. (2, 4 or 6 ft.) in length may be formed, this will eventually develop into a trunk which will display an attractive bark. Even with the tree form the lower branches should be encouraged to develop to eye level or lower in order that the attractive flower display can be appreciated in the spring. *C. officinalis* is closely related to *C. mas*, but the twig system is somewhat untidy. Neither species normally needs pruning.

C. nuttallii is in another distinct group, Section *Cynoxylon*; trained to a single leader, a trunk will be formed, but if low branching is allowed to develop and it is given a clear foreground, the specimen will be seen to the best effect both when in flower and during the autumn when the foliage is often brightly coloured. Normally, pruning is not required or desirable. *C. florida* is more difficult to grow as poor ripening of the wood in the autumn renders it subject to spring frost damage.

C. kousa, in the Section *Benthamia*, will readily form a leader, but the lower branches should be left to develop. The horizontal branches give a flattened, tiered effect and these should be encouraged to develop with a clear foreground. No pruning is necessary unless there is dead wood to cut out. The variety *chinensis* has a distinctly upright, almost fastigiate, habit and no attempt should be made to retain a leader.

C. capitata is an evergreen tree in its natural habitat, but only makes a tall shrub in in the milder parts of England. Little pruning is required, apart from the removal of dead wood following cold winters.

The remainder of the tree species to be mentioned are in the Section *Thelycrania*. *C. controversa* should be trained with a definite leader which will form a trunk in later years. The lower branches may be trimmed close to the trunk as the head develops, with the leader running through the crown. The horizontal branches are tiered and there should be a clear space round the specimen to allow these to develop to their full extent. *C. macrophylla* also responds to leader training. *C. alternifolia* will form a small tree if a leader is selected, or a shrub with a number of upright main branches when left to grow naturally.

The shrubby species

Most of these are in the Section *Thelycrania*. As stated earlier, a number of these are pruned annually and are grown mainly for their coloured stems. *C. alba* with its forms and varieties together with *C. sericea* 'Flaviramea' are outstanding when grown for this purpose, but a number of other species such as *C. rugosa* and *C. racemosa* respond in the same way. The method of culture is to allow the young stock one growing season for establishment after planting from the nursery. In the following spring, just as growth is about to commence, the complete top is cut down to within 50 mm. (2 in.) of ground level. In response to this a crop of young stems is thrown up and these colour brightly and remain decorative during the late autumn and winter. This cutting back in the spring is repeated year after year and vigour is maintained by mulching and feeding, see Fig. 28. Under this system of pruning there will be no flowers or fruit. However, these and many of the other shrubby species are also effective when grown in bush form when, without regular pruning, flowers will be produced. When left to grow freely, many are spreading and are thus suitable for the more natural parts of the garden. An overgrown specimen may be kept within reasonable limits by pruning away the older growths towards the centre of the bush, cutting off whole branches rather than small shoots on the outside. This also encourages a good number of young growths and these lend extra colour to the bush during the winter.

COROKIA

These are tender shrubs that need wall protection in all but the mildest districts. *C. cotoneaster*, the Wire Netting Bush, is best grown as a bush planted 0.3 m. (1 ft.) or so away from the base of the wall. The stems and growths are curiously twisted and are difficult to train against a wire system, hence its appropriate common name. In the nursery the shrub is allowed to develop naturally and the branch system is often a permanent one, apart from minor replacements. The laterals from the main stems develop horizontally and to obtain the full effect sufficient space should be allowed for their extension. With such sparse foliage as this species produces it is difficult to gauge health and vigour, and this condition is best judged by the number and length of the new growths, which are thin, wiry and grey in colour. These show up quite plainly in the late summer and autumn.

C. macrocarpa and *C. ×virgata* are often even more tender and need the protection at least of a wall in the average garden. Corokias generally break freely from the old wood if cut back by the frost or as a part of pruning, though normally no pruning should be needed except as required for training.

CORONILLA

C. valentina subsp. *glauca* is tender and should be planted in the shelter of a wall. It has a dense bushy habit. In the spring as the new growth commences, any dead tips or shoots should be cut back to living wood, at the same time cutting out any very old and worn growths. Otherwise, very little pruning is needed.

CORYLOPSIS

These attractive shrubs or small trees in the family Hamamelidaceae flower on leafless twigs in the spring. Well-shaped specimens of *C. pauciflora*, *C. sinensis*, *C. glabrescens* var. *gotoana* and *C. spicata* are most pleasing to the eye at this period and it is thus important to allow sufficient space for development. If possible the growths should be given freedom to spread out, and when a young plant is finally positioned in a new border, the immediate vicinity should be planted up with Ericas or other dwarf shrubs, so that the horizontal branches can stretch out unimpeded. From this it will be gathered that any pruning required to correct overgrowth in the border should, if possible, be done on neighbouring plants.

In the nursery, the young stock should be allowed to branch freely from ground level. They should also be given a good spacing to allow for natural development.

If it is absolutely necessary, some pruning to restrict size may be carried out, but the greatest care must be taken to retain the natural habit. The best period for this is after flowering. Occasionally it may become necessary to remove old branches but often there are young growths that are suitable as replacements. It is not necessary to thin branches to let in light and air and doing so will quickly spoil the natural habit.

CORYLUS

Only a few species and hybrids in this genus form trees. The remainder, which form the majority, are shrubs. *C. colurna*, the Turkish Hazel, forms a tree up to 25 m. (82 ft.) and over. A leader should be selected at an early stage in the nursery and this develops rapidly when the young tree becomes established in its permanent position. Suckers that may appear from time to time should be removed. The shaggy appearance of the bark is quite attractive and for this reason the lower branches should gradually be removed up to a height of 1.8 m. (6 ft.). The main branches are sparse and grow upwards at a slight or distinct angle, making a pyramidal-shaped crown in the early years, however after about fifty years the main scaffolds begin to grow outwards and a more ungainly, unsymmetrical upper crown is formed. The hybrid *C. ×colurnoides* forms a dwarf tree with an interesting branching habit. The dwarf pendulous growths that often clothe the main branches should be left, as they add to the attraction. Other tree forms include *C. chinensis* and *C. ×vilmorinii* (*C. chinensis* × *C. avellana*) and with these as with any of the tree forms, a leader should be retained and a trunk formed. The shrubby species have a definite stool habit, forming rootstocks from which suckers, and thus new branches, freely arise.

C. tibetica from central and western China should be grown as a small- to medium-sized, wide-spreading multi-stemmed tree.

C. avellana, our native Hazel, is a common example. If the suckers are removed at least annually this species and others with this habit of growth will reach heights of 3 to 6 m. (10 to 20 ft.) with three or more main branches from the base. *C. avellana* is often grown for its display of catkins in the early spring and the best displays are given by mature growths with a strong but compound branch system. Occasionally, it is necessary to cut an old branch right down to ground level, using a young one for replacement. The old wood is best cut out during the winter. This often throws the whole plant out of balance and it may be more effective to cut the bush down to near ground level and to thin and train up a fresh crop of replacement growths. *C. a.* 'Heterophylla' produces interesting, almost laciniated foliage which is at its best on a strong-growing bush furnished right down to ground level. 'Pendula' is grafted on a single stem 1.2 to 1.5 m. (4 to 5 ft.) in height and the most interesting form in which to grow it is by running up a leader for 1 to 2 m. (3 to 6 ft.) beyond the graft-line. The pendulous branches then fall away with graceful effect. The cultivar 'Contorta', the Corkscrew Hazel, is often grafted and if suckers from the base are not removed, it will soon revert back to the rootstock.

C. maxima is stronger-growing than *C. avellana* and the cultivar *C. m.* 'Purpurea' has very dark purple leaves. The pruning policy with this should be to retain the height by keeping mature growths. Vigour may be encouraged by cutting out the weaker wood during the winter.

COTINUS

The most commonly grown species is *C. coggygria*. There are two methods of cultivation.

Grown as a bush with no regular pruning

Under this system the subject will form a large shrub or a small tree with a rounded, bushy head made up of short, twiggy growths. Quite a stout trunk and branch system is built up. Nursery specimens should be encouraged to branch from ground level. The stem system of a mature bush is often covered with clusters of adventitious or epicormic growths, but no attempt should be made to remove these, as this is part of the character and natural habit of the bush. Under this natural system very little pruning is required apart from the removal of dead wood.

Grown for foliage effect with annual pruning in the spring

Under this system the shrub builds up a framework which consists of one to three main stems springing from ground level. These may be allowed to divide or branch again until a height of 0.6 to 0.9 m. (2 to 3 ft.) is reached with substantial wood.

Pruning is carried out annually from this point, cutting down the young wood to the two lowest buds in the spring. This careful positioning of the cut is important, for if cut too low, the growth from the adventitious buds will be later and thus smaller. This is carried out just before growth commences in the spring. Using this system such coloured forms as 'Flame' or 'Royal Purple' are shown to best effect but flower will not be produced from the young wood. Good growth is maintained by feeding and mulching. *C. obovatus* should be grown naturally as a bush.

Care and skin protection should be taken when pruning these plants, as some people can have an allergic reaction to the sap, which may result in a skin rash, similar to that caused by *Rhus*.

COTONEASTER

Most species respond quite strongly even if pruned hard back to the old wood or to the base. Normally, however, there is no need to cut these subjects hard, indeed pruning needs to be carried out very carefully, otherwise the natural form and habit will be spoilt, at least until additional growth has been put on to cover any bad cuts or bare surfaces.

It may be necessary to restrict size, in which case a few long pieces should be removed, cutting back into the shrub so that the wounds and the effects of removal may be hidden by the growths that remain. The selection of the species and position is important so that the need for restrictive pruning is reduced to a minimum, or better still rendered completely unnecessary. In the nursery a bushy habit should be encouraged, although often this develops naturally without any stopping or pruning.

The gardener must take habit of growth into account. This varies with each species, sometimes even between separate individuals of one species. The following classifications will serve as a guide but it is by no means a complete list.

Graceful habit

Most of the cotoneasters have a graceful habit but some more so than others.

C. ×watereri. Indiscriminate pruning easily spoils the fine habit that is at its best when growth is free and unlimited. It is vigorous enough to train to a single stem.

C. insignis. This species may reach 3 to 6 m. (10 to 20 ft.) in height with long slender branches. For the best effect they should be left at full length, cutting out complete branches if necessary, not just a partial snipping back.

C. horizontalis. One important characteristic of this and a number of others is the fish-bone effect produced by the main growths with the regular arrangement of branchlets on either side. This characteristic appearance must be retained if any pruning is carried out. A greater height is gained in the border by tying the main growths to a 0.9 to 1.5 m. (3 to 5 ft.) stake.

C. nitens has a graceful habit with a fine tracery of branches and foliage. If pruning is needed this habit must be retained.

Horizontal or tiered habit

A number of species that produce heavy and conspicuous corymbs of flower have an almost tiered branching habit. An example is *C. lacteus*. If pruning is needed, as for example when this is used for an informal hedge, whole lengths should be cut out after the berry display is over. This will ensure that the informal effect is retained; snipping off short lengths will completely spoil this fine habit.

Dwarf and prostrate habit

There are many species that come into this group. It is important to arrange a proper spacing but despite this, some pruning to restrict spread may be necessary. Rather than a speedy clipping with shears resulting in a straight and rigid line, an informal effect should be maintained by carefully cutting out individual growths, taking them back into the shrub where the cuts may be hidden by the growths which remain. An example is *C. dammeri*, a completely prostrate species. *C. congestus* also has a prostrate habit but, in addition, small incurved branches develop as the mat matures. This gives the whole an attractive appearance and the uneven, mounded effect should be encouraged. It may be necessary to uproot and transplant pieces in order to restrict growth. This is best carried out in the autumn when it is more likely that the rooted pieces can be transplanted successfully.

There are many other instances where habit of growth needs to be taken into account if any corrective pruning is needed, e.g. the stiff, erect habit of *C. simonsii*, the vigour of *C. frigidus* and the spreading, ragged branching of *C. laxiflorus*. Some pruning to improve shape may be necessary with the latter.

A number of the species and hybrids are suitable for planting and training in positions other than in the shrub border or open planting. A number of examples are given below.

Wall planting

C. horizontalis when planted against a wall reacts in a most peculiar manner. The branches press against the wall with a spring-like action. However, as height is reached some support by means of ties is needed. This can be kept to a minimum and is required on the main branches only.

C. wardii. This subject, in company with many others, may be grown on a wall using an intensive and hard system of training and pruning. The branches are spread out, being trained on a fan system as described in Chapter Three and illustrated in Fig. 19 and the training, once the branch system is established, may be carried out by finger and thumb. As the growths develop they can be pinched out when soft and unripened without the use of knife or secateurs, taking them back to the lowest leaves. In this way flower production is encouraged while this display and fruits are more prominent, as they are not hidden by growth development away from the wall. Specimens treated in this way have a somewhat formal appearance, but they are ideal for positions where there is little scope for development away from the wall or similar surface.

C. serotinus, in common with many other species, can be grown as furnishing close to a wall or similar structure. One or two of the main branches may be tied back to correct any tendency for these to grow away from the wall and arch towards the light. In order to retain the berry display for as long as possible, pruning if necessary, should be carried out in the early spring just as the new growth commences. This, however, is only needed if the shrub outgrows its position or if there is any dead or diseased wood. The longer and older pieces should be taken out in order to retain the natural habit, making the cuts back toward the centre of the specimen.

Informal hedging

A number of species and hybrids are well suited for this purpose. One of the first to be used was *C. simonsii*. This is a rigid, upright grower and is a natural choice. Some pruning may be required to keep the hedge shapely and within bounds and this is achieved by cutting out whole lengths that have developed beyond the limits. With the informal hedge this selective pruning is the only method of restricting size for clipping over the entire surface will reduce it to a formal feature. It should be after the berry display is over, although on a limited scale old pieces may be cut out during the growing season with, however, the loss of growth and flowers.

+CRATAEGOMESPILUS

+*C. dardarii* (*Crataegus monogyna* + *Mespilus germanica*). This graft hybrid is usually grown as a 1.8 to 2.4 m. (6 to 8 ft.) standard. Mature trees often develop a mass of twiggy growths in the head, but they should not be thinned as there may be a danger of upsetting the balance between the two tissues.

Should a growth break out which consists entirely of one or the other parent, a careful watch must be kept to see that it does not grow at the expense of the remainder of the specimen, otherwise the nature and shape of the tree may be lost.

The interesting characteristics of the foliage, flowers and fruits can only be appreciated from a close range, and for this reason it is better to allow the branches to develop down to eye level and below.

The cultivar 'Jules d'Asnières' (+*C. +asniersii*), also a graft hybrid, has a natural pendulous habit which should be encouraged.

CRATAEGUS

The majority are small deciduous trees, often with a twisted and matted branch system. In nurseries they are usually raised with a clear stem of 1.8 to 2.4 m. (6 to 8 ft.) with a branching head and no central leader. The feathered tree is also quite popular and it is often to be preferred, for it has a central leader that can extend as the crown is forming. If desired, a clear stem can be obtained by cutting off the lower branches in stages as the crown develops. Nursery-trained trees with a clear stem and a central leader are obtainable and these are to be preferred for planting by public highways etc.

A central leader is particularly important with the larger growers, as with an old specimen the branching is very heavy, for the trunk that is often slender. An open-headed tree with branches arising from one point may become weak in later years. In fact, trunks sometimes split down almost to ground level. Should this happen, the trunk and head may be bolted and braced together, for the wood is very hard and the specimen may go on living for many years.

Once a tree has been planted out and has become established, growth is often rapid and the leader may naturally break up to form the head. This happens with some species earlier than others, e.g. *C. ellwangeriana* has a very flat head but is also spreading. No attempt to retain the leader beyond its natural 'break-up' point will overcome this habit. This is why it is important to have a good knowledge of the natural habit during and after the training period.

In later years as a specimen reaches the mature or semi-mature stage the head may be so matted that it appears to be in need of thinning. It should be remembered that this is the natural habit and to thin would be a mistake. Also thinning might encourage the development of epicormic growths, giving the specimen an unnatural appearance. Over-thinning may actually weaken a tree, both mechanically and in general health.

Many of the species and hybrids will produce outer and lower branch systems that are so pendulous that they will reach ground level. *C.* ×*persimilis* 'Prunifolia' provides one example and it is a habit which can be left to develop when the tree is on a lawn with an open foreground. Such branches also act as a trap for fallen leaves which blow across open spaces during the winter and spring.

Again it is emphasized that habit of growth must be taken into account throughout, both in the nursery and in the permanent position. *C. monogyna* 'Compacta' has a compact growth with stiff branches. This branching may be left to develop just above ground level.

Thorn trees in exposed positions are often leaning and may appear to be unsafe. Such trees should be carefully inspected but it does appear to be a natural habit and they may be perfectly sound and safe.

×CRATAEMESPILUS

×*C. grandiflora* (*Crataegus laevigata* × *Mespilus germanica*). This is a sexual hybrid, an important point, for the tissues are uniform and therefore differs in this respect from the graft hybrid +*Crataegomespilus*.

This tree is commonly grown on a 1.8 to 2.4 m. (6 to 8 ft.) clear stem with an open centre and therefore it is planted as a standard with a branching head. Often, it forms a wide but rather shallow head with many of the lower branches almost horizontal but the twig systems on these become pendulous as the tree reaches maturity. They should be encouraged to develop down to ground level for this adds to the attraction of the tree. Pruning consists of cutting out the dead wood that develops from time to time beneath the branch systems. It is seen at its best with a clear foreground.

CRINODENDRON

C. patagua. This shrub or small tree requires a sheltered position and is often grown in the lee of a sunny wall. In this position it is best when trained as a free-growing specimen without any actual support from the wall. Little pruning is necessary beyond cutting out the dead growths. *C. hookerianum* is even more demanding and requires a partially shaded position in addition to shelter. A healthy specimen requires little pruning beyond cutting back in the spring the dead wood that may develop during the winter.

CRYPTOMERIA

C. japonica forms a definite leader and, with a straight trunk running up through the centre of the tree, the outline is pyramidal. The lower branches should be encouraged by allowing space for light and development. The spread of this tree is very fine, particularly in a lawn setting, but seldom do the branches actually reach ground level. Many forms have smaller growths along the length of their main branches and these should be left, as it is a natural habit.

C. j. 'Elegans' is a juvenile form which produces a feathery branching system but the main stem, although supple, is weak and a large specimen, perhaps 4.6 to 6.0 m. (15 to 20 ft.) high, is often bent down to ground level by the effects of heavy rain or snow. Staking will help to correct such a position but as more growth is put on, the branch systems become very untidy indeed. The alternative to staking is to deliberately cut the main trunk back to within a few feet of the ground, at the same time pruning back the remaining branch systems, even into the older wood. This subject has been proved to be very good as a formal hedge plant and it reacts well to trimming once a year in late summer. The type species prefers a sheltered position, but this is true to a greater extent of many of the forms, particularly such delicate ones as *C. j.* 'Lobbii'.

CUNNINGHAMIA

C. lanceolata appears to be the hardiest species, although it is only really suitable for sheltered positions in the warmer parts of the country. Some of the best trees are based on a straight trunk that runs up through the centre and crown, the branching being horizontal from this. On a well-clothed specimen with an open foreground the lower branch systems may come down to eye level.

Multi-stemmed trees are formed when the original lead is lost perhaps through frost or some other injury, either in the nursery, or when they are established and growing freely. Such specimens are not altogether unsightly, but the stems may weaken and bend over as they become top-heavy with growth and this will obviously spoil the appearance. However, these stems may be cut out as replacement growths are sent up from the base. Old and ragged specimens, which are multi-stemmed and therefore no more than large bushes, may be regenerated by hard pruning in late spring, accompanying this with feeding and, if necessary, watering.

C. konishii from Taiwan is less hardy than *C. lanceolata*, but once established in a sheltered position in the warmer areas of the British Isles may develop into a medium-sized tree. It may require the selection of a strong leader following the development of several due to frost damage.

×CUPRESSOCYPARIS

×*C. leylandii*. This is made up of a number of clones which vary a little in habit yet essentially are very similar in their mode of growth to the typical forms of *Cupressus* and *Chamaecyparis*. A central leader is developed at an early stage, even from cuttings taken from laterals provided that they are sufficiently vigorous. From this leader a central trunk is built up giving the tree a columnar habit with little spread. The laterals, which are thickly placed, often have an ascending habit but there is some variation among the clones.

As specimens they are ideal, but one or two of the clones which are easier to root than others have become popular hedge plants. The young plants are set out at 0.9 m. (3 ft.) apart along the site for the hedge, each being tied to a bamboo cane which in turn is secured to a wire strained along the length of the row. The central leaders are retained until they have reached 150 to 300 mm. (6 to 12 in.) beyond the intended height for the hedge. The tops are then taken off just above a lateral about 150 mm. (6 in.) below this height. The laterals are left to grow up to the intended height. The best period for this topping operation is during summer, indeed, subsequent clippings should also be made at this period. This subject does seem to be very impatient of cutting during the early summer months when growth is very rapid but of course the late autumn, winter and early spring months should be avoided. Unfortunately this tree has been over-planted in small gardens and unmanaged, and is now considered a serious problem due to disputes between neighbours.

Coryneum Canker (*Seiridium cardinale*), a slow-spreading, disfiguring and fatal disease of Cupressaceae, including *Cupressus macrocarpa* and *C. sempervirens*, is seriously affecting the Leyland Cypress, see Plate 48.

CUPRESSUS

The habit of most Cupressus is to develop a definite leader from a very early stage. As this thickens and matures it becomes the central trunk, and the framework upon which the mature tree is built. This mode of growth is readily adopted even by plants raised by cuttings from side growths, but it is advisable to stake the leader carefully in order to encourage a shapely development and as a safeguard against wind-rock or direct damage.

Most species are able to form other leaders if the original one is injured and they will do this most readily from the uppermost laterals. However, with strong and vigorous specimens of *C. macrocarpa*, for example, new leaders may eventually form from growths originating from much older wood if for some reason an extensive reduction has been made. It is usually desirable to reduce rival leaders to one. When a leader has been developed from a misshapen specimen it is often difficult or impossible to hide the effects of earlier troubles. A number of Cupressus species are not as hardy as those of the closely related Chamaecyparis and in a cold or exposed nursery the young growths are subject to frost damage. However, even when the growth is good the anchorage of the root system may be far from satisfactory. *C. sempervirens*, for example, may be weighed down beyond repair or even uprooted in extremes of weather such as those experienced during severe gales or heavy snowfalls. A species is only really hardy when the shoot and root systems are healthy and able to function properly.

C. macrocarpa has been used extensively as a formal hedge plant, but although fast-growing it is not a good subject for this purpose as it will not respond to severe clipping, whole plants sometimes dying out completely. The bigeneric hybrid ×*Cupressocyparis leylandii* produces the same effect and is a far better plant for this purpose. *C. macrocarpa* is good for screening in the milder coastlines, where it may be allowed to grow freely.

Some conifers of this nature will withstand a very hard pruning if it is carried out during the late spring and summer months, but it is a very severe check that is often a 'killer' if it is done at any other time of the year. The reason for this is that the root system suffers extensive damage through the reduction of the food supply manufactured by the foliage and twig growth. *C. macrocarpa* is perhaps more impatient of this check to the shoot and root systems during the winter months than many, and a very high percentage of the trees treated in this way will often die.

It should be pointed out that a severe cutting back of a mature conifer screen is not advocated at any time of the year. It is really lopping, a drastic and undesirable practice.

CYDONIA

C. oblonga is the true Quince and it can be grown to form a large shrub or a small tree for much depends upon the initial training. It is often suckerous, and will quickly branch low at ground level to form a thick mat and stool-like growth with several upright main branches. The extent of suckering depends partly upon the method of propagation originally adopted. Thus the 'stooling' or 'mound-layering' method that has been extensively used in the past frequently results in the free production of growths at or near ground level, unless these are checked and a central leader built up to form a standard. The standard tree is the best form in which to grow this species and its forms and varieties. Grown as a 1.8 m. (6 ft.) standard, the main branches should be developed with an open centre. As the framework of branches is formed, pruning may be necessary to cut out crossing or badly placed growths but as the head develops no further pruning should be necessary. At a later stage the lower branches should be left to develop down almost to ground level. A large intact crown looks particularly fine in fruit and autumn colour.

CYTISUS

The various species and hybrids in this group exhibit quite a wide range of growth, form and habit. This must be taken into account when deciding whether or not to prune.

C. scoparius and the other popular hybrids should be pruned annually immediately after flowering in order to conserve vigour and to direct this into growth instead of the production of a useless crop of seed. These shrubs flower along the length of the previous year's wood and strongly growing plants often produce growths which branch freely during one season and flower the following year. Pruning involves cutting off approximately two-thirds of the previous year's shoots and results in the removal of most of the developing pods. The work is carried out with a sharp knife, cutting the growths as they are collected in a bunch by the free hand. New growths will spring from below the cuts, but care should be taken to avoid cutting too low into the old and hard wood as many Cytisus do not break freely if they are so treated, see Fig. 29.

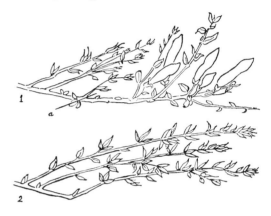

Fig. 29. The pruning of a *Cytisus* after flowering.
(1) The growth has finished flowering and the fruits are forming. (a) is the point at which the pruning cut is to be made. It is just above the young growth that may be found below the flowering portion.
(2) Such a growth a few weeks later after pruning.

Not only does this annual pruning conserve vigour by reducing the strain on the plants at a difficult time of year but it also prevents the bushes from quickly becoming leggy and keeps the plants shapely for a longer period. This is a definite advantage, for straggly bushes often lean over, or may be broken down after a very heavy fall of snow. It is a good practice to carefully brush or shake off snow after it has fallen and before it becomes frozen and perhaps added to by further falls. Summer pruning also reduces the incidence of Black Fly which often colonise from the developing pods. At this point it should be emphasized that a bushy habit is to be preferred with the young plant and is obtained by hard pruning in the nursery before the season's growth.

Among the subjects that benefit from annual pruning are *C. s.* 'Lady Moore', *C. s.* 'Lord Lambourne', *C. s.* 'Andeanus', *C. s.* 'Firefly' and *C. s.* f. *sulphureus.* There are of course many others.

The decumbent species and hybrids are seldom pruned, the reason being that it is more difficult, while the growth itself is usually more compact. A limited amount of pruning can be carried out by cutting out individual fruiting stems after flowering.

C. nigricans flowers on the current season's growths in mid to late summer. It should therefore be pruned back to developing shoots at the base in the spring, and the summer pruning, which is carried out after flowering, restricted to merely cutting off the flowered portion of the stems to prevent fruiting.

C. battandieri is a tall and strong-growing woody subject which may be grown in the shelter of a sunny wall although it is often successful in the open. In the former position it is self-supporting and no training or tying-in is needed. Normally, it throws out plenty of strong growths from the base and these often grow 1 to 2 m. (3 to 6 ft.) in one season. Thus the very old wood may be cut back and also any growths which stray and lean out too far.

DABOECIA

D. cantabrica. This species and its cultivars often develop into a straggly bush if left unpruned for a number of years. This may be overcome to a large extent by pruning back the old flowering heads to the cluster of growths found lower down on the stem. The best period for this is in the spring just as active growth is about to commence.

DANAE

D. racemosa. This shrub throws up 0.6 to 0.9 m. (2 to 3 ft.) high canes from a spreading rootstock during the summer months. The oldest arching growths often become ragged with progressive dieback from the tips of the fine branches. These may be cut out at ground level in the spring as new growth is commencing.

DAPHNE

Normally these do not require pruning and their response if it is carried out is so varied that the advice is, do not try it. *D. mezereum* may be quoted as an example. When it is growing in the open in a suitable soil, growth is close and the bush well furnished. Bushes in the shade or among other, perhaps taller shrubs often develop long bare branches and are straggly. The secret is therefore to select the site carefully in order to obtain typical growth. There are, of course, shade lovers such as *D. laureola* and *D. pontica*, but they are fewer in number.

D. blagayana and *D. cneorum* are dwarf and spreading, and after a few years long, trailing, bare branches develop. Annual pegging down and top dressing of the previous year's growths after flowering prevents this and the plants are happier for it.

DAPHNIPHYLLUM

D. himalense var. *macropodum.* To gain the full effect, this bushy evergreen should be encouraged to branch freely from the base, when it will furnish down to ground level and form a dense, rounded bush. There is little pruning required if this shrub is in full light and can grow unrestricted. Some dead wood collects in the centre of the bush, for the small amount of light which reaches beyond the dense outer canopy will not support healthy growth. Care must be taken if this is cut out to avoid damaging this canopy.

A plant growing in the shade becomes thin and spreading, with a loose untidy habit. This species will, however, regenerate well from the older wood if it is cut hard back.

DAVIDIA

There is only one species, *D. involucrata* and the variety *D. i.* var. *vilmoriniana.* Both retain their leader naturally without any difficulty. The ascending branches are thickly spaced on the trunk but they are rather sparsely sub-divided. The outline of a mature tree is wide and spreading, for the leader finally terminates in branching at an approximate height of

9 m. (30 ft.) or more. The spreading branches should not be restricted by lack of sufficient light or pruning, otherwise the effect will be spoilt. As a tree gains height and grows freely, the lower branches may be removed back to the stem to form a 1.8 m. (6 ft.) clear trunk if desired, doing this in the later summer. This is a good form in which to grow the tree, as the showy bracts, hanging down, may be seen to full effect. The process of forming a clear stem may start in the nursery, but the head will not be complete for at least a year or so after the final planting.

Often with a young tree in the autumn, the leaves on the ends of the branches in the crown, drop earlier than the remainder, and this gives a false impression that the centre and the shoot tips are dying. Wounds on this tree may heal slowly, but seldom does a cavity form.

DECAISNEA

D. fargesii is an upright-growing shrub that throws a number of young growths from the base, and does not branch extensively. The late spring frosts sometimes kill the young growths as they are breaking and this leaves short lengths of dead wood that may be cut out later in the season when new growths below this point are established. Occasionally, the weaker branch systems may be cut out at ground level provided that there are suitable growths to replace them. No regular pruning is required. In the nursery no pruning back is needed as the sparse bushy growth develops naturally.

DECUMARIA

D. sinensis. This evergreen climber from central China clings to supports by means of aerial roots on its young shoots, and it is normally grown against a wall. As the plant extends, the older wood may hang loosely from the wall, in which case a tie will be needed. It is a good plan to allow the growth to top the wall when it will often grow down a foot or so on the other side before turning up again. This will help to give the shrub a wonderful support. Flowering lateral growths are produced from the wall. Any which have extended too far from the wall may be

pruned back after flowering but normally very little pruning is required. There may be some dead growths to cut out after a severe winter.

D. barbara, a semi-evergreen climber from south-eastern United States, can be treated in the same way.

DENDROMECON

D. rigida should be grown against a warm, sunny wall. In the nursery the plants are grown in pots. They develop a bushy habit and these growths are trained fanwise when the final planting is made. Upon establishment, stronger growths appear from the base. These should be trained out so that the plant gradually builds up strength. The flowering laterals are produced from the strong growths. The pruning consists of cutting out the dead and thin wood in the spring as new growth commences.

DESFONTAINIA

D. spinosa. This choice evergreen subject requires very little pruning, apart from the removal of dead pieces that occur from time to time. The shrub is so difficult to please and to grow successfully that one is rightly hesitant to prune it, even though it may be necessary to limit its size. The main essential is to keep the plant growing freely.

DESMODIUM

Of this large genus only a few like *D. elegans* and *D. yunnanense* are hardy enough to be grown outside in the United Kingdom and even these are normally killed down to ground level each winter. They are best grown in a well-drained, sunny border against a wall and may be covered with a layer of loose bracken or straw round the base. In the spring the old growths are cut down to ground level. These shrubs flower on the current season's growth.

DEUTZIA

These have a stool habit, forming branches freely just below ground level. Thus a sufficient quantity of new shoots is produced on a healthy bush to allow a number of the older branches to be cut right down to ground level after the blossoms fade. Flowering on short laterals that grow from the previous year's wood, the best displays are on the younger growths. With some species, however, the bark on the older wood is attractive and a portion of this may be left each year, cutting back the oldest to good replacement shoots. *D. scabra* is one such species. It is a strong grower and the mature branches, which enable it to reach heights of 3 m. (10 ft.) or more, are attractive with a loose, shaggy bark. When pruning these large growers a few small, twiggy growths should be left near the base as furnishing and to lend a more natural effect. Some cutting back is desirable on even the older branch systems that are left, as otherwise the taller growths tend to become wind-blown and straggly. The cuts should always be made to a promising growth.

The strongly spreading species and varieties need plenty of space for their canopy of young foliage is attractive even when flowering is finished. *D. scabra* 'Staphyieoides' may be quoted as an example and pruning to confine this shrub would spoil the effect.

D. gracilis is sometimes damaged by late spring frosts and the flower buds and young growths, particularly on the upper and exposed portions of the plant, are killed. *D. ×lemoinei*, which is a hybrid between *D. gracilis* and *D. parviflora*, often suffers in the same way. These dead pieces of stem should be cut back later, in the early summer, taking the cut back to strong living wood.

In the nursery young plants which are lined out should be pruned hard before their first season's growth in this position, in order to encourage a bushy habit.

DICHOTOMANTHES

D. tristaniicarpa, the lone species in a monotypic genus in the family Rosaceae, is very similar in growth to the cotoneaster and in favoured localities it may be grown as a bush in the open. In this position the pruning consists of cutting out any weak and old wood after flowering in early summer. At this period the strongly growing pieces will be evident and cuts

should be made back to these although sometimes it may mean removing an entire branch. Regular pruning, however, is not necessary or desirable.

This plant should normally be grown on a wall and the framework is first trained out fanwise. Once the area has been covered, all growths coming away from the wall must be pruned back to within 25 mm. (1 in.) of the main stems, unless they are required for replacement, when an older piece has been cut out. This should be carried out in the spring just as growth is about to commence. One stopping at five leaves in the early summer helps to control growth and the shoots may then be taken back hard in the early spring.

In the nursery a bushy habit should be encouraged by stopping or pruning the plants after their first season's growth.

DIERVILLA

The three species in this genus, all from North America, flower on the current season's growth. They should not be confused with the dozen or so *Weigela* species from East Asia which flower on laterals from the previous year's wood, as the pruning needs of the two genera are quite different.

D. lonicera forms a mass of growths from a spreading and suckerous stool. *D. sessilifolia*, *D. ×splendens* and *D. rivularis* have a similar stoloniferous habit. They should be pruned hard back to just above ground level in the spring as new growth is about to start at the base. Old and worn clumps should be dug up, divided and replanted in enriched soil.

DIOSPYROS

The species most commonly met with is *D. lotus*, the Date Plum. It will reach from 9 to 12 m. (30 to 40 ft.) in height with a similar spread. Trained with a clear stem of 1.5 to 1.8 m. (5 to 6 ft.), the outer growths will become pendulous as the tree matures, thus complete coverage to ground level. This displays the beautiful, dark foliage to full effect while, viewed from beneath, the branches often form an attractive and interesting pattern and provide a good position for a garden seat. The tree should be in full sun although it will branch sparsely on the shaded side if grown on the edge of a large clump of trees.

D. virginiana is a larger and more loosely growing tree and with a clear trunk of 1.8 m. (6 ft.) the leader should be retained to at least 6 m. (20 ft.), or more if the tree is growing strongly.

D. kaki should have a sheltered but sunny position, for it is not quite as hardy as the former species and will often lose twiggy growth in a severe winter. These and any growths that have died beneath the heavy foliage canopy may be cut out during the early summer. In former days this species and its forms were given wall protection, being trained and closely pruned for fruit production, but specimens have been left to grow out as this policy was discontinued and have eventually formed small trees, the older wood being perfectly hardy.

DIOSTEA

D. juncea. This unusual shrub in the family Verbenaceae requires little pruning. It is a tall, erect grower and becomes bare at the base. It is therefore advisable to choose a site among other fairly close growing deciduous shrubs so that it can grow above them. The surrounding shrubs need to be 2.4 to 3.0 m. (8 to 10 ft.) high.

DIPELTA

The growth of all three species, *D. floribunda*, *D. ventricosa* and *D. yunnanensis*, is very similar. The main branches from ground level are upright but the secondary growths and the finer laterals arch over as the shoots come into flower. Strong, upright extension growths are often produced from this branch system, but these in turn arch over as flowering begins in the spring. This development deprives part of the older branches of light and causes leafdrop and dieback. Occasional pruning is necessary to remove this dead wood at an early stage to encourage healthy development. In addition, however, strong growths are often produced from the base and this gives an opportunity to remove an old branch to ground level if it is weak and worn.

D. floribunda is a large shrub with a very attractive peeling bark on the older stems and if the lower furnishing branches are retained the effect is very good. Little pruning is necessary on nursery stock, as bushiness is naturally produced by growths springing from ground level and these become stronger as the shrub develops.

DIPTERONIA

D. sinensis forms a large shrub or small tree. It has quite a characteristic habit of growth, for in the first few years after planting the shrub develops a mass of cane-like shoots from ground level. As establishment takes place, strong growths are produced which develop into the permanent branch system of a really large shrub. The smaller growths at the base are then like suckers and may be removed. Epicormic growths that are freely produced on the older branches should be removed unless required for the framework. There should be no attempt to force the early formation of a branch system by pruning and training in the nursery.

DISANTHUS

D. cercidifolius. This choice medium-sized shrub has a spreading habit, with a slender branch system. Shelter is important, especially in the early stages when the young growths are very subject to frost and wind damage. The sheltering screen may have to be pruned in order that the growth of the selected shrub does not suffer in any way, see Fig. 26. The foreground should be clear to allow branching to be as low as possible. This shrub also requires a moist, well-drained soil to do well.

DISCARIA

No regular pruning is required with *D. crenata*, which assumes tree-like proportions. The habit is for the young plant to branch low or at ground level and these branches should be allowed to extend year by year. The laterals have a semi-pendulous habit, a mode of growth that is adopted by the whole branch system as it develops. Any upright shoots which are produced on the branches grow strongly but arch over to deprive the lower ones of light. Over the years, as these lower branches die and are cut back to healthy wood, a rather untidy habit of growth develops. Gloves are necessary to clean out dead wood. The shrub gives every indication that it would be happier in a sunnier climate. The sparse branching allows underplanting.

D. toumatou is a tender shrub for a sunny wall. A permanent framework should be trained from three or four main branches that should be secured flat against the wall. From the sparse branching pendent growths are produced, which should be left at full length to trail down. They will often grow out several feet from the wall and after flowering in late spring the oldest of them may be cut back to the main framework to allow space for younger ones to develop.

DISTYLIUM

D. racemosum. Although a tree in its natural habitat, it is more often of shrub proportions in the United Kingdom. Many of the stiff branches have a horizontal habit with a dense flattened twig growth, which gives an almost tiered effect. Some of the branches in the crown are interlacing, but there should be no corrective pruning for this. In fact, this shrub is most effective when the branches are left to extend over a clear foreground. Should pruning be necessary to restrict size or development in any direction, the cuts should be carefully positioned inside the bush, so that they are hidden and the natural branching habit retained. This should be carried out in mid spring.

DOCYNIA

This is a genus of small trees or shrubs. Under good conditions a leader may be attempted in the nursery, eventually to form a length of clear stem of 1.2 to 1.8 m. (4 to 6 ft.) but more often a natural branching from near ground level is allowed to develop. The head of branches is usually thick and spreading, and in some respects they are similar to the Pyrus, Chaenomeles or Cotoneaster. Pruning may be undertaken to restrict size or spread, taking the cuts back to

suitable growths which are usually not difficult to find. Both D. delavayi and D. indica are similar in general effect.

DORYCNIUM. See Lotus

DRIMYS

D. winteri. This strongly growing evergreen is rather tender and normally it needs at least the shelter of a wall. Its habit is to produce strong upright growths, and the wall or sheltering building should be 3.0 to 4.5 m. (10 to 15 ft.) high to allow sufficient room for development. It should be planted a foot or so away from the structure, as no form of training on the wall surface is required or desirable.

Very little pruning is required, apart from the removal of old twisted branches that interfere with the development of the strong growths from the base of the plant. Branches which have been damaged by the winter should be cut back to suitable growths as they break out in the spring.

D. lanceolata should be treated in the same way.

ECCREMOCARPUS

E. scaber is classed as a semi-woody, evergreen climber. Under glasshouse conditions and in mild districts it often forms a woody base. In warm situations, even in the colder areas, the plant may survive almost untouched provided that the winters are mild. However, the herbaceous stems that are produced from the woody base may be killed back to an extent, even by moderate frosts.

Pruning is best carried out in the spring, when new growth is produced from the living wood. The dead may then be distinguished quite easily and can be cut out. This may mean taking the old growth back almost to ground level.

Pea-sticks or fine wire netting may be used for support, while a sheltered position near a wall is preferred.

EDGEWORTHIA

E. chrysantha. This Chinese shrub should have wall protection and should be planted about 0.3 m. (1 ft.) away from the base, but it only develops into a rather thin bush, and does not respond to tying and training against the wall. It may, however, need a stake. The inflorescences develop in the leaf axils on the newly formed wood in the autumn, but do not open until the spring. Growth often thins out on the older wood over the years, but strong shoots are thrown up from the base that can be used as replacements. Apart from this, no pruning is necessary, even in the nursery stage.

EHRETIA

There are two fairly hardy trees in this genus, *E. dicksonii* and *E. acuminata.* With both species the younger wood is often killed back during a severe winter, but regeneration is usually very free, even from the older branches and should this take place recovery is very rapid. The dead wood should be cut out during the early summer, when it will stand out clearly against the young growth.

Full sunlight is essential for good growth, and in positions of partial shade the tree may lean toward the light through heavy wood being put on that side. No growth is made in the shade and if overgrown by taller trees the affected portions will die back.

In the nursery, stock should be given a sheltered but sunny position as the young wood, particularly that of *E. dicksonii*, is tender and liable to winter damage. This is more likely on sappy and unripened wood and thus a very rich soil should be avoided. In training, a leader should be retained for 1.8 to 2.4 m. (6 to 8 ft.), but there is little advantage in forming a clear trunk and the lower branches may be left.

ELAEAGNUS

This distinctive genus shows quite a wide range of habit, the best known being *E. pungens*. The natural habit is to branch low and extensively at ground level to form a spreading bush. The form *E. p.* 'Maculata' is variegated gold and often displays a tendency to revert back to the type plant by developing a number of shoots with pure green foliage. If allowed to remain, these growths, being faster and stronger growing, quickly take over at the expense of the remainder of the plant. They should be carefully cut out as soon as they appear.

E. commutata is slow-growing and spreads by means of suckers. *E. macrophylla* branches very thickly and a furnishing right down to ground level is required for full effect but it has a very wide spread. *E. macrophylla* develops the low-branching habit to such an extent that the growth is often thicker in this region than elsewhere. Often too, the manner of branching is such that even the main stems become horizontal or almost pendulous as they arch over when young and become woody in this position. Thus the shrub may form a framework of arching branches, gradually gaining height in this way. It is difficult to form a shapely shrub in the early stages.

E. glabra will ramble over neighbouring shrubs by means of long slender growths which are freely produced from the crown. These should therefore be cut annually unless they are required for extension. In the early stages it is better to have a 1.8 m. (6 ft.) pole for support but, as the shrub increases in size, it becomes self-supporting, forming a mass of branches with a domed or pyramidal outline. The long, rambling extension shoots should be cut off each autumn thus forming a fairly compact growth with a slow buildup in height rather than a loose one.

E. ×*ebbingei* (*E. macrophylla* × *E. pungens*) is fast-growing and has an upright habit. As a shrub, it should be left to grow naturally with plenty of space and without any pruning. However, it is very successful as an informal hedge plant. The feature may be kept within bounds by carefully pruning back individual growths to just above a leaf axil or dwarf shoot system in late summer. The leading growths should be left unpruned until the desired height has been reached. *E. pungens* varieties may also be used to form attractive informal hedges.

E. angustifolia produces strong, upright growths, and nursery stock should be trained with a single leader to encourage the formation of a strong trunk and branch system.

A general characteristic of *Elaeagnus* spp. is that they respond well to hard pruning by shooting vigorously from old wood.

ELEUTHEROCOCCUS

These do not require regular pruning, for although they are often untidy in growth this is a natural habit. They should be looked over for dead wood during the summer months for it is often difficult to distinguish this from living material during the dormant stage when free of foliage. Generally, the branch system originates at or just beneath ground level; for example, the medium-sized *E. sieboldianus* is made up of several closely spaced erect stems, which should be left to grow naturally.

E. lasiogyne is one of the larger growers. The lower portions of the mature branches should be kept free of small growths, for the spines which are found on the strong upright shoots develop and become quite broad and thick with age. The extremities of the branches have a pendulous habit and this gives the shrub a well-furnished appearance enabling the foliage, flowers and fruits to be displayed to good effect.

Part of the interest of these shrubs is in their manner of branching and this should not be interfered with by pruning.

ELLIOTTIA

E. pyroliflora often forms a loose bush with clusters of long twiggy growths which develop from the main branch system. By carefully cutting out the longest of these whip-like branches, which tend to make the bush untidy, it is possible to contain the size and shape within reasonable proportions if, of course, this is considered necessary. It will throw out strong renewal growths from the proximity of pruning cuts, provided they are made in promising positions on the branch system. Pruning should be carried out after flowering.

ELSHOLTZIA

E. stauntonii is classed as a semi-woody plant. When established it produces a panicle of small, pink flowers toward the end of the season, on growths that have just been formed. These are killed back during the winter to near the woody base, from which growth starts again the following year. It should be noted that the lower portion of this young stem survives the winter and increases the woody structure at the base of the plant. The pruning, which should be carried out annually, consists of cutting back the old, flower shoots to the lowest one or two pairs of buds. This should be carried out in early spring, when the buds on the living wood are apparent as they commence activity. Gradually over the years the old wood and branch system builds up to a height of 0.6 m. (2 ft.) or more.

EMBOTHRIUM

E. coccineum forms a shrub or a small tree, dependent upon its well-being, position and locality. It is not fully hardy and is suitable only for the milder regions. The Lanceolatum group is hardier than the type. The young plant should be left to grow freely without any pruning when it will often throw up branches from the base. A successful method is to plant in clumps of three or four. This is a subject which, if it is growing strongly enough, will of its own accord form a small tree. Normally there should be no attempt to train a single leader. Should any pruning be needed, for instance thinning out the suckering systems, it is best done in late summer after flowering.

EMMENOPTERYS

E. henryi forms a moderately sized tree with a good straight trunk and leader, the branching from this having a horizontal habit. Great care must be taken to retain the leader while the plant is developing. A careful watch should be kept on the leading growths in the crown of the plant, where most of the extension wood is put on. Part of the answer is to keep the tree growing well, judging the rate of growth by the leading shoots, for lateral growth is very small and slow by comparison. Nursery specimens should have a leader.

EMPETRUM

E. nigrum is described as a procumbent shrub, and eventually bare stems develop in the centre of the plant to give an untidy appearance. When this condition is reached it is wise to replace it with a younger plant, but the need for this may be delayed by trimming back annually in the spring.

ENKIANTHUS

All the species are densely branched, the main stems springing from ground level and often centrally positioned, the laterals from these being whorled and often in layers. In the early stages most species are upright but a spreading habit may develop with age.

These shrubs need very little pruning, although overgrown specimens break freely if cut down quite hard. They will 'stand still' if they are not happy in their situation, but this is not a healthy condition and sooner or later serious dieback will occur. Their condition may be judged by the amount of new growth that is produced annually.

In the nursery no pruning is required for the production of a bushy habit which will develop naturally with good growth.

ERCILLA

E. volubilis. This climber is self-clinging, but it cannot be relied upon to support the extensive growth that it puts on after a few years when it is grown against a wall. In its natural habitat of rocks and trees the young growths by which the shrub adheres are able to loop over angles in the support and thus carry considerable weight. There is, therefore, considerable advantage to be gained from allowing the young wood to grow over the top of the wall and partly down the other side. The main growths should also be tied to the wires. Occasionally, the heavy bunches of growth hang down and become very untidy. This may be corrected by carefully thinning them in the spring after flowering.

ERICA

Even the few hardy members of this genus exhibit a wide range of growth and this must be taken into account when the need for pruning is considered. Many of the low-growing species and forms need pruning annually for at least 3 to 5 years in order to maintain a compact habit. This would appear to be unnatural and severe, until full account is taken of the conditions under which these plants grow in their natural habitat. Heaths and moorlands are windswept and the plants are exposed to full sun in a well-drained and often poor soil. The average garden is made up of richer soil and is often comparatively sheltered. Under these conditions the plants tend to grow tall with a loose habit. When annual pruning is considered necessary it is carried out after flowering, and just as the new growth is about to commence. It is not considered wise to prune in the late autumn or during the winter; in fact with a few species such as *E. vagans* it may kill the plants completely, especially if it is followed by severe weather. As a general rule the following guide may be applied to those in need of annual pruning.

Spring flowering. Prune in late spring to early summer as the flowers fade. This allows the new growths to mature in time for flower production in the following spring.

Summer and autumn flowering. Prune in early spring as soon as the new growth commences. The new shoots develop rapidly and are able to flower a few months later.

Winter flowering. Prune in mid spring as the flowers fade and the new growth begins.

When pruning, it is important to avoid cutting into the old wood, for this does not break freely. Old and worn plants do not regenerate readily and replacement is the better solution, provided that the soil is suitably improved before the new planting is made.

A variety of tools should be used in order to avoid a regular and formal effect. The secateurs, the knife and the hand shears should all be used in the same area. In giving this advice it is recognised that using knife and secateurs will slow the work down. Also care is necessary in using the knife in order to ensure that growths are not broken as a result of exerting a pull rather than a cut. Electric or petrol hedge-trimmers may be used. It will be found that the shoot systems are cut more readily when the foliage is wet. The prunings should be collected in a sack or canvas laid flat and taken up by the corners for moving. It is a task for a light and nimble person, as excessive trampling should be avoided.

While pruning, any seedlings that have appeared should be pulled up by the roots. The beautiful natural effect that results where Ericas are allowed to mingle and grow in association with neighbouring shrubs should also be considered.

The following list gives details of the more common species and their cultivars, and their requirements.

E. arborea var. *alpina.* Annual pruning not required. Very old and leggy specimens or ones which have outgrown their position may be cut back hard in the spring, even to the woody stems at ground level, for new growths will be produced very freely. In the same way, specimens which have been badly broken as a result of damage by severe frost or snow may also be cut back and will break into new growth provided the old wood is living.

E. australis. Annual pruning not required. Readily spoilt and even killed by severe weather.

E. carnea. Annual pruning may be required. These have a naturally compact habit but a limited amount of pruning is often beneficial in the spring after flowering is over. *E. c.* 'Springwood White' is normally low and even prostrate, but given the opportunity it will grow and intermingle with the growths of taller neighbouring plants such as Callunas or Gaultherias and reach a height of 0.6 to 0.9 m. (2 to 3 ft.). It may even be necessary to check it by careful pruning. Should it be necessary to prune to an edge to keep an extending mat within bounds, this must be carried out very carefully to avoid a straight, clipped effect. An informal line may be kept by cutting away the growths individually at different levels. Another effective method is carefully to lift the side of the clump a

few inches, cutting away the under branches. When returned the cuts are hidden.

E. ciliaris. Annual pruning required. This has an untidy growth. The weak stems develop a prostrate habit and upright flowering growths are produced from these. Pruning in March and April as growth commences helps to keep the plants tidier, especially if it is undertaken annually from the time when they are first established. But one should never cut into the old wood. *E. c.* 'Maweana' has a stronger and more erect habit.

E. cinerea. Annual pruning required. This has a stiff, upright habit but, left unpruned, it becomes straggly and rather untidy. Pruning in the spring encourages a closer and more tufted habit just as growth starts and regular annual pruning from the young stage ensures bushier plants. The dwarf, compact forms do not need pruning.

E. ×darleyensis 'Darley Dale' and the other cultivars of this interspecific hybrid. Annual pruning required. This is a vigorous grower, but pruning keeps the plants in better condition. This must be timed carefully, as the subject flowers well into the spring and often into the growing period. The operation should take place at the beginning of the growing season. By cutting back, the new shoots which extend beyond the flowering portions are taken away, and growths break out closer into the bush thus encouraging a compact habit. Should this subject need restricting in size, either because it is growing over a nearby edge, or if a neighbouring plant is in danger of becoming overgrown, the offending shoots should be cut out individually in order to leave a natural effect. Merely clipping round the edge to a hard line leaves a very unsightly finish.

This informal edge pruning should be the aim in the Erica garden. A poor or unsightly edge is particularly noticeable when a neighbouring clump has been cleared for replacement and time spent on the finish is always well worthwhile.

E. lusitanica. Annual pruning not necessary. This species is tender and is happiest in the mild parts of the country. It does not respond to hard pruning.

E. mackayana. Annual pruning required. Although some shortening back may be carried out each spring just as the new growth is about to start, eventually the branches build up and lie on each other to produce an untidy mat. When this happens and growth deteriorates, replacement is necessary.

E. erigena. Some annual pruning required. Some varieties are more compact than others, but often isolated shoots will grow up well above the remainder. These should be cut back after flowering in order to avoid a leggy habit, which may lead to wind damage. If after a severe winter the shrubs are killed back, they will usually regenerate from the base, making up well even during the first season. *E. e.* 'W. T. Rackliff' has a compact dome-shaped habit, but very old plants have a worn and gappy appearance. This form seldom responds well to cutting back and a complete replacement is the only answer. No regular pruning is required.

E. scoparia. Annual pruning not required. This has a loose upright habit and sometimes suffers from wind damage, especially in exposed areas. It is advisable to prune it hard in the initial years in order to encourage a bushy habit. This should be carried out in the spring.

E. terminalis. Annual pruning not required. This species has an erect habit and is rather a loose grower. If it is desired to keep it more compact the pruning back of the longer and taller growths may be undertaken in the spring. It may be more necessary to do this with specimens that are shaded.

E. tetralix. Annual pruning required. Cutting back in the spring before growth starts helps to keep a more compact habit, but with older plants the stems are spreading and the plants become untidy. No attempt should be made to induce the plants to break by cutting into the older wood and replacement with young plants is the best solution. *E. t.* 'Alba Mollis' has a compact upright habit, and a limited shortening of old, flowered growths in the spring is advisable.

E. vagans. Annual pruning required. This species develops a close, clump-like growth but, left unpruned, it will become overgrown and woody and flowering deteriorates. Pruning should take place just as the new growth is showing signs of starting. It must never go back beyond the lowest point where this is breaking out. Specimens that have become old and worn despite annual pruning should be replaced.

E. ×williamsii. A limited annual pruning required. This hybrid has a close habit, but leggy shoots, particularly those that have flowered, need to be shortened back to the general level as the new growth commences. One of its main attractions is the young growth that is yellow, particularly in the spring. This effect is spoilt if a general clipping over of the entire clump is carried out.

A number of species and hybrids have not been included in this list, but, provided the habit of growth is recognised, the principles as outlined above may be applied.

ERIOBOTRYA

E. japonica. This strongly growing evergreen shrub often reaches tree-like proportions, but it needs the protection of a wall in regions with hard winters. With a large wall space that has considerable height, a leader may be retained to form a main stem and the main branches and stem should be loosely secured to the wall. In a more restricted space, branching from near ground level may be encouraged, while good, strong shoots which are thrown up from the base can be used for replacement purposes.

In the milder regions, this subject may be allowed to grow away from the wall, when the branches will spread out for 1 to 2 m. (3 to 6 ft.). In this case the shade beneath it will be very dense and only an evergreen ground-cover plant will survive.

ESCALLONIA

One almost general characteristic is the arching habit that develops as a growth hardens and goes into the second year when it flowers. There are exceptions, however. For example, *E.* 'Iveyi' has a completely upright and rigid growth. But the few variations are easily recognised.

Most species and hybrids produce abundant new growths each season from one-year-old shoots and even from older wood near or at the base. Often, at least one new growth is found on the upright portion of a mature stem, or even on the bend as it arches over.

For the most part they flower in early to mid summer from one-year-old wood. Any pruning that is necessary may be carried out as the blossoms drop, removing these growths and making the cut just above a promising shoot or branch. Another characteristic is their ability to break into growth from old wood after most of the shrub has been killed by severe winter weather. Badly damaged shrubs should not be cut out until they have been given a chance to break in the late spring or early summer.

The reasons for pruning Escallonias may either be to conserve vigour or to control their growth and shape. It is not necessary to prune every year, and the general condition and habit of the species or variety must be taken into consideration. The shrubs should be looked over at least once a year after flowering, first removing the dead and very weak growths. Often it is better to cut in deeply, taking out a considerable portion of a branch, rather than to snip at separate small growths which will give a hedge-like effect.

The warm, sunny wall is a fine position for most Escallonias, but in particular for such tender species as *E. rubra* var. *macrantha*. In the first years after planting the main growths should be tied in, which will ensure that the full height of the wall is reached.

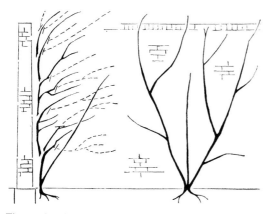

Fig. 30. *Escallonia* trained to a wall. The main branches are tied out to cover the space. The broken lines indicate where the old flowering growths would be cut out after the blossoms fade.

The strongest species and hybrids will grow up to heights of 3 m. (10 ft.) or more when supported. From this framework strong branching develops to give a considerable spread from the wall. This outward spread needs to be kept in check by pruning after flowering, occasionally cutting out an entire branch, for renewal shoots are often freely produced from the base, see Fig. 30.

In the warmer parts of the country many of the species and hybrids are successfully grown in the open border. Pruning is often necessary after flowering to conserve vigour and to encourage the young growths, but it may also be necessary to check an invasive habit of the very pendulous forms whose growths, on touching the ground, will root to make separate plants, often to the detriment of their neighbours. The careless application of mulch that weighs down and buries parts of the lower branches also has the effect of encouraging such rooting and spread.

The following remarks on individual species will help to give a more complete picture. *E. illinita* is one of the hardiest. It is fairly upright and is unusual in that it flowers terminally on the current season's wood. Any pruning on this and other late-flowering species should be carried out in mid spring, as otherwise, if done immediately after flowering, soft growth will be produced which will not stand the winter. *E.* 'Iveyi' has a very bushy habit and it is difficult to grow hard against a wall. Growth in an outward direction from the wall may be limited by cutting back whole branches.

In a wet, mild summer and autumn some varieties will give a second if reduced display of flowers from short laterals. These are distinct from extension growths. This second flowering, cutting back the old growths after flowering, but not severely may encourage habit. The harder pruning is left until later. Only a few varieties respond in this way, e.g. *E.* 'William Watson'. The later pruning is important, as otherwise a close hedge-like surface will result which will look unnatural.

In the mildest regions Escallonias are commonly used for hedging. Under annual clipping, a good surface is formed and the whole genus is able to withstand the salt-laden winds of coastal districts. *E. rubra* var. *macrantha* in particular has a dense rigid habit and is ideal for this purpose.

EUCALYPTUS

E. gunnii is one of the few species which are hardy enough for the United Kingdom.

Within recent years there has been a revival of interest, which has been partly due to the establishment of improved methods of training and pruning. These are described in detail below.

The plants are raised by seed which is sown in the late summer, and they are kept growing coolly throughout the following winter until planting time in the early summer, when all danger of frost is past. By this time they may be in 130 to 150 mm. (5 to 6 in.) pots and they should go straight out into their permanent quarters. There must be no delay in doing this, as otherwise the main roots will be wrapped extensively round the pots, which will spoil the chances of a good anchorage. Trees that start life with a root system that has been cramped and distorted in this way, are more likely to be blown down in later years.

The site selected should be sheltered from the north and east winds and additional protection is advisable during their first winter outside, using tree shelters, sacking for screening purposes and a heavy mulch to reduce the chances of the ground freezing in depth. During very severe periods fleece, straw, bracken or similar loose and dry organic material could be piled round the basal portion of the stem as a further protection. Effective staking is necessary as the plant grows away, however if trees are planted small enough, a stout cane with the Max Tapener system can be used to effectively secure the tree.

The second season's growth should be very rapid indeed, and if satisfactory, the plant should be able to stand well on its own without requiring further support. If not, or if there is any doubt, the young tree should be cut back hard to within 0.5 m. (1.5 ft.) of ground level in the spring. This may seem to be rather drastic, but an established plant should respond to this treatment by breaking freely from the base. Often these regenerating growths occur from the swollen

base that is normally present on a young tree, which is referred to as the ligno-tuber.

Once these young shoots grow away and are a foot or so in length, the strongest one can be selected and an adjustment made with a final cut on the old stem. This should result in better anchorage, although if it becomes necessary it should be repeated. Alternatively, several stems can be retained to produce a multi-stemmed specimen.

Trees that have been badly frosted or killed back during the winter can be expected to react in the same way, unless of course the vital tissues at the base have also suffered. The dead growths may be shortened in the spring, the final cut back being delayed until the regenerating shoots have developed, when some decision as to which are the most promising growths is possible.

There is another method of culture in which the growths are cut down annually or quite frequently to near ground level on a coppice system. This should be carried out in the spring. Tub-grown plants may be treated in this manner, and this will provide attractive juvenile foliage. Bracken and leaves are placed round the tubs during the winter after standing them in a sheltered place.

EUCOMMIA

E. ulmoides forms a tree up to 18 m. (60 ft.) in height. It should be raised in the nursery as a 1.8 m. (6 ft.) standard. The reason for this is that the head opens out very quickly once branches are left to develop, and there may be difficulty in retaining a central leader. A good height to the branch system allows the outer and lower branches to develop a fully pendulous habit. Heavy with twig growth and foliage, they are most attractive. This type of growth needs a sheltered position as wind may cause damage.

EUCRYPHIA

These are informal shrubs or small trees that have their own peculiar habit of growth, and they do not take kindly to pruning or training. It is therefore advisable to allow and encourage a natural growth.

Often, the leader splits up low down or at ground level, and the main stems are upright. E. ×nymansensis in particular is a very upright grower with laterals which have a semi-pendulous habit. Often there is some dead wood to cut out beneath these.

Eucryphias are often grown in woodland settings, and care should be taken that low, overhanging branches from neighbouring trees are removed before the general shape and health are affected. In the nursery the young shrubs should be allowed to develop a natural habit, staking if necessary to prevent wind-rock. They do not respond to hard pruning and any pruning necessary should be carried out in spring.

EUGENIA

E. cheken is not fully hardy except in the warmer localities, but it can be grown in the shelter of a wall in all but the colder regions with hard frosts. It should be planted about 0.6 m. (2 ft.) away from the base and with its extensive, lateral branching it will occupy a large area. It is upright and close branching but it will be completely self-supporting. Normally it should be encouraged to branch low by stopping, and it is most effective when furnished right down to ground level. The shrub may be restricted in width by careful pruning, so that the cuts are hidden and an informal surface preserved. The shrub maintains many living growths inside the bush. If severely checked or cut down by frost it will often break freely at ground level from old wood.

EUONYMUS

Normally, the deciduous species require very little pruning, but it should be borne in mind that there is quite a variety of growth even among these. E. alatus is a low, close-branching shrub with a spreading habit and corky wings on the branches, which must have scope for development if it is to be grown to full effect. E. bungeanus has an erect habit and may develop into a small tree. By way of contrast, E. latifolius has a weaker branching system and the leading growth needs staking, at least when it is young. There

are other variations and it is better to see a mature tree or shrub before the choice of species is made. Some of the deciduous species, E. europaeus in particular, act as hosts for Black Fly (Aphis fabae). The developing colonies of insects will often cripple early growths and should be controlled.

E. japonicus is one of the most common of evergreen species and it will either form a dense shrub or a small loosely growing tree. E. j. 'Robustus' has a stiff, upright growth. This subject is often used for hedging purposes, especially near the south and west coasts. It is very good grown as an informal hedge when individual shoots or branches may be cut back, if it is necessary to keep it in shape, in mid to late spring. It does not form an attractive surface when closely clipped although it will withstand this treatment. The coloured forms are attractive; a watch should be kept for reversion that must be cut out as soon as it appears. The forms of E. j. 'Macrophyllus' are attractive when young, but they should be replaced, as they become old and woody at the base.

E. fortunei is a creeping evergreen, and in common with the Ivy and some other shrubs it has an adult or flowering stage. In nature, the shrub climbs tree trunks etc. and only when the light is reached, is the mature flowering material produced. E. f. 'Carrièrei' and E. f. var. vegetus are mature forms which are bushy and bear fruit. E. f. 'Coloratus' forms quite a large spreading shrub which covers a very wide area of 4.6 to 6.0 m. (15 to 20 ft.) wide when it is mature. E. f. 'Silver Queen' is most attractive when trained to climb and ramble over the main branches of small trees as Acer negundo. E. f. 'Gracilis' is also a variegated form which climbs. Loose ties may occasionally be necessary for both of these. It is very attractive when planted against a close columnar conifer such as Juniperus communis 'Hibernica'. The trailing growths are assisted in climbing by threading them through the close branches of the Juniper. The Euonymus is not of course allowed to overgrow the Juniper completely.

E. f. 'Minimus' is a low, creeping shrub, but it will climb. Even the smaller-leaved form of this, 'Kewensis', will climb for 4.6 to 6.0 m. (15 to 20 ft.)

up a tree trunk, to produce a mature branch system with larger leaves, when it reaches the light.

Many of these forms may also be grown against a wall where they require the minimum of support. The coloured forms of *E. japonicus* are also suitable for this situation and in warmer and more sheltered areas a north wall is suitable. Occasionally with the latter, the older growths are cut away in the spring to allow the younger ones to be tied in. Other surplus growth is pruned hard back.

EUPHORBIA

E. characias subsp. *wulfenii* may be regarded as a subshrub. It forms a mass of erect stems, and this close habit no doubt helps to keep the plant intact and windproof. However, the old growths as they pass out of flower develop small laterals, and this may spoil the general effect. These old flowered stems may be cut down to a really strong growth or to ground level. The plants should be looked over annually, for a drastic pruning in one operation may result in overthinning and thus wind damage on the remaining growths.

The main attraction of this plant is in the impressive effect that is gained when young and well-furnished stems are massed together. It has great powers of regeneration and quickly recovers from damage that may result in the removal of all the top growth.

EUPTELEA

This is a genus of small trees or shrubs. The habit of growth and appearance of *E. pleiosperma* and *E. polyandra* is similar in some respects to that of the Hazel stool. Sucker shoots are thrown up from the base in just the same way, but they are usually not as plentiful and the shrub as a whole is more sparsely branched. In the nursery an attempt may be made to run up a leader with the aim of forming a single trunk and head, but this is not always successful. Little regular pruning is required but the oldest growths may be cut out at ground level or to a suitable growth, if they are weak. Specimens with a single trunk should have their suckers removed as necessary.

EURYA

E. japonica is a stiffly branched shrub which needs to grow unpruned and unrestricted in any way; the spread is then considerable, being 1.8 to 3.0 m. (6 to 10 ft.) from the centre of the bush. The branches ascend from ground level at a low angle, while the minor growths are arranged herringbone fashion down the main stems. In the nursery a naturally bushy habit should be encouraged. This shrub will respond to pruning but the characteristic natural habit will be lost unless great care is taken.

EVODIA. *See* Tetradium

EXOCHORDA

These shrubs have a fairly upright habit, the branches often being slender and covered with epicormic growths. In addition, numerous suckers may spring from round the base at ground level. These superfluous growths should be cut off annually unless a number are required for the replacement of older branches, in which case selected shoots may be left to extend and develop so that they are suitable for this purpose. The winter period is good for cutting away this crop of annual growths but, in addition, young developing shoots may be quite easily rubbed off, or removed with finger and thumb in the spring, just as three or four leaves have formed. Another time for looking over these shrubs is after flowering in late spring when useless old wood may be cut out and surplus young growths removed.

The most erect species is *E. korolkowii*, while *E. racemosa* has a more spreading habit.

FABIANA

F. imbricata is normally grown at the foot of a south-facing wall. Apart from the main stems that are upright, the shrub produces a twisted and distorted branch system. It is better in most cases to restrict the shrub to one main stem that will require staking as a head develops with maturity. Should a branch system crack, or break in the wind, the shrub may be cut back into really old wood, as regenerating growths are produced very freely. Any cutting back to shape should be carried out after flowering in midsummer.

FAGUS

F. sylvatica, the Common or European Beech, is the most common species and is a native of Britain, and when well grown is ideal from the arboriculturist's standpoint. Typically, when grown out in the open as an isolated specimen, the upper main branches in the crown are ascending, while the remainder are more horizontal, with the outer and lower ones pendulous. These often sweep down to reach the ground and may eventually root to become a thick, extensive clump round the mother tree. On large estates where there is sufficient space this habit should be developed. The leaf canopy is very dense and quite often the smaller and lower branches die back. These should be removed when this dieback commences, for the healing will then be complete in a young and vigorous specimen, and a length of clear trunk, one of the great beauties of this tree, will develop. Large wounds on an old specimen heal well although the scars will remain on the trunk for the remainder of the tree's life, see Plate 7.

One unfortunate characteristic, particularly with old and mature specimens, is the liability to shed heavy limbs suddenly and without warning. More often this occurs on hot, still mornings in early summer. Invariably, the wood on the exposed surfaces is very dry in appearance. Often, large, ugly tears on the main trunk are made in this way, but they should be cleaned up and smoothed as much as possible. An even more thorough inspection should be made of trees that have shed limbs in this way, and if possible the target should be moved away from the hazard in order to keep people away from danger. Alternatively, of course, a dangerous tree in a high-risk area should be removed.

The good arboriculturist takes soil preferences into consideration when planting young trees and the beech thrives best in well-drained soil. Growth in a young tree is rather slow in the early years, but upon establishment the leader shoots up very rapidly. The addition of soil ameliorants which include mycorrhizae will help beech to establish with a higher success rate, as there are natural symbiotic associations between the two. Much can happen to spoil the leader with the result that rivals quickly develop, for example, the beech is liable to damage from late spring frosts. Rival leaders should therefore be cut out at an early stage, for shedding limbs, the one great weakness of this tree, will be more likely to occur where the whole weight of the crown is carried by two or three main branches. Planted in a group, 12 to 15 m. (40 to 50 ft.) apart, beeches retain their leaders more readily than in the open, eventually forming smooth, straight pillars of great beauty.

F. s. 'Riversii' appears, because of the colour of the foliage, to cast an even denser shade than the type. Generally, it also has very dense branching. Occasionally, reverted growths appear in the centre of the crown, but this is difficult to check and it does not harm the specimen in any way. The forms of *F. s.* 'Purpurea Pendula' are small and compact, forming dense umbrellas of growth. On the other hand, the green weeping beech, *F. s.* 'Pendula', has a distinctive habit, with the tree gradually gaining height and spread, with heavy branches. Many of the older branches are kept alive in the centre of the tree and form branches of dwarf, fastigiate shoots. These should be left, as they add to the character of the tree. *F. s.* Heterophylla Group are densely but gracefully branched trees. In order to appreciate this habit to the full the foreground should be open to allow the branching to reach ground level. Some of the forms in this group are periclinal chimaeras and growths arising from a cut may show considerable variation. *F. s.* 'Dawyck', the Dawyck Beech, retains a leader naturally with twisted side branches. There should be no attempt to form a length of clear trunk. *F. s.* 'Rotundifolia' is slow-growing and forms a low crown with ascending main branches. This tree will furnish thickly to ground level and will even layer itself at the points of contact. *F. s.* 'Tortuosa' may appear to be untidy to the conscientious arboriculturist, but no attempt should be made to clear the congested growths beyond retaining the lead and clearing the dead wood. *F. s.* 'Zlatia' has an upright, almost fastigiate branching, with a curious bark-splitting habit. The leader should be retained for as long as possible.

The European Beech is often grown as a hedge plant. When kept in a dwarf state it responds to annual trimming in late summer, autumn or winter. In order to allow the young stock time for establishment, no trimming should be carried out for at least two seasons after planting. After trimming, the dead leaves are retained throughout the winter.

The beech seems to be very prone to infection by White Rot, *Ganoderma applanatum*, while the presence of the huge fructifications of *Meripilus giganteus* in the neighbourhood of the root system is indicative of a fatal rot on the root system, for this fungus is a saprophyte. A tree in this condition may be unsafe and will need careful monitoring. During periods of drought, the beech is also open to secondary infection from Beech Bark Disease, which will cause slow dieback of the upper crown and bark death on the main trunk. Seriously infected trees will eventually fail and die.

Of the remaining species, *F. grandifolia* is quite a strong grower, but the leader should be retained for as long as possible, as it often shows a great tendency to form a crown early in life. *F. orientalis* and *F. crenata* form a similar tree and both should be trained with a 1.8 m. (6 ft.) clear stem. *F. japonica* forms a small slender tree with a very light, twiggy branch system. It should be allowed to branch into several stems at the base, as this is a natural habit.

FALLOPIA

F. baldschuanica. This rapid-growing deciduous subject climbs by twining. It does this so freely that seldom is training needed, even when young, provided that there is a wire or branch support. It is difficult to restrict it to a confined space, but if it is necessary, pruning may be carried out during the dormant season. The ideal support for this subject is an old tree where it has almost unlimited space for development. Eventually long, trailing growths hang down to give a completely natural effect. Under this condition a considerable amount of dead wood builds up in the centre, as more and more trailing growths

are produced which deprive the older ones of light. With care some of this can be cut out.

×FATSHEDERA

×*Fatshedera lizei* (*Fatsia japonica* × *Hedera hibernica*) is a spreading, low-growing shrub which seems to develop at random, rather than to any pattern. As the shrub grows over the surface, strong shoots are produced which are at first upright, but, as they extend during their second season, are weighed down. The whole process is repeated over and over again in later years as the clump extends. This untidy habit may to a certain extent be controlled by stopping these upright growths in late summer. Sub-laterals will be produced, but the shrub as a whole will be closer to the surface. A pair of long-arm or standard pruners may be used for this work, if the clump is extensive and to save walking on the bed.

FATSIA

F. japonica is a quite outstanding late autumn-flowering shrub which has a wide spread of some 3 m. (10 ft.) as it reaches maturity. The outer branches are weighed down as they extend, although their subdivision into branchlets is very sparse. Most of the branches and the new growths, one or two of which are produced each year, spring from ground level, thus giving the shrub a stool-like habit.

Although it is most impressive when left to grow naturally, it is often necessary to restrict the size by pruning. If this is essential, it is carried out in the spring, when the offending branches may be taken down to ground level. This subject will throw growths from dormant buds, even on the older wood, but provided that there are plenty of replacement shoots, the shrub assumes a more natural shape if they are cut right down.

In the nursery this subject assumes a natural growth without stopping.

FEIJOA. *see* Acca

FICUS

F. carica, the Common Fig, was formerly grown in the larger private gardens for its fruit, and often under these conditions it was subjected to a specialized pruning system.

When grown as an ornamental feature, an upright growth with the main branches should be encouraged, as if there is considerable spread an untidy habit will develop. An overgrown specimen may be cut hard back to ground level; in fact top growth is often killed completely during a severe winter. This subject has great powers of regeneration and will break very freely. It is possible to restrict the size by very careful pruning, taking the cuts into the bush so that they are hidden, and at the same time leaving an informal surface. This may be carried out at any time other than the spring or summer.

FIRMIANA

F. simplex develops into a large tree but it can only be grown successfully in the mildest localities. It has attractive foliage, but this is only seen to full effect when allowed to develop freely without being hemmed in by neighbouring trees. It is a fast grower, but the leader should be retained to form a good trunk and strong crown.

FITZROYA

F. cupressoides is usually found as a large shrub in cultivation rather than a tree with a definite clear trunk. At its best it is conical, well furnished down to the ground with the ends of the branches drooping. The main branching system may consist of a number of upright stems that often spring from near ground level.

Undoubtedly, in a very favourable climate and under good growing conditions, it is possible to build up a small tree form with a definite trunk. Training for this should commence in the nursery when they are but 150 to 300 mm. (6 to 12 in.) high, for there is a tendency even at this stage for the young plants to become bushy and to form several competing leaders.

The selected growth should be staked, the uppermost tie being on the mature portion of the wood where the stem has ripened. This allows the growing tip to droop naturally.

FOKIENIA

F. hodginsii closely resembles *Calocedrus* in foliage and in fact is closely related to *Cupressus* and *Calocedrus*. It makes a slow-growing small- to medium-sized shrub and very little pruning will be needed. It is best grown in a sheltered position.

FONTANESIA

F. phillyreoides and *F. p.* subsp. *fortunei* are similar to Privet in habit and appearance. They branch low from ground level. The former has the more delicate and graceful branching habit. Some dieback may occur as a result of severe winters, but apart from cutting this back in the spring very little pruning is needed.

FORESTIERA

F. acuminata and *F. neomexicana* are similar in appearance to Privet, although they are not as free-growing. They form branches at or just below ground level, and occasionally strong growths are thrown up from the base, which can be retained, either to provide extra furnishing or to replace growths that are weak or overgrown.

FORSYTHIA

The habits of growth and flowering of this genus are that mature plants freely produce blossoms in the early spring, directly from growths made during the previous season. Even the strongest of wood on young and vigorous plants often flowers profusely, but occasionally this is devoted entirely to growth. Most species produce a quantity of branches from ground level, and it is their natural habit to grow strongly from this point with growths that, in time, will develop and replace older branches as these

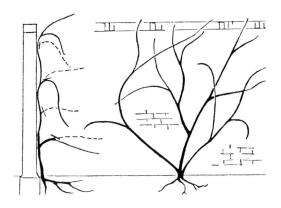

Fig. 31. *Forsythia suspensa* trained to a wall. Owing to the habit of growth it is rather difficult to produce a shapely plant. The broken lines on the left-hand figure indicate the growths, which are to be cut out after flowering. Entire lengths of the old flowered wood are cut out at that time. The pendulous habit of the remaining growths is retained.

become worn and weighed down by a mass of twiggy growths, which have a poor flowering potential.

The object of pruning these shrubs is to encourage this habit by cutting out the oldest wood immediately after flowering, just as the new growth has commenced. This means that annual pruning is not necessary or even desirable. In a young plant, the future branch system is being formed, and this should be encouraged to spring from ground level by planting slightly lower than in the nursery. As the plant reaches maturity the balance between old and young wood should be satisfactory, little or no pruning being required. The growths must be left full length in order to encourage a natural and free habit.

It is at a later stage, when the plant has been at full size for two or three years, that a proportion of the older branches may be taken out completely, making the cut as low as possible on the bush, just above a strong shoot or bud. This should be carried out immediately after flowering. A furnishing of small branches and twig-like growths should if possible be left near the base of the shrub, as these look attractive in flower and in leaf and help to give a natural appearance.

It will be recognised that over the years this policy amounts to quite severe pruning, and that very little

wood will be left on the plant which is more than 6 to 10 years old. In order to maintain vigour, therefore, regular mulching and feeding is necessary.

In cases of neglect, when a specimen is very old, unshapely and weak, it may be cut back hard to ground level in the winter or early spring. Provided that it is not too old it will shoot up strongly to produce an entirely new branch system within two or three years.

Although the relationship between the growth and flowering habits and the pruning has a general application throughout the whole genus, variations in size and outline are found among the species and varieties. *F. giraldiana* is often a thin grower with a graceful branching habit, a complete contrast in this respect to *F.* ×*intermedia* 'Spectabilis', which is stiff and upright, although, as it matures, many of the outer growths become semi-pendulous. *F. ovata* forms a very dense, rounded bush with a compact habit and is seldom more than 1.2 to 1.5 m. (4 to 5 ft.) in height. Surprisingly, against a wall the character of the plant changes and longer growths are produced, which if supported add to the height considerably. *F. viridissima* 'Bronxensis' is a dwarf and compact grower that seldom needs any pruning.

F. suspensa is a tall grower, reaching 3 m. (10 ft.) or more with long, pendulous laterals and sub-laterals which may reach lengths of 0.6 to 0.9 m. (2 to 3 ft.). In the open this shrub quickly becomes untidy and it is much better as a wall specimen. The main branches, if trained up and supported, will reach heights of 4.6 to 6.0 m. (15 to 20 ft.) and the long pendent branchlets may be left to trail down to ground level. Young branches may be trained up and tied in to replace the older ones as complete lengths are cut out, and thus overall the plant is kept young and vigorous, see Fig. 31. *F. s.* var. *sieboldii* is even more slender and pendent in growth, and may collapse in the open without support. The two latter subjects are suitable for a shady wall.

F. suspensa f. *atrocaulis* may be grown for its coloured bark, but for this it is necessary to maintain a good supply of young and vigorous canes by hard pruning. These are coloured dark purple.

Forsythias will flower quite well beneath a light canopy of foliage, provided that there is sufficient moisture for growth. They are sometimes grown for hedging purposes and *F. ×intermedia* 'Spectabilis' is the best one to choose for this, as it has an upright, rigid growth. It will even flower when clipped formally perhaps two or three times during the growing season, but the best effects are from a more natural growth and outline. For this the standard pruning is adopted immediately after flowering, but care must be taken to preserve the outline of the hedge.

FOTHERGILLA

These have a stool-like habit, sending up woody and very twiggy growths from ground level, which have an attractive display of flower spikes in the spring, with a fine autumn display of coloured foliage before the leaves fall. For this autumn colour to be shown to full effect, a bush should be well shaped with a good furnishing of growth down to ground level. The short twiggy shoots at the base are therefore important and should not be cut off. These shrubs as a group need very little pruning and often it is necessary to cut neighbouring growth to prevent overcrowding. Should an old and worn branch need removal it should be carefully cut out during the winter, for the growths at the base are crowded and, unless care is taken, unnecessary injury may occur. Usually there are a number of young shoots at the base that can be trained for replacement. *F. major* is an upright but slow grower, strongly resembling a coppiced hazel stool. *F. major* Monticola Group has a well-furnished and spreading habit.

FRANKLINIA

F. alatamaha requires a sheltered woodland position in a very mild and favourable locality. It naturally develops an upright habit, and may reach a height of 3 m. (10 ft.) or more. Specimens often display a tendency to branch from near the base, but there is no need to restrict growth to one stem. No regular pruning is necessary, apart from cutting back any growths from sheltering shrubs that overgrow it and

compete for light. This should be done carefully to conceal the cuts, and to leave an informal effect.

FRAXINUS

It is important to retain and preserve the leading growth for as long as possible, for once rival leaders occur, a rounded head is quickly produced and this will be difficult to correct. This habit is encouraged by the winter buds being opposite, which means that they develop with equal vigour once the terminal bud is lost through pest damage or a late frost after it has broken into growth. The main branches in a prematurely formed head grow very long and heavy with foliage. These are liable to break during severe summer gales.

Some species, even on generally well-shaped trees, produce long branches with masses of foliage and in exposed positions these may be broken during wet and windy weather. Among the species that are liable to do this are *F. latifolia*, in some forms where the laterals are semi-pendulous, and *F. angustifolia*.

F. excelsior, the Common Ash, is a strong well-branched tree, but when heavy branches are broken or sawn off, large upright growths frequently develop, adding considerable weight to a weakened and often rotted system. Also the general shape of the tree is spoilt. Careful balancing by thinning may be used to correct this. The weeping form of this species, *F. e.* 'Pendula' develops a low, spreading mass of growths, while *F. e.* 'Pendula Wentworthii' will retain an upright leader with pendulous branches. Should an attempt be made to reduce this leader, other upright growths may form on the horizontal branches. *F. e.* 'Myrtifolia' forms an attractive dwarf tree with stunted branching and clusters of small epicormic shoots, which should be left. Occasionally, strong growths with larger leaves are produced, and these should be cut out at an early stage.

Both *F. americana* and *F. pennsylvanica* retain their leaders well, and will form shapely trees with branches sweeping down often to form a thick canopy at ground level. This should be encouraged. One or two of the forms of the latter are very strong in growth, with a dense, almost mop-head of growth.

This means that there is plenty of dead wood to cut out from beneath as it dies back through lack of light.

F. ornus and the other species which are in this group have a closer, sturdy growth which should on no account be thinned. A clear trunk of 0.9 to 1.2 m. (3 to 4 ft.) is desirable and eventually the branches will reach the ground. *F. platypoda* is a small tree with rigid branching, which has little trouble from wind damage.

Generally speaking, the *Fraxinus* species display a considerable degree of hardiness, but some dieback sometimes occurs among species that have been introduced from warmer climates. Not only do these tend to develop into smaller trees, but owing to the frosting of the young growths which sometimes occurs in the spring, it is difficult to form shapely specimens. Examples of the species that may suffer in this way are *F. dipetala*, from California, *F. mandshurica* from Northeast Asia, and *F. angustifolia* subsp. *syriaca*, from West and Central Asia.

F. angustifolia 'Raywood' has a graceful, upright habit and is worth experimenting with for roadside planting.

FREMONTODENDRON

F. californicum. This subject needs little or no regular pruning. Nursery stock should be grown in pots and trained up to a single leader. This should be staked, a precaution which is also necessary after planting if it is grown as a bush in the shelter of a wall. The alternative method is to train the main stem and branches hard against a wire support system. Wall culture is necessary and the shrub must have full sun.

FUCHSIA

This group of attractive shrubs or small trees cannot be considered hardy except in the mildest regions of England. However, the so-termed Hardy Fuchsias may be grown out-of-doors permanently in the more sheltered parts of the garden especially in the southern part of England. Normally they are killed down to ground level each year, but the old stem should be left intact until the spring and when the new growths appear the cut may be made down to

living wood. As a protection, a loose layer of fleece, bracken or a 150 mm. (6 in.) layer of ashes may be placed round the bases of the stems for the winter, this being raked away as growth starts in the spring. Among the hardier forms are the *F. magellanica* cultivars, the old wood being retained in a normal winter, thus building up a framework.

When the main branches do survive to build up year by year, the laterals are pruned back to the lower buds in the spring, just as they are breaking out. Vigour is taken into account, the weaker growths being cut back harder than the stronger ones. Very old overgrown bushes may be pruned back hard to encourage growths from the base.

The hardy forms are commonly grown as hedge plants in the South West of England and Ireland. This feature is pruned hard back to a formal outline in the spring just as growth is about to commence. The Fuchsias flower on the current season's wood as it extends. Plenty of good growth should therefore be encouraged.

GARRYA

G. elliptica is almost hardy and in the south and west of England it may be grown in the open as a bush,

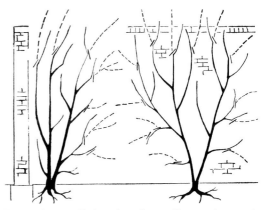

Fig. 32. *Garrya elliptica* when given wall protection may be grown as a free-standing shrub, perhaps with one or two ties on the main branches to keep it in closer to the wall if this becomes necessary. No pruning is necessary unless it is desired to restrict size. The broken lines indicate how this should be carried out after flowering.

provided that a sheltered site is chosen. Normally, however, the protection of a wall gives better results. Although this shrub responds to pruning after flowering, even when cut back quite hard to a branch system which is trained close to the wall surface, the best results are from a free-growing bush which has been trained initially to one or two leaders, see Fig. 32. It may, however, become necessary to restrict the spread and size of the subject by pruning, and this should be carried out after the catkins fade and before the new growth commences. The cuts should be taken to a suitable growth well inside the general outline of the foliage and shoot system, so that they are hidden and an informal effect is retained. With an overgrown bush this pruning should be spread over a three to five year period, though an alternative in this latter case is to cut hard back in the spring to the main framework, when it will throw new growths quite freely.

G. ×thuretii is a vigorous hybrid and will form quite a large bush to 5 m. (17 ft.) out in the open in the south. Should it be damaged by frost it will throw new, strong growths very readily in the spring. G. laurifolia subsp. macrophylla is normally only suitable for the warmest parts of the country. It may be trained up to a single leader.

GAULTHERIA

Normally these require very little, if any, pruning. The dead or weak growths would naturally be cut out of the choice species, such as G. hookeri, but this would be difficult and indeed unnecessary with G. shallon, as it generally grows really strongly, and is difficult to curb on a definite line without making it apparent by producing a dense, hedge-like surface. An overall clipping with a pair of shears will produce a close formal line of growth, and it is better to cut or even dig out whole pieces in the spring as the new growth is getting under way. Also, there should be no hesitation in cutting out individual pieces with the secateurs during the summer months if this is required.

A number of Gaultherias produce a dense habit, but G. procumbens is one of the creeping species and forms a mat which is only 50 to 100 mm. (2 to 4 in.)

high. Gaultherias with this type of growth do not need pruning, but mice will sometimes congregate and live in large numbers beneath the close mat during the winter. For food they will nibble away at the bases of the short stems, but the only sign that this has happened, apart from observations made on an occasional inspection, is in the spring when large patches gradually wither and die revealing the extent of the damage. By using a long bamboo cane in a sweeping action to brush over the tops of the growths, any loosened and detached pieces are disturbed and an attack can be detected. In the early stages the mice can of course be dealt with, while the nibbled growths, if taken early enough, can be rooted as cuttings.

The habits of growth of G. mucronata and forms are all very similar. Many spread by means of suckers and form a dense thicket. Normally, very little pruning is necessary unless it be to prevent the overgrowing of neighbouring shrubs. They will often grow in close association with G. shallon to form a pleasing cover. It will also grow well with Erica carnea 'Springwood White'.

Growths which are dying back should be cut off at ground level in the spring. When it becomes necessary to restrict the size of a clump, perhaps along one edge, the growths should be cut off at ground level, carefully removing any roots or suckers, but ensuring that a natural form and habit is retained and not a straight, clipped edge.

G. ×wisleyensis. This shrub is very bushy and spreads extensively with arching growths and by means of suckers. On the right soils and in suitable situations it is best when allowed to grow and romp in the wilder parts of the garden. However, by careful pruning in the spring, size may be restricted and it is not difficult to decide on the positioning of the cuts, as there are plenty of growths within the bush. Even the low, horizontal growths have upright shoots to which the cuts can be made.

Normally there is little pruning required on a mature bush which has plenty of room for development. The upper branches occasionally develop dead ends and an untidy appearance that needs correction. Also fallen leaves from nearby trees may collect in the branch system in such numbers that they are not even dislodged during gales. The movement of the stiff branch system with a stout stick causes them to fall to the ground where they will act as a mulch and thus be of benefit.

A very old, straggly bush may be pruned hard back in the spring to encourage the production of new wood from the base.

GENISTA

Genistas are sun-lovers and the most typical growth is obtained in a sunny position. *G. aetnensis* becomes quite a large shrub, or even a small tree up to 6 m. (20 ft.) in height. The ultimate height it reaches depends to some extent upon the form and training in the nursery. A low branching, either as a result of a natural break or by stopping, leads to a bushy growth. A leader of a few feet, perhaps by careful staking, produces a standard-like effect. Little or no pruning is required as the shrub matures.

G. monspessulana becomes straggly and overgrown, but annual pruning is not needed for when a plant becomes unsightly it is better to replace it. Seedlings are often found in the vicinity of a bush and these will transplant readily. It is not fully hardy.

G. cinerea and *G. tenera* 'Golden Shower' are similar to each other in habit and appearance. In the nursery and even in the early stages after planting, pruning may be necessary in order to encourage a bushy habit. Once the shrub is growing away, pruning consists of shortening the growths over the whole bush after flowering. They should be taken back to the young growths that develop at the base and along the length of the previous year's wood, see Fig. 33.

Fig. 33. The basal portion of a growth of *Genista cinerea* that has just finished flowering. The pruning cut may be made at (a). Care must be taken to avoid over-pruning.

This removes most of the developing seed pods and thus improves growth and vigour. The cuts should not be made beyond the previous year's wood, as the older parts do not break readily. Very old plants that have become unsightly and do not respond to pruning should be taken out and a fresh start made with young ones.

G. hispanica forms low and compact hummocks, but as they become older, dead patches often appear which completely ruin the appearance. This often happens after a severe winter. Any that are in this condition may be taken out for replacement, but another method is to cut away the dead wood, pegging the living portions down as close to the ground as possible. This may be followed by a dressing of leaf mould over the bare stems to encourage rooting. Regeneration and coverage is often speedily obtained in this way. A light clipping immediately after flowering helps to keep a compact and healthy growth. *G. lydia* has a distinctive habit which could quite easily be spoilt by pruning; in fact, this is true of many of the remaining species such as *G. horrida* and *G. sagittalis*.

GINKGO

G. biloba, the Maidenhair Tree, is quite distinctive by reason of its sparse branching and the short spur-like growths on the older portions, in addition to the long shoots which extend from year to year on the extremities of healthy branch systems. There is, however, considerable variation in habit, for some are much more upright with semi-erect branchlets and an absence of heavy branching; they are almost fastigiate in habit and there is a recognised form, *G. b.* 'Fastigiata', which is columnar with semi-erect branches. Others have a more natural form of branching, the main limbs coming away at right angles, the sub-branches from these being semi-pendulous. In a well-shaped specimen with a strong central lead the main branches are often formed when the tree has reached a considerable height and is many years old.

Essentially, this tree should have a good, well-defined leader running up through the centre. Fortunately, it readily responds to training and naturally forms a good leader in the nursery. The nurseryman only needs to ensure that growth is good and that rival leaders, if they do form, are reduced to one. This policy should be continued after the final planting. This is a very long-lived tree, but a weakness caused by the formation of rival leaders will inevitably tend to shorten its life as the wood becomes older and the strain greater.

GLEDITSIA

G. triacanthos is the most outstanding tree in this genus. It will retain a good leader and will thus form a long, straight trunk. As the tree develops, this may be cleared of growths to a height of 3.0 to 4.6 m. (10 to 15 ft.). The trunk is also quite interesting, as short but stout spines develop in clusters. These should be left, as they add character to the tree. This species is also grown in several other interesting forms. *G. t.* f. *inermis* is thornless but can be trained and grown in the same manner as the type. This is also true of 'Sunburst', although it is not such a vigorous grower as the type. It is trained with a 1.5 to 1.8 m. (5 to 6 ft.) clear stem in the nursery. 'Elegantissima' is shrub-like and no definite leader or trunk can be formed. It seldom has thorns and has upright branching. *G. t.* 'Nana' can be trained to a definite leader when young, but the trunk is short and it forms a dense narrow crown.

A good straight leader and a well-formed tree may be trained from the following species: *G. caspica*, *G. delavayi*, *G. japonica*, *G. macracantha* and *G. sinensis*, although the results are variable according to health and well-being. *G.* ×*texana* often forms a small flat-topped, spineless branched tree in England.

Gleditsias should, if necessary, be pruned in the late summer for bleeding is a danger with spring pruning.

GLYPTOSTROBUS

G. pensilis is the only species in this genus. It is a deciduous conifer related to *Taxodium* and will not grow in regions with hard winters. With some protection it will make, albeit very slowly, a small tree. It

should be planted as a small single-stemmed feathered tree. No pruning should be needed.

GORDONIA

G. axillaris is a tender evergreen tree or large shrub from China and Taiwan that can only be grown in the mildest localities. Often a specimen is restricted to one main stem, but later other upright growths may develop from the base. These should be allowed to grow as they increase the strength and vigour of the bush. Very little regular pruning is needed, but occasionally weak and untidy growths are better cut out to strong and well placed branches. Most of the pruning is needed on sheltering plants if they tend to overgrow and deprive the specimen of light, see Fig. 26. This should be carried out carefully in order to retain a natural and informal surface.

GREVILLEA

This genus is represented in England by a few shrubs that normally need the protection of a wall if they are to succeed. They are planted close to the foot of the wall for maximum protection, but should not be trained in any way. One essential is to keep growth as compact as possible by allowing full sunlight. If the subject is overgrown or shaded in any way by stronger neighbours, growth will be drawn towards the light and away from the warmth of the wall. In this case it is more likely to be caught by severe weather. Careful pruning may also be carried out in the spring, to cut off straggly growth, thus keeping the bush compact. Also, if growths have been damaged by a severe winter they may be cut back to suitable breaking shoots in the spring.

GRINDELIA

G. chiloensis. It is only in the more favoured places that this survives the winters sufficiently to become a definite shrub, retaining wood to a height of 0.6 to 0.9 m. (2 to 3 ft.). More often the growths are killed to the woody stems at the base. They should be pruned by cutting out the dead growth in the spring, when it can be seen just how far down the bush the winter's damage has extended.

GRISELINIA

G. littoralis forms a rounded, evergreen bush 2.4 to 3.0 m. (8 to 10 ft.) high, although it will grow higher in sheltered and favourable conditions. In the nursery it will branch naturally from the base. As it develops, laterals are freely produced which in turn become very thick with foliage and additional growth.

This characteristic of breaking freely and strongly, even from short growths makes it an ideal shrub for use as a windbreak along the milder coastlines. It may also be used as a hedge plant in the milder areas. For this latter purpose, an even bushier habit may be encouraged in the initial years by pruning. This subject grows quickly, and density, with increased rigidity, is encouraged by its habit of throwing up strong shoots through the centre, from the base to the top of the hedge, even during one season.

Although it will respond to 'clipper pruning', it is better with an informal surface, the secateurs being used to cut off individual shoots. This should be carried out in the early summer.

This subject retains a considerable amount of foliage, even in the centre of the bush. The variegated form has a similar growth.

G. racemosa is a small, suckering shrub to 1 m. (3 ft.) and requires no pruning.

GYMNOCLADUS

G. dioica forms a large, coarsely branched tree. Even the twig growth is thick and sparse. From the nursery stage a leader should be run up for as long as possible. Eventually, as the head forms, the lower branches can be removed cleanly, thus encouraging a clear trunk of 1.8 to 2.4 m. (6 to 8 ft.). Often the outer branches on a mature tree have a semi-pendulous habit and the attractive foliage is thereby brought down to eye level. In addition to the summer and autumn display of foliage, the effect of the midribs, which remain attached long after the leaflets have fallen, is both pleasing and interesting.

G. dioica 'Variegata' has a distinctive, upright habit, forming a dense head, while, in addition to the variegated foliage, the attached midribs in the winter are quite attractive. Both this and the type species love the sun and a warm sunny spot should be selected where they are isolated from other trees.

To reduce danger of bleeding, any major pruning operation should be carried out in midsummer and never in the late winter or early spring.

HALESIA

The most common species is *H. carolina*, the Snowdrop Tree. It can be trained in the nursery to form a short trunk, but a more natural habit is a free branching from the base. With the latter habit of growth a low, spreading bush is formed and the lower branches assume a horizontal habit. This free spread, with growth down to ground level is delightful, and with a clear foreground, it may be allowed to develop naturally without pruning. If pruning is needed to restrict growth it should be carried out after flowering. It is natural for the branches to be thickly placed and they should not be thinned.

H. monticola has a tree-like habit and may be trained to form a definite leader. Eventually a mature specimen may have a clear stem of 0.9 to 1.2 m. (3 to 4 ft.), but with long trailing branches the growths reach down to ground level. They hang down in an untidy manner, but should not be thinned. *H. diptera* is trained as a shrub from the nursery stage.

×HALIMIOCISTUS

This small group of bigeneric hybrids, in common with *Cistus*, seldom responds well to pruning. Should a straggly and woody growth develop, it is better to re-propagate and then to plant up with young stock. However, dead wood and the old flower heads may be cut off in the spring.

HALIMIUM

This small genus shows considerable variation in habit, but generally the species do not respond well to pruning. This should therefore be confined to the removal of dead growth in the spring. *H. lasianthum* and the cultivar 'Concolor' spreads extensively without gaining more than a foot or so in height. It should be planted 0.6 m. (2 ft.) from the edge of a border, so that there is good space for natural development. It is possible to carefully prune the leading growths if it is necessary to restrict size in any way. This should be carried out in the spring as growth is beginning, making the cuts well into the shrub so that they are hidden and an informal effect is retained. *H. lasianthum* subsp. *alyssoides* is also spreading. Often, when either of these two plants are grown near to and develop against larger shrubs, the long prostrate growths will climb through the branches, gaining a height of 0.8 to 0.9 m. (2.5 to 3 ft.) and flowering profusely when they reach the light. *H. halimifolium* will gain height in this way too, but may also be grown against a wall. As a contrast, *H. umbellatum* forms a fairly compact bush with finer foliage.

HALIMODENDRON

H. halodendron. This shrub has a spreading habit with spiny branches. It should be allowed to develop naturally, and usually it branches freely at ground level, having this free branching habit as a seedling. Normally no pruning is required.

This plant, however, thrives better when grafted upon seedling stocks of *Caragana arborescens* as the root system is not well adapted to conditions in the British Isles.

HAMAMELIS

Normally, the members of this genus require very little pruning. One of the most desirable features, that of winter flowering, is displayed to the best effect by free and natural growth. Some pruning may be required at the training stage in the nursery, especially with *H. japonica* 'Arborea'. Trained to a single leader for 0.9 m. (3 ft.) or more, it will assume the proportions of a small tree, although it should be recognised that the habit of this form is naturally rather ungainly, with the branches assuming a horizontal habit.

H. virginiana is also sufficiently strong-growing to form a small tree; the main branches are ascending and it has an attractive habit. This latter species may also be grown as a bush. Most of the remaining species, cultivars and forms also have quite distinctive habits of growth that must be allowed for in training. It is definitely a mistake to thin branches or to prune with the intention of reducing each to a uniform shape. Should any pruning be necessary in order to reduce size, for example, if a specimen is too close to a path, this should be carried out after flowering and before growth commences. It should be done very carefully with the cuts being made annually just above two growth buds, missing out the odd year if little growth has been made by the plant, see Fig. 18.

When grown in even slight shade the bushes become very straggly, and the habit and flowering are much better in full sun. Mature specimens have a considerable spread and in a group planting may need to be 5.5 to 6.0 m. (18 to 20 ft.) apart.

The practice of grafting *Hamamelis* cultivars onto *H. virginiana* stock is widespread, and a watch must be kept for suckers that may spring from the base. They are best dealt with as they appear, for if they are left until the end of the growing season they are often several feet in length, and may spoil the inner growths of the bush itself. Plants suffering from stress, lack of feed, light and moisture usually produce more suckers, whereas healthy plants, over the age of four to five years rarely produce suckers. One means of distinguishing the suckers is that the leaves remain attached to these strong shoots long after the bush as a whole is completely defoliated. Shrubs that are on their own roots are usually, of course, free from this trouble, although *H. vernalis* often has a natural habit of suckering. Branches that are at eye level are very much appreciated as the flower display can then be admired from close quarters.

HEBE (VERONICA)

One of the most important characteristics of this genus as far as pruning is concerned, is the ability to break freely from the old wood when cut back, either by frost or by hand. This is fortunate, for many of the large-leaved species such as *H. speciosa* are tender, and are often cut back severely, almost to ground level, in a hard winter. Should a specimen be badly frosted in this way it is better left with its top, withered and scorched though it may well be, until the spring, for it will afford some protection during the latter part of the winter. Also, when the new growths break out it will be apparent just where the pruning cuts should be made. It is important to cut back to the strongest of these, although it may be apparent when growth is under way a few weeks later that the final cut should be lower, in order to leave a neater bush. There should be no hesitation in doing this, but the earlier in the season it is done the better, for with more light and air there will be a better chance for the growths which remain to ripen.

Form and habit of growth vary considerably, but many species such as *H. odora* are naturally compact and therefore seldom need pruning to correct a straggly habit. Occasionally however, even such species as *H. brachysiphon* benefit from hard pruning in the late spring in order to correct an untidy habit, or if the bush has been broken down by snow. *H. dieffenbachii* is one of the more untidy growers and restrictive pruning may be necessary, in which case it should be carried out in the late spring. However, as with all plants in an informal setting, it is important to retain the natural habit of growth as far as possible.

It is sometimes necessary to prune back a specimen in the neighbourhood of a path, but this needs to be very carefully done as otherwise an abrupt and ugly edge is produced. Often, it is better to cut the entire shrub hard back and make a fresh start, or even to take it up and plant a more suitable species. A careful watch must be kept on the variegated forms such as *H.* ×*franciscana* 'Variegata'. Any growths showing reversion to the pure green type plant should be cut out as soon as they appear.

H. macrantha has a poor, straggly habit, but this may be improved by cutting back after flowering.

Many Hebe species and varieties set heavy crops of fruits, and the vast numbers of developing capsules place a considerable strain on these shrubs, particularly during periods of drought. Plants that are suffering in this way will benefit from the removal of the withered heads, and they will look neater during the winter months if this is done, though it is only possible on a small scale. *H. hulkeana* certainly benefits from their removal, for otherwise it may be short-lived. Sometimes this and many of the other species die back for an unaccountable reason, often progressively, one shoot after another. Little can usually be done to correct this, apart from removing the offending growths, but a bush may be cut about so badly that it is better to propagate from healthy shoot tips and remove the old one completely.

HEDERA

H. helix. The natural habit of this subject is well known, the creeping and climbing growths producing bushy branches when the plant ultimately passes into the mature stage. This sequence of growth allows the developing plant to reach the light before the branches that produce the flowers and fruits are formed.

There is a great need for caution when the health and safety of an Ivy clad tree is considered. Such a tree may be attractive, but it must be safe. There is little danger of strangulation, for the habit of growth is for the main Ivy stems to develop along the length of the trunk and scaffold-branch system. The extra weight, as the Ivy branches freely, may, however, strain a weak framework causing a loss of one or more of the main limbs. This danger may be overcome by preventing an extension of the growths into the upper

Fig. 34. The short growths which are produced by Ivy on a wall when it is clipped hard annually.

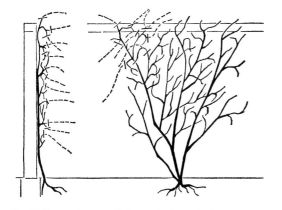

Fig. 35. Ivy against a wall, but only the main branches are shown. The broken lines are the young growths which would be removed by clipping hard back in late spring to early summer, after the nesting period for birds.

branch systems, and once the Ivy has developed beyond the creeping juvenile stage this is not difficult. However, by far the greatest danger is that the matted growths and stems may hide a cavity that will ultimately affect the health and well-being of the tree, making it unsafe. This should give the person responsible great cause for concern, and, if the Ivy is to be retained, the tree must be inspected very carefully—a difficult task!

Ivy is often found on the walls of buildings, etc. where it will, if there is room, reach considerable heights. Actually, it does no harm to such structures until the mature stage is reached. Then the branches, as they become heavier, may strain and loosen the brick or stone as they sway in the wind.

Annual clipping overcomes this trouble, for the subject is kept close to the wall and never in fact has a chance to produce mature growths, see Fig. 34. This should be carried out during late spring to early summer, for this allows time for the new growths to develop and ripen before the winter sets in. If it is left until later the young growths may be damaged by the winter frosts. The clipping should be taken as close to the wall surface as possible, despite the fact that for two or three weeks it will look rather bare, see Fig. 35. Ivy which is grown over fencing, pillars or similar

structures should be treated in the same way, if a topiary-like effect is desired.

'Arborescens' is the tree form of the Common Ivy, obtained by propagating from cuttings of mature growths. Pruning is not required, but some form of staking may be advisable from an early age. This seems to be a difficult subject to nurse back once it has slipped into a poor, unhealthy condition. The remainder of the species can be treated in much the same way as *H. helix*.

HEDYSARUM

H. multijugum has a bushy habit, but it is sparsely branched, and after a few years it becomes rather unsightly, with bare, woody stems. The pruning back of long branches to suitable growth in the spring may help to correct this. Long branches may also be pegged down in the spring just as the buds are breaking, and this will produce new, young plants.

HEIMIA

H. salicifolia. This light and graceful bush normally needs the protection of a sunny wall, where it should be planted about 0.5 m. (1.5 ft.) from the base. It should be allowed to break freely when young, both with main branches and smaller furnishing growths. The flowers are produced along the lengths of the current season's wood in the late summer. Pruning consists of cutting out one or two lengths of the older wood, as this becomes necessary, in the spring just before the new growth commences. If pruning is confined to merely snipping over the head of the bush, a close broom-like effect is produced which completely spoils the graceful habit of the shrub.

HELIANTHEMUM

These respond well to pruning after they have finished flowering, which is usually in midsummer. Growths which are straggly and make the plant look untidy may then be cut back, and they will even break freely from the old wood. Often too, older growths that need removing are found beneath the clump.

These should be cut off carefully, and it may be necessary to lift the mat of growth to do this.

HELICHRYSUM

These shrubs generally need the shelter of a wall and are suitable for the smaller border. Often, they survive the winter, but in a very ragged condition. However, even without the winter's damage they may become woody with age. They will often respond to hard pruning in the spring as growth is about to commence, but reaction is variable and a very old plant in poor condition may not respond favourably. In the same way, frost-damaged wood will not break out, and this may in part explain some of the failures that have been experienced. Cutting back need not, in all cases, be carried back to the actual wood, thus gaining the advantage that the younger tissue breaks out more readily.

HELWINGIA

H. japonica is the species normally found growing in gardens and arboreta. It has little horticultural merit and is grown for the botanical interest of its unusual flowers, which are found in the leaf axils. It makes a small deciduous suckering shrub of stems to 1 m. (3 ft.) and requires no special pruning apart from the occasional thinning of dead or weak stems.

HEMIPTELEA

H. davidii forms a small tree, related to *Zelkova*, with twiggy and thorny branching. It is best to encourage a clear trunk to 1.8 m. (6 ft.) and a leader for as long as possible before forming a head. No regular pruning is desirable beyond that required for corrective training.

HEPTACODIUM

H. miconioides, the sole member of a monotypic genus from China, makes a very large, upright deciduous shrub. It produces fragrant flowers in late summer, into autumn at the ends of the current year's growth.

No pruning is necessary to encourage flowering, however this is a vigorous grower and may need some pruning to restrict its growth. This should be carried out in early spring, just as the new season's growth is about to be produced. One of the features of this plant is the attractive peeling bark on the main trunks that can be exposed to view by removing some of the lower branches.

HETEROMELES

H. salicifolia makes a large multi-stemmed evergreen shrub, or small tree on a single stem. Any pruning, which will be to restrict the size of this plant, should be carried out in late winter or early spring. Very little pruning should be necessary; however, it will tolerate hard pruning to a framework for rejuvenation when out of control. *H. salicifolia* also makes an interesting hedge plant and can be encouraged to thicken up by pinching out the growing tips.

HIBISCUS

H. syriacus is recognised as a good late-flowering shrub and is available in several cultivars. These vary in habit and form but generally they are upright, often branching low from near ground level. Flowering is on the current season's wood. For good growth they must have a well-drained soil, while a sunny position is necessary for healthy wood which will flower well and stand the winter in sound condition. In particular, this species is prone to infection by various forms of dieback including Coral Spot (*Nectria cinnabarina*).

Pruning consists first of cutting out dead or diseased wood during the spring or summer, but when there is large scale dying back it is often better to replace the plant completely. If it is thought that the dieback is due to an unsuitable site or soil, it is advisable to select a better one for the replacement. Little other pruning is required, although overgrown specimens may be thinned and cut back quite hard, choosing the spring for this operation. Extra light reaching the bush as a result of nearby thinning will have the same effect, for vigorous breaks often appear from very old wood.

In the nursery, a low bush should be encouraged by hard pruning in the spring.

Often, the anchorage or rooting of these plants is not particularly strong and in exposed positions they may rock considerably creating an air space to develop around the root collar, which will lead to the bark rotting and eventual failure of the shrub.

HIPPOCREPIS

H. emerus. This shrub has a very pleasing habit, the slender and rather crowded branchlets springing from a woody framework. Many of these are upright with the tips bent over and almost pendulous. The regular pruning policy should consist of cutting out any old and worn growths during the winter. Specimens which have become too large and overgrown may be cut down close to ground level, when they will break out quite readily. This should be carried out in the late winter.

HIPPOPHAE

These deciduous trees or shrubs are dioecious, but there is very little difference in the manner and habit of growth between the two sexes. They are spiny, especially when young.

H. rhamnoides, the Sea Buckthorn, is a native and is often found growing in coastal areas, where it may be partially buried by drifting sands yet continue to survive. It is also grown inland and, under favourable conditions, by reason of a suckerous habit of growth, it will often form large clumps. Under these conditions very little if any pruning is required.

It may also be nursery-trained to form a small tree with a 1.2 to 1.8 m. (4 to 6 ft.) length of clear stem. It is difficult, however, to retain a leader and to form a shapely head, in fact, it would be against the character of this subject to do so. Instead, the branches are curiously twisted, while the head is composed of stiff, semi-pendulous twig growths. Unfortunately when grown as a tree, it becomes susceptible to strong winds and often the root plate blows out of the ground. It can soon regenerate into a new plant from suckers developing from old roots left in the ground. It is also difficult to distinguish dead from living wood during the winter and the cutting out of this is better left until the summer.

H. salicifolia will form a medium-sized tree. It should be nursery-trained to form a clear stem of 1.2 to 1.8 m. (4 to 6 ft.). As the tree matures the bark is attractive, being deeply furrowed. The trunk should be kept clear, but any epicormic growths may be allowed to remain on the branches as they give character to the tree. The branch system is often quaintly twisted and this very habit may lead to weakness in later years, when some form of bracing may become necessary. The stiff outer branches have a semi-pendulous habit.

HOHERIA

H. glabrata and *H. lyallii* are the hardiest. However, they are not completely so and may be killed right down to ground level during a severe winter, though, provided that there is living tissue at the base, strong regeneration and growth can be expected.

Both species have an upright habit, branching from ground level and occasionally vigorous growths are thrown from these low branches or from the base. After cutting out the surplus, the remainder should be left to add to the branch system, or to be used as replacements for the older branches when these are cut out. There should be no hesitation in cutting out a proportion of the older and weaker wood in the spring if this is considered necessary. Both species are subject to Coral Spot (*Nectria cinnabarina*), and this is more likely in a damp and shady position.

The evergreen species *H. populnea* and *H. sexstylosa* are definitely tender and in all but the mildest districts they should be grown as bushes in the shelter of a wall. Both species should be left to branch freely from the base. If necessary they may be carefully pruned to restrict their size, making the cuts at a suitable point inside the bush in order to retain an informal surface. This should be carried out in the spring. *H. sexstylosa* has a shiny sap immediately under the bark, which leads to the bark stripping and tearing, leaving an untidy cut when secateurs are used. To overcome this, finish off the cut with a razor-sharp knife and extra care.

HOLBOELLIA

These are evergreen, twining shrubs. They will freely produce a large number of slender stems, and are so vigorous that if a suitable means of support were available they will reach a height of 6 to 9 m. (20 to 30 ft.).

H. latifolia is quite a tender species and thus needs a sheltered position such as a sunny wall. The main support should be a horizontal wiring system, some of the growths growing between the strands and the wall. Others may be laid on the wires and tied in position. Vertical wires are also useful, particularly for the young plant as it grows to cover the available space. When the full height is reached, the pendulous growths provide an attractive furnishing. At this stage it has a considerable spread outwards from the wall. Some thinning of the weaker growths may be carried out in the spring and this helps to keep the shrub within suitable proportions. Dead wood may also be cut out at this time or later during the summer, when another thinning of the long growths may be necessary.

H. coriacea is hardier and may be used to climb small trees or a system of tripod stakes in the border.

A neglected specimen is often full of dead wood in the centre. This may be cleaned out by pulling away the brittle growths by hand.

HOLODISCUS

The best known and most attractive species is *H. discolor*. The growth is spreading and arching, and the flowers in the form of heavy panicles are produced on leafy shoots that spring from the previous year's wood. Young canes are produced from the base of the plant each year and thus the older stems may be cut out annually after flowering. This has the effect of maintaining the flowering display year by year and allows the strong growths to arch over freely to produce the best effect. Sufficient older wood must be left on the bush to maintain furnishing and a good framework and the best of the young

growths from the base are used to replace this framework as necessary. Usually, just part of the branch system is cut back to suitable young growths, leaving an adequate furnishing. An unusual, but very suitable, setting for this subject is a north-facing wall, where with the minimum of support it will reach a height of 3.7 to 4.5 m. (12 to 15 ft.). *H. dumosus* is a dense, twiggy grower. The old canes may be thinned at the base after flowering. This will result in a neater plant, and the young canes can develop freely and produce an improved flower display.

HOVENIA

H. dulcis, the Japanese Rasin Tree, forms a large shrub or small tree, although it is more often the former as it is not fully hardy in most parts of England. As a result, unripened and even woody growth is killed back during the winter. The wood is also very subject to Coral Spot (*Nectria cinnabarina*). Often, therefore, there is a considerable amount of dead wood to cut out in the spring. In a sheltered and suitable position, a leader with a 0.9 to 1.2 m. (3 to 4 ft.) clear length of stem may be developed.

HYDRANGEA

One characteristic which is common to this genus, is that the species and varieties grow freely from the base, thus allowing old and worn branches to be removed, even from those which are not normally pruned regularly. For pruning and management purposes, the genus may be divided into four groups based on their habits of growth and flowering.

Group 1. Those which flower terminally on the current season's wood

H. paniculata 'Grandiflora' may be taken as an example. Growths that extend during the season from the dormant bud stage produce large heads of blossom in the late summer. Left to develop year after year without any pruning, the many growths which result will produce only small heads of flower. The hard pruning which is advised each spring, usually in

February before growth commences, is in effect a
form of disbudding, for the cut is made just above the
lowest pair or two pairs of buds. Thus only two or
four buds can grow from each position. An interesting
point is that this plant does exercise some control
over its flowering, for often only one bud of each pair
grows out strongly to flower. Very seldom do four
growths develop completely unless the plants are very
vigorous. Eventually this treatment, extended over the
years, will result in the buildup of a short, stout
branch system a few inches or more in height. In an
exposed position, lower branching should be encouraged on the plants on the outside of a clump, as these
will protect the taller ones which may otherwise be
broken. It is emphasized that growth and vigour must
be maintained by feeding and mulching as necessary,
usually on a planned annual basis.

The other species that responds to annual pruning
is *H. arborescens* and its varieties, including *H. a.*
subsp. *discolor*.

Group 2. Those which are low growing, producing a clump-like growth freely with young growths from the base (Lace-cap and Hortensia, or Mophead, varieties)

H. macrophylla may be given as an example. It flowers
from the strong buds which have wintered, and which
were produced terminally on growths that sprang up
from the base during the previous season and on
growths that flowered then. If the plants are examined
after the flowering period, the large, fat buds are those
likely to produce an inflorescence the next year, the
smaller ones being confined to growth only. It should
be noted that a flowering growth might also form
flower buds for the following season.

As a result of this habit, which is at first sight rather
confusing, the following pruning method can be
adopted to assist flowering. It should first of all be
understood that, left unpruned, this group will often
flower well, especially in a well-drained, sunny position. Pruning carried out on careful lines will,
however, improve flowering. The old flower heads
should be left on during the winter for protection
against very severe weather. In the spring, before

Fig. 36. A climbing growth of *Hydrangea anomala* subsp.
petiolaris with the adventitious aerial roots on the undersurface of the stem which allow a secure attachment to a
suitable surface.

growths from the buds have advanced, the weaker and
older branches may be cut right down to ground level
and the old flower heads cut back to strong buds. The
removal of these old heads may mean cutting back
150 to 300 mm. (6 to 12 in.) of stem. The heads of the
Lace-cap varieties may be cut off as the flowers fade to
prevent wasted vigour in seed production.

In effect, the strong flower buds are retained,
crowded growth is avoided, the wood ripens better
and this assists flowering. The varieties vary considerably in their flowering capacity.

In addition to the large number of cultivars in the
Hortensia group that may be pruned by this method,
H. serrata also responds. Should any of this group be
cut back to ground level in the spring, the regenerated growths will be strong, but will not flower until
the following year. The cluster of growths may need
thinning at an early stage as they develop.

Group 3. Those which form large shrubs, retaining a more permanent framework

The following subjects are among those in this group:
H. heteromalla, *H. h.* 'Bretschneideri', *H. quercifolia*,
H. aspera and *H. a.* subsp. *sargentiana*. These and the
other species that are similar in growth need little
pruning. The weaker growths may be thinned or cut
out in the spring, or after flowering. A weak or poor

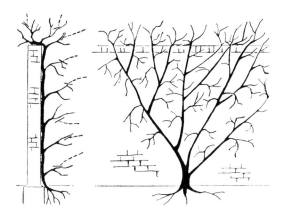

Fig. 37. An established plant of *Hydrangea anomala* subsp. *petiolari*s growing against a wall. It is well furnished with flowering laterals. The diagram on the left shows how these may be shortened if necessary, the pieces to be removed being indicated by broken lines. Notice the strong attachment to the top of the wall.

bush may be pruned hard and then strong renewal shoots will be thrown up from the base, provided the plant is encouraged by way of mulching and feeding.

Hydrangeas suffer during late spring frosts, and some adjustment by pruning may be necessary when new growths break out.

H. quercifolia is rather an untidy grower and staking is helpful in the spring before the new growth is made.

Group 4. Those species which climb by aerial rootlets

These rootlets are produced by the young extension shoots to enable them to cling to any support as they develop, see Fig. 36. Their hold is often retained for many years as they thicken, and the shoots that flower develop laterally from them. The three subjects commonly grown in this group are *H. serratifolia*, *H. anomala* and *H. a.* subsp. *petiolaris*, the latter being the most common.

When grown on a wall they will cling naturally without any support, but an even greater stability is gained if the plant is allowed to develop its extensive branching on the top of the wall. This it will do with great freedom.

Normally, pruning consists of carefully cutting back extension growths which are not required, as they are produced during the summer. In time, the flowering branch system has a considerable spread from the wall. These branches may be pruned back closer to the wall by carefully cutting back a proportion of the spurs to a suitable bud. This should be carried out in the spring, but in order that flowering is not affected, the work over the whole surface may be extended over a 3 to 4 year period, see Fig. 37. This group may also be planted against trees or other supports.

Another effective method of growing shrubs in this group is to plant them against a boulder or tree stump, so that a low mat of branches and growths are produced. No attention is needed, beyond cutting off any extension growths that are not required.

HYMENANTHERA. *See* Melicytus

HYPERICUM

A considerable variation exists among the shrubs in this genus, for while a number are hardy and retain their wood from year to year, others are semi-woody and are almost herbaceous in nature. Most or all of the wood above ground is lost, the growth being made up from ground level each year. The most common species is *H. calycinum*, which is seldom more than 0.3 m. (1 ft.) in height. Being stoloniferous it spreads extensively and is a good ground-cover plant. By cutting hard back in the early spring to within an inch or so of ground level, the areas colonized by this plant may be given a general clean-up before the new growth commences. This looks quite attractive when it develops a few weeks later. It is, however, a good plan to go round the clumps from time to time during the growing season in order to check the invasive spread of this subject over weaker plants. Large areas may be clipped over for the annual pruning, using the garden shears. Power hedging shears are useful for covering extensive areas.

H. ascyron is almost herbaceous and should be cut back each spring. *H. ×inodorum* 'Elstead' is now rarely grown due to rust problems but may also be treated in this way as a possible means of control. A form called 'Rheingold' is less susceptible to rust and is grown as cut stems for its bright orange-red fruits. These two plants may weaken over the years as the soil is exhausted, and the clumps extend, with the area becoming hard and weedy. Regular mulching will delay the need for replacement.

H. androsaemum need not be cut back as hard, but it will throw up shoots strongly if occasionally it is reduced to ground level in the early spring in order to clean the area generally.

The distinctly shrubby species, hybrids and varieties include *H. hookerianum*, *H. ×moserianum*, *H. kouytchense*, *H. beanii*, *H. forrestii* and *H. pseudo-henryi*. The extent to which the wood is killed back depends upon the severity of the winter, but in the spring there is no difficulty in recognising the living wood, for the new growth will then be breaking out quite readily. The method of pruning is to cut out the weaker and thinner growths, afterwards shortening the remainder to suitable buds or shoots. Often this will mean only the removal of the seed heads. To some extent this pruning regulates the size of the bushes.

The semi-evergreen hybrid *H.* 'Rowallane' is not really hardy and will be killed down to ground level in all but the mildest areas. Normally, therefore, it should be planted against a sunny wall, and the dead wood cut down to ground level. It grows up to flower each year in the late summer. Should wood survive the winter it may be left to build up height.

In the nursery, the woody members of this genus should be cut hard back as they break into growth in the second season, in order to encourage a bushy habit.

IDESIA

I. polycarpa has a distinctive habit. It forms a single, straight trunk and leader, the radiating branches being horizontal and in tiers. The branching is also rather sparse. Provided that it is given a good position with no overhanging branches or competition for light with neighbouring shrubs, it will form a shapely

tree and pruning is not necessary. Shading causes dieback on the affected branches.

Even in the nursery, the young trees quickly develop a good leader and a tier system of branching. This should be encouraged by careful handling, spacing and staking.

ILEX

I. aquifolium, the Holly, a native, is found almost throughout the whole of the British Isles. Both the type and the many garden varieties are commonly used as garden features.

This subject reacts well to close annual clipping and large specimens as well as hedges are sometimes found which have been kept to a formal outline. Unless, however, the surrounds are completely formal, a more natural growth is desirable. The pruning policy may thus be based upon the need to maintain a general outline, cutting back any growths that are obviously extending beyond the intended limits. This pruning should be carried out during mid to late summer, using a knife or pair of secateurs and making each cut well back to a suitable growth. Thus an informal and natural surface is obtained. The aim should be to have a thick coverage right to ground level, for not only does this appear more attractive but bare soil at the base is unkindly, and loose, thin twig growth may brush the soil in the wind, to produce erosion.

It should, however, be borne in mind that varieties behave differently; some, if left unattended, may even lose their character and grow vigorously into tree forms. Account must be taken of this, and if it is thought undesirable, the tendency should be corrected at a very early stage.

Sometimes, despite efforts to conceal them, cuts appear unsightly, but hollies, if they are healthy, respond to this treatment very vigorously and the pruning points are hidden after a few months.

Hollies are tolerant of shade, but the density of growth is often affected and it may be thin. Thus over-shadowing and faster growing neighbours may quickly spoil a surface, even to the extent of making it bare and ragged. Corrective pruning on the neighbouring tree or shrub may be thought desirable, rather than that the specimen itself should suffer. It should be remembered that starvation and drought might also cause defoliation, thin growth and dieback.

If cutting out of dead wood is attempted, it should be carried out over a period of 2 to 3 years, otherwise there is danger of living wood being cut too. To carry out this work thoroughly it is often necessary to crawl into and beneath the specimen, which can prove very dirty work.

The nursery training should be based upon the need to form and retain a leader, and this should continue after planting, for as long as possible in the life of the tree. A stunted specimen may not at first have a leader, but with good growth, suitable shoots appear and selection is possible at a later stage. Frost damage may also kill leading growths, especially if they are vigorous and sappy. A further selection of growths may therefore be necessary at a later stage, when new ones have developed.

Finally, it should be remembered that many forms produce naturally pendulous growths from their outer and lower branches as they reach maturity. The extensive lateral spread of large specimens that is sometimes met with, is often caused by seedlings that have germinated and grown beneath the lower branches. Unless the coverage is insufficient they may be removed.

I. aquifolium is often used as a formal hedge plant. Clipping should be undertaken in late summer, but an earlier start may be made if there is much to be done. The holly hedge, if overgrown, will respond to very hard cutting back, provided this is spread over 2 or 3 years. First one side should be cut back, then the other, and finally the top. Great care must be taken when reducing the height of a really old hedge with pendulous growths. Cutting back to a definite level may sever these, causing a collapse of several feet. This is the main reason for cutting back the sides first, for there is less weight and length of growth and the position is clearer.

Just as the varieties of *I. aquifolium* vary, so do the other species and full account of their natural habits should be taken when a training and pruning policy is decided upon. *I. ×altaclarensis* naturally forms a strong leader and an impressive pyramidal tree. *I. ciliospinosa*

forms a good leader, but may only reach up to 4.6 m. (15 ft.). *I. dipyrena* is similar but is much stronger. *I. cornuta* forms a dense, rounded bush. *I. pernyi* has a very wide and stiff branching habit. *I. verticillata*, a deciduous shrub, branches at ground level with rather fine, stiff growth. *I. crenata* is variable, some forms being tree-like, others quite dwarf and compact.

ILLICIUM

I. anisatum is the best known species. It is slow-growing, but often eventually forms a large shrub or small tree. *I. floridanum* is a shrub with very thick growth. Little pruning is required, but it may be necessary to restrict growth in certain positions. For example, these subjects should be grown within the shelter of a wall in countries with the mildest of winters, and the borders to such walls are often quite narrow and shrubs may thus need to be confined. The growths for this type of pruning should be carefully selected, making the cuts at suitable points behind others so that an informal surface is maintained. With *I. floridanum*, whole branches, if they are weak and old, may be cut out at ground level. Much depends upon the condition of the shrub, but usually new growths are freely produced from ground level.

I. simonsii naturally forms a narrow conical-shaped shrub and requires very little pruning, usually flowering at an early age.

INDIGOFERA

A few of the shrubby species are hardy enough to survive our winters in the open, but they may lose most or all of the wood which they make during the late spring and summer months. Usually they are killed right down to ground level, but *I. amblyantha*, for example, will retain a low, woody branch system and perhaps build up height from year to year. The flowers are produced during the late summer and early autumn on the current season's wood. Pruning is carried out in the spring, cutting away the previous year's growths down to near ground level. Any which have retained wood above ground may be pruned hard back to this, leaving just the basal portion of the younger wood. If wood is left in this way, it should be checked over later, as the buds become prominent, in order to cut out any that is dead.

ITEA

I. ilicifolia. This subject is grown as a wall shrub in regions with hard winters where it may be grown as a bush in a sheltered area. Where space is unrestricted both along the length of the wall and in front of it, this shrub will develop up to a height of 3.7 m. (12 ft.) or more and have a considerable spread. In this case very little pruning is required, but a number of ties should be made from the wall on to the main branches to prevent these from being damaged by strong side winds or heavy snow falls. Alternatively the growths from the previous year can be pruned back by one third to a half to keep the plant tidy and prevent it from falling away from the wall. In the colder areas or where space is restricted, some pruning and tying-in is necessary. The best displays of the long catkins are produced on the strong, young growths made during the previous year. Once the framework has been formed against the wall, the policy should be to cut out the older and weaker branches to allow the best of the new growths to be tied in. The young developing growths are often tinted an attractive bronze colour. This type of training is very similar to that advised for *Escallonia*, see Fig. 30. In the nursery the production of a plant with three or four low branches should be encouraged, so that these may be trained out against a wall when planted in their permanent position.

I. virginica will naturally form a bushy plant right down to the base, which allows some of the oldest and weakest wood to be cut out altogether, although this is only occasionally necessary. However, some of the oldest wood on the ends of the branches may with advantage be cut out annually after flowering which is completed in midsummer. The cut should be made back to promising young growths, the majority of which originate from just beneath the flowering shoots. The young growths produce the best foliage and autumn colour.

JAMESIA

J. americana. This is a rather stiff shrub with erect branches, and grown in the open it produces a close habit. It produces growths freely from the base in the nursery stage, and these may be used as replacements if necessary for any of the older branches that are cut out. However, this subject usually requires very little pruning and the crown should be kept as intact as possible, with foliage down to ground level.

JASMINUM

In general the hardy species are vigorous growers, and freely develop young growths that are produced as readily from the topmost branch as from near the base. A number are climbers that cling to a support by twining, but others have a loose scrambling or arching growth.

J. nudiflorum, the Winter Jasmine, is best grown as a wall specimen. In the early stages this should be trained fanwise to bamboo canes that are tied to the horizontal wire supports. Later, as growth increases, the leading shoots may be loosely tied to the wires. The laterals from these hang down and the pruning of these should be hard, directly after flowering in the early spring, taking the growths back to promising shoots at the base which break out at this time. This policy must be rigidly carried out on an annual basis otherwise the subject quickly gets out of hand, with the new growths falling over the old ones and killing them by depriving them of light. This results in a buildup of untidy masses of dead wood. At pruning time the ties should be carefully checked. A plant that is untidy and out of hand may be pruned severely and it is also a good plan to cut out a really old branch, using a young one as a replacement.

The pruning is the same when this plant is grown on a fence or pergola, but it may also be tied to a single stake 1.2 to 1.8 m. (4 to 6 ft.) high in the open border. Again, the framework branches should occasionally be replaced.

J. mesnyi has similar growth and pruning requirements, but is tender. *J. humile* has a stiffer habit than *J. nudiflorum*. It may be grown against a wall, and as it flowers on the previous year's wood, this may be cut out after the petals fall, tying in the new growths as they develop on the framework. It may also be grown in bush form as a border plant. Old and worn growths may be cut out after flowering.

J. officinale, the Common White Jasmine, is a vigorous climber which must have a strong support, especially if left to grow to heights of 6 m. (20 ft.) or more. It is difficult to train and to prevent it from becoming a tangled mass; indeed a more natural effect is gained when it is left to grow and develop on its own. This climber flowers from laterals produced from the previous year's wood, but also terminally from growths produced during the summer. If it is thought necessary, some of the oldest wood may be cut out during the summer as it passes out of flower, but great care must be taken to preserve the natural furnishing and foliage effect.

J. beesianum is similar, but is not such a strong grower as *J. officinale*. Both are climbers that twine in an anti-clockwise direction for support. *J. ×stephanense*, a hybrid between these two, also has this habit.

JOVELLANA

J. violacea is a half-hardy shrub that should normally be grown near the base of a sunny wall, and then only in regions with a milder climate. Even in such positions growths are usually killed back to ground level during the winter. A protective layer of fleece or loose bracken should be placed round the base of the plant before the winter sets in. Pruning is carried out annually in the spring, just as the new growths are breaking from the base. Should there be any old wood which is living it may be retained, but generally the shrub responds better to hard pruning. It also spreads by means of suckers.

JUGLANS

All the species in this genus have much in common. They are prone to damage from late spring frosts, but particularly so in the nursery stage, when careful pruning back and reselection of the leader is needed if this occurs. In the nursery and in their final positions,

a good growing soil is needed in order that strong growth may be produced and that, if the leading shoot is lost, a sufficient number of good leaders develop in its place to ensure a suitable selection. It is also important to transplant when young, for they move badly, growth is checked and a poor tree often results. Another important point is that walnuts bleed badly if cut in the spring, and they should, therefore, only be pruned in the late summer.

J. nigra, the Black Walnut, forms a graceful and shapely tree, retaining the central leader better than many others. This allows the lower branches to be removed as the tree develops, forming 4.6 to 6.0 m. (15 to 20 ft.) of clear trunk. Even from this height the lower branchlets sweep down to ground level to produce a fine effect.

J. regia, the Common Walnut, *J. ailanthifolia* and *J. cinerea* often form rival leaders after frost damage. It is important to correct this by selection and stopping at an early stage, as otherwise they quickly become heavy branches and the trees may later become unsafe.

J. californica and *J. microcarpa* are small trees which do not always grow well in the United Kingdom and the wood is prone to rot from cavities. They are best left to grow into small multi-stemmed trees. *J. mandschurica* is also a poor grower in many parts and much depends upon the early days in the nursery.

With this wide variation in growth rate and final form, it is important that the characteristics of the species or variety are taken into account during the training and shaping period.

JUNIPERUS

There are many varieties of dwarf junipers, but this section is concerned mainly with the tree and large shrub forms. *J. virginiana* is perhaps the most common of the tree species. In its best form, it has a central leader and is well furnished with branches, the lower of which may almost reach the ground. Many of the larger growers that will develop into trees have a similar habit and a central leader is desirable for a good proportion of the height. With both these and the shrubby species and forms it seems important to allow specimens sufficient light and space for healthy development, as otherwise the buildup of dead material among the branch systems makes them very unsightly. No regular pruning is normally needed.

KALMIA

These shrubs must have the correct growing conditions and pruning will not in any way compensate for a failure to provide them. It is true that some regeneration often takes place as a result of pruning hard a neglected specimen, but the response will only be maintained if conditions and culture are suitable.

K. angustifolia, which normally requires very little pruning, may become old and woody, and with the main stems bent over and exposed, the effect is rather unsightly. These may need to be cut right down to the base, leaving only small, thin and perhaps woody growths in this region. The strong growths that are needed will not develop from these, but from completely new shoots that will form at their bases or on the old wood. Often too, several years after establishment, strong growths are thrown well above the ordinary level of foliage. These should be left, as they are a sign of extra vigour and well-being.

K. latifolia forms a rather dense bush with a stout branch system, and no pruning is needed with a healthy specimen. The policy should be to preserve a furnished effect over the bush as a whole. A straggly plant is the result of poor growth and a weak branch system and the general appearance is unhappy. Unsuitable growing conditions are the most frequent cause of this, and if the shrub is in a poor state of health it may not respond well to cutting back. A large specimen which has overgrown its position is difficult to deal with, but careful pruning back over a period of 3 to 5 years will be effective, choosing a few growths at a time and cutting them at a suitable point beneath the canopy of foliage. The only other method is to prune hard to a suitable size, but the rate of regeneration is often slow, even on a healthy bush.

KALOPANAX

K. septemlobus. This beautiful Acer-like tree should be trained up to form a single leader, for not only is the bark more attractive on a large trunk, but the framework is also very much stronger. The main scaffold branches have an ascending habit and thus rival leaders will form very acute angles with the main stem. The tree as a whole is sparsely branched, with very short spur systems. The latter even form on the main branches and trunk. The trunk should be kept clear of these and of branches up to a height of 1.8 to 2.4 m. (6 to 8 ft.), but the remainder are better if left.

This tree is outstanding for its fine foliage and this is seen to full advantage with an open foreground. Grown in this setting, the lower branches sweep down to eye level, despite a rather stiff habit. It is often very slow to establish, but once happy will soon make a small- to medium-sized tree.

K. s. var. *maximowiczii* has a similar habit, but more deeply lobed leaves and should be treated in the same way.

KERRIA

K. japonica forms a close, bushy shrub, throwing up new canes from the base at ground level, which reach the height of the shrub at 1.2 to 1.8 m. (4 to 6 ft.) in one season. They flower in the following year. The shrub also spreads by means of suckerous growths and thus the whole area round it becomes a mass of intertwining stems and foliage. Often, the old, flowering shoots die back to strong, young growths that appear on the stem. This habit of flowering well on the young growths allows some of the old shoots to be cut out, either to a strong, young cane on the stem, or down to ground level, as the blossoms fade in late spring.

'Pleniflora' is similar in habit, but the pruning is more extensive, there being a greater need for this as the flowered growths which die back look unsightly. Often the young growths produce a scattered display of flowers in the autumn. 'Picta' is variegated with an attractive spread or tracery of branches. This variety does not sucker readily; in fact, there is a danger of reversion if this happens. Any growths that show reversion should be cut out.

KOELREUTERIA

K. paniculata is the species most commonly grown. At its best it will form a tree 9 m. (30 ft.) or more in height, with a definite trunk and a sound branch system. Good nursery stock should have a clear stem of 0.6 to 0.9 m. (2 to 3 ft.) at planting time, with a central leader. After planting out, this leader should be retained, and as the tree develops the lower branches will often die through lack of light, thus allowing a clear trunk to form which may be 1.2 to 1.5 m. (4 to 5 ft.) or even more in height. At a later stage the lower branches will sweep down to within 0.6 to 0.9 m. (2 to 3 ft.) of the ground, if unrestricted by shade or growth. This tree is light-demanding, and growths that are shaded will not flower and may even die. This tree will not respond to hard reduction of the main scaffold branches. 'Fastigiata' is a rare form with a habit similar to that of the Lombardy Poplar. It is extremely slow-growing with a very tight columnar habit, requiring no pruning at all.

KOLKWITZIA

K. amabilis. From the nursery stage, when a bushy habit should be encouraged, this plant sends out strong, arching growths as it becomes established. These should be left to grow freely and unpruned, for the arching habit continues at maturity. From these main branches, whole lengths of old and weak wood should be cut out immediately after flowering in midsummer. Many of these will be found on the underside of the branch system and they should be cut back to a suitable point. The lower, furnishing branches should be left, as they are quite attractive and add to a natural effect.

This shrub may reach 1.8 m. (6 ft.) or more feet in height with a considerable spread and yet, with its upright, arching habit, it can be grown fairly close to the edge of the border, for example, 1.2 m. (4 ft.), without interfering with mowing operations.

+LABURNOCYTISUS

+*L.* 'Adamii'. This graft hybrid (*Laburnum anagyroides* + *Chamaecytisus purpureus*) is normally grown as a standard and is similar in habit to *Laburnum*. No pruning is required other than the removal of suckers. Occasionally, however, a specimen will grow out of its chimaera form, eventually becoming a complete specimen of *Laburnum*. This appears to be the result of pure *Laburnum* tissue growing out very strongly and any such tendency should be checked by pruning.

LABURNUM

This is a small genus of trees. They are small and quite fast growing, but often only remain in perfect condition for a short period when compared to longer living trees. Forms and hybrids are often propagated by budding on lined-out stock and may produce suckers from the rootstocks below the graft union. These should be removed by rubbing out at the earliest opportunity. Growth from this graft is so rapid in the first season that a 1.8 m. (6 ft.) leg is quite easily formed. This is quite a popular form, although they are often grown as bushes or feathered trees. Once the head and main framework has been developed they need very little pruning. Any large branches that need to be removed should be attended to in mid to late summer as bleeding may occur if this is done in the spring. Large wounds do not heal rapidly, especially with a mature specimen, and a careful watch should therefore be kept on these, for deterioration of the heartwood often sets in rapidly once air and moisture gain access.

L. anagyroides, *L. alpinum* and *L.* ×*watereri* 'Vossii' respond to spur pruning, the young growths being taken back almost to the older wood, leaving only one to two buds. This should be carried out during the early winter. They are often trained in this way to cover archways and pergolas. In the early years, the positioning of the main growths should be studied carefully. Crossing branches, and those that are badly placed, should be removed at an early stage. Low-branching fan-shaped specimens are best suited for this purpose. Wisterias, also winter pruned, are effective when allowed to climb and grow in conjunction with Laburnum that has been trained in this way.

LAGERSTROEMIA

L. indica, the Crape Myrtle, will not grow unprotected in regions with hard winters or cool summers, as it requires long hot summers to ripen the wood and encourage flower in terminal panicles at the end of summer. They can be trained as a short single- or multi-stemmed tree or against a sunny wall and pruned annually between autumn and early spring to an established framework. They can also be pruned to an open habit to show off the smooth attractive mottled bark on the main stems and scaffolds.

LAPAGERIA

L. rosea is a twining, evergreen shrub from Chile, which can only be grown outside in very mild districts on a sheltered wall and in partial shade. There should be vertical strands stretched between the horizontal wires. Pruning consists of cutting out the weaker stems in the spring before the new growth commences. Naturally, the best of the growths break from the thicker and healthier stems, and by careful timing, injury to the new growth can be avoided. Should any of the remaining stems become loose on their support during this operation, they should be carefully tied back in position.

LARDIZABALA

L. funaria. This evergreen shrub climbs vigorously by means of long, twining stems. It is only satisfactory against a wall in warm, frost-free climates. Vertical strands should be stretched between the horizontal wires to facilitate climbing in the early stages.

Pruning consists of cutting away old and weak growths and dead wood in the spring. This must be done carefully to avoid disturbance and damage to the remainder of the shrub. Young growths that develop from low down on the stem system should be encouraged. Any which develop beyond the bounds should be cut off, if they cannot be tied in without crowding.

LARIX

The Larches are very distinct in habit, and when grown under good conditions a straight trunk is formed through the centre of the tree, the branches radiating from this. A good leader should be encouraged, but it is noticeable that with a vigorously growing tree, a broken leader is replaced by growths from adventitious buds or by the upper branches which develop an upright habit.

Larches are light-demanding, and with close planting the lower branches are lost one by one, as height is gained and the light taken from them. Thinning at such an advanced stage is not the complete answer, for although new growths are produced from the bare trunks, they develop very slowly and may never reach the proportions of the original branches. Thinning, unless carefully carried out, may also lead to considerable gale damage.

Single specimens in sheltered positions may be quite heavily branched, provided there is no shading, but a distinct and straight trunk is essential. *L. decidua*, the European Larch, is fine when grown as a specimen, with its large branches sweeping down almost to ground level. The Japanese Larch, *L. kaempferi*, is also recommended for this purpose, but the branches often spread more horizontally.

LAURELIA

L. sempervirens. This evergreen plant must be grown in the shelter of a wall, where it will form a self-supporting tree or large bush. It may be run up on a single leader. It needs considerable headroom, but restrictive pruning may be carried out on the width, cutting back into the branches in order to conceal the cuts. Often, the main stem needs one or two ties back to the wall to prevent the specimen from being blown about.

LAURUS

These are thickly branched trees or shrubs with a plentiful supply of young growth. *L. nobilis* is hardier than *L. azorica*, which should definitely be grown in the shelter of a wall. The leaders should be left to grow up strongly without pruning, although if it is necessary to restrict the size, this may be carried out in the spring, carefully positioning the cuts inside the bush to hide them. These shrubs regenerate very strongly and will often break into growth even if killed back to near ground level by severe winter weather.

L. nobilis, the Bay Laurel, is often grown in tubs and clipped to a formal design. The shape is maintained by carefully cutting back the new growths several times during the summer, using a pair of secateurs. This species also withstands exposed positions near the south and west coasts.

LAVANDULA

L. angustifolia is the most common species, but there is a number of cultivated forms available which vary in height and vigour, a factor which must be taken into account when pruning. Left unattended without any pruning, the shrub eventually becomes weedy with many bare stems. Regular pruning keeps it more compact and decorative. This should be carried out in early to mid spring, just as the new growth has begun, when the branch system may be shortened to a point where only a sufficient number of new shoots is left to develop and furnish the bush. The hand shears may be used for this work. It is unwise to cut back hard into the old wood, as this does not break freely. It is therefore better to keep a plant in condition from an early stage by pruning annually than to allow it to grow unpruned for several years, when it is easier to make a replacement and start again. Young plants are pruned hard, even in the nursery, to encourage a bushy habit. In order to make the shrub appear tidy for the winter the old flower stems may be cut back in the late autumn.

Lavender is often used as formal hedging, but it is pruned according to the same system.

The advice is sometimes given to prune after flowering, but as a general rule the spring is the better time. The young growths are then protected by the mature foliage for the winter, while they grow away without check with the improved weather conditions.

The other species may also be improved by pruning, but a number are tender and need a sheltered and sunny position.

LAVATERA

The hybrid *L. ×clementii* and its cultivars, including 'Barnsley', 'Kew Rose' and 'Rosea', are vigorous medium to large subshrubs. They are not fully hardy and should be grown in a sheltered position. Usually, a woody framework of older branches survives and the new growths break freely from these in the spring. The flowers are produced along the terminal length of the current season's wood and this flowering portion dies back naturally as the fruits ripen. Unpruned, these shrubs develop a loose, untidy habit and once the framework is formed, the young growths should be cut back annually in the spring to near their bases, waiting, however, until there is little danger of severe weather.

LEIOPHYLLUM

L. buxifolium. In order to keep this small, evergreen shrub tidy, the clusters of dead flowers may be cut off as the blossoms fade in the summer. Eventually, when the plant becomes old with a worn, untidy appearance, hard cutting back should be resorted to. This should be carried out in the late spring and new growths will be produced during the summer. At this stage it may, however, be considered better to start again with rooted pieces that may sometimes be found round the plant, or with freshly propagated material.

LEPTODERMIS

L. kumaonensis. This shrub loves to grow in the shelter of a sunny wall in a well-drained position. It should be allowed to grow and branch freely when young as most of the growth is put on by the leading shoots. Often, the furnishing at the base of the shrub is poor. While it is young it may be necessary to stake the rather slender growths. It does not always break out well when damaged by frost. Normally, little pruning is required.

LEPTOSPERMUM

This genus is made up of sun lovers which must also have a mild climate. Wall protection is often necessary, but they should be grown as bushes in this situation and not trained against the surface.

Normally, very little pruning is necessary, and they do not break readily from old wood if they are cut down to it. In order to encourage a bushy habit, pruning should be carried out in late spring, on young growths, before hardening and ripening take place.

LESPEDEZA

The woody members of this genus are killed down to ground level each winter. They are best grown in a sunny, well-drained and sheltered border, with a protective layer of fleece, bracken or loose straw placed round the bases for the winter. In the spring the old growths are cut down to ground level. These shrubs flower on the current season's growth in late summer.

LEUCOTHOE

Very little pruning is required. Those species such as *L. fontanesiana* that have an attractive arching habit should be planted well back from the edge if in a border, in order to show this to full effect. Pruning to restrict the shrubs can easily spoil their appearance. If it does become necessary, a few of the oldest and weakest growths may be cut out after flowering in late spring, provided that the bushes are left well furnished with younger growths. The aim should be to make the cut at ground level, thus retaining a natural, branching habit.

LEYCESTERIA

L. formosa has a stool-like habit of growth, breaking freely from the base with strong, green, hollow-stemmed shoots which reach the full height of the shrub and flower in one season. If it is left to grow completely unpruned it will become thick and congested with many weak growths.

Pruning consists of thinning out the older and weaker shoots in the spring before growth commences, taking these right down to ground level. An alternative plan is to cut all top growth down hard each spring, to within 50 to 80 mm. (2 to 3 in.) of ground level. This treatment, however, must be accompanied by heavy mulching and feeding, with watering if necessary.

In an exposed position, the hollow stems are sometimes broken in strong winds.

LIBOCEDRUS

L. bidwillii and *L. plumosa* are the two species under this genus, both small trees from New Zealand. Both require a sheltered location in a mild area. They need very little pruning and should any be needed, they should be treated as *Calocedrus*, which see.

LIGUSTRUM

This genus is most commonly represented in gardens by *L. ovalifolium*, the Oval-leaf Privet, as a hedge plant, but there are quite a number of species which will, if allowed to grow freely and pruned correctly, form shapely bushes equally as decorative as many other shrubs. Perhaps it is because it is such a good hedge plant and responds so well to clipping, that it is never thought of as a free-growing bush and it is concluded that the whole genus is therefore worthless for any other purpose. Most of the species regenerate very strongly if hard pruned and many throw young shoots freely from the base.

L. lucidum is the strongest grower, with erect main branches, and can make a fine, large round-headed tree to 25 m. (82 ft.). The laterals from these main branches are spreading and are gradually weighed down by extending growths. It is at its best when allowed to branch low on the edge of a lawn. The young shoots, which develop from the main branches, as they become horizontal, should be left, as they will help to thicken up the centre.

The remaining species and varieties, if allowed to grow freely, should be pruned when necessary so that the natural habit is retained. The mode of growth varies considerably within the genus; for example, *L. obtusifolium* var. *regelianum* has a spreading habit, while *L. japonicum* 'Rotundifolium' has a compact, stiff habit and also needs shelter. There is even considerable variation in habits of growth among the varieties of such common species as *L. vulgare*. Three which are stiff upright growers are 'Densiflorum', 'Fastigiatum' and 'Glaucum'. Their habit makes them suitable for close planting to form a screen in exposed coastal districts. The type plant could also be planted more extensively in these and other windswept conditions. This plant is found colonizing the lee slopes of sand dunes where the winds do all the pruning which is necessary.

L. ovalifolium and the cultivar 'Aureo-Variegatum' are commonly used as hedge plants. After planting for this purpose, the young shrubs should be pruned back to within 300 mm. (12 in.) of ground level and taken back hard for 2 or 3 years afterwards in order to fill out the base before too much height is put on. This hedge needs clipping frequently during the growing season, but if it is overgrown it will respond to hard cutting back on both the top and the sides. The response will be very quick if it is carried out in mid spring.

L. delavayanum is now often used as a hedging plant in the milder areas and has replaced *Buxus sempervirens* in many cases as a plant used for topiary in the nursery industry, due to its small evergreen leaves and spreading growth.

L. quihoui is also becoming a popular, elegant medium-sized shrub that should be left to grow naturally with little pruning unless it becomes too large for its situation and then it should be thinned, selectively removing the more vigorous stems in early spring.

LINDERA

These seldom require pruning, apart from the removal of any dead tips or branches that may have been killed back during the winter. Their powers of regeneration are often very good and they can be expected to break into growth, even from the old wood at the base, after a severe winter has killed all the top growth.

L. praecox, hardy only in the warmer localities, is bushy from the base and has a stool-like growth with dense upright branches. In the most favoured positions it may be trained, with one to three stems only, to form a small tree.

This species may also be trained against a sunny wall. At an early stage it is pruned hard back to encourage the development of a number of growths which are then trained out fanwise. Informal, twiggy growths are left to develop from this framework. They require little pruning, unless they extend too far from the wall, in which case they may be carefully shortened to hide the cuts. A hard pruning of these lateral growths back to the main branches usually results in a free production of young growths round the edges of the wounds that may require thinning. Under this system of culture a cluster of suckerlike growths often springs out annually from the base. It is better to remove these as they appear during the growing season, than to leave them until the end of the season.

L. benzoin also forms a rounded bush, while *L. megaphylla* is more upright in growth, often making a large evergreen shrub or small tree.

LIPPIA. *See* Aloysia

LIQUIDAMBAR

The hardiest and most widely grown species is *L. styraciflua*, forming a large and beautiful tree. In the nursery stage it should be encouraged to grow freely with a strong central leader as a feathered specimen. It should be transplanted at an early stage, but larger trees are said to withstand a move better, if the side branches are drastically pruned just before the move is made in the early winter. A good, mature tree forms a long, straight trunk with a beautiful bark effect. This characteristic may be enhanced by cutting off the lower branches flush with the trunk up to 4.6 to 6.0 m.

(15 to 20 ft.) as the overall height increases. Even from this height the lower and outer branches, which are pendulous, will, with encouragement, spread and drop down to eye level, allowing the full beauty of the foliage, especially when tinted in the autumn, to be seen to best effect.

L. orientalis is a slow-growing tree very similar in general appearance and habit to *Acer campestre*. When young, this tree or large shrub is full of twiggy growth, but from this the leader and the main branches form. A sharp watch should be kept to ensure that a central leader is kept for at least 6 m. (20 ft.), otherwise the branching becomes very heavy which leads to weakness later in life. At maturity, the pendulous outer branches reach right down to ground level. It is a tree for the edge of a planting.

L. formosana and the Monticola Group are both liable to be injured by late spring frosts, if they occur just as growth is breaking. This, to a lesser extent, also is likely with the other species. Following such damage, it may be necessary to train another leader by stopping rival branches during growth.

L. acalycina quickly loses its leader and wants to produce a head very early; however, if possible, a single leader should be encouraged. It will require strict training to make this into a specimen tree with formal training, little and often, in the early years until a head forms.

LIRIODENDRON

L. tulipifera, the Tulip Tree or Yellow Poplar, is commonly found in tree collections. The best form in which to grow this is with a strong central leader. The branches are then well spaced and are able to carry a considerable amount of growth when the tree reaches full size at maturity. The extreme ends of the branches are often semi-pendulous and will reach ground level with encouragement. This will allow the interesting flowers to be inspected at close quarters.

The best form in which to plant this tree is as a feathered specimen, for establishment will be easier than with an older tree. The trunk is cleared of growths up to a height of 2 to 3 m. (6 to 10 ft.) as the head develops. However, young trees are available as

standards and with care they may be successfully established. These should never be without a leader. Specimens that are left to branch low without a central leader, reach a stage when each limb carries considerable weight and weakness may develop in a crotch with disastrous results. Bracing is often necessary with a mature specimen in this condition.

Apart from the training, there is little need for pruning. However, some trees show a tendency to throw strong, upright shoots, even from mature horizontal branches. This should be corrected by pruning, otherwise the head will be thrown completely out of balance. Epicormic growths need not be removed unless they are thick and unsightly. Provided that the tree is healthy with a naturally thick canopy, these are not troublesome.

With the cultivar 'Fastigiatum' which is narrow and upright in habit, branching should be left to develop from ground level.

L. chinense will also form a good leader with little training, and appears to have a slender branching system.

LITHOCARPUS

L. densiflorus is the only species that is normally hardy. In the earlier years it forms a pyramidal, evergreen tree with a slender branch system. If possible, the leader should be retained, for a strong framework is needed as the foliage is very heavy and the slender stems of rival leaders are easily weighed down and broken, especially under snow or during a gale. Even a properly trained specimen should be given a sheltered position. There will often be small pieces of dead wood to cut out, especially after a severe winter.

L. edulis if given reasonable shelter will make small evergreen tree or large shrub.

LITHODORA

L. diffusa. Two cultivars of this species are popular, 'Heavenly Blue' and 'Grace Ward'. Left to grow unattended year after year this species often develops into a large but untidy mat. In addition, exposed parts of a clump die back during the winter. A restricted amount of pruning is beneficial after flowering, taking out the weaker and dead growths and letting light into the clump. An inspection may also be made in the spring. It is possible to lift the mat of growth and cut the dead wood out from beneath.

LOMATIA

This genus of the family Proteaceae is uncommon in our gardens, for the species are difficult to grow in regions with hard winters and can only be grown in the mildest of climates. Very little pruning is required and the shrubs furnish up well and throw up new shoots from the base. Thus there is a chance of replacing old growths which may need cutting out.

LONICERA

The members of this genus exhibit a wide variety in habits of growth and yet, as far as the horticulturist and pruning policies are concerned, there are three distinct groups: (1) the shrubs or bushes with branches and growths springing from the base; (2) the climbers which flower on the current season's wood; and (3) the climbers which flower on the previous year's wood.

Group 1. The shrubs or bushes with branches and growths springing from the base

These are found in three of the sections of the Subgenus I. *Chamaecerasus*, namely Section 1. *Isoxylosteum*, Section 2. *Isika* and Section 3. *Coeloxylosteum*. Their habit generally is typical of shrubs that regenerate well by sending up young growths after being cut back, both from the base and from the mature branch systems.

Pruning consists of removing old wood when it is weak and perhaps partly dead, taking the cut back to a suitable point just above a promising growth. Branches that arch over will often produce upright growths from their lower portions, and these may be in an ideal position to be used as replacements. Care should be taken to retain the natural habit, otherwise by frequently cutting all arching branches to an upright growth, bare sections of the old wood will be visible, especially during the winter months. It is, however, difficult to restrict the growth of a large-spreading shrub by pruning and at the same time retain the natural effect and habit, and far more attention should be given to selection in the first place, before planting.

A considerable variation in habit is found even among the shrub species. For example, *L. quinquelocularis* and *L. maackii* produce a few branches at the base which later become quite large and, being often twisted and gnarled, are full of character. The same is true of some others, but many more branch freely from ground level and in addition produce a mass of new growths, also from the base such as *L. korolkowii*. Thus the difference in pruning, for the oldest wood on the latter species may, if necessary, be cut down completely to ground level after flowering. As the species with weaker growths and main stems extend, they sometimes arch over and even spread on the ground during wet weather or as a result of a snow-fall. *L. fragrantissima* should be pruned following flowering in late spring, by removing the older weaker wood at the base of the shrub to encourage the new growths from the base to make a younger plant.

L. nitida, one of the evergreen, shrubby honey-suckles, is very easily propagated, is fast-growing and responds well to frequent clipping on a rigid line, and is therefore suitable as a formal hedge plant. It is, however, liable to be blown over and out of line at the top, especially if the feature is in an exposed position. This fault may be overcome at planting time by the erection of a fence consisting of two or three strands of wire over the actual planting line. The hedge plants grow on either side of this and are thus held firmly in position. After a number of years as a hedge plant, this subject often loses foliage from the older and lower branches and thus becomes bare at the base. Hard pruning, even down to within 150 mm. (6 in.) of ground level, is an effective answer to this and work of this nature should be carried out in the early summer. As stated earlier, this subject is a vigorous and rapid grower, and requires frequent clipping during the summer months. *L. pileata* requires very little pruning.

Group 2. The climbers which flower on the current season's wood

This group is made up of the few evergreen species that twine, with their flowers in pairs, they are in the Section *Nintooa*. The most common species is *L. japonica*. It is a vigorous grower and will climb and ramble over stumps or small trees. Sometimes it is grown on a pergola or archway, but it is not an easy subject to prune by accepted methods. However, it is possible to keep it within bounds by hard clipping over the entire surface in the early spring with a pair of shears. In this way it may be kept within bounds and be grown along a fence, e.g. chestnut paling. Treated in this way, new growths soon break out to flower some weeks later. Renovation of the plant can be done by cutting the whole plant back to about 0.6 m. (2 ft.) during late winter or early spring. *L. henryi*, *L. acuminata* and *L. hildebrandtiana* also fall into this group.

Group 3. The climbers which flower on the previous year's wood

Species in the Subgenus II. *Periclymenum* are in this group. The Woodbine or Honeysuckle, *L. periclymenum*, is an example. They are pruned by cutting out a portion of the vines which have produced the flowers as soon as these fade, see Fig. 38 (1 and 2). It should be noted that the flowers are formed on short laterals from a vine that has been made during the previous year. It is this vine or twining stem which is cut out, but great care must be taken to avoid injury to the young, developing ones. These are often intertwined with the older ones. When these climbing subjects are growing in a natural setting, some of the smaller growths may be left to hang down from the supporting branches. In this position the flowering heads are attractive. When these are pruned after flowering, young replacement growths are left hanging down in their place to produce the flower display the following season. *L. ×brownii*, *L. caprifolium* and *L. etrusca* also fall into this group.

Species for wall culture.

Generally they are not ideally suited for wall culture. *L. fragrantissima*, one of the winter-flowering shrubby species, is sometimes

wall-trained for the earlier display produced under the more sheltered conditions. It is only really successful if the shrub is attended to especially as far as pruning is concerned. The main branches are tied out to cover the feature and may be replaced later, if necessary, by the promising growths that often spring from the base. The flowering laterals are left to develop from the wall and are pruned back to suitable growths in the spring after flowering. By this system the extension of the lateral branches is restricted and kept reasonably close to the wall. Strong growths, which spring from the base and which are not required for replacement, may be cut out as they develop during the growing season. A wall specimen which is out of control through years of neglect may be pruned back very hard during the winter, either to suitable growths on the main branches or even harder.

The climbing species may also be grown against a wall, but under hot, dry conditions pests are often troublesome. Pruning is on the lines already described, the *L. japonica* types being clipped back hard over the surface in the early spring, and the *L. periclymenum* group pruned after flowering by the removal of the older wood. A vertical system of wires

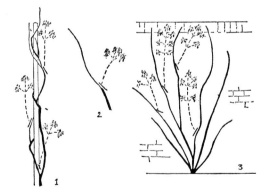

Fig. 38. A simplified diagram showing the pruning of a climbing form of *Lonicera periclymenum*. This flowers on the previous year's wood.
(1) Trained to a pole.
(2) A close-up showing how the flowering portion, indicated by the broken line, may be pruned as the flowers fade.
(3) The pruning of a wall-trained specimen.

should be attached between the horizontal strands for additional support to the young growth, see Fig. 38.

The tender species *L. sempervirens* appreciates wall protection. It belongs to Group 3.

LOTUS

L. hirsutus may be regarded as a subshrub, but the stems that are produced die back to the woody root-stock each year. The dead top branches serve as a protection for the young basal shoots during the winter and should be pruned back to these in the spring.

LUMA

L. apiculata, an evergreen tree or large shrub from Chile, is grown for its aromatic foliage, cinnamon-coloured bark and scented white flowers, attractive to butterflies in late summer in the milder regions. In the milder climate it can be grown as a tree with a central leader, but in the cooler areas it should be grown as a multi-stemmed tree with three to five stems. The lower laterals should be removed as soon as possible and the crown gradually lifted, as the tree develops to reveal the attractive bark on the main stems. Once the crown develops and is lifted to the required height, the only necessary pruning in the future will be to remove the dead wood and to open up the centre of the crown by some light thinning.

LUPINUS

L. arboreus. This rapidly growing shrub normally branches freely when it is young. Pruning consists of cutting off the old heads of flower, leaving sufficient for seed if desired. This is followed by spring pruning, when the younger growths may be shortened and some of the oldest and weakest wood cut out completely. Despite this treatment the shrub is often short-lived and it is wise to raise young plants for succession.

LYCIUM

These rather untidy shrubs, *L. barbarum* being the commonly grown species, respond well to hard cutting back and this should be resorted to when the mass of shoots gets completely out of hand. This may be considered part of their treatment every few years. The growth generally is rather spreading, but corrective pruning, carried out annually, delays the need for a more drastic operation. This annual pruning may be carried out during the winter. It consists of cutting away any dead growths, searching for these beneath the branches where they tend to collect, and at the same time reducing heavy horizontal growths back to suitable young and upright shoots near the centre of the bush. Any young growths that are too long may be shortened.

These shrubs are often grown in open spaces near the sea, where they can be used to fix sandbanks where they do not require pruning. They are also used for hedging purposes, being cut back hard in the spring, although at least one trim may be necessary during the summer if the feature is to be kept close and formal in outline.

LYONIA

L. ligustrina is the most commonly grown species. It is dense growing, branching freely from ground level, and strong young growths are also sent up from the base if the shrub is doing well. This does give an opportunity for a limited amount of pruning, as the oldest growths may be cut out completely at ground level. The extent to which this is done should depend entirely upon age and vigour of the shrub. The natural habit is close and the bush should be left well furnished. This advice also holds for the varieties of this species.

MAACKIA

M. amurensis. This species is often shrubby but it may develop into a small tree. The leader should be retained on a young nursery plant. Branching is naturally sparse and vigour and health will be the deciding factors in determining the ultimate height a specimen reaches before the head opens completely. The branching has a flattened appearance and there appear to be few trailing branches. *M. hupehensis* has an ascending branch system, and may be trained to a definite tree form. The branching is also sparse but the ends are more twiggy. It may be grown on a 0.6 to 1.2 m. (2 to 4 ft.) leg.

MACLURA

M. pomifera, the Osage Orange, is a very hardy, small- to medium-sized tree with thorny branches, ultimately forming a congested head. For this reason it is often grown as an impenetrable hedge in the United States. It is best grown as a feathered tree with a strong central leader, soon slowing down to form a broad upper crown. Very little pruning is required apart from keeping this plant within its bounds, however this should be carried out between autumn to early spring while the plant is dormant. The white milky sap can be harmful to some people, so care should be taken and gloves worn. When grown as a hedge plant, shears can be used to retain a hedge effect.

M. *tricuspidata* forms a dense thorny shrub or small tree. It is often easier to accommodate if it is trained to a definite clear stem 1.8 to 2.4 m. (6 to 8 ft.) in height. Dead wood should be pruned out during the summer, when it can easily be distinguished from living material.

MADDENIA

M. hypoleuca. This relative of *Prunus* is grown as a shrub or small tree and should be encouraged to branch at soil level in the nursery. The main branches are ascending, while the laterals tend to be horizontal in habit. In the initial years of training the centre of the bush should be kept open. Occasionally, strong growths appear from near the base and grow up through the centre of the bush, but unless any of these are needed for replacement purposes they should be cut out, as they may ultimately spoil the shape. Otherwise, no regular pruning is necessary.

MAGNOLIA

Magnolias grow and develop best in a well-sheltered position, for the wood is brittle and the branches are liable to be torn off by severe winds. They must be planted with as little damage to the root system as possible, which can be kept to a minimum by not firming the backfill during the planting stage with the heel. It is important to use healthy nursery stock that is not pot bound; nor should the root system of nursery stock have suffered any damage by drying out or frost. Magnolias must be kept growing well in order to produce a good shape. They usually show great powers of regeneration and may throw strong young growths from really old wood. Advantage may be taken of this by cutting damaged specimens back carefully, if necessary correcting the positions of the final cuts a year or so later, when the most suitable growths may be selected. This power of regeneration is also a great help in overcoming the effects of bad training in a young specimen, especially with bush types such as *M. ×soulangeana*, which branch low. Large scale pruning, if it becomes necessary, should be carried out in midsummer, thus avoiding the risk of bleeding, while leaving sufficient time for the healing processes to get under way before the winter sets in. The heartwood is soft and rot quickly sets in so the smaller the pruning cuts and the least damage from large limbs tearing out, the less chance of cavities forming.

The need to keep Magnolias growing well applies to all plants, trees and shrubs, yet many an old specimen has flowered so extensively that its vigour has been exhausted, particularly when a heavy crop of seed has followed. The result has been little or no growth, followed quickly by death as the energies were completely dried up. The avoidance of such a disaster is sometimes possible by carefully picking off the flowers as they whither and by feeding and, if necessary, watering. As with so many subjects, the main pointer to watch is the amount of growth that is being put on early in the season.

The form of tree or bush should be carefully considered. In the nursery the young plants should be left to grow naturally and to form a leader. Strong rival branches should not be left unattended and the necessary action must be taken early. With the bush forms such as *M. ×soulangeana*, the vigour of the leader will soon weaken as the branches increase in girth and extent. As specimens of both the bush and tree types reach maturity, the lower branch systems should be encouraged to grow and develop, even down to ground level. The individual flowers are of great beauty and they can be appreciated better if they are within reach.

Many of the vigorous growers throw strong suckers and sometimes epicormic growths, which run up through the centre of the bush. This needs careful judgement for they should be encouraged, perhaps with some thinning, if the older branches are weak or in need of replacement. Otherwise, they should be regularly removed before they become too large, or spoil the character and shape of the bush. Also they may, if left, reduce the vigour of the older branches. If grafted plants send up suckers from the rootstock, they should be removed as soon as possible, as they are usually more vigorous than the scion and will very soon take over. Eventually very low and heavy branches may need some support, either by bracing, or by the use of a forked prop.

M. campbellii and the other species and hybrids, including *M. c.* subsp. *mollicomata*, are strong growers which can be trained very easily to form a central leader. The tendency to form a really strong leader is greater among seedlings, and thus the initial years of training young nursery stock obtained by grafting is important. Young plants of this group take many years to come into flower, but there appears to be some evidence that plants with a leader flower earlier than those which are forced to break and branch low. Seedlings often produce growths from the base when 4 or 5 years old, but if the leader is strong there is little chance of these spoiling the shape. One of the most untidy growers is often *M. ×thompsoniana*, for the branches are very widespreading and they rest on each other as they become heavy. It is difficult to correct this habit if it develops.

M. grandiflora is ideal for growing in the shelter of a large, sunny wall. For this purpose it should be trained up for at least two-thirds of its height with a central leader. Often, it is necessary to tie only the main branches to the wall. In the warmer climates it can be grown as a free standing tree with a conical crown if a central leader is maintained.

M. delavayi usually needs wall protection. It produces very strong wood and requires a large wall, where a strong central leader can be encouraged.

M. macrophylla requires summer heat to ripen the wood, otherwise it will be damaged beyond repair with winter cold. Plants checked by winter cold suffer from dieback and Coral Spot (*Nectria cinnabarina*), never making a strong healthy plant.

M. sieboldii, *M. sinensis* and *M. wilsonii* require only minimal pruning, such as the removal of crossing branches and dead wood, and should be trained to make as tall a plant as possible in the early years in order that the nodding flowers are shown to their best effect from underneath.

×MAHOBERBERIS

×*M. neuberti* often develops an untidy habit which may be corrected by pruning back loose, straggly growths to suitable buds. This should be carried out in the spring after flowering.

MAHONIA

The most commonly grown species of this genus is *M. aquifolium*. It is a strong-growing subject and will extend and colonise by means of suckers. It should therefore be planted where there is scope for development, but it can be restricted by pruning and by removing the suckers.

It is very tolerant of bad conditions and can be planted on banks and in shady positions, but often, in such situations, the upright growths are weak and produce little flower. In addition, they may become untidy and full of fallen leaves and dead twigs etc. Such areas and clumps may be cut over in mid spring, taking all the upright growths down to 100 to 200 mm. (4 to 8 in.). This may either be carried out at intervals of a few years, or on an annual basis if required.

In the open, a thick mass 1 to 2 m. (3 to 6 ft.) in height is formed and very little pruning is necessary. Some of the varieties and forms such as 'Undulata' have an upright habit, often without suckers, and thus form a bush rather than a clump.

Many of the larger-leafed species and hybrids such as *M. japonica*, *M. lomariifolia* and *M. ×media* have a stiff, erect habit and a beauty of form which would be spoilt by pruning. It may become necessary to cut out dead wood, but the need rarely arises. Breaks should be encouraged along the length of the stems and from the base, if they arise. In the same way, branching from ground level should be encouraged in the nursery. Should there need to be a reduction in height, as they become leggy and bare at the base, they can be shortened back to side shoots or strong buds lower down the stems.

A number of species, such as *M. napaulensis*, need a mild climate and all the large-leaved forms appreciate shelter. *M. nevinii* is not sufficiently hardy to be grown in the open in most districts and usually needs wall protection. It may be grown as a bush in the shelter of a wall or actually tied up to the face fanwise on a supporting wire system. Growths are freely thrown up from the base, and this allows the longer and older branches to be cut out at ground level, replacing them with younger shoots.

MALUS

The species comprising this genus are mainly small or medium-sized trees, the larger growers reaching up to 9 m. (30 ft.) or more. They are strong and reliable and the main branches on an old specimen, even when holed or full of cavities, are able to withstand considerable strain. This, of course, is no excuse for allowing a tree to get into this condition, or for allowing such a state to continue once it has occurred. The well-balanced tree, maintained in a good condition, will always have much to commend it, and it will be a much better long-term proposition.

The form of tree is important and there is much in favour of the feathered type that has a strong central leader. This may seem at first to be contrary to general practice, for many very good nursery trees are produced which are standards with an open branching head. Yet fruit trees with a central leader are preferred by many, and this does seem to be the more natural mode of growth. The branches will be equally spaced round this leader which eventually opens out to form the topmost system on the crown, thus the weight is more evenly spread along the length of the leader. Also, by using the feathered tree, for *M. baccata*, *M.* 'John Downie' and *M.* 'Golden Hornet' it is possible to encourage a much lower branching and under certain circumstances this may be desirable. A tree with a central leader on a short 0.8 m. (2.5 ft.) clear leg can be very attractive. In other cases, however, a 1.8 to 2.4 m. (6 to 8 ft.) clear length of trunk may be preferred. It may be more difficult to restrict the lateral spread of an open-centred, wide-branching tree, while there is also another important point—often another leader develops and is left to grow through the centre of the tree, making the removal of the first one seem to have been unnecessary.

As the trees mature, epicormic growths may develop on the more horizontal branch systems and will develop more profusely following any pruning. These are indeed unsightly, yet they are more likely to be found on specimens that have been thinned out in the centre to let in the light and air. There seems to be little point in doing this; in fact, a twisted and crowded head of branches in *M. floribunda* is to be expected and is thus more natural, typical and also more interesting. Once the main framework has been established, a natural head of growth is advocated. Often, this may mean that the outer and lower branches become pendulous. This, for example, is the habit of *M. pumila* whose trunk and main branches are often very crooked with a matted head, which is characteristic of the species. *M. trilobata* and *M. tschonoskii* are distinct from many others in having an upright growth with a pyramidal habit. Both of these trees develop a crown naturally with very little pruning. *M. sieboldii* is a small naturally weeping tree, often making no more than a large shrub and no form of pruning will ever make this into a specimen tree.

M. toringoides produces vigorous growths in the early years that twist and bend the main central leader, eventually making an ungainly specimen with lots of twisting and crossing of branches. When this is planted as a grafted plant, it is often unstable and after several years will begin to fall over with the top weight. Retrospective staking will not overcome this problem.

As in many cases Malus are budded or grafted, it is important to remove all suckers as soon as possible, particularly those that spring from below the union, which is usually at ground level.

MANDEVILLA

M. laxa is a slender, twining shrub and is only suitable for a very sunny corner or wall in the mildest regions. On a wall, vertical strands should be stretched between the horizontal wires.

Pruning consists of cutting out the dead wood and weaker growths in the spring, as the shrub becomes active. There should be no hesitation in cutting out some of the older wood, provided that no damage is done to the growths that remain, for they are often wound very tightly together. This shrub breaks out readily from the older wood.

MARSDENIA

M. carvalhoi. This deciduous climber produces long growths that twine in an anti-clockwise direction. It is not hardy and a sunny wall or a sheltered position is necessary. Neither is it particularly ornamental and, owing to the danger of blistering on the skin caused by the milky juice which the plant exudes when it is pruned, it is rarely grown. It is also very poisonous. If it is grown there will be some need for pruning, for the twining shoots will overgrow all but the largest of positions. They should be cut back during the summer and autumn, using the long-arm pruners to keep clear of the cuts. A final check over the plant at closer quarters with the secateurs may be made in the spring, cutting out some of the older wood. This work should be undertaken from the top of the plant downwards, as this reduces the danger of the cut ends coming into contact with the skin. Gloves should be worn.

MEDICAGO

M. arborea is not completely hardy and in most gardens it thrives better in the shelter of a wall.

Normally, no pruning is required. Some cutting back is necessary after a severe winter, but it may not break out if the damage extends into the old wood.

MELALEUCA

These are tender evergreen shrubs and need a very mild and favoured locality. *M. squarrosa* seems to be a little hardier than the remainder and it may be successful in a sheltered sunny corner against a wall. It should be left to grow freely, for it will not conform to rigid training. The younger wood may break into new growth following winter damage, but the old wood is more reluctant to do so when grown in the open. No regular pruning is required.

MELIA

M. azedarach, the Bead Tree, is a sun-loving plant and will not grow well in regions with hard winters. It makes a small elegant tree, requiring hot sun to ripen the wood and should be grown as a standard with a central leader and a clear stem up to 2 m. (6 ft.). Any formative pruning should be done in late autumn to early spring.

MELICYTUS

The species in this genus have very distinctive habits of growth which would quite easily be spoilt by regular pruning and therefore should only be pruned if it is necessary to confine them to a limited space. *M. obovatus* is very bushy from the base, most of the branches being rigid and fairly upright. It may be confined to a narrow border by careful pruning, with the cuts being hidden by the thick foliage. *M. angustifolius* forms a mass of thick, fairly upright branches. The young, whitish growths are an attractive feature of this shrub, and it should be allowed a width and height of several feet to show this to good effect. *M. crassifolius* forms a low mound of congested growths and any form of training would not be practical. It should therefore be in a position where it can develop freely, gradually building up height to 1.5 m. (5 ft.) or more. If it is restricted in width, the main growths, naturally twisted and weak, are without support and may need staking. These shrubs need the shelter of a sunny wall and should be planted about 0.3 to 0.6 m. (1 to 2 ft.) from the base.

MELIOSMA

There are two groups in this genus, one having pinnate and the other simple leaves. Generally, the species in the former group are tree-like, while those in the latter are more shrubby. It is important to recognise these two forms in the nursery, for a definite leader must be formed with the tree species.

Group 1. Species which should be grown to a single leader

M. beaniana is a very rare species. *M. veitchiorum* is slow-growing, but produces branches which radiate naturally from the central stem with a sparse, almost spur-like habit. Ample all round space should be allowed for development. *M. pinnata* var. *oldhamia* has an ascending branch system, but again neighbouring trees or shrubs should, if necessary, be pruned back to allow for development. These are prone to frost damage in the spring as growth commences.

Group 2. Species which should be left to branch naturally at the base

M. parvifolia freely produces upright growths from which almost horizontal branches extend. The twig system is often tangled, but there should be no attempt to correct this, as it is a natural habit. This species often regenerates well from around cuts. Both *M. dilleniifolia* subsp. *cuneifolia* and *M. d.* subsp. *flexuosa* freely produce young growths from ground level, and these can, if necessary, be used for replacing old branches.

MENISPERMUM

M. canadense is a vigorous, suckering twining shrub which will quickly cover a wall, trellis or similar structure up to a height of 3.7 m. (12 ft.). Vertical wires may be necessary to assist climbing. Once established, this subject is so vigorous that it can be cut down to nearly ground level each winter, when short woody stems will often build up below the point of pruning.

The alternative method is to cut down to the ground periodically, perhaps every two to three years. One other method is to avoid this drastic pruning completely and rely upon the cutting out of dead and weak wood to keep the shrub in condition, but this task, with such a tangle of growth, is a very difficult one.

MENZIESIA

During the winter these shrubs have the appearance of rather thin-wooded, deciduous azaleas. They are fairly erect in growth, with main branches that originate from below ground level. They are slow-growing, but as the bushes gain strength new growths are thrown up from beneath the soil. Little regular pruning is needed on the rather twiggy branch system, but dead wood and some of the weak growths may be cut out. There is only limited scope for this and it must be carried out carefully. Some pruning may be done after flowering, when the dead blooms may be cut off in order to prevent seeding and thus to encourage the shrub, but it is advisable to look over them again in the spring.

MESPILUS

M. germanica is normally grown as a 1.8 to 2.4 m. (6 to 8 ft.) standard. Usually, it has an open head without a central leader. The strong branches spread out laterally in rather an interesting manner and the tree as a whole has great character. The growths should be left to sweep down as low as possible. Often, if horizontal branches are cut short, strong epicormic growths appear which will, if left, thrust up through the crown to spoil the character of the tree completely. Dead wood should be cut out during the late summer. Normally, very little pruning is required.

METASEQUOIA

M. glyptostroboides, so recently discovered, has proved to be quite distinct from many other conifers in its habit of growth. One outstanding feature is the ease with which a new leader is formed, even from the older wood, if the injuries are extensive and provided, of course, that the tree concerned is young and vigorous. The habit appears to be columnar with a definite leader, which is naturally and readily maintained for the whole height of the tree. A furnishing down to ground level should be encouraged, as one of the beauties of this tree is the branch and twig growth, when seen at close quarters, which is effective at all seasons. Some variation in habit and growth can be expected among seedlings.

This subject is effective as a screen, where a planting distance of 3.7 to 4.6 m. (12 to 15 ft.) is recommended if it consists of a single line. If necessary, the laterals may be reduced in spread.

As a hedge plant this subject has not proved entirely successful, yet it makes an interesting feature and is so beautiful at all seasons. One of its faults is that hard pruning results in a considerable amount of top growth, this being very pronounced on forms that have an ascending branch system. A selection of the best forms for hedging is therefore advisable. A height of 1.5 to 1.8 m. (5 to 6 ft.) is suggested for this feature, and clipping should be carried out in midsummer.

The form 'National' is more narrowly conical, more suited for street planting.

METROSIDEROS

Even *M. umbellata*, one of the hardiest species, requires a sheltered position in a very mild and favourable district. No pruning is necessary; rather, it is a fight to retain the shoots and foliage intact through the winter. A well-drained and warm soil is essential.

MICHELIA

These evergreen trees or shrubs are more suitable for the milder climates, free from hard winter. *M. compressa* will, under favourable conditions, develop a leader, and every effort should be made to retain this for at least a metre or so until a head of branches is formed. *M. doltsopa*, *M. maudiae* and *M. yunnanensis* may form a small tree or shrub, depending upon the environment, although in a very

favourable situation with shelter, it is possible to retain a leader for some time.

M. figo forms a very leafy medium to large shrub and occasionally the lateral branches have a horizontal habit. Often therefore, it is spreading, the young growths toward the centre of the bush being very upright. It is possible to restrict size by careful pruning in spring, concealing the cuts and leaving an informal surface. In the mildest of localities it needs wall protection, but even so it is better grown as a free-standing shrub rather than hard trained against the surface. The cultivar 'Jack Fogg' makes a large shrub or an upright, conical small tree.

MICROBIOTA

M. decussata is the only species from this genus, closely related to *Juniperus*. It is a small prostrate conifer to 0.5 m. (1.5 ft.) with wide-spreading branches, pale green in summer, turning bronze in winter. It needs minimal pruning and should be given the space to develop into a fine specimen on the rock garden or as a spot planting in the colour clump. Its home is in East Siberia, so it is hardy in most climates.

MICROGLOSSA. *See* Aster

MIMULUS

M. aurantiacus. This is a woody subject from California, but it is tender and is most successful as a wall plant subjected to warm, sunny conditions. In this position and locality it may be trained to a support system, and pruned fairly hard back to the woody framework each spring. Alternatively, it may be grown as a bush. Often, it survives in less favourable areas if the wood at the base is protected with a mound of coarse sand. Young growths are thrown from the old wood very readily and the shrub will respond to hard pruning in late spring if this is necessary to correct a ragged appearance. When young, the shrub should be stopped once to encourage a bushy habit.

MORUS

M. nigra, the Black Mulberry, is often found in the older gardens, usually as ancient trees and thus of historical value. These old specimens may be heavily branched, this being a characteristic of old or mature trees. The danger that these will break, especially during summer gales when the branch system is heavy with fruit and foliage, is a very real one. Thinning, which should be carried out in the early winter, will help to reduce this danger, but it must be done with great care, as otherwise it will spoil the shape and character of the tree. Bracing is often the better plan, for the branching usually gives way in one of the main crotches.

The standard is the ideal form in which to plant this and the other species but the leader should be retained for as long as possible in order to reduce the weight of branching. One of the advantages of a standard is that it is more difficult for children to climb in search of the fruit than a low-branching tree. Even with a standard, however, the lower branches may, with encouragement, grow down close to ground level.

M. alba, the White Mulberry, is also heavily branched and the same advice applies. There are a number of varieties but, in general, there is a tendency for this group to throw epicormic growths, often in great quantity, especially from the horizontal branches. These must be pared back annually, otherwise they may spoil the character of the tree and may also cause dieback on the branch tips, especially during a drought. The cultivar 'Pendula' has tightly grouped weeping branches and needs to be trained by tying up the leading shoot until the desired height has been reached.

M. cathayana is quite distinct in growth and is more adaptable to training to a central leader.

MUEHLENBECKIA

M. complexa produces a mass of thin, wiry stems which will intertwine to form a close canopy over the ground. When sufficiently established it will also invade nearby shrubs, covering them thickly with a tangle of thin growths. Should it be necessary to restrict this subject, it will look most effective if care is taken to leave an informal edge. This means cutting away individual growths. A clipped effect, which results from masses of growth being cut off at one level or line, should be avoided. It may be necessary to do this two or three times during the growing season. In a severe winter it may be cut down to ground level, but it should regenerate. Very old plants should be replaced with new, young vigorous stock instead of carrying out hard pruning.

MUTISIA

M. oligodon, *M. ilicifolia* and *M. decurrens* climb by means of tendrils that are modifications of the midrib. Unless the district has a mild and favourable climate they should be grown against a sunny wall, at first being encouraged to climb on pea sticks planted nearby, or tied onto the wires. Should growth be healthy and vigorous, they may invade nearby plants, but this will not be excessive or harmful. Pruning consists of cutting out dead or weak growths in the summer, but great care is necessary in doing this or vital connecting growths will be severed.

MYRICA

The members of this genus as a whole need very little pruning and usually this only consists of the removal of dead twigs during the summer. They are best grown in moist acid conditions. *M. gale* and *M. cerifera* need to be grown in a clump with several plants together, as both are to some degree suckerous and therefore invasive. Tall and straggly branches will give a planting an untidy appearance, and such growths may be cut right down to ground level, for there are usually plenty of small suckerous shoots to train as replacements. There is no point in clearing the suckers among established plants as they act as ground cover. *M. californica* forms a large bush or small tree but does not sucker to any extent. In a severe winter this shrub may be killed back to near ground level, but usually growth will break out from any living tissue which is left in the spring.

MYRICARIA

This small genus, including *M. germanica*, is closely related to *Tamarix*. All species flower on the current season's wood, and they respond to hard pruning back to the main framework in the spring. Without hard pruning, even while the frame is being built up, they quickly become straggly and unsightly.

MYRSINE

One of the hardiest species in this genus of mainly tropical, evergreen trees is *M. africana*, which forms a compact bush 0.6 to 0.9 m. (2 to 3 ft.) in height. It should be given wall protection and planted approximately one foot from the base. However, after severe weather or through old age, the shrub may develop an untidy appearance. Often, this takes the form of long, woody, bare shoots terminated by small bunches of bushy growths. Hard pruning in the spring will correct this.

MYRTUS

M. communis is the most commonly grown, and it is one of the hardiest of a genus of evergreen shrubs or small trees, all of which are tender. In all but the most favoured districts it needs wall protection, but even in this situation it cannot be grown in regions with hard winters. Normally it is not trained hard up against the surface of the wall, but is grown as a bush, being planted about 0.5 m. (1.5 ft.) from the base. It has a dense habit with branching from ground level. The main branches are somewhat erect and it is completely self-supporting. Normally, no pruning is required, unless it becomes necessary to restrict the shrub, in which case the longer branches may be cut back to a suitable growth inside the bush, so that the wounds are hidden. This should be carried out in the spring. Should it be severely damaged or killed down to ground level by frost, it will often break freely from the old wood right at the base.

This shrub is sometimes grown hard up against the surface of a wall, where it will grow to considerable heights with only the minimum of support.

Sometimes the walls of old cottages in the West Country of England can be seen completely covered in this way. The surface is clipped over once during the spring or early summer and again at a later period if it becomes necessary. The dwarf forms such as *M. c.* subsp. *tarentina* are compact and seldom need pruning, even to prevent encroachment.

The advice given for this species may also be applied to others that may be attempted in the milder districts, they seldom need any pruning.

NANDINA

N. domestica. This bamboo-like subject, grown for its large panicles of red berries, is only really at home in the warmer localities, where it requires a sheltered position. In other areas, even though it may survive, it often has a ragged appearance, especially after a severe winter. With a strong-growing specimen, vigorous growths are freely produced from the base and these may be used as replacements for the ragged growths, which can be cut out at ground level in the spring. Even young plants in the nursery will branch freely. The upright stems are unbranched and pruning at any point down this stem is not effective. They should be cut right off at ground level, if pruned at all.

NEILLIA

These shrubs have a stool-like growth, freely producing young canes from the base. Often, too, suckers are produced one foot or so from the parent, originating as adventitious buds on the roots. Pruning consists of cutting back some of the oldest wood to ground level, at the same time shortening the other mature branches back to suitable growths. Thus the old flowered portions are removed at the same time, letting light and air into the bush. This should be carried out immediately after flowering.

The extent of the pruning will depend upon the amount of young wood being produced; for example, *N. sinensis* var. *ribesioides* does not always have sufficient for all the old wood to be cut away annually. The essential thing is to leave these shrubs well furnished with young growths that spring from the base and from older wood.

NERIUM

N. oleander, a large sun-loving evergreen shrub, is often grown in containers in order that it can be grown outdoors during the summer for the summer heat and brought in under glass during the winter, as it will not tolerate any temperatures below freezing. They can be grown in a variety of ways, including as standards, hedges or free-growing specimens, or against a sunny wall.

Very little pruning is required, unless some form of shaping is needed and this should be done in late summer to autumn. Care should be taken: the sap is toxic and the leaves are poisonous, so some form of protection should be worn when working on them and arisings disposed of sensibly away from animals or small children.

NEVIUSIA

N. alabamensis. This shrub, related to *Kerria*, develops a stool-like growth, gradually spreading as new canes are produced on the outside of the bush from ground level. These extend to the height of the shrub, 1.2 to 1.8 m. (4 to 6 ft.) in one season. Pruning consists of cutting out the older and thinner wood, either back to suitable growths or right down to ground level in summer after flowering. In the nursery, the stool-like habit develops naturally.

NOTHOFAGUS

N. obliqua, the Roble Beech, is a fast grower but care must be taken that a single leader is maintained. Trained in this way, the branches are well spaced round the trunk and the whole habit is attractive, as they sweep down at an angle. Eventually, as the tree gains height, additional lower branches may be removed to expose the trunk for 4.6 to 6.0 m. (15 to 20 ft.), as it has an attractive bark. In exposed positions growth is more stunted. *N. alpina* can suffer frost and wind damage and is more successful in the sheltered climates. Good short staking is important to prevent wind-rock in the early stages.

N. antarctica. The arboriculturist should make due allowance for the fact that growth is not always free with this species, and that often the main shoot and branches will adopt a twisted habit; it quickly losing its main central leader and should be grown as a feathered tree.

N. dombeyi usually forms a small evergreen tree in the United Kingdom, with a spread that is often equal to the height. This species, especially if it is growing in an open site, develops rival leaders and the whole tree becomes very bushy with many of the lower branches horizontal and just above the ground. There is evidence that a definite leader develops more naturally, if there is competition for light with other trees of a similar age in the early stages after planting out. Grown either way, it forms an attractive tree. Established trees do not respond to hard pruning.

NOTOSPARTIUM

The species are not fully hardy and generally need wall protection. They are particularly tender when young, and should be grown on in the nursery for 2 to 3 years where they can be protected during the winter. When the stems are definitely woody, they may be planted out in a sunny position approximately 0.5 m. (1.5 ft.) from the wall. Branches may be allowed to form from ground level, and they maintain an upright habit of growth to begin with, but the growths from them are pendulous. Often, as the bushes grow older, staking is needed, otherwise the heavy branches lean badly. Very old bushes that are unsightly may be cut right down to young growths, which are often found at the base. Normal pruning consists of carefully cutting out any dead wood, or growths that appear to make the bush untidy.

N. carmichaeliae will reach 1.2 m. (4 ft.) or more in height, and *N. glabrescens* forms a rather larger shrub.

NYSSA

N. sylvatica, the Tupelo. When mature, this species will form quite a large tree, 15 m. (50 ft.) or more in height. However, there appears to be some variation in height and, where the crown forms at an earlier stage in development, a more compact tree is produced which has shorter growth. This variation may well be due in part to soil conditions and a good deep loam is most likely to give the strong growth essential to the production of a leader which will run right up through the crown as height increases. As the tree becomes established in its permanent position, the lower branches may be gradually removed, eventually to a height of 1.8 to 3.0 m. (6 to 10 ft.). This allows the remaining branches to develop their typical semi-pendulous habit and display their fine autumn colour at eye level. Also, access beneath the branches allows the autumn foliage to be viewed from the inside against the light and this is very pleasing.

In the nursery, good, strong growth and a leader should be encouraged, for a stunted specimen, when established in its permanent position, may break out with a strong shoot from low down or near to ground level which will run right up through the centre of the head and spoil the shape. However, should this happen and it is thought that this growth has sufficient vigour to develop beyond the existing branch system, it may be left to supply the future framework of the tree.

N. sinensis should be treated in the same way as *N. sylvatica*.

OEMLERIA

O. cerasiformis. Although this shrub is unisexual both the male and female forms are similar in habit. The shrub suckers freely, and a single specimen soon develops into a clump which also layers freely. With this habit it is suitable for the more natural part of the garden. In this setting an enlarging clump is formed and pruning is difficult to carry out effectively. In a more limited space, some pruning of the older wood may be carried out after flowering and the cuts may be taken right down to ground level. It may also be necessary to remove offending suckers. With age, as they carry more and more wood, the growths often arch over and spoil neighbouring plants. Pruning these to upright young shoots relieves weight and thus corrects the position.

OLEA

O. europaea normally requires wall protection, even in regions with mild winters. Generally six to eight main branches are trained fanwise, with additional laterals tied in as growth extends over the wall. The growths, or 'breast-wood', which develop from this system must be restricted and thinned by careful pruning, always allowing an adequate and natural furnishing. This furnishing should consist mainly of young growths that are the most attractive parts of this plant. Promising shoots may also be used as replacements for any older branches that show signs of failing.

With age, large, woody stems or branches develop and the shrub may become unsightly. The remedy for this is to cut the whole back close to ground level, in the spring so that a fresh start may be made with the young growths which break out freely. Alternatively, the old shrub may be removed completely, planting up a young one in a fresh position.

This species may also be planted out in a sheltered position in the open, provided that the climate is sufficiently mild and sunny. However, after severe winters there may be considerable dieback and dead wood to contend with. A central leader should be trained for this purpose.

OLEARIA

This is a genus of evergreen trees, shrubs and subshrubs. There is a great variety of growth, but the majority will only survive in the mildest climates. Many are happiest in coastal areas where the full sun and wind results in a closer habit, which is more typical.

One general characteristic is that they break freely from pruning cuts, a response which can be made use of in various circumstances. Thus, worn and untidy bushes may be pruned very hard in the spring when growth will break out very freely from the old wood. In the same way, severe injury by frost may be followed by hard pruning. However, the operation should be left until new growths appear, which will indicate just how severe the damage has been. Specimens that have grown too large for their positions may also be carefully pruned in the spring, making the cuts inside the bush at suitable points in order that an informal surface is retained. This restrictive pruning is, for example, needed with such large growers as *O. avicenniifolia* when grown in a fairly confined space near a wall. The gradual process of shortening may need to be extended over two or three seasons, unless a more drastic hard pruning is given over the whole shrub in the first instance. Olearias in such a situation are not trained hard against the surface of a wall, but are left to form free-growing bushes, see Fig. 32.

O. phlogopappa may, with advantage, be cut back after flowering by several inches once the bush is two or three years old and has grown to full size. An even harder cutting back is necessary following damage by frost.

It will be seen, therefore, that the same principles apply throughout the genus. Even *O. nummulariifolia* may at times need pruning, for although it has a stiff and rigid growth, the outer branches sometimes have a tendency to spread and spoil neighbouring shrubs.

ONONIS

O. fruticosa is a hardy, shrubby species which is sometimes found in collections. The actual growth is quite compact, but it does benefit from a light clipping over after flowering, as useless seed production is thus avoided. The pieces should be brushed or picked off. *O. rotundifolia* is semi-woody and should be cut down in the dormant season.

OPLOPANAX

A small genus of the family Araliaceae containing *O. horridus*, Devil's Club, from western North America, a small- to medium-sized stout, spiny shrub with spiny Acer-like leaves. Hardly any pruning is necessary and should any be needed to tidy this plant up, it should be carried out in the spring.

ORIXA

O. japonica is a very densely foliaged shrub that grows from 1.2 to 2.4 m. (4 to 8 ft.) in height, and sends out spreading growths. These are horizontal at first, but the extended branch ends become pendulous. As they touch the soil they root and form strong shoots, and so the mass of twig growth and foliage moves forward. This shrub shows great promise of becoming a first-class ground cover subject. If necessary, the spread can be checked by careful pruning so that the cuts are hidden and the natural habit is retained. The layers may be uprooted in the dormant season and planted elsewhere.

OSMANTHUS

A common characteristic of all the species of Osmanthus is that they regenerate very freely from old wood. Thus they may, if overgrown, be cut back quite severely.

O. heterophyllus is slow-growing. It should be left to branch freely from ground level, the lower branches being almost horizontal. Small growths are produced freely on the old wood, even inside the bush. This shrub may be restricted in size by cutting any long growths back to suitable laterals inside the general branch system, and thus preserving the beautiful effect of an informal surface. This should be carried out in late spring, but hard cutting back of the whole bush, if hopelessly overgrown, is better done in mid spring.

This subject is quite good as a hedge plant, but trimming should be carried out before midsummer. A formal hedge cannot be expected to flower a great deal. The flowers are produced in the axils of the previous season's wood and are followed a few weeks later by more flowers from the bases of the young growths. As a hedge it is often slow to fill out. Plants of *O. h.* 'Purpureus' are often grafted onto a rootstock of *Ligustrum*, and a watch must be kept for suckers, which should be removed as soon as possible.

The remainder of the species also respond to pruning if it is necessary to restrict size, using the same method as with *O. heterophyllus*. Where the individual leaves are larger and the growth stiff and upright, even more care is necessary in carrying out this operation.

O. delavayi, although it may be grown in the open border in the milder regions, is often planted as a wall shrub. The main branches are trained out fanwise and the laterals produced from these provide the furnishing as they extend and branch. This subject flowers in the spring from the previous year's wood. Pruning may be carried out immediately after flowering in late spring and it consists of cutting out any overgrown branches, which may even be weighed down and spoil lower growths. The pruning cuts should be made to suitable growths and, at a later stage, the long, strong shoots may be tied in with the aim of using them as replacements for the older branches forming the framework against the wall. On no account should the wholesale snipping back of growths take place during the summer months, as this will spoil the next season's flowering.

This subject will, however, conform to close clipping several times during the growing season, and is thus suitable for a formal hedge in the milder regions.

O. ×burkwoodii. This is a compact and slow-growing shrub, particularly in the first year or so after planting out from the nursery where it has in the course of training been regularly transplanted. When it does become established in its final quarters, strong, upright growths are put on which stand well above the remainder of the close branch system. Following this, growth often tends to slow down.

If it is necessary to restrict the size of this shrub in any way, pruning should be carried out after flowering in mid to late spring. The longer branches should be cut back inside the bush, taking care to leave an informal surface.

This subject regenerates well after being cut back, and it forms a very close surface as a hedge plant when it is given an annual clipping which should be carried out in midsummer. A later clipping results in secondary growth being put on in the autumn, and this, being soft, may be damaged by frost.

O. decorus, with large leaves, is spreading and rounded in outline. The branching is very rigid, even to the extremities of the system. The spread may be restricted, if necessary, by pruning in late spring after flowering, the longest growths being pruned back to suitable points well inside the bush. With a badly overgrown specimen the pruning may be spread over several years, selecting the growths carefully so that the process is a gradual one and the whole surface is kept well furnished.

OSMARONIA. *See* Oemleria

OSTEOMELES

O. schweriniae is not fully hardy and needs to be grown against a sunny wall in most parts of England. However, the long branches conform quite readily to training, which should be fanwise and hard up against the surface. Pruning in midsummer, once the framework is formed, consists of cutting out the older branches in sufficient quantity to allow the younger ones to take their place, perhaps after further growth and training.

OSTRYA

These are medium-sized trees that in a suitable setting can be trained up with a central leader and become very shapely. A 1.8 to 2.4 m. (6 to 8 ft.) length of clear stem is to be preferred.

O. carpinifolia, the Hop Hornbeam, will perhaps produce the most shapely round head, the branching being light and evenly spaced round the central lead. One of the main beauties of this medium-sized tree is in the finer branching, and the lower limbs should be left to sweep down to eye level, where the beauty of the fruits and later the catkins can be appreciated after the leaves have fallen. This species does not take kindly to competition for light from neighbouring trees, and branches will be lost on shaded parts of the specimen. It is not advised that every specimen should be perfect, in fact, it is an interesting tree to plant on the edge of a natural clump where a tree with rival leaders which leans toward the light, produces a more natural effect.

O. virginiana, the Ironwood, is similar in habit but the branching tends to be heavier. *O. japonica* is a small- to medium-sized tree, retains a very good leader and has slender branches. The shaggy bark of this species is very attractive and it should be grown with a good clear stem.

OSTRYOPSIS

O. davidiana forms a stool-like habit and occasionally throws strong growths from the base. The new growths that extend from ground level often appear 0.3 m. (1 ft.) or so away from the main clump. If necessary, thin and old wood may be cut out at ground level during the winter, but regular attention, even on an annual basis, is seldom required.

OXYDENDRUM

O. arboreum, the Sourwood, requires little or no pruning, but this is often needed on neighbouring, sheltering trees and shrubs to prevent a specimen from being overgrown and spoilt. This subject needs good treatment in the nursery to promote free, feathered growth with a single leader, and this policy should be maintained after it has been planted in its final position. In the early years, short staking may be necessary and transplanting will result in the loss of the central leader. Branching should be encouraged to ground level to provide an adequate furnishing. Any pruning should be carried out in the winter during dormancy, however they do not tolerate pruning, especially established trees. The side of a lawn in an open, sunny site is an ideal setting.

OZOTHAMNUS

This genus is allied to the Helichrysums. Normally the species need wall protection and even in this position they may be badly damaged during the winter. An attempt to improve a damaged or straggly specimen may be made by pruning hard in the spring, just as growth is about to commence. *O. ledifolius* often responds better than many to this treatment if it is considered necessary.

O. scutellifolius in particular is often very reluctant to break out after severe damage during the winter.

PAEONIA

The shrubby species that include *P. delavayi* and *P. suffruticosa* normally require very little pruning.

After the fruits have ripened, the old flower stalks die back to the terminal bud on the new shoot. If fruits are not required, deadheading during the summer can be carried out to encourage further, stronger growth. The shrub has a tidier appearance if these old stalks are cut off after the leaves have fallen. At the same time, any old and worn growths may be removed at ground level. The summer is also a good time to search for dead wood, as it is sometimes difficult to pick out during the winter.

PALIURUS

P. spina-christi. As a shrub this has a spreading habit, the main branches often spring from ground level. In this form, the lower branches are often weighed down to a horizontal position and even lie on the surface as more and more growth is put on laterally. It is also an untidy grower with many crossing branches, but it is not worthwhile attempting to correct this fault in any way, as it does not appear to affect the health of the shrub.

This subject may also be trained as a small tree with a 0.9 to 1.5 m. (3 to 5 ft.) clear stem, by retaining the leader and by cutting out the rivals at the nursery stage. When grown either as a tree or a shrub, this subject can be restricted in size by careful pruning hiding the cuts and retaining an informal effect. If very overgrown, a specimen may be cut hard back, even close to ground level, when it will respond by breaking out strongly. Pruning should be carried out during the dormant season.

PARAHEBE

These natives of New Zealand and Australia, suitable for the rock or gravel garden, need very little pruning apart from a light clip-over after flowering in summer.

PARROTIA

The common species in the genus is *P. persica*, the Persian Ironwood. It is usually classed as a small tree and is capable of growing 9 to 12 m. (30 to 40 ft.) in height. However, once branching commences, even on a nursery specimen, the head quickly opens up and the leader is lost. As a result, the specimen becomes a large bush without any trunk, even when mature. In most cases the best form for planting is a standard on a definite leg of at least 1.8 m. (6 ft.), which has been selected and trained in the nursery. A dense canopy of foliage is formed, making a perfect spot for a garden seat set in the shade against the beautifully mottled trunk and main branches. A watch must be made for any suckers, which should be removed as soon as possible.

The branches have a spreading habit and many are horizontal and even pendulous, growing along the ground as they reach it. In order to retain the full beauty of this plant, these growths should be left to grow unrestricted. A grass foreground is ideal, but care must be taken when mowing on the perimeter of the branch system, for injury to the growths will spoil the effect. Mulching around the dripline of the canopy to reduce the need for close mowing will help to preserve a natural effect with the lower canopy. There should be no attempt to thin the branching, however much this appears to be crowded, for the overlapping and often crossing system is the natural habit of this tree and is also one of its beauties. Often a deep shade is cast on the lower branches of this canopy, but usually they retain a full covering of foliage. This ability to survive in shady conditions is again displayed when branches develop under neighbouring trees with quite a dense canopy. However, full sun is preferred. Two cultivars are grown for their habits, *P. p.* 'Vanessa' for its erect form and *P. p.* 'Pendula' for its pendulous dome-like habit.

The second species in the genus, *P. subaequalis*, should be treated like *P. persica*.

PARROTIOPSIS

P. jacquemontiana forms quite a dense, twiggy head, developing into a large shrub, rarely a tree. In the nursery, the head may be formed on a short leg 0.3 to 0.6 m. (1 to 2 ft.) in length. Branching is very extensive and the head forms very quickly. The beauty of this shrub is in the branching, and this should be encouraged to develop, even on to the ground. Once

the head is formed, any suckers which appear, as they sometimes do from the region of the trunk, should be removed unless grown as a multi-stemmed shrub.

PARTHENOCISSUS

One characteristic of this climbing genus is that the tendrils usually flatten upon contact with solid objects and form discs or pads that cling very tightly to the surface.

P. quinquefolia is one of the strongest species and it is typical of the majority, which are suitable for growing over trees, sheds or other buildings, walls or fences. Pruning is unnecessary when they are grown in the wilder parts of the garden, although a careful watch should be kept to see that nearby shrubs are not smothered unintentionally.

These self-clinging vines are sometimes planted against buildings, *P. tricuspidata*, Boston Ivy, being the most frequently grown, but this can lead to damage if they are allowed to grow beyond the eaves and among the tiles. The thickening stems disturb these, while the annual leaf fall can lead to blocked gutters and the surface of rough-cast walls can be torn away and damaged by the weight. It is certainly advisable to keep the growths below the eaves and guttering by pruning annually in the autumn.

Pergolas may also be used as supports, the pruning being carried out annually. The young growths are taken back to the rods, which are trained onto the uprights and crosspieces, the point of pruning being just above the lowest bud. The period for this is in early winter, when there is no danger of bleeding. Under this system, spurs build up on the vine, while the growths hang down to form a curtain of attractive foliage, see Fig. 20 (6).

P. henryana is best grown against a wall and produces bright silver veins on the leaves when grown in the shade.

PASSIFLORA

P. caerulea is commonly grown in the south of England, particularly on walls where it may be trained up a trellis or wire system. It is best when taken up to a height of 2.4 to 3.0 m. (8 to 10 ft.). The available space is covered by a framework of main branches that are trained hard up against the structure. This is not difficult, as this subject climbs naturally, using tendrils for support. The main stems are spaced approximately 150 to 250 mm. apart, but it may become necessary to thin these later.

The laterals from these are allowed to hang down at full length and are pruned back to a good bud at the base. This is carried out annually in the spring; it is in fact a type of spur pruning. The subject flowers on the long growths that are produced during the summer.

PAULOWNIA

The three subjects most commonly grown are *P. fargesii*, *P. tomentosa* 'Lilacina' and *P. tomentosa*, although the latter is the best known. Some authorities are of the opinion that *P. fargesii* is more suited to the climate of the British Isles but this certainly does not always hold good and, so far as the arboriculturist is concerned, there appears to be little difference in their training and pruning. The following details will therefore hold good for all three.

They are all fast growers and are especially tender when young. Often, they will reach a height of 1.8 to 2.4 m. (6 to 8 ft.) after two years from seed. They prefer a rich soil, but the large, sappy growth which is produced is often unripe at the tip when the winter sets in and is thus damaged or killed. This does not matter a great deal, for the dead growth may be cut back to a strong developing shoot; in fact, it is seldom that a terminal bud is produced on the tip of the shoot and an axillary bud beneath invariably takes over in the spring. It is important to build up a single leader for as long as possible and the first main branch should be formed with a clear stem of at least 1.8 m. (6 ft.).

Occasionally, after a wet year, a shoot is thrown up through the tree that may eventually rival the leader. Normally, this should be pruned at an early stage, but such a growth ought to be left on a weakly specimen as it may eventually prove to be the tree's means of survival and development. It is difficult to grow shapely trees on wet, cold soils. Under these conditions, uncontrollable cavities form in the soft wood,

while whole branches often die back. Paulownias do not do well in shade, for a sunny position is required to ripen the wood.

Formerly, Paulownias were frequently grown for their tropical foliage effect. The way to produce this is to cut the stems down to within 50 to 80 mm. (2 to 3 in.) of ground level in the spring each year before growth begins. The resultant shoots are then thinned out to one. Feeding and watering, if this is necessary, ensures rich, luxuriant growth.

PERIPLOCA

P. graeca is a vigorous twining shrub that may reach a height of 6 to 9 m. (20 to 30 ft.). It branches freely from ground level. When grown against a wall, vertical wires are necessary in addition to the horizontal strands to give support in the initial stages. However, this subject is more suitable for pergolas and similar structures, though it will also climb small trees that are weakly or dying.

Little pruning is required and it is difficult to keep this shrub tidy. However, some of the weakest growths may be cut out in the spring.

Care should be taken when pruning, as it produces a poisonous milky sap that can also be an irritant.

PERNETTYA. *See* Gaultheria

PEROVSKIA

The most commonly grown species in this small genus is *P. atriplicifolia*. This late-flowering, semi-woody member of the family Lamiaceae produces long flower spikes terminating the growths which develop rapidly during the spring and early summer from the woody rootstock. During the winter these are killed back severely, often to within 50 to 80 mm. (2 to 3 in.) of their bases, but in the spring buds break freely from the living portion.

There is a definite advantage in hard pruning annually in the spring, just as the buds break, for the dead wood which has served as a protection during the winter is then removed to allow the new growths to develop unrestrictedly, and the plant is left tidier. Also, with the buds breaking the severity of the pruning may be adjusted with accuracy, cutting hard back to the base of each shoot, leaving only one or two developing buds on each. This is really a form of thinning and results in few shoots but better spikes.

The remaining Perovskias may be dealt with in the same way.

PERSEA

P. americana, the Avocado Pear, is the most commonly grown, but is not hardy outdoors in regions with hard winters. *P. borbonia* and *P. ichangensis* make small evergreen trees in the milder climates, producing small white flowers in late spring or early summer. Very little pruning is needed, apart from the removal of crossing and damaged branches, which should be done after flowering if there is no need for the fruits.

PERTYA

P. sinensis. Provided that this interesting shrub is well positioned in an open situation, it is a neat grower and very little pruning is necessary.

PETTERIA

P. ramentacea. This shrub should be left to grow and branch naturally, when it will develop into a sturdy bush. Normally no pruning is required.

PHELLODENDRON

These trees are fast-growing and thrive best on a well-drained but rich soil. They have rather a stiff, sparsely branched habit and providing that good growth is encouraged in the nursery they train very readily. A good leader should be maintained throughout the stages, until the crown has been formed when, with the main branches taking much of the vigour, it will quickly be lost. Late frosts may damage the young growths.

P. amurense var. *sachalinense* is the most outstanding, forming a good leader from which a clear trunk of 1.8 to 2.4 m. (6 to 8 ft.) may be trained. The lower branches develop sparsely, even down to eye level. The foliage is attractive, especially in the autumn, the leaflets turning bright yellow and dropping later to reveal the bright yellow midrib that eventually falls as well. The remaining species have a similar habit but they are not as large growing in cultivation. *P. amurense*, the Amur Cork Tree, and *P. chinense* seem to be more prone to damage from late frosts than the others and, as a result, the branching is not so clean and definite, but is twiggy with a covering of dwarf shoots over the system. Due allowance must be made for this development. *P. lavalleei* produces a beautiful canopy of foliage and when viewed from beneath against the light, the mosaic effect is perfect.

PHILADELPHUS

Most of the shrubs in this genus grow freely from ground level and form a stool. They flower on laterals produced on growths made in the previous year. This stool habit may be encouraged by planting slightly deeper, after a bushy habit has been developed by close pruning in the nursery.

A good soil and sufficient moisture, with feeding and mulching, provide the conditions necessary if these plants are to remain healthy and flower well year after year. Their general condition can be judged by the amount of new growth, which should develop rapidly during and after flowering.

In most cases some annual pruning immediately after flowering is necessary. The wood that has flowered may then be cut away to a suitable growth. Sometimes an entire branch may be cut out to ground level, but there should be a new growth from this region for replacement. In this way annual pruning should be seen as a necessary operation to regulate growth and flowering, keeping a good supply of young wood coming up from the base. As a general rule most of the wood above ground level should be no older than five years.

In the case of really old bushes which are spent and overgrown, most of the top growth may be cut down to ground level during the winter and early spring, or after flowering. However, it is often a better policy to replace such plants with young ones.

It is important to take the natural habit of growth and vigour of the species or variety into account, for there is a considerable variation in this respect. As an example, *P. coronarius* is a strong grower, reaching up to 3.7 m. (12 ft.), while *P. c.* 'Variegatus' is much smaller, producing thin almost wiry stems. Many other instances of variation could be quoted among the Lemoinei Group (*P. ×lemoinei*) yet the general method of pruning is common to all, provided that habit is taken into account.

P. microphyllus is a low-growing shrub with fine growths and small leaves. With this species it is necessary to carefully prune back any branches which trail and overhang other plants but generally an informal shape should be retained.

P. c. 'Variegatus' has already been mentioned. Both this and *P. c.* 'Aureus' are grown mainly for their foliage. The best colour is found on the younger growths and it is therefore important to maintain a good proportion of these on the bushes.

Aphis is a serious pest of *Philadelphus* and the young growths that are so important often suffer badly. A control should therefore be applied in good time, before the damage is extensive.

PHILLYREA

One reaction which is common to all the species and cultivars in this genus is that they regenerate freely and produce a plentiful supply of new growths from the region of pruning cuts, even if they are made on the old wood. They also produce substantial branches from ground level, eventually becoming large shrubs or small trees.

P. angustifolia has a close habit, but with the variety *P. a.* f. *rosmarinifolia* the density of individual branches is such that there is a considerable buildup of dead twig growth inside the bush. This in turn increases the weight to such an extent that the upper branches are bent down onto the lower ones. Also, the inside branches are deprived of light and thus there are few living growths in this region of the bush. Owing to the dense habit it is difficult to prune with the aim of restricting size, and it is better to give this subject a grass foreground where its natural habit can develop. Should very severe damage occur as a result of a gale or a heavy snowfall, hard pruning to near ground level is often the best policy.

P. latifolia, an elegant small tree or large shrub, has a similar habit.

Phillyrea can also be used successfully for topiary, as it will tolerate regular tight clipping.

PHLOMIS

Although these are classed as shrubs and consist of a woody branch system, the leafy shoot tips are soft and are liable to injury in a severe winter. However, one characteristic which is common to all the species is that new growths break freely from the old wood, provided that this is in a healthy condition. Thus, after a severe winter the injured growths may be cut back as the young shoots break out in the spring. Very old and woody specimens may not break freely and should be replaced.

Overgrown specimens also respond to hard cutting back, again choosing the spring period. It is possible, however, to keep these shrubs in good condition for many years by pruning back a selected number of growths each spring, for example, cutting back any which have become weak and woody or have overgrown into neighbouring plants. *P. chrysophylla* becomes very heavy with growths which are eventually weighed down to the ground. These will even root and form fresh plants well away from the parent. *P. italica* has a woody habit and develops a very ragged appearance unless this is controlled by an occasional pruning. *P. viscosa* has a loose habit which is kept more compact by a limited amount of cutting back each year, again in the spring.

PHOTINIA

P. villosa is a large, deciduous shrub or small tree which often consists of several upright branches.

Normally, this subject needs little regular pruning, but strong young growths are often thrown up from ground level. These can be thinned and trained to eventually replace old branches if this is considered necessary. As they become old, the top growth often does not produce much young wood and thus the shrub loses strength.

P. davidsoniae is an evergreen for a sheltered position. It should be trained to form a leader, but should be allowed to branch from ground level. It may be cut back by severe weather, but it will break freely from living wood despite the fact that this may be old.

P. davidiana, another evergreen species, is commonly grown. It has a stiff, erect branching habit and appears to be rather an ungainly grower when compared with many other shrubs. However, this is a natural habit and there should be no attempt to correct it by pruning. In fact, this subject and its varieties need little pruning beyond the removal of dead wood as it is unfortunately very susceptible to Fireblight (*Erwinia amylovora*). Like so many Rosaceous shrubs it will break freely from cuts, even on the older wood. It is also quite attractive when trained fairly close to a wall, with the main branches tied fanwise to wire supports. In this position pruning should consist of cutting away the oldest wood and branches, if they are worn and spent, provided that healthy young shoots remain which can be trained as replacements. Otherwise it may be necessary to wait for the old wood to break after cutting them out. The young growths not required for tying in may be stopped during the summer to 6 to 8 leaves, pruning these back hard to near their base during the winter.

P. nussia develops into a small tree, but is only suitable for mild localities. *P. serratifolia* is similar in this respect. This latter species and *P. beauverdiana* are really at their best when grown in the shelter of a wall. One or two main stems should be trained up and tied loosely to the wall but otherwise they are self-supporting. The side growths may need pruning back carefully from time to time as they grow extensively. This should be carried out in mid spring, taking the cuts back into the bush to a suitable point so that they are hidden and leaving a furnished appearance.

P. ×fraseri and its various forms like 'Birmingham', 'Red Robin' and 'Indian Princess' are usually grown for their attractive brightly coloured young leaves in the spring. Minimal pruning is required, apart from shortening back out-growing branches to keep the shrub tidy. This should be done in spring. When grown as a hedge, clipping should be carried out in late spring to early summer.

PHYGELIUS

P. capensis 'Coccineus' is the most popular form of this plant. It is often grown as an herbaceous plant in the open border, being killed down to ground level each winter. It spreads extensively by stoloniferous growths that develop just beneath the soil surface.

This is also a good subject for a wall with a southerly aspect. The wood is retained from year to year up to a height of 1.5 to 1.8 m. (5 to 6 ft.). Pruning is carried out in the spring, back to the main stems that are secured loosely to the wires. In very mild districts it will survive as a woody shrub in the open. Pruning is carried out in the spring back to the living wood.

PHYLLODOCE

Normally, very little pruning is needed on these small shrubs which are rather exacting in their cultural requirements. A bushy habit should be encouraged in the nursery and in the permanent position and, as a result, plenty of strong growths will be thrown up from the base of the plant each year. Any dead growths that do occur should be cut out, but often there is a wholesale browning over the whole of the plant which is a sign that it is dying. Often, one or two branches in a clump extend well beyond the remainder and these may be layered down with pins, when they will serve a useful purpose in forming fresh plants and increasing the size of the clump.

PHYLLOSTACHYS. *See* Bamboos

PHYSOCARPUS

P. opulifolius. This shrub adopts a stool-like habit and it throws up many young growths among the older branches at ground level. Pruning consists of cutting out a proportion of the older wood after flowering. The extent of this pruning must depend upon growth and condition, but the shrub should be left well furnished. The older branches are quite attractive with peeling bark during the winter and this should also be considered. The pruning policy may consist of cutting out the oldest wood at ground level taking away whole branches, of cutting out some of the old wood on the remaining mature growths to a suitable point and of thinning out the young canes which originate at ground level. When cutting back part of a branch system it is often better to take the cut back to an outward growing young shoot, as the bush then assumes a more natural appearance.

P. capitatus is even stronger growing, and with a large number of young canes springing from the base it may need a more drastic thinning. This species also suckers extensively and it is more suitable for the more natural parts of the garden. *P. monogynus* has a small stool head with a spreading but stiff branch system and it should be given sufficient space for a 1.8 to 2.4 m. (6 to 8 ft.) spread. A greater proportion of the older wood will need to be left on this and on *P. malvaceus*. *P. stellatus* throws up plenty of new growths and the old ones may be cut out quite severely after flowering. The natural arching habit should be retained.

PICEA

As with many other conifers, the spruces have a strong central leader that is built up from the seedling stage in the nursery. They vary greatly in size and shape, however most have a conical habit. Most of the species will only thrive well with at least some shelter and a sufficiently moist soil. A free and adequate branch spread down to ground level is to be desired, but for this, adequate light should reach the whole tree and the immediate surround must be kept free of shrub growth, etc. It is important to grow them well from the seedling or transplant stage for the best results.

PICRASMA

P. quassioides is a small tree or shrub grown for its foliage effect. The branches are ascending and preferably it should be trained with a short leg 0.6 m. (2 ft.) high. Even the lower and outer branches on a mature tree are horizontal and seldom droop. Cuts heal very well, but in a mature tree the long branches with little furnishing except at the ends sometimes split at the narrow crotches and bracing may eventually be needed.

PIERIS

There is quite a variety of growth within this Ericaceous genus, but all the species have one or two requirements and characteristics in common. Growth is more likely to be healthy and typical in a sheltered position and, provided the plants are strong and healthy, they will respond well to hard pruning although it should not be resorted to more often than is necessary. Free natural growth is ideal and it is often necessary to cut back neighbouring shrubs in order to ensure this. Low overhanging branches or difficult positions where the light comes only from one side may bring about unequal growth and a poor shape. *P. floribunda* and *P. japonica* seem in particular to suffer in such conditions, and the heavy one-sided growth which follows may pull the whole bush out of shape. Under such circumstances, in addition to correcting the cause of this unnatural growth, the excessively heavy branches may often be cut back to suitable upright branches, but if the latter are not available they will normally break out in response to pruning. Another justifiable reason for hard pruning is when it is necessary to cut off growths that have been severely damaged during the winter. Often these shrubs will break forth, even when they have been cut hard back close to ground level. *P. formosa* and its forms perhaps show a more ready response than the others. Concerning the species generally, a good bush should be well furnished to ground level and the aim should be to keep this surface intact by good culture. If it is necessary to prune, do this in the spring.

PILEOSTEGIA

The species commonly grown is *P. viburnoides*. It is self-clinging, producing long extension growths that become attached to a support by means of masses of roots, see Fig. 39. Thus it is a suitable subject for rambling over an old tree stump or a wall. If the latter, it is advisable to allow the growths to develop on the top as this gives additional support to the mature flowering wood that is built up. A wire system is also necessary for supporting ties as the heavier branch system develops.

Fig. 39. A young growth of *Pileostegia viburnoides* showing the free production of adventitious roots along the stem which enable this subject to cling to a suitable surface.

Pruning consists of cutting back any surplus extension growths that develop once the allotted space has been covered. The flowering branches also need shortening if they become heavy and in danger of breaking, or grow too far from the wall. This should be carried out in the spring, although the extension growths may be stopped as they develop during the summer months.

PINUS

As with most of the conifers, the retention of a leader is very important to the form and well-being of the vast majority of this large group, but their habits vary considerably. It is important to have some knowledge of the species under consideration, especially when the final position is being selected, for little pruning or training is possible without spoiling the trees completely.

Following up the point that it is important to retain the leader in a healthy condition, this is only possible if the tree is growing vigorously. The radial branches produced round the central stem must be healthy and vigorous to give support and shelter to the main extension shoot.

Should the main leader be lost for any reason, a vigorous tree will often produce several growths that will grow up in its place. These should be thinned down to one in the following spring, retaining the strongest and bearing in mind the desirability of selecting a growth that is in direct line with the main axis. The best time for pruning is in the spring when the new growths are 50 to 80 mm. (2 to 3 in.) long. Once a flat-topped effect has developed and the tree has reached its ultimate height, there is no point in trying to select a leader, as it is seldom successful.

A group of the Pines, mostly the larger and more vigorous growers and including *P. nigra* and *P. sylvestris*, appear to have two distinct phases of growth, but the transition from one to the other is a very gradual process. The first phase is an extension in height within the limits set by the environment and exposure generally. It is during this period, which lasts until the ultimate height for the tree is reached, that the preservation and well-being of the leading growth is important. In the second phase many or all of the lower branches die, partly through lack of light and also because the vigour is taken into the upper system. Often in the higher portions a definite crown forms as a number of the branches thicken, as a result of which the smaller ones usually die out completely. The extent to which the thickening occurs and the crown develops varies, even within a species, but a crowded specimen is less likely to form an extensive head. The amount of all-round light is the most important deciding factor.

This may appear confusing, for there is no definite advice to give upon the species or varieties which develop this habit, but the general rule to follow is to keep the specimen growing healthily and to cut any dying branches back hard to the trunk. Thickening and extension into main branches will soon become evident when it occurs. The arboriculturist may often welcome the ultimate development of a head, in contrast to the forester who does not look kindly upon heavy branching.

It should, of course, be remembered that a number of species have an attractive bark that is shown to full effect on a long straight trunk, clear of branches. Examples are *P. nigra*, *P. sylvestris* and *P. bungeana*.

The many other forms of growth among the various species are often quite distinctive; for example *P. muricata*, *P. pinea* and *P. radiata* may branch heavily from low down to form a wide crown with little or no trunk, especially if planted in the open. *P. mugo* is also variable, being either a shrub or a small tree, but it is low branching.

P. wallichiana, the Bhutan Pine, retains and builds on the lower branch system if it is in an isolated position and receives sufficient light. These branches often spread horizontally and even lie on the ground. A mature specimen with this habit needs special care, for during periods of extreme drought or impoverishment the topmost branches tend to die back and this spoils the general shape of the tree.

P. rigida is quite distinctive in that even a mature tree will freely produce adventitious shoots. This is a characteristic of this species and there should be no attempt to remove them. *P. serotina*, a related species, also produces these growths.

PIPTANTHUS

P. nepalensis is the hardiest and most widely grown species, but wall protection is often necessary. The shrub has a stool-like habit, producing strong growths from the base, a habit that in time results in overcrowding and this may spoil the effect.

As this shrub may suffer during severe winters, pruning should be left until the spring so that the young growths have maximum protection. At this period, when the danger of severe frost has passed, the old and worn growths are cut out completely down to ground level, but sufficient mature shoots should be left for furnishing. The laterals on the main upright and healthy branches are only tipped back if they have been injured.

This shrub should be left to grow freely as a bush, and not be trained on the wall's surface.

PISTACIA

P. chinensis is the most reliable species for growing in the open but sometimes it is not altogether happy. The main stem should, if possible, be trained up to form a trunk 1.5 to 1.8 m. (5 to 6 ft.) in height before the branch system is formed. The lead should be maintained for as long as possible but this species does not often form a large tree in England. There is often a considerable amount of dead wood to cut out, and it may be desirable to leave the epicormic growths to balance up this loss of wood. Prune in midsummer if this is necessary.

P. terebinthus is slow-growing and is not altogether satisfactory in the open as it really needs wall protection. It should be trained up with a single leader and apart from one or two loose ties to the wall it is capable of self-support. The laterals are pendulous and become untidy.

PITTOSPORUM

Normally, even the hardiest species require the protection of a wall in all but the warmer localities. They are not trained hard against the surface but are grown as bushes, being planted 0.6 to 0.9 m. (2 to 3 ft.) from the base. The habit of growth varies not only with the species but also with local climatic conditions. The well-drained, open and sunny position tends to produce a more compact and well-ripened growth that is more typical of many species, and such plants have a better chance of wintering successfully.

Those species, such as *P. ralphii*, which produce a bush with a spreading habit, may be pruned in the spring if this is considered necessary, in order to encourage a more compact habit. The cuts should be taken to a suitable point inside the bush in order to maintain an informal surface. By contrast, *P. patulum* has ascending branches and is more upright in growth.

P. tenuifolium is a tender species which reaches the proportions of a small tree. It should be left to form a single stem but will branch very thickly, both from this and on growths which are sent up from ground level. It is used for hedging in mild districts.

Pittosporums regenerate freely from the old wood and therefore respond to hard pruning in the spring. So often, however, a severe winter will kill the tenderer species outright.

PLAGIANTHUS

P. regius is very like a birch in general appearance, especially in the early stages when it has a straight leading trunk with thin, intertwining, semi-pendulous laterals. More definite side branches appear as the shrub matures. *P. divaricatus* produces masses of thin growths. Both subjects normally need wall protection. No regular pruning is necessary.

PLATANUS

The Planes are strong-growing, majestic trees which are much prized by arboriculturists as they respond well to good, early training and develop into shapely specimens.

P. ×hispanica retains a leader very readily and young trees are often shapely. However, rival leaders often develop and these should be dealt with at an early stage. It is considered good practice to grow a 1.8 to 2.4 m. (6 to 8 ft.) clear stem in the nursery, although at a later stage, as the crown extends, the length of clear trunk may be increased to 4.6 to 6.0 m. (15 to 20 ft.). The clean growth and bark effects of the main trunk and branches are the great attractions of this hybrid. When the tree reaches the mature stage the ends of the lower branches are pendulous, and although this habit cannot be encouraged in a thoroughfare where it would impede traffic, it produces a fine effect in the garden. These growths may be 6 m. (20 ft.) or more in length and reach the ground. The base of the trunk thickens considerably in a large mature tree and a low mound of soil develops beneath this, but seldom do the individual buttress roots develop to the surface. *P. ×h.* 'Pyramidalis' does not develop the same pendulous habit in its lower branches.

P. orientalis develops a more rounded head with heavier branches and a shorter trunk. It is a strong tree, but there is some evidence that older wood on specimens beyond their prime produces cavities, which might in time result in the loss of a large limb. The main branches of very old trees should therefore be braced as a precaution and a thorough overhaul and shortening is often advisable.

P. occidentalis is not a satisfactory tree in the United Kingdom, as the young growths suffer severe damage from the late spring frosts.

Platanus species regenerate very freely from the tissues surrounding cut surfaces. This amazing response to frequent cutting is proved beyond all doubt when it is used as a street tree and is cut back year after year to form a dense crown of young growths. This practice is not advocated as a long-term policy and the reader in need of advice is referred to Chapter Two.

PLATYCARYA

P. strobilacea is a small, slender tree or even a large shrub. It needs great care and attention when young, with shelter and protection, for it is subject to damage by late frosts. Trained properly, it will retain its leader well and a clear trunk of 1.5 to 1.8 m. (5 to 6 ft.) can be formed. The slender branches are naturally well spaced round the leader while the crown is fairly dense.

PLATYCLADUS

P. orientalis has a formal columnar habit built up with a central leader and erect branches when young. No attempt should be made to form a leader with *P. orientalis*, for with many forms of this species the trunk naturally splits up almost at ground level.

PLEIOBLASTUS. *See* Bamboos

PODOCARPUS

Many of the species are grown successfully in milder climates, although a few are suitable for the more favourable regions.

   P. lawrencei and *P. nivalis* require no training and need only sufficient space and light for development. *P. salignus* normally develops into a large shrub in all but the most sheltered areas. It should be allowed to break freely from ground level if it shows a tendency to do this.

POLIOTHYRSIS

P. sinensis. This interesting, late-flowering subject forms a small, slender tree with a very bushy crown. It should be trained to a single leader, eventually forming a clear trunk of 1.2 to 1.8 m. (4 to 6 ft.). However, once branching has become strongly established, it is difficult to retain a leader. Stopping is therefore important in order to build up height and length of stem while young. The flowers terminate the short, twiggy growths of the current season. No regular pruning is needed.

POLYGONUM. *See* Fallopia

PONCIRUS

There is only one species in this genus, *P. trifoliata*, the Japanese Bitter Orange. It does in fact bear 'range blossom' flowers in late spring on the growths produced during the previous year. The shrub forms a very thick bush when it is growing freely and in the early stages strong shoots are thrown up from near the base. A bushy habit should be encouraged in the nursery stage by at least one pruning. At a later stage in its growth a maturing bush thickens up considerably, often with crossing branches. There should be no attempt to thin the bush or to cut out the offending branches, for this dense growth is one of its attractions. In the same way, any small furnishing branches near the base should be left and the lower and outer ones will almost reach ground level.

This shrub loves the sun and a shaded branch sometimes dies back, especially in a severe winter. Any such dead wood may be cut out in an annual inspection each spring.

   It is sometimes grown as a formal or informal hedge. Under close clipping, which is carried out in early summer, a very dense surface is produced. Often, growths are produced later in the season, particularly on the sunny side, so that a second light pruning may be necessary.

POPULUS

Many of the species and hybrids are rapid growers that will quickly develop into quite large trees and are much favoured for this reason by the timber industry. Mostly too, they respond well to training and will rapidly form a leader and trunk.

   For ornamental purposes they are often grown with a clear length of trunk, but the branches should not be trimmed back for a greater height than 6 to 9 m. (20 to 30 ft.) unless it becomes absolutely necessary through dieback. Epicormic growths develop freely, even on mature trunks once they have been trimmed up, and this involves considerable work if it is to be carried out to any height. The epicormic growths that do develop on the trunk must really be trimmed annually during the winter, as otherwise if they are left for some years the problem becomes an even greater one.

   Poplars generally hold their limbs remarkably well and are seldom ruined by gales in the same way that Ash trees are, for example. They do suffer minor twig damage but this does not seem to matter a great deal.

   Any trimming that is to be carried out should be completed by mid winter as bleeding can be troublesome. The wood itself is soft but tough and does not saw easily unless the teeth are very sharp.

   Many Poplars produce main roots close to the surface. As they thicken, these may be on or even above the ground. This often leads to difficulty when mowing and the only remedy is to raise the soil level carefully to cover such obstructions. With really large trees a mound often builds up round the base of the trunk as the buttress roots thicken and push the surface soil up.

Among the diseases that are most serious is the bacterial organism that causes the condition termed Poplar Canker. It may be so serious that even large branches are killed. Varying degrees of resistance are shown by some species and hybrids. The appropriate Forestry Commission Leaflets give an account of these.

Poplars are grouped in sections botanically and it is convenient to deal with the pruning according to this system.

Section 1. *Leuce* (White Poplars, Quaking Aspens)

The tendency of this group to sucker is more marked in some species and forms than in others. *P. alba* is effective when planted on the edge of a clump of trees as the white undersurface of the leaf is often exposed even in a light breeze and makes an attractive feature. For the same reason a good furnishing should be encouraged as low down as possible. This species suckers freely. *P. ×canescens* also suckers and will thus form large clumps if allowed to grow freely. With both species the suckers must be regularly removed unless a clump effect is required. Both species are good on the coast and in exposed places and are most effective if in natural clumps in such a situation. In this way the smaller, suckerous stems give protection to the larger ones. The lower branches of *P. ×canescens* often have a semi-pendulous habit and the tree will furnish up with an attractive growth that shades most of the trunk. *P. tremula* is definitely at its best when grown as a natural suckering clump.

Section 2. *Leucoides* (Large-leaved Poplars)

One of the most ornamental of Poplars is in this group, *P. lasiocarpa*. It forms a round-headed tree and has a stiff, branching habit. The individual branches are mainly either ascending or horizontal. Poplars generally are light-demanding, but normally this species is so shapely that a poor, badly shaped specimen is very evident by contrast. A tiered effect is often produced by strong development of the terminal bud and those immediately below it. *P. wilsonii* also falls into this group.

Section 3. *Tacamahaca* (Balsam Poplars)

P. balsamifera and *P. ×jackii* sucker freely and these must be kept down if ornamental specimens are desired. *P. trichocarpa* and the hybrid *P. ×generosa* are strong, large growers and it is important to maintain a leader for as long as possible. *P. ×jackii* 'Aurora' produces an attractive cream-mottled leaf when coppiced or pollarded regularly.

Section 4. *Aegeiros* (Black Poplars)

The above is also true for the strong-growing species and hybrids in this group. Failure to retain a leader results in very heavy and unnatural branching. The ability to retain one varies considerably with the species and variety; for example, *P. ×canadensis* 'Eugenei' forms a long, straight trunk quite easily with comparatively light branching, whereas *P. ×c.* 'Marilandica' will often produce very heavy branching and a wide head. These various branching habits should be taken into account by the arboriculturist responsible for their care and maintenance, who should be acquainted with the habit of trees in his charge.

The arboriculturist who is looking for ornamental poplars rather than large and vigorous hybrids may prefer the smaller growers such as *P. ×berolinensis*. This has an attractive, burred trunk, the branchlets often being pendulous with the growing points turned up. As with *P. nigra*, the burrs should be trimmed over annually in order to remove any dwarf shoots that may arise. *P. ×canadensis* 'Serotina' has the interesting habit of turning the leader away from the direction of the prevailing wind, although this habit is also displayed to some extent by others. This hybrid comes into leaf late and thus escapes the late spring frosts. The danger of spring frost damage must be taken into account when making a selection of Poplars to plant up.

Such fastigiate forms as *P. nigra* 'Italica' require very little pruning, being most effective when furnished down to ground level.

POTENTILLA

P. fruticosa. There are numerous varieties of this popular shrub grown in our gardens but the type species forms a dense shrub about 0.9 m. (3 ft.) in height. The main branches are upright or ascending, increasing in size to form a permanent branch system. Many of the forms, hybrids and varieties follow this habit, e.g. *P. f.* 'Friedrichsenii'. Left unpruned, they develop a mat of growth, the older and weaker branches being weighed down by the younger. Fallen leaves collect in the fine mass of branches, making the bush very untidy.

Pruning should be carried out in the spring and consists of cutting out the weaker wood and smaller growths to stronger wood or to the base. The strong, young growths, often sent up from the base or from older wood in the centre, should be shortened to half or two-thirds of their length. It is the laterals from these that flower the most and over the longest period. The old, small and twiggy growths do not flower extensively, nor for so long a period.

However there are a number of low, dwarf forms that are very popular. A modified form of this type of pruning should be adopted, for it is still a good policy to cut out the weakest wood and at the same time cut back the strong, young growths.

This subject may also be grown to form an informal hedge and it is pruned in the same way in the spring.

PRINSEPIA

P. sinensis forms a dense thorny bush with a large number of young growths originating from the older wood, particularly from the more upright portions of branches which, as a result, become weighed down to and below the horizontal. Very little pruning is possible, apart from the removal of dead wood in the summer; indeed, the natural habit can easily be lost by unnecessary thinning. The larger branches have scaling bark that is attractive. *P. uniflora* is even more disorderly in growth. *P. utilis* needs wall protection in regions with hard winters, where it should be grown as a bush. It has a graceful, arching habit. These shrubs must have sufficient space for free and full development.

PROSTANTHERA

Even the hardier species require the protection of a wall, and may be tried in this situation in the zones with mild winters. They do not conform to a rigid training and should be planted 0.3 m. (1 ft.) away from the base and grown as bushes. Their normal habit is to break low down at or near ground level and produce upright growths that branch very freely, forming a thick and bushy shrub.

Any pruning that is necessary, either to restrict size or to prevent overgrowth onto neighbouring specimens, is carried out after the flowers have dropped in the spring. However some attention may be necessary after a severe winter when much dead growth may have to be cut back. This should be left until the new growth is breaking.

PRUMNOPITYS

P. andina is hardy in many regions provided that it is sheltered. Typically, this species forms a very low but dense and spreading crown. At the best it will normally only form a very short trunk before splitting up into a number of upright stems, but often these spring directly from ground level. The branches grow out from these horizontally, but the lowest ones will sweep to the ground over a lawn or open space adding greatly to the attraction of this beautiful tree. This species may also be used as a low, formal hedge, approximately 0.9 m. (3 ft.) high. For this purpose they should be planted about 300 mm. apart, and should be encouraged to branch low near the base by hard pruning. The very young growths, especially those on the top surface, are susceptible to frost damage and it is not advisable to clip later than midsummer in order to allow sufficient time for subsequent growths to harden. It may be necessary to clip twice during one season, in which case the best times are late spring and early summer.

PRUNUS

In this genus are various subgenera that are based on well-known groups: Subgenus I. *Prunophora* (Plums, Apricots); Subgenus II. *Amygdalus* (Almonds, Peaches); Subgenus III. *Cerasus* (Cherries); Subgenus IV. *Padus* (Bird Cherries) and Subgenus V. *Laurocerasus* (Cherry Laurels).

Very few of the prunus need annual pruning. In fact, the majority seldom need attention once the tree or bush has been formed in the nursery, apart from the removal of dead or diseased pieces. It is difficult to over-stress the importance of sound propagation and good training, for a bad start through the choice of a poor or incompatible stock cannot be corrected by culture and pruning in later years. Again, should the grafting be set at the wrong height on the stock no form of training will hide this. It is therefore preferable with ornamental trees generally, for the union to be made near ground level, so that if an unsightly bulge forms in later years it can be hidden by grass or suitable plantings.

While it is true that most prunus do not need annual pruning, many horticulturists believe that even an occasional pruning when needed is definitely harmful. It is difficult to produce any direct evidence that this is so, but there is a danger of certain diseases entering a wound, e.g. Silver Leaf, especially during the winter when the trees are dormant. The best period for large prunings to be removed is before midsummer, see Chapter Two.

In order to reduce the need for pruning to a definite size and shape, it is important to select the species or variety most carefully before the planting is made. Among the prunus there is a great variety of form and size to choose from and thus with the ideal selection, perfectly natural and unrestricted growth can be left to develop.

Subgenus I. *Prunophora* (Plums, Apricots)

Prunus spinosa, the Blackthorn, a spiny shrub or small tree, is usually found in thickets on waste ground or in hedgerows. It spreads rapidly by means of suckers and eventually each clump will colonize extensive areas. If trained to a single stem and grown in grass which is mown short, the sucker development is kept in check and a small, slow-growing tree may be formed. The other forms may also be trained in the same way. This species will colonise extensive areas even on poor soils in exposed districts and near the coast, but if it is necessary to keep to a definite line of demarcation, there should be an annual cutback of the suckers.

This species could be used extensively to give shelter and protection to young trees in the early years for it is difficult to imagine that vandals and hooligans would risk being torn and scratched just to damage a tree. The competition would also induce the specimen to grow up to the light and thus produce a good stem. The clearance of the Blackthorn would take place after 10 to 15 years.

P. cerasifera, Myrobalan or Cherry Plum, forms a small tree with a dense crown. Often during good growing seasons very strong branches are thrown directly up through the centre of the crown. This is a natural habit and it is difficult to maintain a neat and tidy crown. If they are cut out the resultant proliferation of growths requires the 'clean-up' to be carried out annually. This is a good subject for hedging and screening purposes. The forms and varieties have a similar habit.

There are many other species in this subgenus but their habits vary, some becoming tree-like and similar to *P. domestica*, the Garden Plum, others forming thickets like *P. spinosa*; but it is important to have some knowledge of their natural growth at planting time. The Apricots are also in this section and include *P. armeniaca*, which on a well-drained soil is hardy, but needs a wall to ripen its fruit. *P. mume*, the Japanese Apricot, and its cultivars may be trained to form a 1 to 2 m. (3 to 6 ft.) standard, but it needs shelter and usually a stake for a longer period.

Subgenus II. *Amygdalus* (Almonds, Peaches)

The Common Almond, *P. dulcis*, and several of the cultivars all make shapely trees, the exception being 'Macrocarpa', which has very large flowers but is often a tall straggly grower, especially in a shaded position. These, with the coloured varieties of Peach, *P. persica*, are often grown as half-standards. With peaches some of the oldest, twiggy branchlets may be cut back to suitable growths after flowering, thus letting light and air into the bush to encourage a better display in the following spring. The hybrid *P. ×amygdalo-persica* 'Pollardii' and *P. davidiana* also display this characteristic habit of growth. For the best effect, balance is important and secure staking and shelter is very necessary for this, especially in the early years.

On their own roots, peaches and almonds often die back by whole branches at a time, especially on a heavy soil, or after a very wet winter. The shape is quickly spoilt, and regenerating growths tend to spring from the main trunk and these are out of character with the remainder of the tree, being strong and upright. In many such cases it is better to grub up such a tree and replace it with one which has been grafted onto a plum stock.

P. triloba 'Multiplex' may be grown as a bush, but it looks very fine against a warm wall. In this position the branches are trained fanwise to provide a framework over the allotted space. After this, the growths that are produced at right angles to the surface of the wall are cut back hard to one or two buds immediately after flowering. Even during the formative period, growths not required for the framework are cut hard back in like manner. As this subject flowers freely from the previous season's wood, a good annual display is given each spring, provided that growth and vigour are maintained. By this method the shrub is kept hard against the wall, but the temptation to dig over and to plant bedding plants up to the foot of the wall must be resisted, as the roots will be disturbed with disastrous results. It is sometimes grown as a half-standard and pruned annually in the same way.

P. tenella, the Dwarf Russian Almond, is also in this group, but this and the cultivar forms need no pruning.

Many peaches and almonds are attacked by the fungus that causes Peach Leaf Curl (and this will seriously impair growth, especially in a bad season). The necessary spraying to combat this should be carried out in the early spring.

Subgenus III. *Cerasus* (Cherries)

The species and varieties display great variation in growth and size and this is seen even among the Japanese Cherries, most of which are forms or varieties of *P. serrulata*. The beauty of these trees is in their natural spread and this is shown to full effect with 'Fugenzo', which forms a flat head with spreading branches, or with 'Tai Haku' whose pendent branches will reach the ground as the tree matures. With the latter variety these branches often appear untidy, but much of the flowering beauty will be lost if they are cut off. As a contrast to these varieties, the well-known 'Kanzan' has ascending branches, while 'Amanogawa' has an erect, almost fastigiate growth. A neat appearance with this latter variety is maintained by using single strands of wire at intervals to keep in offending growths that break from the general outline. The size of the tree will depend to some extent upon the length of the trunk, and the height at which the head is formed. The type of tree that branches low from close to ground level is useful for planting on the edges of groups or in an exposed position.

With the species, too, it is a matter of allowing free growth after the initial training has been carried out in the nursery and if need be continued during the first year or so after planting. The aim must be to maintain health by good culture, for if growth is produced most cherries will flower.

Cherries are usually trained as open-headed specimens, but the large tree-like species such as *P. avium* may be trained with a central leader running up to 6 to 9 m. (20 to 30 ft.). This is likely to occur naturally where the tree is in light woodland competing with others. *P. serrula*, grown for its beautiful mahogany-like bark, should be trained as a half-standard, the lower part of the branches and the trunk being kept clear to show this beauty to the full. Thus the feathers (branchlets) should be cut off during training and soon after planting, choosing midsummer for this pruning. In this way the size of the wounds is kept small and they heal more readily than large ones which seldom close completely. *P. incisa* is almost alone among the cherries in that it does not produce gum in the region of wounds and thus reacts better to pruning.

P. glandulosa forms an attractive, small bush if planted at the foot of a warm wall and pruned hard back immediately after flowering, taking away all the old wood to the stool at the base. Dieback occurs during the winter if the growths do not ripen properly.

Subgenus IV. *Padus* (Bird Cherries)

It is advisable to train *P. serotina* with a central leader that will develop through the greater part of the tree, the length of clear trunk being from 1.8 to 2.4 m. (6 to 8 ft.). In this way it will grow into a fairly large tree 18 m. (60 ft.) or more in height. If rival leaders are allowed too early, the branch systems that develop from them will have a very narrow angle, and will thus be weak. The same is true of other large growers in this group, e.g. *P. padus*. One habit of this species is that strong, upright growths are often thrown up by mature specimens from horizontal branches, through the centre of the tree. On no account, if this occurs, should thinning be attempted for this will check the tree and may even cause its death. *P. maackii* and in particular the cultivar 'Amber Beauty' has a finely coloured golden-brown bark and stem, and the main branches should be cleared of feathers and twiggy growths before these become too large.

Subgenus V. *Laurocerasus* (Cherry Laurels)

The Common Laurel, *P. laurocerasus*, is frequently used to provide a formal surface, but clipping results in the disfigurement of a high proportion of the large leaves which remain on the surface. The alternative is to remove individual shoots and leaves one by one, using the secateurs, but this is very time-consuming. This subject is better as a screen plant when, if it is left unpruned, it will develop into a large specimen of considerable height and spread. Grown this way, any pruning that is necessary to restrict size should be carried out with the aim of retaining an informal effect. Brambles and other woody plants often grow on the edges of these clumps and these should be checked before they get out of hand. Laurel regenerates and grows very strongly and, if cut hard back and coppiced periodically, will make an excellent cover shrub, even in a dry situation. The best period for this hard cutting back is in the spring or early summer.

P. lusitanica, the Portugal Laurel, is similar in many respects to *P. laurocerasus* and it is at its best if left to grow freely when it will develop into a small tree. It does, however, respond to formal clipping and may be used in colder districts to provide a Bay Laurel effect in suitable settings.

Pests and diseases

Those that commonly attack the various species when they are planted on a commercial scale are fortunately not as troublesome in the ornamental garden. This is undoubtedly the result of the better balance that exists in this community and all possible means should be taken to conserve this happy state of affairs. Neglect of feeding and mulching for the maintenance of good healthy growth is one of the commonest causes of trouble. The too free use of a drastic insecticide may be equally disastrous. If growth is impaired by insect attack, suitable insecticides are usually effective if applied in the early stages and until the balance is restored. Diseases can in most cases be contained by cutting out affected branches as soon as they are noticed during inspections making sure that the cut is made sufficiently low down to remove all the infected wood. Diseased wood should be burnt at once.

Disease and dieback is more prevalent in badly drained or unsuitable soils, and the requirements of individual species and varieties should be studied before a selection is made.

PSEUDOLARIX

P. amabilis, the Golden Larch. This beautiful tree will respond well to training, provided that the environment and growing conditions are suitable. A good, central leader is desirable and the horizontal branches that spring from it should be allowed a full spread in open surroundings. In this way the beauty of this deciduous conifer can be fully appreciated, as the lower branches, perhaps laden with cones, sweep down almost to ground level.

Often, after transplanting from the nursery into their final position, the young trees remain stunted for a few years, perhaps even losing vigour in the leader. However, provided that the planting site was adequately prepared and every attention is given to watering and feeding when necessary, such young trees usually grow away strongly, even to the extent of forming a new leader which often springs from beneath the older and perhaps weaker one. The secret of success is, therefore, to maintain good growth, thus enabling the tree to overcome any disaster that may befall the all-important leading shoots.

PSEUDOPANAX

This small genus can only be grown in very mild localities, but it may survive against a sunny wall in many parts of the south of England. The species appear to exhibit four distinct stages of growth. *P. ferox* in the second stage is occasionally met with. In this form it grows up to a height of 1 to 2 m. (3 to 6 ft.), but is usually completely unbranched. It is noticeable that the parent plant will branch if cuttings are taken off the top. Regular pruning is, however, out of the question. It is necessary to see that the shrub is firmly staked, as it becomes top heavy with increased height. Mature bushes of *P. lessonii* throw strong, young growths from the base and branch system. It may therefore be pruned in order to restrict size or spread by carefully cutting to the most promising of these growths.

PSEUDOSASA. *See* Bamboos

PSEUDOTSUGA

P. menziesii, the Douglas Fir, is capable of rapid growth and reaches a considerable height provided conditions are suitable. This plant is the tallest tree in the United Kingdom. Growing well, it can be a delight to the arboriculturist, but on a poor dry soil it will cause him to despair. A healthy young tree will develop its leader and produce tiers of branches that should be encouraged to spread to their full extent.

The tree is naturally irregular in growth and outline and no attempt should be made to trim it into shape by cutting back individual branches. Generally, if any cutting back needs to be done, it means that the cut is made right back to the main trunk, that is, apart from the removal of small, dead twiggy material.

PSORALEA

P. glandulosa is a half-hardy shrub with slender, upright and almost cane-like growths. It should be grown as a bush in the shelter of a sunny wall. The flowers are produced from the previous year's wood and from the young growths late in the season. This shrub has the curious habit of retaining clusters of buds in a living condition on the old wood. It is capable of breaking out quite strongly if cut down, even to ground level, by a severe winter. If it is necessary to confine the bush, this may be done in mid spring, taking care to preserve as many growths at full length as possible.

PTELEA

This genus of small trees or shrubs is made up of only a few species. Apart from training in the nursery, very little pruning is necessary. *P. trifoliata* is the most common representative. It has a spreading habit and in the early stages of crown formation the branching is upright. Later, with a generally slender branch system this effect may be lost. One of the most important features of this species is the fruiting display that is quite conspicuous during the autumn and early winter months. The petioles that remain attached to the parent stems for a short time also add to the attraction. This display can be better appreciated when the specimen is well balanced against a background of deciduous trees. Some pruning on neighbouring trees may be necessary to retain this balance.

In training, a short leg 0.6 to 0.9 m. (2 to 3 ft.) is to be preferred. Staking is necessary, often for many years after planting, for this and other *Ptelea* species sometimes adopt a leaning posture, perhaps as a result of a weak root system. The powers of regeneration are good and should a tree be cut down to ground level, growth may be expected to break out freely to form a new head of branches.

The habits of growth and treatment of the remaining species are very similar.

PTEROCARYA

These trees are strong-growing when young and should be raised in the nursery under good conditions but in a sheltered position, as the young shoots in particular suffer in a severe winter or in a late spring frost. Damaged growths should be carefully cut back to living tissue as the buds break. A sunny position ensures that the growths are ripened and will winter better. It is important to retain the leader and to develop a 1.5 to 1.8 m. (5 to 6 ft.) leg. The reason for this is that the young trees show a tendency to branch low and for the crown to develop without a leader. The branching, however, is strong.

P. ×rehderiana is the most common representative of this genus. As with the species, this hybrid will produce a furnished effect down to ground level, even with a 1.5 to 1.8 m. (5 to 6 ft.) trunk. Planted by the waterside, the branches spread out 0.3 m. (1 ft.) or so over the surface and the large, pinnate foliage produces a tropical effect. Eventually the branches dip beneath the water as the extending growth makes them heavier. Under these conditions even the more mature parts of the branch system form massive bunches of roots on the portions that are submerged and the whole surface becomes a jungle. This can be remedied by cutting back to remove such growths and at the same time to lighten the weight, leaving a fully furnished and natural effect. This hybrid suckers extensively, as does *P. fraxinifolia*, one of the parents and unless an absolute thicket is desired, they should be cut down annually. Owing to the extensive and shallow root system that this subject produces, it is ideal for retaining banks by the waterside.

Epicormic shoots are sometimes produced on the more horizontal branches, but these should be left unless they are very thick, as their removal will result in the production of a heavier crop in a year or so.

The species have similar habits, although normally they do not sucker as extensively. Even mature trees are prone to frost damage in the late spring. Owing to the danger of bleeding, large pruning cuts should be made in the late summer; never prune in the autumn.

PTEROSTYRAX

P. hispida, the Epaulette Tree. The form which this subject takes depends to a large extent upon the nursery training in the initial years. It may be trained to a single stem, when it will definitely form a small tree. On the other hand, the more common and perhaps better form is achieved by allowing the natural development of a few main stems which grow upright from ground level. With this habit it gains height more slowly, but will eventually reach 4.6 to 6.0 m. (15 to 20 ft.).

A healthy specimen may freely produce young growths from the main branches and from ground level. These may be thinned out and the strongest trained as replacements or as additions to the branch system. No regular pruning is needed to the main head of branches.

P. corymbosa makes more of a spreading tree or large shrub and is difficult to train to a tree with a central leader.

PUNICA

P. granatum is normally a shrub for a warm, sunny wall. It may be trained up to the support or grown as a bush. The latter method is the better one, although it will have considerable spread, perhaps 1.8 to 2.4 m. (6 to 8 ft.) from the wall, and is also low-branching. It will respond to pruning and some of the older and weaker wood may be cut out during the late spring or summer. Wood should not be cut out during the winter as it is then difficult to distinguish living from dead. In severe winters this shrub may be cut back into the old wood which if alive will break out strongly.

When trained up close to a wall the main branches are tied out fanwise. Growths coming away from the wall are pruned short as the buds break in the spring. The free production of strong, young growths along the branch systems allows for some replacement of the old wood.

PYRACANTHA

The natural habit of the species is to form a system of closely knit branches, and they are very effective when grown as specimen shrubs in the border and in the more natural parts of the garden. Under these conditions they require very little pruning. If any is carried out for any reason, the cuts should be taken back into the centre (wear gloves for protection against the long thorns) so that the wound and the effects of the pruning are hidden. The stiff, rigid ends of cut and mauled branches look very unsightly and the effect of free growth is spoilt.

Pyracanthas conform well to extensive wall training, for the flowers and fruits are freely produced from spurs on the old wood. Thus the main branches may be trained fanwise to cover the support, although it will be found that they conform well to any system of training. There are several methods of pruning as the structure is covered. A free form of bush is obtained by very little pruning at all. The main branches are loosely tied to the wiring system, and if necessary invasive branches are cut back in the spring after flowering to points hidden within the bush.

A closer system of training consists of cutting back all the growths that are not tied in for furnishing or replacement. This is done after flowering. Another system of rigid control is to clip over the whole surface annually in the spring or even two or three times during the growing season. Under this system the surface is given a very close covering, but the actual flowering may suffer.

Pyracanthas are susceptible to Fireblight (*Erwinia amylovora*) and any infected branches should be pruned back beyond the staining. Hard pruning as a form of renovation often makes plants more vulnerable to Fireblight and the replacement with disease-resistant cultivars may be the better option.

PYRUS

This is a genus of small or medium-sized trees, one of the largest growers being *P. communis*, the Common Pear, which may reach a height of 15 to 18 m. (50 to 60 ft.).

The species are normally propagated from seed or by grafting onto seedling stocks, usually *P. communis*. They are mostly strong-growing and it is important in the early years to train carefully, the best form of tree being a 2.4 to 3.0 m. (8 to 10 ft.) standard with a central leader. Often they grow so strongly that rival leaders are easily formed and these need to be spotted and dealt with at an early stage. When the growth is free after the final planting it is difficult to avoid crossing branches. The natural growth of many of the species is very thick indeed. When the head finally matures the outer and lower branches have a pendulous habit. *P. ussuriensis* is typical of the larger growers with a dense head and pendulous outer branches. Some knowledge of the growth and final habit is necessary; for example, *P. amygdaliformis* has a spreading shrub-like habit while *P. salicifolia* 'Pendula' forms a small tree with a branching that is distinctly pendulous. For this habit to develop and be appreciated to full effect the foreground should be clear of any but dwarf shrubs. It should be grown as tall as possible before being allowed to weep, to get the maximum benefit of the grey foliage. The inner crown should be regularly cleaned out of dead wood, as this will build up if left and eventually form three fifths of the crown, spoiling the overall effect.

P. calleryana 'Bradford' and *P. c.* 'Chanticleer' are commonly grown as street trees due to the upright pyramidal form that they show. 'Bradford' tends to have weak crotches that sometimes fail, whereas 'Chanticleer' has stronger crotches that are less prone to fail.

Many of the species are susceptible to Fireblight (*Erwinia amylovora*), and a careful look out should be kept for this, especially after flowering, see Chapter Five.

QUERCUS

This great genus of trees contains species that vary enormously in size and, while a few of the hardier species are evergreen or semi-evergreen, the majority are deciduous. From the arboriculturist's point of view their culture is very rewarding, for on good soils the hardy species grow well and, provided that a good leader and shape is formed in the nursery and the situation is not too exposed, fine trees are quite easily produced. It is more difficult to grow shapely trees in exposed sites but a few such as *Q. petraea*, the Sessile Oak, and *Q. ilex*, the Holm Oak, will succeed well even on the coast, although the latter does not prove to be hardy in the colder districts.

Generally the oaks are safe trees to work on and they hold their framework well, even during severe gales. During such weather it is more likely to be the odd small branch which is twisted off than a large one, provided the tree has been well trained. Even dead branches are retained for a long period, as the inner core of wood does not rot quickly. These often fall in considerable quantities from neglected oaks during severe gales.

Most of the oaks heal well, but even large wounds made on really old specimens which may never cover over completely, remain healthy, provided that the surface of the exposed wood is firm and intact.

Many of the oaks produce epicormic growths, often on an extensive scale. These commonly occur on the branch systems and provided they do not become too large and out of proportion, they may be left. Usually their removal is quickly followed by a more vigorous outcrop. They should, however, be removed from the trunk unless the specimen has been cut hard back to the extent that there is little growth left other than in this region.

Oak Wilt (*Ceratocystis fagacearum*) affects the vascular system of Live Oaks and several of the Red Oaks, including *Q. rubra*, *Q. velutina*, *Q. shumardii*, *Q. marilandica* and *Q. nigra*, causing death in a few weeks or months. Prevention of the spread of the disease is the most appropriate method of control and as beetles carry the fungus to fresh pruning wounds, the timing of pruning operations is essential. Prune when the beetle is less active: the most suitable timing is during the winter between late autumn and early spring; never prune between mid spring and midsummer. The use of a thin coating of wound sealant is now being recommended on Red Oaks to prevent the attraction of sap-feeding and disease-carrying beetles.

The oaks are classified botanically in a number of subgenera, all requiring different approaches to pruning, as the subgenera range from very large trees to shrubs. The following notes deal with those most commonly met.

Subgenus II. *Erithrobalanus* (North American species)

These vary considerably in their reaction to our climate. *Q. rubra*, the Red Oak, is one of the best growers. The leader is retained very well, although the tendency for the ascending branches to rival this at a later stage demonstrates the importance of raising trees that have been formed well in the early years. *Q. r.* 'Aurea' is much slower in growth and requires shelter. However, the background should not be too close otherwise the tree develops a poor leaning shape. A distance of 15 m. (50 ft.) is suitable. Other rapid growers in this section include *Q. palustris*, but the pendulous branches which often develop on mature specimens, although desirable in the garden, lead to increased work if used for roadside plantings. *Q. phellos*, the Willow Oak, will grow to a large size, often with very heavy branching and it is important to keep the leader running up through the head in a young tree.

Generally the species in this group which come from the southern United States are not completely at home in England. This may not be due so much to the severity of our winters as to the rather indefinite seasons and a lack of sufficient sun to ripen the wood. *Q. agrifolia*, the Coast Live Oak, may be quoted as an example. It comes from California, is evergreen and is often shrubby. Yet in the warmer and more southerly parts of the United Kingdom, if carefully looked after when young, it will form a leader from which a trunk may finally develop. It is therefore wrong for the nurseryman and the planter to be too set in their methods and, with trees and shrubs that are on the borderline of hardiness, some modification of the original plan may be desirable. A mature tree will often lose a considerable amount of small growth after a severe winter and an annual check in the spring is advisable. The bark on the trunk often lifts in blocks and large patches and this needs attention before cavities form. The healing powers of this species are usually very strong. *Q. wislizeni*, a related species, is also found in California. It produces dense, twiggy growth and there is often considerable dieback to attend to after a severe winter.

Subgenus III. *Lepidobalanus*

This is divided into six sections which are also quite distinct from the arboriculturist's point of view.

Section 1. *Cerris*

Two species that will often grow into giants if given the position are *Q. castaneifolia* and *Q. cerris*, the Turkey Oak. Both should be trained with good trunks and leaders. The latter species produces outer and lower branches that are almost pendulous. The result of this is that the inside branches are likely to die off through lack of sufficient light and will then need to be removed.

Q. variabilis is worthy of special mention as it shows how the good arboriculturist is able to bring out the best in a tree by correct training. The species is slender and light branching, but the main attraction is in the bark of the main trunk which is flaked in a beautiful diamond pattern. To show this to full effect the trunk should be run up as straight as possible and should be cleared of lower branches up to 3 m. (10 ft.), before these get too large.

Section 2. *Suber*

The species in this section are evergreen and many suffer severely during a hard winter. *Q. suber*, the Cork Oak, to some extent provides an example for the remainder, for if the climate and conditions are not ideal, it seems impossible to grow anything but a miserable specimen. *Q. alnifolia* and *Q. coccifera* are usually shrubby and unless nursery specimens show a definite tendency to form a leader they should be left to grow freely.

The one distinctive tree in this section is the hybrid *Q. ×hispanica* 'Lucombeana', the Lucombe Oak, and it should be trained to form a large tree.

Section 3. *Ilex*

This is a section of evergreens of which *Q. ilex*, the Holm Oak, is the most important. In earlier days it was much used in formal designs and very large specimens were often clipped annually in the late summer to maintain a dense, rigid outline. Even as a hedge the Holm Oak will maintain a good surface. However, the beauty of this tree is shown to perfection in free growth and heavy branching. The outer growths and branches should be left to grow down to ground level, when they will look particularly fine with the light green growths set against the dark foliage. A trunk of 1.8 to 2.4 m. (6 to 8 ft.) is preferable, but the shade that is cast is very dense, and there should be no attempt to have a border beneath or near a large specimen. It is better to use grass as a foreground, running this up to the base of the tree or, if the growths are already touching the ground, up to the outer perimeter of foliage. It will also take many years for this subject to reach the ground again once the lower branches have been removed and therefore this should not be done lightly without serious consideration. Where large formally clipped specimens still exist under conditions where there is insufficient labour to attend to the annual trimming which is so necessary, they will quickly develop a free, natural growth with very little attention. As free growth develops after two or three years the trunk can, if necessary, be cleared and formed, while at a later stage some of the smaller growths may be thinned out in the centre as the stronger branches become more evident.

Q. phillyreoides should be left to grow freely in the nursery as it is more often shrub-like.

Section 5. *Robur*

Most of the species in this group are strong growers and will develop into large trees. *Q. frainetto*, the Hungarian Oak, *Q. canariensis*, the Algerian Oak, *Q. macranthera*, *Q. pyrenaica*, *Q. petraea*, the Sessile

Oak, and *Q. robur*, the English Oak, all form good leaders and with training will branch well to form a good length of clear trunk with a large head. *Q. pubescens* is a smaller tree, but it is usually possible to retain a leader of 4.6 m. (15 ft.) or more through the tree before it is left to open out. *Q. pontica* branches low on a short trunk and is, in nature, often shrubby. It should therefore be left to form a head even though the leg may only be 0.6 to 0.9 m. (2 to 3 ft.) in length. *Q. robur* in particular suffers from dieback on the topmost and outer branches, a condition which is referred to as 'stag-headed'. A tree that has this does not necessarily show a general decline in health, for much depends upon the causes of this condition. Often the primary cause is a lowering of the water table or soil compaction, and the fact that the living part of the tree may remain in reasonably good condition is an indication that, with encouragement, the effect can be delayed or even offset for many years. Eventually, of course, rot and decay gain a foothold on the cut ends formed by the removal of the dead wood, but at least a number of years usually elapse before such trees die completely, and this gives time for new plantings to mature. Impoverishment or a check to the root system may be another cause of dieback.

There are many forms of *Q. robur* and their habits of growth must be recognised during the training stage. 'Cristata', for example, forms a small crowded head and it is usually difficult to retain the leader for long. 'Atropurpurea' is found in several forms, but in one it produces a dwarf stunted tree whose branches are covered with epicormic growths. These should be left as it is a characteristic of this variety and an attraction. 'Filicifolia', which tends to produce a branch system in layers, has most beautiful foliage and should be allowed to branch low in an open space for this to be seen to best effect. The fastigiate form 'Fastigiata Koster' must be allowed to grow freely unpruned.

Section 6. *Prinus*

So many of this group do not succeed well in England that there is a temptation for arboriculturists to dismiss them completely. However, at least one, *Q. bicolor*, is worthy of consideration, for it produces a good leader and the trunk, if it is kept clear of branches, will display a shaggy bark to full effect. *Q. montana* produces thin, wiry branchlets and the general effect of the foliage is seen to best advantage if there is full light on at least one side, for the branching to come down to eye level. *Q. dentata*, the Daimio Oak, tests the skill of the arboriculturist to the full, for it has the reputation of being short-lived in the United Kingdom. Dieback often occurs on the younger wood during the winter, causing bushy growths on the tips of the branches as a result of regeneration.

RAPHIOLEPIS. *See* Rhaphiolepis

REHDERODENDRON

R. macrocarpum. This rare tree eventually reaches a height of approximately 6 m. (20 ft.). It should, if possible, be kept to a single leader, but should be allowed to furnish as fully and as close to ground level as possible. Little pruning is needed.

This is a subject for a sheltered part of a woodland garden but nearby trees and shrubs should if necessary, be pruned, rather than that the growth of this choice tree should be impaired in any way, see Fig. 26.

RHAMNUS

Although the species within this genus are grouped botanically there is not sufficient difference in the pruning to warrant an elaboration of this classification. It is however essential to be acquainted with the final habit and form while the young plants are in the nursery stage.

Many of the larger growers will develop into small trees, particularly if a short leg of 0.9 to 1.2 m. (3 to 4 ft.) is kept clear of branches as the head is being built up. *R. purshiana* will even grow to a height of 9 to 12 m. (30 to 40 ft.), but if allowed to develop low branching from ground level, it will be much shorter. The species that develop into large shrubs or small trees are most attractive when growing on the edge of a clump, when the pendulous habit of the ends of the branchlets can be seen to best effect. With this habit dead wood is formed on the undersides of such branch systems and this must be cut away cleanly.

R. alaternus is quite a distinct grower. It has an attractive evergreen shoot and leaf system which is seen at its best when the shrub is grown in the front of a border, and allowed to furnish right down to ground level. By careful pruning in spring, a perfect informal surface may be maintained, as this subject branches very freely. 'Argenteovariegata' is somewhat tender and needs a sheltered position.

It is worth noting that there are dwarf species such as *R. pumilus*, which is procumbent and suitable for the rock garden.

R. frangula, a slender-growing shrub or small tree, is suitable as a support for such climbers as *Lonicera caprifolium*.

RHAPHIOLEPIS

These are slow-growing, stiff shrubs with leathery leaves. *R. umbellata* forms a fairly compact and rounded bush in full sun, but under even slightly shaded conditions it tends to be more spreading with an untidy habit. There also seems to be a greater tendency for the shrub, when under these conditions, to produce long growths, often at random, which throw it completely out of shape. If desired, some pruning to shape may be carried out in mid spring by taking off such growths to a suitable point well inside the bush. Dead branches that appear from time to time should also be cut out. Otherwise, no regular pruning is needed.

R. indica is less hardy and needs wall protection in all but the milder localities. The same is true to some extent of *R. ×delacourii*.

Wall protection is best afforded these shrubs by allowing them to grow as a bush rather than by training them rigidly to the wall face. They should be planted about 0.5 m. (1.5 ft.) from the base of a warm, sunny wall.

RHODODENDRON

Normally this large genus requires very little pruning, the main essential being to maintain healthy growth by the provision of correct growing conditions. Not only is it necessary to study and provide for their soil and moisture requirements, but some will tolerate quite exposed and sunny positions, while others require shade and shelter. These factors are of course directly connected with cultural conditions, but it is most likely that failure to provide a suitable environment will result in ill health and dieback, which in turn will necessitate pruning. This cutting-out of dead branches which should in fact be living, can be very disheartening, for almost invariably the whole plant is unhealthy and it is just a question of time before the poor specimen is cut away completely. The rule should be to follow the use of the secateurs or saw with improved culture.

From time to time it becomes necessary to cut out dead wood which has developed inside the bush as a result of the loss of light. This is most likely to occur on crowded specimens, when the result is often a mass of trunks and branches, perhaps near the path or on the edge of the border, with the foliage and flowers well above head level. This is a difficult position to correct, the best method with the larger-leafed species being to slowly reduce selected specimens by pruning in order to give the remaining ones more light. This should be carried out over a period of at least 3 to 4 years, when a final decision to clear any undesirable specimens may be taken. It is possible that the bushes which have been cut back will have regenerated and be in better condition than the unpruned ones. The one danger of thinning and clearing in one operation without any preparatory pruning is that the remaining bushes will be unduly exposed and more likely to be blown out during a gale. It is sometimes possible, by replanning the beds and paths, to avoid cutting back altogether, in which case this may be the more desirable course.

It should be noted that many species and varieties of Rhododendron will regenerate with young growth after being cut hard back, but it is difficult to be more precise than this, as it then becomes a matter of trial and error with experience playing a big part. *R. augustinii*, *R. davidsonianum*, *R. yunnanense* and *R. concinnum* are very responsive indeed and they will break out freely even after being cut back to the old wood or to near ground level. It should be noted that those mentioned above are in the Series *Triflorum*, a group which, among others, responds readily to hard pruning. It is possible that the response would be far greater than is generally realized, but it is a sounder policy to cut back the commoner subjects, leaving the rarer and more choice ones intact with sufficient space for development. Who would think of cutting back a large specimen in the Series *Grande*, such as *R. macabeanum*, when the overcrowding could be relieved by reducing thick and towering clumps of *R. ponticum*. Often such a surround, although reduced, is needed for shelter and thus there is need of balanced pruning in relation to microclimate, see Fig. 26.

Rhododendrons are sometimes used for informal hedging and screening; *R. ponticum* in particular is planted for this purpose. Pruning to restrict size, if necessary, should take the form of regular, annual pruning after flowering. The cuts may be made well into the bushes on growths that extend beyond the limits, thus concealing the fact that they have been cut at all. It is emphasized that, if this controlled and systematic pruning is carried out regularly, there is no need for the drastic cutback, which, although effective, is rather unsightly for a time. However, should this hard cutting back be necessary, perhaps as a result of overgrowth through years of neglect, it should be carried out directly after flowering and before the new growth is put on.

Clumps of *R. ponticum* in a natural setting have a habit that can be divided into two distinct phases. Firstly, new growths extend and arch up from near ground level, often creating the effect of a low border round a clump. This is the stage at which pruning should take place, for these quickly send up new and extensive growths, which gain height quickly to enlarge the clump considerably.

It is a common practice to remove the old flower heads as the blossoms fade and before energy is spent in useless seed production. This is a form of pruning and it is very effective in helping the new growth,

particularly if a dry spell sets in. It is done quite easily by holding the old flower truss firmly in the hand with the fingers and thumb on the lower part of the main stalk but above the developing growth. Sometimes it is necessary to use the free hand to steady the growth and to assist generally. Provided that sufficient care is taken, the heads come away cleanly without damaging the remaining growths and foliage.

It is important to watch for suckers and grafted plants, and these should be cut off as soon as they appear, as close to the root as possible.

R. groenlandicum, *R. tomentosum* and *R. neoglandulosum* need very little pruning, especially if they are growing healthily. In fact, once it becomes necessary to cut out dead wood, it is often a sign that the shrub is deteriorating. They are often happier when growing in association with other shrubs that have similar requirements and pruning may then be necessary on these neighbouring subjects to prevent encroachment. However, it may be preferable to cut back the occasional long, straggly growth that spoils the appearance of the bush, or even pulls it out of shape. Such cuts should be made in the spring as growth is commencing. Thin bushes may regenerate, if they are cut back and there are sufficient growths left, but conditions generally should also be improved and it is often better to begin again with fresh plants.

They will produce young growth during and just after flowering, and their health and vigour is improved by removing the heads as the blossoms fade in order to prevent seed production. Care is needed to avoid damage to the young growths, but with a little practice this can be done by hand. Mulching and watering if necessary may be beneficial at this stage.

RHODOTYPOS

R. scandens. This shrub is allied to *Kerria japonica* and has a similar habit of growth. Wood is thrown up from the base of the shrub so freely that it is advisable to cut a portion of the older wood down to ground level. The shrub flowers on short laterals from the previous year's wood and therefore young canes produced in one season will flower in the next. The intensity of the pruning should depend upon condition, growth and flowering. Sometimes the cuts are made to suitable growths on the old wood, at other times at ground level. Pruning is best carried out after flowering but as a second best it may be done in the winter.

RHUS

The species within this genus vary considerably in their habit and mode of growth but, apart from specialized systems of culture, very little pruning is necessary. The tree species need training to a single leader in the early stages of their formation. *R. verniciflua* forms a large, wide-branching tree and is similar from the aboriculturist's point of view to *R. potaninii*. Both callus and heal well if cuts have to be made, although it is better to do this just before leaf fall in order to minimise the risk of bleeding. Both may have a 1.2 to 1.8 m. (4 to 6 ft.) length of clear trunk. *R. punjabensis* var. *sinica* and *R. vernix* are also in this group, the sap of the latter being reputed to have toxic properties. Some of the other species, *R. toxicodendron* and *R. ambigua* for example, may on contact also cause irritation and rashes, some people being more susceptible than others. It is advisable to work on any suspected tree or shrub for two or three short trial periods before any major task is undertaken. Rubber gloves should also be used for protection. Disposal of arisings can also be a problem, particularly with *R. verniciflua*. They should never be burnt, as the fumes given off can be very toxic, and composting may simply postpone the problem to a later date, as the irritant will remain with the compost. Burying the arisings on a spare piece of ground is the best practice, although this may not be the easiest or most practicable solution.

A number of species may be looked upon as forming trees or shrubs, for example *R. typhina* often develops into a small tree, particularly if it is trained with a short, clear stem when it is young. *R. trichocarpa* with stiff upright branches is another example and no pruning other than training is needed. *R. glabra* is similar to *R. typhina*, but is smaller. To be seen at their best these three latter species should have an open foreground, when the furnished effect to ground level will be particularly attractive with autumn foliage tints. Hard pruning of *R. typhina* encourages vigorous sucker production, which can be a problem in a lawn or border.

Those species that are definitely shrubby, for example, *R. trilobata* and *R. aromatica*, should be allowed to branch freely from ground level. Often a number of young growths are thrown up from the base and these may be used for replacement purposes.

The lower, shrubby species such as *R. toxicodendron*, Poison Ivy or Poison Oak, sucker freely, forming spreading clumps and are thus more suitable for the more natural parts of the garden, but never where children are likely to play.

R. glabra 'Laciniata' and *R. typhina* 'Dissecta' may be grown purely for foliage effect. Under this system the young growths are cut back to within approximately 100 mm. (4 in.) of the old wood. Thus, a low framework is gradually built up. Shrubs so treated should be heavily mulched and fed each year. If the growths are considered to be too crowded, they should be thinned as they shoot up in the spring.

RIBES

Within this genus are three subgenera: I. *Berisia*, mostly unarmed, II. *Ribesia*, the Currants, which are unarmed, and III. *Grossularioides*, the Gooseberries, which are armed. All have a stool mode of growth, freely producing shoots and branches just beneath ground level. Most are alike too in requiring a sunny position in which to develop and ripen their wood. The most ornamental forms flower freely from almost the whole length of the shoots made during the previous season. A number of the less decorative forms, for example *R. rubrum*, flower near the base of the previous season's wood and also from spurs on the older branches.

However, this minor difference matters very little, for their general habit does allow whole branches to be cut down, even to ground level, thus giving light and air to the new growths springing from the base. By this means a balance is maintained between old and young wood.

Many of the Currants, for example *R. sanguineum*, are best pruned immediately after flowering, taking away the older branches and cutting them down to a bud or growth as close to the ground as possible. It may be necessary to remove from a quarter to one-third of a mature bush each year, aiming to leave no wood above ground level that is older than five years.

With the Gooseberry section the framework is more permanent, but some pruning must be carried out to remove old branches and to restrict growth within reasonable bounds. They should be looked over for any pruning that may be needed at least twice during the year, in the dormant season and again at the height of growth. The latter period is particularly useful, for when in foliage their full size and effect can best be judged. Also it does ensure that neighbouring shrubs are prevented from being overgrown if growth is heavy.

Most members of this genus respond well to hard pruning when they are neglected and overgrown. This may be carried out during the summer or winter and all but the youngest shoots or branches may be removed. If all top growth is to be removed completely this should only be done during the dormant season in order to give them the best chance of recovery. Often the growths that are produced as a response to this treatment are lush and soft for the first season, and are liable to be broken by severe winds. They should therefore be staked in time to avoid this, while some thinning may also be necessary.

The natural habit of growth must also be taken into account and the method varied accordingly. For example, most of the *R. sanguineum* varieties produce a strong and fairly rigid framework and are a complete contrast in growth to *R. odoratum*, which has a loose habit and whose supple branches may even lean over onto neighbouring plants. Again, *R. alpinum* 'Pumilum' is dwarf and dense-growing, and pruning, unless dead branches occur, is not necessary. *R. sanguineum* 'Brocklebankii', with golden-yellow leaves, is not a strong grower and slight shade with good cultural conditions are more essential than pruning.

R. speciosum is sometimes treated as a wall shrub and in this position it often reaches 3 m. (10 ft.) in height. Full account must be taken of its habit of growth. The young shoots produced from the base should be used for the replacement of the older ones, otherwise over the years the vigour of the specimen may diminish. The replacement pruning may be done during the late summer after the new growths have been produced. The growths must be tied hard against the surface of the wall and trained fanwise.

The *R. sanguineum* varieties make good hedge plants. By pruning after flowering, using secateurs to cut the older wood, the dimensions are restricted, but the whole effect is informal. If the outline is cut rigidly to a definite height and width, a buildup of old wood reduces the amount of young growth, which in turn affects flowering. Also the secateurs are selective and the strongest and most forward growths can be saved, whereas with the shears these are often cut off and the shrubs are forced to develop weaker and retarded buds. This species has a good reputation for wind resistance and even thrives near the coast despite periodic scorching from sea gales.

Many of the Ribes genus suffer badly from attacks by aphis in the spring and early summer. The tips of the young growths are badly distorted and thus the health of the bushes as a whole is affected. Corrective sprays must be applied in the early stages of an attack. The Gooseberry Sawfly will also attack many species.

ROBINIA

This genus of leguminous trees and shrubs is distinctive by reason of the very light and attractive foliage canopy, in addition to the branched system which is beautiful at all times of the year. The wood has a reputation for being brittle and large limbs are sometimes torn off during gales at the junctions with main stems or branches, leaving bad tears that often extend considerable distances. This is more likely to happen with an old tree that is declining in health. Trees that are suspected of being dangerous should have their limbs shortened, or more drastic action taken if this is considered advisable.

Owing to the danger of bleeding all pruning should, if possible, be carried out during the mid to late summer period. Dead wood should also be cut out at this time.

Robinias in general are healthier after a sunny summer when the young wood is well ripened and a tree in this condition winters better than one that is poorly ripened. The wood will also be healthier on a well-drained soil. Sometimes the young growths are damaged by the late spring frosts and it is therefore better to avoid frost pockets when choosing a site.

In the nursery the tree forms and species should be trained up with a single leader and this should be retained through the crown. A clear stem of 1.8 to 2.4 m. (6 to 8 ft.) is advisable. Rival leaders produce a forked or divided main trunk, and in later life these trees in particular are very weak at such points. Old trees that have this weakness should be braced for safety.

R. pseudoacacia is the most common species. It is a rapid grower and suckers freely, especially from roots left in situ after the parent tree has been cut down. This species also regenerates and throws out very strongly after being pruned or cut back. Upright growths will even develop inside the cavities of old stems if they extend for some considerable distance to the light.

It is grown in many forms. 'Umbraculifera', the Parasol Acacia, forms a very close and compact head. This close habit is normally maintained without pruning, but a careful watch should be kept for strong growths from the stock which sometimes break out at the graft-line normally situated just below the head. If they are left the whole mop-headed nature will be destroyed as they develop and extend. 'Pyramidalis' has a habit that is very similar in form to that of the Lombardy Poplar. It is most effective when it has a clear foreground with low branching, even close to ground level. With an old specimen some form of branching between the main branches may be necessary. 'Tortuosa' is slow-growing, but despite this a leader should if possible be retained as the crown forms. 'Rehderii' is not grafted but is grown on its own roots and is normally allowed to branch from ground level. There are a number of other well-known forms, but the main point to remember is to take the habit of growth into account when training and pruning. 'Frisia' is so conspicuous by reason of its yellow foliage that any malformation will detract from the overall beauty.

The remaining species also display variations of growth and habit. *R. ×ambigua* 'Bellarosea' forms a small tree with upright branching and twiggy shoot system. *R. ×slavinii* 'Hillieri' also forms a small tree. *R. luxurians* will often form a large shrub unless a leader is selected and trained.

The definitely shrubby species seem to be more difficult to grow well and they demand better conditions with a warm, sunny position on a well-drained soil. Shelter from strong winds is also desirable, for the growths and branches are brittle. This is also a difficulty when they are grown as standards, for the branch system is then more exposed.

Robinia pseudoacacia wood is very durable, and the trunk of a tree that is condemned will serve as a useful support for such a climber as *Celastrus* or *Lonicera*, and will last for many years. It should be cut down to 3.0 to 4.6 m. (10 to 15 ft.), leaving the remainder of the trunk and the root system intact.

ROMNEYA

These thrive best in a sunny, warm, well-drained position. They spread by means of buds on thick fleshy horizontal roots. The extent to which the stems are killed back is dependent upon the severity of the winter. The growth above ground is often killed right down to ground level, but the stems should be left until growth commences in the spring, when the cuts can be made to living wood, or taken down completely. In either case the subject will flower, as the blossoms terminate the current season's wood. Wood that is growing hard up against a wall is more likely to be retained and a greater height may then be built up. Even so it is advisable to renew the wood by cutting out old stems and retaining young growths from the base.

ROSA

This vast genus, including many species and related hybrids, displays three distinct habits of growth and flowering:

(i)   Those which flower best on the growths made during the previous year. Long growths are thrown up, often from the base of the plant each year. *R. wichurana* and the Rambler Hybrids are examples.

(ii) Those which flower on laterals which are produced from growths made during the previous season. However, all the growths are part of a framework that is retained in a vigorous condition for many years. New growths are also sent up from the base. Many of the species and allied hybrids are in this group, for example, *R. moyesii*. The framework is retained but is invigorated by strong growths from ground level, while there is usually a definite period for flowering, followed by fruiting. It should, however, be noted that summer pruning, or an extended period of mild weather in the autumn, sometimes results in flower production on the new growths soon after their development is completed.

(iii) Those which flower from laterals produced from the previous year's wood, but also directly from growths made during the current season. Thus there is a continuous flowering from early summer until the first frosts in the autumn, starting with the growths produced on the last season's wood and continuing with the young shoots that are produced often from near the base. Those in the Section *Chinenses*, which includes *R. ×odorata*, the Tea Rose, have this habit.

Pruning related to growth and flowering

It will be seen at a glance that the group which flowers best on laterals, which are produced by the young shoots made during the previous year, may have much of the old wood cut out after flowering, provided there is sufficient of the new. With the two remaining groups, on the other hand, to cut this older wood out would be wrong when it supports a good flower display, and when there is not sufficient replacement wood. However, this is perhaps an oversimplification, and it may be dangerous to apply these rules generally. It should, however, be looked upon as an attempt to give the reader an overall understanding of the subject.

Most roses grow naturally by a system of replacement of the older flowering branches by young ones. The nature of the pruning depends in many cases upon the vigour of the plant and the extent of this ability to replace old wood. With this understanding an intelligent pruner, using his powers of observation to the full, will adjust the pruning according to the vigour and type of wood of each bush in turn, in order to obtain the maximum display the following season.

The rose species are divided botanically into subgenera and sections, each of which displays a typical habit of growth and has its own pruning requirements.

Subgenus *Hulthemia*

R. persica, a very rare shrub indeed, is normally grown under glass or in a very warm and sheltered border. It spreads by means of suckers and these should be left to develop as they produce the strongest growth and are more likely to succeed. There is little actual pruning apart from cutting out the dead wood.

Subgenus *Eurosa*
Section *Pimpinellifoliae*

The roses in this section are mainly of the Old World, flowering white or yellow. *R. pimpinellifolia* is a species which normally suckers, especially in a light, sandy soil where it is very much at home. For this reason it is difficult to restrict this species and many of the varieties to a given area, and the suckers need constant attention during the summer months. Occasionally, some of the older wood can be cut out of the larger growers such as *R. p.* 'Grandiflora'. The form *R. p.* 'Andrewsii' makes an attractive, informal hedge about 1.2 m. (4 ft.) high. Of the stronger-growing species in this section, some have graceful, arching branches such as *R. hugonis*, but they may become untidy as they grow older, for as extension growths are produced on the older wood these too arch over and thus the shape is spoilt and a bare stem exposed. By looking over the bushes after flowering, this habit may be checked, cutting out the oldest wood low down and near ground level. The remainder of the branches and the laterals are left intact, many of the latter having a definite horizontal habit and with the foliage being almost fern-like an attractive effect is produced.

The following taxa may be treated in a similar manner: *R. primula*, *R. ecae*, *R. elegantula*, *R. xanthina* and *R. sericea* subsp. *omeiensis*. A study of the growth that these make will serve as a guide for others. *R. xanthina* f. *spontanea* is sometimes grown as a standard on *R. rugosa* rootstock. Pruning is much the same, but staking needs to be very rigid, for a heavy head of foliage is produced. A wire frame or cross-piece secured to the stake may be concealed and yet hold the head rigid, thus preventing wind sway which would otherwise occur. *R. foetida* itself, with some of the stronger forms, produces strong, arching growths which readily extend over neighbouring shrubs and become a nuisance. This can be corrected by thinning out the older wood that weighs the new growth down and encourages this habit.

Section *Gallicanae*

The Moss Roses and many of the other old-fashioned garden hybrids belong to this group.

R. gallica. The varieties in this group vary in growth and habit. Most need good growing soil and conditions but the branches often become thick and crowded, especially as the new growth is put on during and after flowering. Some thinning is therefore necessary, taking out the older shoots after flowering down to good healthy growths or buds, often to ground level. Final adjustment may be made in early spring before the new growth commences, taking out more of the thinner and older wood and even shortening a number of the young growths if this is considered necessary. Hard pruning will not, however, help these roses to make good if the growing conditions are not suitable.

R. ×centifolia, the Cabbage Rose, is also related to many of the old hybrids including *R. ×c.* 'Muscosa', the Moss Rose. If it is considered necessary some of the weaker and older wood may be thinned after flowering and a final look over the shrubs made before growth commences in the spring. Vigour must be

taken into account, for example, the variety 'William Lobb' reaches up to 3 m. (10 ft.) and needs the support of a pillar or wall. *R. ×damascena*, the Damask Rose, has similar pruning requirements, but again the importance of taking vigour into account is stressed.

R. ×alba is quite a strong-growing shrub, and the branches are often so heavy with fruit that they spoil the general shape of the bush. These may be pruned back to suitable upright growths after the fruiting display is over.

Section *Caninae*

All the roses in this section are the European species with the exception of some in the *Synstylae* and *Pimpinellifoliae* sections. In growth the species in this section vary considerably, some being sturdy, others producing long, arching branches. Those with a sturdy habit are suitable for border culture, but the scrambling species are difficult to control and satisfy in such a situation and need a small tree or artificial structure for support.

R. pulverulenta is dwarf and compact and spreads by means of suckers. It should be planted in a group in the front of the border. There is little pruning with this beyond the removal of the obviously dead wood. *R. villosa* and *R. mollis* have a fairly erect and sturdy habit and are suitable for border culture. After the fruiting display is over, the older wood may be thinned out before the new starts. *R. tomentosa* has an arching habit and will rest on neighbouring shrubs. It is therefore better suited to the more natural parts of the garden. *R. glauca* is suitable for the border or a coloured foliage feature. There is little pruning, except to thin out the oldest wood after the fruits have vanished.

R. corymbifera, *R. micrantha*, *R. stylosa* and *R. canina*, the Dog Rose, have arching growths and if growing strongly they are a nuisance in the border unless a stake or support is given. They are better in the wilder parts of the garden, for it is difficult to prune them on a restrictive policy and yet do them justice. Growths can be looped over and around stakes, but unless some pruning is carried out before the season's growth commences each year, the bushes develop into an impossible tangle of shoots, which will in the end prove difficult to control. The early spring period is selected for this pruning operation as many of these species have an attractive fruiting display. *R. rubiginosa*, the Sweet Briar, has an erect habit with arching branches, but it is easier to keep under control. It is also grown as a hedge plant, being tied down to the fence or supporting wire system. Pruning takes place in the late winter or early spring when the fruit display is over. Some of the older wood is then cut out and the new growths tied in.

Section *Carolinae*

This group of roses naturally occurs in the eastern and southeastern United States. *R. carolina* and *R. virginiana* are somewhat similar in habit as they both form dense clumps of erect stems, the former spreading by means of suckers. Both species are more suitable for the more natural parts of the garden, for the branches arch over as they become laden with fruit. In the border, unless they are surrounded by shrubs that are of equal size, they need staking, as otherwise this habit spoils their effect. Pruning consists of cutting out the oldest branches after the fruits have disappeared, but the stems tend to support each other and they should not be over-thinned. *R. foliolosa* has the same habit although it is only 0.9 m. (3 ft.) in height. Its branches are thin, it spreads by means of suckers and in the border needs quite a large and sheltered area. *R. nitida* has similar requirements although it is not as invasive or untidy in its habits. With both species, just the oldest wood should be cut out after the fruiting display is over.

Section *Cassiorhodon*

These roses naturally occur across the northern hemisphere and generally freely sucker. This section shows considerable variation in habit and size, but the general rule is again to cut and thin out the older wood after the fruiting display has finished, remembering the all-important essential that the natural habit of growth must be taken into account. The habit lof *R. rugosa* need only be compared with that of

R. davidii for one to realize how wide this variation is—wider in fact than in any other section. However, pruning to confine these strong growers spoils their free and vigorous habit. This is also true of other strong growers such as *R. moyesii* and *R. gymnocarpa* var. *willmottiae*. Some species such as *R. arkansana* sucker so freely that the only way to prevent it from roaming across the bed through other plants is to provide it with its own bed and allow the mower to retain it within its confines. Another alternative is to insert a form of barrier material around the clump.

Section *Synstylae*

The roses in this section are the climbing, creeping or prostrate shrubs. These are strong growers and many of the species and hybrids in this group may reach considerable heights, provided that a suitable support is available. They will even climb 9 to 12 m. (30 to 40 ft.) over large trees. *R. multiflora* and *R. moschata* are good examples. Both, with others, have been used for hybridisation purposes, the Rambler Roses having been derived partly from the former species. Little pruning is necessary if these are growing unrestrictedly unless its purpose is to invigorate, when old wood may be cut out after flowering back to suitable young wood. Normally, if the plant is strong the old wood should be left for the fruit display. *R. wichurana* and *R. maximowicziana* have long, prostrate or trailing growths which are ideal for covering banks. Again, pruning is unnecessary provided growth is strong.

Many, even the most vigorous in this group will also trail well over banks when no support is available. As an example, *R. multiflora* will, under these conditions, form a large, dense clump that would defy all efforts to produce a tidy bush by pruning; indeed, under natural or semi-wild conditions it would be wrong to try. It is only when they are grown in a confined space, perhaps tied to a single stake or tripod in a border or a pergola in a formal setting, that annual pruning becomes necessary. By cutting out lengths of the old wood after flowering the development of young wood is encouraged, that which originates from near the base being especially valuable. The amount of old wood to be cut out depends entirely upon the condition of the young, developing growths. The long, arching growths that are left may also be looped over and tied in, a good method of containing large climbers in a small space.

It is an advantage to hard-prune a young plant intended for this restricted training and habit for the first season or two after planting, for this ensures the production of sufficient young growth from the base. Flowering does not matter at this early stage and pruning can therefore be carried out in the spring back to growths or buds near the base of the plant.

R. soulieana produces long arching stems and can be left to form a natural bush without any support, cutting out old woody stems to the ground, allowing new young growths to grow through and fill in the gaps.

Section *Chinenses*

The species and hybrids in this section flower over a long period during the early summer on growths from the old wood, and later in the year from shoots produced during the current season, often from near the base of the plant. *R.* ×*odorata*, the Tea Rose, and *R. chinensis*, the China Rose, both have this habit. Pruning in late winter to early spring should consist of cutting out some of the oldest and weakest growths and branch systems, often close to ground level. In this way the bushes are thinned out, allowing less crowded conditions for the growth and flowers which are produced later. Some of the previous year's growths are left on the more promising branch systems. These laterals are shortened back by a third or more, thus removing the old heads and the unripened portions.

R. ×*noisetteana* has a climbing or spreading habit from one of the parents, *R. moschata*, and thus much of the framework is retained from year to year. The laterals are pruned back in the spring together with the oldest and weakest branches, provided there is new growth coming up from the base that can be used for replacement.

R. ×*borboniana* is a strong, upright grower for the milder zones. The oldest and weakest wood is cut out in the spring. The unripened and flowered tips of the laterals which remain are cut back.

Section *Banksianae*

The roses in this section are tall climbing plants and include *R. cymosa*. The most important rose in this section is *R. banksiae*. It is a strong climber and may reach a height of 12 m. (40 ft.). It is not likely to be successful in the open garden, even with a suitable support, for it is not sufficiently hardy. A sunny, warm wall is necessary, using the ordinary strained wire method of support in order that the plant may be tied in as close to the wall as possible.

As maturity is reached some annual pruning is advisable, otherwise the plant becomes very untidy with long trailing growths which extend for 1 to 2 m. (3 to 6 ft.) from the protective surface of the wall. It is also necessary to keep the young growths close to the wall for protection during the winter, as otherwise they may suffer considerable damage.

The main pruning period is after flowering when some of the very old wood may be cut out and the young growths tied in as replacements, thereby preventing overcrowding. Much of the main framework, however, remains for the life of the plant, although sometimes strong growths several feet in length are produced from the base in one season, and there need be no hesitation in cutting out even the main branch systems if they are considered to be old and weak. In the late autumn, before the winter sets in, any growths that have developed away from the wall should be tied in. Pruning in mid spring consists of cutting out any wood or shoot tips which may have been frosted during the winter.

The method of pruning by spurring back all the young growth after the petals fall results in a loss of flowering potential in the following season. The forms *R. b.* 'Alba Plena' and *R. b.* 'Lutea' are more common than the type *R. b.* 'Normalis'.

Section *Laevigatae*

R. laevigata, the strong tender grower in this section, is more suited to wall culture, except in the mildest regions where it may be grown in the open with a tree or strong tripod for support, see Plate 43. Trained on a wall, the young growths should be tied in to replace some of the older wood after flowering. The same method of pruning may be applied to the hybrids in which this species is involved such as *R.* 'Anemone' and *R.* 'Silver Moon'.

Section *Bracteatae*

R. bracteata, the only shrub in this section, is large and evergreen. It is not fully hardy and must be given wall protection. Even with this safeguard it is only suitable for the warmer localities. In the nursery it should be encouraged to form laterals low down on the plant, by stopping if necessary. These are trained out fanwise to form the permanent branch system. As these branch, the space allocated to the plant is covered.

At a later stage the laterals produced from the framework grow out from the wall and flower. Pruning should be carried out annually in the spring, the aim being to keep the plant tidy and as close to the wall as possible for maximum protection. Also, the extent of the winter's damage is then evident, and any dead pieces may be cut back to living tissue. The laterals that have flowered during the previous season may be shortened to strong, healthy growths which should be developing near their bases. Some of the older branch systems may be cut out entirely, provided that there are young growths that have wintered and are suitable as replacements. These young growths are more certain to winter well if tied in against the wall as they develop during the summer and autumn. The old branches that they will replace are not cut out until the spring, as they will protect the young growths which are more likely to be killed by severe weather.

The hybrid 'Mermaid' is hardier and may be grown in colder areas, provided that a wall is selected. In the milder districts a stake or pergola is suitable. This hybrid is often budded onto one of the rose stocks, but it may be grown successfully on its own roots, and has even been known to sucker strongly from these. Pruning is similar to that carried out on the species, *R. bracteata*. A low branching should be encouraged in the nursery. By having the lower part of the shrub shaded, perhaps by suitable shrubs, the wood is prevented from hardening, and is thus more likely to throw strong, young, basal shoots that can be used for replacement purposes.

Subgenus *Platyrhodon*

The only rose in this group is *R. roxburghii*, the Burr Rose, which is distinct with its prickly, orange-yellow hips and peeling bark. If left to grow naturally, this rose will make 3 m. (10 ft.) in height and the same in spread. There is no pruning needed for this rose, apart from the removal of dead wood or to open up the plant to view the attractive flaking stems. *R. r.* f. *normalis* can be treated the same way.

Subgenus *Hesperhodos*

R. stellata is in this small group. It is a small plant with thin stems forming dense thickets, difficult to grow, liking a well-drained, sunny position. *R. minutifolia* has similar requirements and is even more difficult. Both species are better suited to the warmer and sunnier climates.

R. s. var. *mirifica* is a stronger grower but also prefers a sunny, well-drained position. It has a suckerous habit and flowers better on this younger and stronger wood from laterals produced in the second season. Pruning consists of cutting out the old and dead wood in the spring and looking over the plants again after flowering, when the new season's growth may be taken into account in deciding just how much of the old should finally be removed. The suckers often appear among neighbouring plants as the clump becomes established and, if these are valued, must be removed at an early stage, tracing the root back to the parent plant if possible. A shrub with this habit is better in an isolated bed surrounded by grass or among taller shrubs that will not suffer in any way. This rose should not be grown closer than 0.6 to 0.9 m. (2 to 3 ft.) from a path, as the thorny branches will be weighed down over the edge as they extend and become older, and will thus be a nuisance.

THE PRUNING OF THE MODERN HYBRID BUSH ROSES

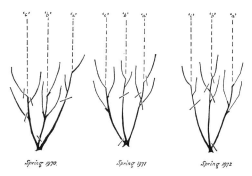

Fig. 40. Diagrammatic representation of pruning a modern Large-flowered Rose (Hybrid Tea Rose). A bush with three branches, 'a', 'b' and 'c', is shown, each branch being at a different stage of a three-year cycle of growth and pruning. The cycle for branch 'a' is as follows:

(1) Spring 2002. The branch is almost all new wood produced in 2001 and will probably have flowered late that summer. It should be lightly pruned in spring 2002 as shown.

(2) Spring 2003. The new laterals produced in 2002 will flower early that year and should be cut back to two or three buds in spring 2003 as shown.

(3) Spring 2004. More laterals will be produced in 2003 and will flower early that year. But now, the lower part of this branch is three years old and it should be cut hard back to near ground level in spring 2004 as shown.

Branch 'b' has reached the third stage described above by the spring of 2002 and therefore must be cut hard back then to near ground level as shown. In 2002 a new shoot will be produced which may flower late that year. In spring 2003 this is cut back lightly and in spring 2004 the new laterals are cut back more severely to two or three buds.

Branch 'c' has reached the second stage by the spring of 2002 and consists of one- and two-year-old wood. The laterals are therefore pruned to two or three buds and in the following spring of 2003 the whole branch is severely cut back as shown. In spring 2004 only light pruning will be required.

It is emphasized that this is a very much oversimplified example, its purpose being to illustrate the three-stage cycle of pruning.

This method of pruning can equally well be applied to a modern Cluster-flowered Rose (Floribunda Rose).

Large-flowered Bush Roses (Hybrid Tea Roses)

This is a very large group of mixed origin, and one that in recent years has absorbed many of the older hybrids such as the Tea, Hybrid Tea, Hybrid Perpetual and Pernetiana groups. Hybridization for colour, scent, disease resistance, vigour and continuity of flowering has taken place to such an extent that it is impossible to define or to classify many of the modern roses. At first sight this seems very confusing to the pruner but there is one safe guide. This is continuity of flowering during the growing season that may even extend into late autumn or early winter. This characteristic has been handed down from at least one parent which is common to most— *R.* ×*odorata* in the Section *Chinenses*. The reader is referred to this section and the pruning advised for this species and for *R. chinensis*. The early crop of flowers is produced on laterals from the old wood, while a later display is provided by the young growths during their first season, these often being long and originating from low down near the base.

If left to grow on from year to year the bushes will become large and congested, with a mass of growths that often form an impenetrable thicket. By contrast, a well-managed plant is healthier and more balanced and the flowers although fewer are better shaped and more typical. The annual pruning, which is advised for most if not all of the Large-flowered (Hybrid Tea) types old and new, is designed to control growth and bush formation, and is based upon the cutting out of the old, weak and dead shoots and the preservation of the new wood.

It is helpful, especially for the beginner, to carry out the annual pruning of this type of rose in stages, which are well defined. These are described below.

Stage I. The cutting out of dead, diseased and frosted wood. Sometimes dead or dying snags from previous prunings are found. These should be removed together with any other dead material. Frosted wood is likely to be found on the tips of the unripened, young wood produced late in the season. These should be cut back hard into sound wood. With practice, the work entailed at this stage may be reduced, for there is no point in removing the dead wood from a growth that is to be pruned back at a later stage.

Stage II. The removal of the older branch systems. This is an important, if not the most important, stage of the pruning. A healthy bush produces a crop of new growths annually, often from the lower portions of the bush or even from the base. By cutting out the branch systems which are made up partly of old wood perhaps three or more years old the young growths are encouraged. The beginner would do well to examine these older branch systems after they have been removed. Living branches will, of course, be made up of some young wood, but, when this is compared with the younger shoots coming from the base, it will be found to be much weaker. In some cases only a portion of such an old system can be cut out; but often it is possible to make a complete removal at or near ground level. The pruner must decide just what proportion of the older systems should be removed, taking the cuts back either to good dormant buds or to younger and more promising growths. In other words, a balance must be maintained which can be adjusted from year to year, taking response and the previous season's growth into consideration at the time of pruning. No hard and fast rule can be laid down, for behaviour varies both with the soil and with different varieties. The weaker the bush the greater the care needed in cutting back the old branch systems to a suitable point, for some of the older and weaker wood may need to be retained in order to keep an adequate furnishing.

It is emphasized that the cutting out of the old wood merely takes the place of a natural process whereby hybrids of this nature, which have the *R. ×odorata* habit and origin, eventually shed their older branch systems. By the process of replacement already described, these older branch systems would be naturally crowded out and, deprived of food, would eventually die. The rose grower, however, cannot afford to allow this process to occur naturally for poor and crowded growth often means an increase in pest and disease troubles. Also, many of the hybrids would never survive or bloom well without specialized and intensive methods of culture, which include pruning.

Stage III. The shortening of the previous year's wood which is to remain on the bush. The growths of the previous season that are to remain should be shortened, as a general rule, to half their length. Thus the number of buds which remain and possibly develop is reduced, as the cuts are made into stouter wood. It must be clearly understood that this shortening takes place after the weakest wood has been cut back to a suitable bud, or to the base as described in the previous section.

At this stage it should be noted that the height of the bush is to some extent controlled by the measure of the pruning, but no attempt should be made to keep a large and strong grower down by severely cutting back. In fact, the strongest growers need only light pruning, taking the young growths back by a quarter or less. The weaker growers are pruned harder, leaving only a third or less of the young wood, see Fig. 40.

Choice of bud or growth above which the cut made. It is important to select the position of the cut very carefully. This has already been mentioned in the opening chapter of this book, and to some extent in earlier paragraphs in this section on roses. The bud or growth left just beneath the cut is, by virtue of its position, the leading growing point. It must be healthy and strong enough to take the lead. In addition, in order to keep the centre of the bush open as a means of countering congestion, it is advisable to prune to an outward-pointing bud. Ideally, the cuts should be sloping and made just above the buds, in order to avoid dead snags which are not only unsightly but may encourage diseases to gain a foothold and spread later into healthy wood.

No plant will grow to order but if necessary the annual pruning may be corrective. A bud that grows in towards the centre of the bush, for example, may result in crossing branches. This position may be corrected during the winter's pruning that follows for, if left, other branches may eventually be weighed down and broken, spoiling the shape and general effect.

Period for pruning Hybrid Tea types.   Normally these are pruned in the dormant period, between late autumn and early spring just before growth commences. If left till later when growth is actively under way much of this is wasted, as the shoots most forward and active are those on the topmost portions which are cut away. Damage may also be done to the plant by knocking off shoots that would otherwise have been retained. Many rose growers prune in the autumn after the leaves fall or during the winter but this should not be attempted by the beginner. Experience is necessary for the selection of suitable buds when they are dormant.

Summer pruning and deadheading.   This operation, which entails looking over the bushes at regular, perhaps at weekly, intervals during the growing and flowering season, improves the appearance and display and, if carried out carefully, it is also a partial growth regulator.

Deadheading is often referred to as entailing the removal of withered blossom. This prevents seed production and thus conserves energy in addition to giving the plant a tidier appearance. When the withered blossoms are on the head it should be carried out very carefully, ensuring that the remainder, which may be fresh or even unopened, are left intact.

When the whole head, or in some cases the single blossom, has withered, it may be shortened back to a suitable bud or growth. Often this means removing several centimeters of flower stalk with some leaves attached. This may be referred to as summer pruning although in part it overlaps deadheading. It should not be carried to the extent that there is a considerable loss of foliage and branch growth otherwise the health of the bush may suffer.

Autumn pruning.   In exposed situations, following a good growing season, roses may be susceptible to frost damage or winter cold and wind rock. Prior to severe winds in early autumn it is advisable to prune the plants by a third to reduce the possibility of wind damage. If the plants have rocked, carefully re-firm around the base of the plant.

Pruning after planting and before the first season's growth.   This operation is very important, for if the bushes are left unpruned before the first season's growth they become straggly with few if any low breaks. In order to carry out the subsequent pruning properly the breaks must be low down or at ground level. To encourage this, the stems are cut back to approximately 150 mm. (6 in.), choosing outside buds. This may be carried out any time after planting and before the new season's growth begins.

Cluster-flowered Bush Roses (Floribunda Roses)

As with Large-flowered Bush Roses (Hybrid Teas), extensive hybridization has taken place within recent years. The modern varieties are mostly vigorous growers and throw up strong shoots, often from near the base. If left unattended, the bushes become very congested with wood that is old and has lost much of its vigour.

Firstly, the dead and diseased wood is cut out. The removal of a proportion of the older wood follows, if possible making the cuts low down to a suitable bud near the base. This in fact means that branch systems based on three- or four-year-old wood is removed to make way for the younger wood. Growths that remain are also cut back and, as with the Large-flowered, the extent of this depends upon age and condition. When the growth is very strong the pruning is light, the harder pruning being reserved for the weaker growers when as much as two-thirds or even more is removed. With moderate pruning the growths may be cut back by one-third or a half. Young growths, which are based upon any older wood which remains, are cut back harder than new shoots which spring directly from the base. Under this system the older wood supporting the weaker, exhausted or close-growing laterals is thinned and pruned, the cuts being made above a promising shoot or buds. Thus more light and air is left for the younger material which remains, this being pruned according to vigour. Thus each branch and

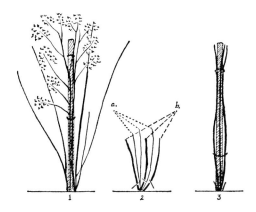

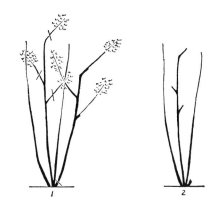

Fig. 41. The pruning of Rambler Roses which send up a sufficient crop of canes each year to allow the old ones to be cut out.
(1) Before pruning, just as flowering has finished.
(2) A close-up of the base, showing (a) the young growths and (b) the old canes with the positions of pruning cuts made after flowering.
(3) After pruning, the new growths tied in.

Fig. 42. The pruning of a Rambler Rose type which does not make a sufficient number of new growths in one year to allow the old wood to be cut out completely.
(1) This shows the position of the oldest growth, while the laterals which have also just flowered on the younger cane are cut back to near their bases.
(2) The same bush after pruning.

growth is judged upon its age and vigour, and it is only when the bushes concerned are of one variety either in a group or bed that uniformity is considered. Great care is needed even in this situation, for a uniform level and appearance at the time of pruning does not mean that the bushes will grow uniformly. Careful and selective pruning is a means of encouraging weaker bushes so that the planting as a whole is uniform.

Summer pruning is of great benefit to the bushes and to their appearance. It is carried out on the same principle and by the same method as for Large-flowered.

Miniature Roses

These popular plants are miniature versions of the Large- and Cluster-flowered Bush Roses and should be treated in the same way as their full-size counterparts. If the plants are growing well, they can be lightly pruned, but if the plants are struggling and are in need of some renovation, they can be cut back hard to stimulate new growths from the base.

Rambler Roses

The reader is referred to the opening paragraphs on the flowering habits of the genus *Rosa*, see page 264, and in particular to the account of the growth and flowering of the Section *Synstylae*, see page 267. The habit of growth of the majority of the species in this section is to throw up a strong crop of shoots annually, but the new canes produced are much stronger in some species than others and it is the same with the varieties and hybrids of this section. However, it is possible to establish two definite groups:

(i) This group is made up of those varieties which throw up long growths abundantly each year from the base. These are the true Ramblers being hybrids of *R. wichurana*, for example, 'Dorothy Perkins'. These young growths produce their best crop of flowers in their second year. The pruning, which is carried out annually, is based on this habit of growth and flowering. The complete lengths of old growths over two years old are cut out at ground level immediately after flowering and the new ones tied in. It is an example of replacement pruning, see Fig. 41.

(ii) In this group are the varieties which do not make a sufficient number of young growths in any one year to allow the old wood to be cut out completely. Often too, the strong growths spring from high up on the old wood. The aim in pruning must be to keep the bush, which is usually tied to a support, well furnished with young wood. Sufficient of the old wood is cut out to allow this. Occasionally, to prevent the base of the plant from becoming bare, an old growth is cut down hard to a dormant growth or bud at ground level. The pruning is carried out after flowering.

The pruning of these two groups after planting is based upon the need to encourage breaks from low down. The canes are therefore cut down to approximately 200 to 250 mm. (8 to 10 in.), see Fig. 42.

Climbers

In this group are the types of climbing roses not already mentioned. Among these are the climbing sports and hybrids, all producing a similar growth that makes them suitable for training over a support such as a fence or pergola or on a wire system against a wall surface. The framework or branch system is tied out and is often kept for a number of years. Flowering laterals are produced from this and these are cut back to the lower buds in the spring before the new growth commences. From time to time young growths are produced which may be used for extension. These should be carefully tied in and later, as they grow, used as replacements for older and spent branch systems.

Unlike most of the other types of roses, the varieties and hybrids in this group should not be pruned after planting or during the first season's growth, unless it be to cut out any dead wood. This is an important rule to observe with the climbing sports in paticular, for there is a danger of reversion to a bush habit if pruned back too hard.

Standards

Usually these are made up of large-flowered varieties that have been budded onto stems of *R. canina* or *R. laxa* rootstocks, although other stocks are also used. Apart from the removal of suckers and the need to keep the stem clean and free from stock growths, pruning follows the same principles as for the Large-flowered.

Weeping Standards

These are often formed from Rambler, climber or ground-cover varieties, the stems being trained over a hood or umbrella framework. The new growths are tied in after old stems have been cut off when the blossom display is over.

Forms other than Ramblers trained in this way are treated according to the methods advocated for their own group.

Hedges

Roses like *R. rugosa* and *R.* 'Nevada' grown in this way are treated informally, the pruning following the lines already described for each species. With many of the hybrids and varieties that flower throughout the summer, the withered heads may be cut back as they form in a series of weekly operations. The cut is always made above a suitable bud. In this way and by feeding and watering if necessary, a continuous display is assured. Should pruning be needed, it can be carried out in early spring. Mechanical hedge-trimmers are commonly used on hedges today.

ROSMARINUS

R. officinalis. This shrub is not fully hardy and it may be damaged in severe winters, especially in a damp area. It will however regenerate very freely if there is living wood to which it should be cut down. This strong and ready response to cutting back is more certain with a young and vigorous plant, and there need be no hesitation in cutting back a straggly overgrown specimen. The spring is the best time for this.

When the shrub is very old it is often advisable to replace it with a younger one, choosing the spring as the planting time. It is less likely to become overgrown and worn out if a sunny, open position is selected.

Bushy plants should be encouraged by stopping at least once in the nursery and once again at the start of the growing season after planting.

Some pruning after flowering may be undertaken with advantage when long branches may be cut to suitable growths. These are plentiful on a vigorously growing bush and by this means it is kept more compact. A Rosemary hedge is trimmed after flowering.

There are a number of cultivars and their individual habits must be taken into account when deciding upon a pruning policy, for example, the cultivar 'Miss Jessopp's Upright' has a very erect growth.

RUBUS

These flower on laterals which are produced from the previous season's wood, but many species will retain their long canes for three or four years, producing new laterals from buds at the base of the flowering growth. As a general rule, however, the practice is to cut out all or much of the old wood, as a characteristic of the genus is to throw up a plentiful supply of young growths from the base during the summer. It is important to study growth and behaviour, both from the point of view of pruning and of training.

The white-stemmed species are most distinct. As an example we may quote *R. cockburnianus*. The young growths are very attractive during their first winter, but they lose this pure white colouring as they ripen in the second season after the flowering period. However, by this time a fresh crop of canes has been produced from ground level, and the old ones may be cut out completely. If they were left they would spoil the effect of the young growths. Most of the young canes are vigorous and should reach full height, provided the shrub is healthy and is well fed and mulched, but the smaller growths may also be left, as they provide furnishing and thus contribute toward a more natural appearance. The natural arching habit of the long growths should also be retained. Other species with a similar habit and effect may also be treated in this way, for example, *R. biflorus* and *R. thibetanus*. Staking may be necessary but the natural habit should be preserved as far as possible.

R. odoratus belongs to another distinct group. It is upright in growth and the flowers, which are borne by the canes in their second season, are attractive. Immediately the display is over the old canes should be cut out. Thus the young growths are given more light and air for ripening and the flaking bark, which is quite attractive, is displayed to full effect during the first winter.

R. deliciosus may be quoted as an example of a species which does not produce enough young growth from the base to allow all the old wood to be cut out each season after flowering. Sufficient of the old wood must therefore be left to form a framework. Young growths for replacement should be encouraged from ground level. The beautiful hybrid *R.* 'Benenden' needs similar treatment, cutting away the flowering growths and some of the older wood if possible.

Many species have a scandent habit and produce long growths which need staking if grown in a restricted space or border. The stake may take the form of a stout pole, although a tripod support is more secure. Pruning consists of cutting the old growths down to ground level, usually in the autumn, after the fruits have been gathered. The new shoots are then tied in. If insufficient new wood is produced, some of the older canes may be left after the flowering laterals have been cut back. This group is grown more for its fruit than for its ornamental value.

RUSCUS

These require very little pruning, apart from the dead and discoloured 'foliage' and stems, which need cutting off when the shrubs are looked over each spring. A proportion of the large 'leaves' of *R. hypoglossum* in particular, may be discoloured during the winter and appear very unsightly. The whole stem should be cut away at ground level.

Some adopt the practice of cutting established clumps of this species right down to ground level each spring just before the new growth commences, but such drastic treatment is not always successful, especially on the drier and poorer soils. Normally, with this species and *R. aculeatus*, it is not necessary to cut out healthy stems even to thin the growths as they have a naturally close and tufted habit.

RUTA

These are referred to as herbs or subshrubs, but although some wood is produced it is seldom sufficiently strong to reach more than 1 m. (3 ft.). The pruning, which should be rather hard, is carried out in mid spring, cutting back to good growths and taking out weaker wood altogether. The flowers are interesting, but the corymbs are often cut off with the stalk down to the leaves with the object of keeping the plants tidy as they are grown mainly for their foliage effect. A compact form of *R. graveolens* is named 'Jackman's Blue'.

Care must be taken when pruning, especially during sunny periods, as the sap can cause a skin disorder.

SALIX

This is a large and botanically a confusing genus, but as far as the arboriculturist and horticulturist are concerned there are three distinct groups:

(1) strong-growing species and varieties suitable as trees;

(2) medium growers taking the form of bushes, the height and form varying with the species;

(3) strong or medium growers which are cut down annually for stem effect.

Most species are adaptable and will throw growths freely even after being cut back hard. This characteristic is a great advantage in training.

Group 1. Strong-growing species and varieties suitable as trees

These can be subdivided into (i) those forming upright trees; and (ii) those with a weeping habit.

In the first category, *S. alba* 'Liempde' is typical. It is a large upright grower often pyramidal in outline

and it is quite a simple matter to retain a central leader. *S. alba* also produces ascending branches and again a leader can easily be retained. *S. fragilis* forms a spreading head with wide-angled branching, a habit which makes it difficult to retain a leader. The lower and main limbs quickly reach a girth equal to or even exceeding that of the central and leading system, which may then quickly lose its dominance. Such a spreading and heavy framework is sometimes prone to damage during gales as the tree becomes old and declines in health. Cavities also have a weakening effect, and in this respect it should be remembered that the wood is soft and the rot is therefore likely to spread rapidly. Cavities must always be inspected and promptly dealt with whatever the species, but it is a matter of even greater urgency with the softer-wooded subjects such as willow.

Among the smaller trees is *S. babylonica* var. *pekinensis* and the cultivar 'Tortuosa'. During the formation of the framework both in the nursery and after planting, it is important to select and train the leading growth most carefully, as otherwise there will be a tendency for rival leaders to develop. This applies in particular to 'Tortuosa'. *S. pentandra* is often quite a small tree, but there is a natural tendency for low branching and a clear stem must be trained if a good height is required. The same is true of *S. daphnoides*. Both are effective either as a large, bushy shrub or a small tree with a clear stem. This latter species is mentioned again in Groups 2 and 3 below.

In the second category, *S. babylonica*, *S. alba* 'Tristis' and *S.* ×*sepulcralis* var. *chrysocoma* all have a weeping habit; the latter is considered the best of the group. Weeping Willows often produce a few main branches that are large and heavy. Once branching is left to develop on a length of clear stem, the leader is quickly lost as more and more vigour is diverted into this extending system. The habit of growth is such that the main branches arch over, additional height being built up by strong, upright shoots that in turn droop over and so the process is repeated. The main danger is with a very old and large tree which may lean, often with considerable weight, perhaps over water, when one or more of its heavy limbs may be torn away from the trunk by a severe gale. Bracing will help to alleviate this danger, but it is also advisable to check any tendency for a tree in this position to develop in one direction where there is more light, thus throwing the crown out of balance. It is often possible to anticipate trouble and take corrective action even on an old tree, although it is better carried out while the tree is young.

S. purpurea 'Pendula' forms a small but spreading head of fine thin growths. Usually this is grafted onto S. purpurea stocks at a height of 2.4 to 3.0 m. (8 to 10 ft.). In the early stages particularly, it is important to keep the stem and crown clear of growths from the stock, rubbing these out while they are young and undeveloped.

Group 2. Medium growers which take the form of bushes, although on occasion they grow into tree form

One common species in this group is S. caprea. The natural form of growth is for the branching to be low, often from ground level. Little pruning is required. S. daphnoides, a species with attractive young growths, may also be grown as a bush. After pruning to encourage a bushy habit in the nursery, the subject is left unpruned for a number of years. Ultimately as the young growths become more numerous they are shorter and less conspicuous. When this happens the younger growths may be encouraged by cutting out a proportion of the older wood. It is usually advisable to continue this on an annual basis in the early spring, maintaining a natural form by carefully positioning the pruning cuts. In no way must it be confused with the method of pruning this and other willows hard back to a main stump for a completely young stem effect. The need to retain vigour in the young wood is also important with S. aegyptiaca. This subject is grown for the decorative effect of the catkins, which are freely produced on strong, young growths of the previous season in late winter. A vigorously growing bush or multi-stemmed tree will therefore be the most effective. Pruning should be devoted to cutting out any weak or dead branches remembering the need for a shapely bush, an essential for a subject which is to provide a display in the dormant season, when every branch shows up in relief against other

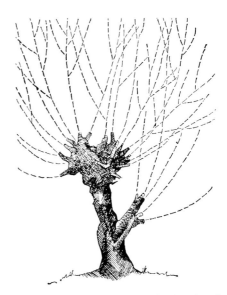

Fig. 43. A *Salix* stool that is cut back hard each spring, being grown for the decorative stem effects. The broken lines indicate the growths which are cut back.

subjects. Feeding and mulching is also necessary to retain vigour.

Much could be written about many of the other bushy species, but they can be covered briefly by the advice to study and retain the natural habit of growth. Each species and variety varies in this respect. The Kilmarnock Willow, S. caprea 'Kilmarnock' is a weeping form top grafted as a weeping standard, to 3 m. (10 ft.) high with a show of catkins in spring. Pruning will take place annually in the form of thinning the curtain of pendulous branches to open up the framework, removing any dead branches and shortening back any remaining branches that are too long. Many of the species have the habit of layering naturally and this may not be desirable, as it is often difficult to keep the ground thus occupied free from strong-growing weeds and saplings such as bramble or ash. It may therefore be the better policy to correct this habit.

Group 3. Strong or medium growers which are cut down annually for stem effect

A number of species and varieties are grown for the colour and decorative effect of the young shoots as they ripen after their first season's growth. The method is to cut the growths hard back in the spring of each year, which results in a crop of young shoots which extend during the season to provide a display of stems the following winter.

The species and varieties that are grown for this effect are pruned to a definite height of 0.6 to 0.9 m. (2 to 3 ft.) each year and this in time results in the building up of spurs which increase in size until a large number of coloured stems are produced. It is often found desirable to keep the short leg clear of growths, although some prefer one or two small spurs to be left on the lower part to increase the decorative effect, see Fig. 43. The intensity of the colouring is more pronounced in the late winter and early spring and the stems are therefore left as long as possible until the buds break to commence the new season's growth. They are then pruned back to within one inch of the old wood or spur. The following are among those that respond well to this system of culture: *S. alba* subsp. *vitellina* and its cultivar 'Britzensis', *S. daphnoides* and *S. irrorata*.

The stools may be over-vigorous in the early years, in which case a root pruning operation is advisable.

SALVIA

S. officinalis, the Common Sage, described as a subshrub, is the only really hardy species which is definitely woody. When young, it forms an attractive plant, but as it becomes older, patches of bare wood are exposed at the base leaving the plant straggly and unsightly. However, in this condition when it is old and woody, the shrub responds to hard cutting back in the spring, for even in the older wood buds remain alive and develop very quickly if called upon to do so. An alternative is to discard such specimens, replacing them with new young plants. The need for such drastic treatment may be delayed by cutting back after flowering almost to the base of the younger wood. This advice also holds for the variegated forms.

The remainder of the woody species needs the protection of a warm, sunny wall. Examples are *S. microphylla* and *S. elegans*. Often, especially with *S. elegans*, a woody system may be built up over the

years reaching a height of 0.3 to 0.6 m. (1 to 2 ft.). Species in this group should be pruned back to the older wood in the spring just as growth is about to break out. In severe weather the growths may be killed back to near ground level. Left unpruned, these shrubs become weak and untidy. Some form of support will also keep them in a tidier condition, but no attempt should be made to train them to a wall as they are more successful when planted a foot or so away from the base and allowed to develop a bushy growth. Often sucker-like growths are produced as the shrub spreads. A covering of garden fleece, straw or bracken round the bases in the winter is advisable.

SAMBUCUS

These are often short-lived shrubs and thus periodic propagation is necessary in order to replace the old, weak specimens. The pruning consists of cutting out the older wood and branches, a task that may be carried out during the dormant season. A healthy bush has sufficient young wood to cut to, but a weak and overgrown specimen may be taken hard back to near ground level, when a supply of young shoots will spring from the base.

Some of the foliage forms such as *S. nigra* 'Albo-variegata' may be trained as small standards on a 1.5 to 1.8 m. (5 to 6 ft.) leg. The suckers, which tend to spring from the base in particular, should be cut off as they appear. Other forms include *S. racemosa* var. *sieboldiana*, which is strong growing and, if kept well supplied with young growths by cutting out the oldest branches, the strong shoots that are left spread out to give a tropical foliage effect. These shrubs are sometimes grown purely for foliage effect, in which case they are cut down hard each year. One method is to prune down to near ground level each winter, but this does not always result in a full and well-furnished plant. By leaving the one-year-old canes pruned down to half their length, and, at the same time cutting down to ground level those which have been treated in this manner the previous year, a larger and more spreading plant is obtained, see Fig. 44. The coloured forms of *S. nigra* may be treated in this manner, but vigour is all the more important when these shrubs are grown for

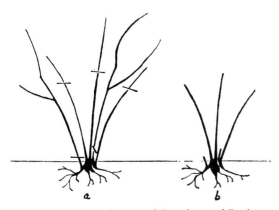

Fig. 44. The method of pruning foliage forms of *Sambucus* which do not send up sufficient growths each year, to provide an adequate furnishing when cut hard to near ground level. The one-year-old canes are left after being pruned back while the older growths are cut down hard to near ground level.

colour and foliage effect. Mulching and feeding are an important part of their culture. *S. canadensis* 'Maxima' benefits from hard pruning down to near ground level each spring, and the strong canes resulting from this produce large heads of flower in the late summer.

S. nigra is a very good shrub in exposed coastal areas, where it will help to form the first line of defence against the wind.

S. ebulus and *S. formosana* should be treated like herbaceous plants and cut back to ground level each year, during the dormant season. Flowering will occur during late summer. It may be necessary to insert a form of root barrier around the planting to prevent it from running through the bed, as it can be quite invasive.

SANTOLINA

These small shrubs, when young, form close masses of leafy shoots. As they grow older, however, the heavy branches are weighed down and the whole appearance and shape is spoilt. If left unattended the upright growths produced on the now horizontal branches are in their turn weighed down, until the whole becomes a mass of stems, dead growths and fallen leaves. In a wet winter this may cause the plants to die.

Occasional hard pruning will prevent this unhappy condition occurring. The regular annual pruning should be carried out in the autumn and consists of cutting off the old flower heads and stalks, at the same time cutting back any tall and straggly growths to prevent them from being weighed down by snow and rain, thus spoiling the remainder of the shrub during the winter.

Eventually however, despite this attention, the general condition of the plant appears overgrown and worn. It is then that it should be cut hard back into the old wood in the spring. The recovery from this harsh treatment is very rapid and it may be necessary to repeat this every two or three years. Often however, it becomes necessary to replace old plants every two or three years.

Growth tends to be shorter and more compact in a rather dry and sunny position.

This advice applies generally to *S. chamaecyparissus* and *S. rosmarinifolia* which are normally grown in gardens.

SAPINDUS

S. drummondii and *S. mukorossi* are the only two members of this genus that can be grown in a sheltered, sunny garden. They will make small trees and should be grown with a central leader and apart from the removal of the lower branches and dead wood, need minimal pruning.

SAPIUM

S. japonicum is grown for its foliage colour which can be quite a spectacular red in the autumn. It can be grown with a central leader, requiring very little pruning, apart from keeping the plant in shape, should it outgrow its planting site.

SARCOCOCCA

The Christmas Boxes are useful shrubs that require very little pruning, apart from the removal of dead or worn-out growths. Usually these should be taken off at ground level, but sometimes it is better to cut back to a strong growth inside the bush. It is not desirable to thin, because the growths are crowded, as this is the natural habit.

S. hookeriana often throws strong growths well above the remainder and these may lose their leaves during the winter and appear dead. Cutting back is, therefore, best left until the spring, when the dead wood can be readily distinguished from the living. The habit of a mature bush of this species is often very spreading, as the branches extend and bend over with the extra weight. This is a natural habit and should not be spoilt by pruning. *S. confusa* with a spreading habit often develops one or two ragged growths that spoil the general appearance. These may be cut back in the spring to a growth which originates well down inside the bush or at ground level.

SASA. *See* Bamboos

SASSAFRAS

S. albidum. The best form in which to grow this species is to a single stem, retaining the leader through the crown for as long as possible. The branches often have an ascending habit as they arise from the trunk, while the individual branches form close heads of twig growth and foliage, which gives the crown an unusual but pleasant appearance. As the specimen develops, the trunk should be cleared of branches to a height of 1.8 to 2.4 m. (6 to 8 ft.), for the furrowed bark is also of beauty. Grown as a lawn specimen the lower branches tend to sweep down in a pleasant manner and these should be retained.

Often this species suckers in neighbouring borders and at the bases of nearby trees should these be in grass. These form a ready means of propagation if potted up singly and placed under a mist unit. They may however be left to form a colony.

SCHIMA

The only species that are to any degree hardy are stiff-branching, evergreen shrubs. In addition, the whole framework and twig system is covered with dwarf shoots that are spine-tipped. *S. wallichii* var. *superba* may be grown in a sheltered position while *S. w.* var. *khasiana* really needs wall protection. The latter can either be grown as a bush within the shelter of the structure, or be trained up close to the wall with the main branches and laterals spreading out fanwise. Growth is kept hard up against the wall by careful pruning in the spring. Shoots that extend too far from the surface are pruned back to suitable points where the cuts are concealed.

These two shrubs show a remarkable response to hard cutting back, and there need be no hesitation in doing this with an overgrown shrub or with one which has been damaged by severe weather.

SCHISANDRA

This is a genus of twining shrubs, which are suitable for growing against a shaded wall. In the early years after planting, some form of training is necessary in order to cover the available space adequately with the main branch system. Usually this entails tying out five to eight growths fanwise from the shrub at ground level. The laterals and extension growths from this system should be left to hang down, when short spurs that form the flowering growths will develop. The topmost growths are very vigorous, especially if the height of the wall is limited to 1.5 to 1.8 m. (5 to 6 ft.). It is therefore important that they should not hide those that spring from lower down on the branch systems, as if they are deprived of light they will die. Pruning consists of thinning out the older and weaker of these pendulous growths during the winter before the buds break out. Some of the young wood, the extension growths which it naturally produces as a climber, may need to be cut away completely. A limited number, however, will be needed for replacement purposes.

Although they are climbers, the branch system will need tying, as the main means of support are the young twining growths that under wall culture cannot be left in quantity to develop.

These shrubs may also be grown on trees, poles or tripods for supports. The stub ends of the branches should be left on the poles as these form a good support and a hold for the twining stems without which, as the weight increases, the mass would slip down to form a tangle at the base, see Fig. 20 (1 and 2). A pendulous habit from the top of the stake should be encouraged. Pruning with this system of culture consists of cutting out the older wood in the winter, using the young growths as replacements. The young growths that are not needed may be cut out.

Certain species are stronger and are more suitable for culture under normal conditions; *S. grandiflora* and *S. rubriflora*, for example, are able to reach 3.0 to 3.6 m. (10 to 20 ft.) in height while *S. chinensis* is much weaker by contrast.

SCHIZOPHRAGMA

S. integrifolium is the species commonly found in gardens. It may be grown against a wall for support and it is self-clinging by means of the adventitious roots that are freely produced, like Ivy, from the young growths. However, some additional support by means of ties to a wire system is often necessary. In its natural habitat, it would be found growing up the trunks of large broad-leaved trees. The main framework is trained out to cover the available space, but the habit is often somewhat ungainly, and it is not often possible to space the branches out neatly.

Two types of growth are produced: (i) extension shoots that are long and self-clinging. These often grow many feet in the one season with short laterals on their basal portion and (ii) branched laterals that grow from the main framework and have a semi-pendulous habit. These are the flowering growths and during the winter the blossom buds may be found terminating the short spur systems.

Pruning may be needed during the dormant season to remove any long extension growths that may be surplus. The cut should be made just above a lateral, which may also need shortening. It may also be wise to remove weak growths.

This species is sometimes grown over a low stump, where it will form an attractive bed or informal drift. Under this system flowering branches should be encouraged, but there must be a number of extension growths to allow older branches and dead wood to be cut out if need be.

S. hydrangeoides has a similar habit.

SCIADOPITYS

S. verticillata is a slow-growing tree that in its best form has a central leader from which the smaller branch systems spring directly. They have a crowded appearance and may be semi-pendulous. However, many specimens show a tendency to throw out strong branches, which first grow out at an angle from the main stem and then assume an upright position. In time this habit may result in the production of one or more rival leaders. A number of specimens produce leaders freely from ground level, a habit that develops during the nursery stage. Early training and selection are therefore important if a single leader is desired. Timely corrective training is important even with an established specimen, for once rival leaders have developed and are perhaps 2 to 3 m. (6 to 10 ft.) in height, it would be unwise to remove them. A good specimen is often clothed with a dense branching down to ground level. While it may prefer light, partial shade, especially when young, this does not seem to be essential, while over-shading may quickly cause loss of foliage.

SECURINEGA

S. suffruticosa. Either of two methods of pruning can be adopted with this shrub. One is to cut down almost to ground level in the spring of each year. The growths that are sent up during the summer flower in late to early summer. Treated in this way it becomes an ideal subject for positioning near the front of the border. The other method is to allow the subject to grow more naturally, thinning the weakest branches only by cutting them down to ground level.

SEMIARUNDINARIA. *See* Bamboos

SENECIO

S. cineraria is a leafy subshrub which flowers terminally on growths made during the previous season. Growths are also produced along the lengths of these shoots and at their bases. Pruning consists of cutting off old flower heads in the autumn and at the same time very long straggly growths should be removed. This prevents the plants from being blown about excessively, although limited staking may be necessary. A heavier cutting back may be carried out in the spring if necessary.

S. scandens is a vigorous semi-woody climber that can be grown over other bushes and trees in a sheltered position in the garden. Any pruning should be to remove weak shoots or to reduce long shoots after flowering by about a third.

SENNA

S. marilandica is the only species which is normally grown outside in the milder climates. It must be given wall protection and should be planted about 300 mm. (12 in.) from the base. It is treated as a herbaceous plant, being cut down in the autumn to within 25 mm. (1 in.) of the base. As a protection for the winter the crowns and the surrounding soil should be covered with garden fleece, bracken or straw lightly held in position with string and pegs.

S. corymbosa may be grown as a wall shrub in the mildest climates. One method is to train the framework of branches to the wall supports. When the buds are active in the spring the growths made during the previous year are pruned back close to the framework. These in turn flower in the late summer.

SEQUOIA

S. sempervirens is a tall species and will, under suitable conditions, reach considerable heights. It prefers shelter and in exposed positions the tree is ragged and the growth stunted. There is considerable variation in the growth of the branch systems, some producing sub-branches that trail down for many metres, often reaching the ground. This habit, if it develops, should be encouraged and the extremities safeguarded when mowing or carrying out other work round the tree, for the effect is most desirable. Trees of this species often produce suckerous growths that usually spring from round the base of the trunk. These should be removed at least annually during the autumn or winter, both as a means of improving appearance and for the benefit of the tree, as they will take nourishment away from the crown if they are allowed to develop.

Young trees, both in the nursery and for a few years after planting, need exceptionally well sheltered conditions. The leading growth is also susceptible to frost damage.

SEQUOIADENDRON

S. giganteum is a large and tall grower, provided the soil and situation are suitable, and the natural habit is to retain the leader until the ultimate height is reached. This may, in sheltered positions, be well over 30 m. (100 ft.). The height to which this species grows is directly related to the degree of exposure to strong winds. Once the general height of the surrounding trees is reached, unless there is some other form of effective shelter such as a hillside, the topmost growing point often loses vigour and further extension is reduced or stops altogether.

When in good condition, the trunk is often furnished with branches for almost its entire height. However, any of the lower branches that show signs of serious and extensive dieback should be sawn off to the main trunk. If there are only a few dead ends on the branches these may be cleaned up, making these branches and the tree look much tidier. This is a difficult task on a large tree.

It is desirable to provide exceptionally well sheltered positions for young trees both in the nursery and in the years immediately after planting.

SHEPHERDIA

S. argentea is a slow-growing dioecious shrub which has a spiny, twiggy growth. In the nursery it should be trained with a single stem and this is retained for the life of the shrub. The growth coming away from this consists of small branches, giving the shrub, as it matures, a miniature tree—like appearance, growing up to 3.7 m. (12 ft.) in height. No pruning is needed beyond the removal of dead wood. Occasionally, multi-stemmed specimens are grown and these are quite attractive if allowed to develop from ground level.

S. canadensis is, by contrast, a spreading shrub.

SHIBATAEA. *See* Bamboos

SIBIRAEA

S. laevigata. This shrub is closely related to the spiraeas and it produces terminal panicles of blossom in the late spring or early summer.

Pruning consists of cutting out the weaker wood after flowering, making the cuts as low down on the bush as possible. Two or three years of experimental pruning are needed, for it is dangerous to cut out more than the shrub can make up with young growth in one year.

SINARUNDINARIA. *See* Bamboos

SINOCALYCANTHUS

S. chinensis has a habit of growth similar to that of *Calycanthus*, freely producing young shoots from the base which will make a shrub to 3 m. (10 ft.). Thus quite a dense canopy is produced, the lower branches spreading, which should be encouraged. The flowers are nodding and are best viewed from underneath the plant, so the maximum height should be encouraged to get the best out of this wonderful plant.

The habit of growth is such that old branches that are cut out are quickly replaced and this pruning is carried out, if necessary, in the spring. The flowers are produced terminally on the young wood during the early summer.

SINOFRANCHETIA

S. chinensis is a vigorous, hardy subject which climbs by means of long, twining stems. Grown where it can climb a small tree, which is perhaps declining in health, or a trunk left after a large specimen has been cut back, it is no problem and requires little or no pruning. When it is grown in a restricted space, for example on a single stake or a tripod some pruning of the long, climbing growths is needed once the support has been covered. They can be cut back to the lowest two or three buds in the spring. A better alternative is to stop the developing extension growths at 6 to 8 leaves in midsummer, cutting these back to two buds in the spring. Under this system short, spur-like growths build up and these should be encouraged.

For wall culture the same system can be adopted. It is advisable to have vertical wires tied to the horizontal strands as these are a considerable help to the developing shrub in the first instance. Ideally, the young shrub should have two main branches that can be secured to the lowest horizontal wire. In this way the twining growths quickly take to the vertical wires, which may be set at 0.3 m. (1 ft.) apart.

SINOJACKIA

S. rehderiana forms a small tree or a large bush, usually with many branches springing from ground level. Also a considerable number of young branches are often thrown up from the older wood and these can be used for renewal purposes. The two-year-old wood has the curious habit of shedding bark in strips during the winter, giving the bush a ragged appearance.

There is little need for pruning unless there is dead wood to cut out, for it is difficult or impossible to produce a shapely bush as there are so many crossing branches. The lower branches should be left to provide furnishing, as they will do almost to ground level.

S. xylocarpa is a small tree and has a similar habit of growth.

SINOMENIUM

S. acutum is a vigorous, twining shrub that is better when grown up a small tree for support, for it is too strong and rampant for the average pergola or stake or tripod system. Masses of twining stems form long chords to the climber's topmost growths. Little pruning is required, in fact it is risky to remove the dead vines as, twined with the living, they help to support the shrub generally.

SKIMMIA

These compact, bushy evergreens rarely need pruning, for informality is their character and beauty. Provided that there is sufficient room, they are effective when planted in a group with the bushes growing together to form one large clump. Such a clump is even more effective when it is made up of a mixed planting of the forms of *S. japonica*.

When these shrubs are established, taller growths are thrown up well beyond the general height and canopy of foliage. These should be left intact, as their development is a sign of vigour and well-being.

Sometimes long, bare and bent branches appear which should be cut back well into the shrub leaving a well-furnished, informal surface. When these shrubs are grown too close to an edge they often require a periodic cutting back, but it is difficult to do this without spoiling the surface. If it is necessary, pruning should be carried out in the spring.

SMILAX

These climb by means of tendrils which occur as modified stipules, but they also scramble over neighbouring bushes gaining advantage from the extensive growths often produced from the base in one season. The thorny, wiry stems undoubtedly helped in this connection.

Tall posts are suitable for training and it is better that the short 0.3 to 0.6 m. (1 to 2 ft.) stub ends of the side branches are left on them as more support is gained in this way, see Fig. 20 (2). In the early stages it may be necessary to tie growths in. Some species such as *S. rotundifolia* are very vigorous indeed and should be given positions where they can ramble over neighbouring shrubs with perfect freedom. Such strong subjects are therefore more suited to the natural parts of the garden.

It is possible to restrict growth and size by pruning, but this must be very carefully carried out, otherwise the shortened canes can appear very unsightly. The cuts should be made where they are hidden and it is often better to cut out complete lengths rather than shorten every one to the same level. Some thinning of the weaker growths is also advantageous in the spring. There may be dead growths to cut back after a severe winter.

S. aspera and *S. megalantha* can both be treated in the same way.

SOLANUM

S. crispum has an arching habit and will ramble over low supports such as tree trunks or the roofs of low buildings. It may be trained as a bush, a suitable form in which to grow this plant in a sheltered place. However, in this form it is an untidy grower. Grown either way, some pruning may be carried out although considerable patience will be needed. It consists of cutting out the weak wood in the spring, taking this back to promising young growths. It should not be carried out after flowering, as the subject is tender and liable to suffer during a severe winter. The mature wood is more likely to survive than the younger growths.

When trained against a wall the framework should be tied out fanwise. The young growths are tied in loosely in the autumn and the final pruning and tidying up left until the spring. This consists of cutting out lengths of the weaker wood and tying in the best of the young shoots as replacements, before the surplus ones are cut off.

In the nursery a bushy habit is encouraged by pruning at least once before planting out.

S. laxum is definitely tender and can only be grown outside in the mildest districts. The thin shoots grow rapidly and are thus adapted for rambling over supports, when a mass of shoot growth will result. Grown on a large sunny wall, the aim should be to cover the area with the main branches and both horizontal and vertical wires are necessary for this. At a later stage some of the thinner and weaker wood should be cut out in order to relieve the congestion, doing this before the new growths develop in the spring.

SOPHORA

The various species and cultivars are at their best in sunny positions. Under these conditions the wood is ripened more thoroughly and the tree or shrub is better able to withstand the winter.

S. japonica, the Pagoda Tree, forms a large tree with a spreading crown, making it a useful street tree. There is a tendency for the lowest branches to put on a larger proportion of growth in comparison to the remainder of the tree and as a result they become unduly heavy which may cause weakness at a later stage. It is important therefore to retain the leader for as long as possible, and for a nursery-trained tree a clear stem of 1.8 to 2.4 m. (6 to 8 ft.) is preferable. The lower branchlets often have a semi-pendulous habit and sweep low to ground level making it a very beautiful tree which is ideal as an isolated lawn specimen. A mature specimen may be in need of bracing, as large limbs sometimes rip off at the main junctions during gales. Pruning should be carried out during the late summer and never in the spring, as there is a risk of bleeding from the cut surfaces. Old trees do not respond well to hard crown reduction.

S. tetraptera and its form 'Grandiflora' are not really hardy, but they will often survive in the warmer regions when planted against a warm, sunny wall. The shrub must have plenty of headroom where it may grow up to 6 to 9 m. (20 to 30 ft.). It does not conform well to pruning. If left unpruned to form a bush it is self-supporting. It flowers heavily in the spring on the strong growths, the flower buds being formed in terminal clusters in the autumn.

S. davidii is hardy and forms a large shrub with a woody trunk and main branch system. One of the beauties of this species is in its stiff branching, many of the smaller ones having a naturally arching habit. Pruning may destroy this habit, but should it be necessary to sever or clean up a torn limb, the shrub often responds by throwing a quantity of young shoots.

SORBARIA

The species within this genus were formerly included under *Spiraea*. However, the leaves are pinnate and they are very strong in growth, suckering and flowering on the current season's wood in large, terminal panicles. Provided they have sufficient nourishment they respond well to annual pruning, for growth and vigour is directed into the production of fewer shoots, the result being better and more luxuriant foliage with an increased flower display. The species are alike in producing new flowering growths both from the crown and from the base. Often, the strongest growths of all originate as suckers from below ground level.

A general pruning policy can be based on the principle that much of the young wood must be shortened to reduce the number of buds which grow out

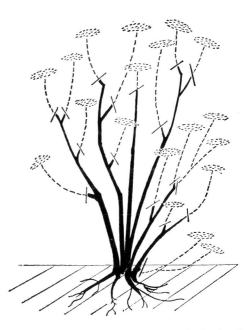

Fig. 45. A mature bush of *Sorbaria kirilowii*, showing the pruning which is carried out in early to mid winter. The broken lines and discs represent the previous summer inflorescences and these, as indicated, are cut back severely close to their point of origin on the main framework. Unless it is desired, notice how the spread beneath ground level may be prevented by making a cut hard back to the main stool.

to flower. This pruning should be carried out in early to mid winter. Once the framework for the bush has been formed the previous season's wood is cut back to 150 to 230 mm. (6 to 9 in.) according to vigour. The very strong growths, especially those springing from the older branches or at ground level, should be left longer, perhaps 0.6 to 0.9 m. (2 to 3 ft.). These can be used to replace older wood and branches, see Fig. 45.

The species vary in growth. For example, *S. kirilowii*, one of the tallest, suckers very freely, and these suckers must be removed unless the shrub is growing in the more natural parts of the garden where extensive colonisation might be welcomed. *S. sorbifolia* is shorter and more erect in habit, suckering very freely. *S. tomentosa* is less hardy than the others. *S. tomentosa* var. *angustifolia*, the most popular, also suckers extensively.

×SORBARONIA

This group of bigeneric hybrids are classed either as small trees or shrubs. To a large extent the ultimate size and form is dependent upon the initial training in the nursery. They may be taken up with a single leader to form a clear stem; ×*S. alpina* is an example. With a clear trunk the lower branches, having a semi-pendulous habit, sweep down, and the whole head forms a close network of twigs and branches. Thus a perfect umbrella of foliage is produced, and the only pruning necessary is to cut out the dead wood that develops on the underside. This should be done during the summer months.

×SORBOPYRUS

×*S. auricularis*. This interesting, bigeneric hybrid should be propagated by grafting. Normally, growth is run up to form a clear stem and a definite head with a central leader. However, as the crown forms, this leader will often quickly break up to become part of the branch system making a small- to medium-sized tree. A watch should be kept for the stock suckering and for dead wood, which may form beneath the dense crown as it develops.

SORBUS

It is useful to use the various botanical sections of this genus as a basis for studying cultural, pruning and training methods.

Section 1. *Sorbus* (Mountain Ash)

S. aucuparia, the Mountain Ash, typifies this section which has pinnate foliage. The species and varieties are fast-growing and are thus popular, especially in smaller gardens. They should be well trained with a good central leader, for there is considerable strain on the framework when the tree is fully laden with fruit. Some damage is also likely on young trees freshly planted in an exposed position after being raised in a sheltered nursery. There is a good case for specially raising trees which are to be planted in these exposed positions in nurseries on the poorer, dryer soils, where the rainfall is light and the situation somewhat exposed. Such conditions encourage a short-jointed, strong branch structure. Further evidence of this is provided by the well-formed specimens of *S. aucuparia* which are often found in the higher and more exposed parts of the British Isles. They are perfect in shape and are able to withstand such conditions because they have grown in the situation from the very start.

When planting in the final position, good growth should be encouraged by careful planting and adequate short staking. The species in this section reach maturity so quickly that a fault in training in the early years is difficult to overcome. This applies particularly to the ill effects of stunting in the early years. *S. a.* 'Beissneri' is grown for its warm orange trunk and the stem should be cleaned up early in the nursery to show this off to best effect. The most desirable form of tree depends largely upon the position and role for which it is intended. In a completely informal setting the multi-stemmed tree, which branches low from ground level, is attractive and lends itself to the situation. Furthermore the species in this group seldom grow sufficiently large to be dangerous.

There is considerable variation in habit, and the intending planter should take this into consideration before making the final choice. No amount of subsequent pruning and training will alter a habit that is thought, after trial, to be undesirable. As examples of the variation, *S. a.* 'Aspleniifolia' forms a graceful tree, but has an upright habit, *S. a.* 'Sheerwater Seedling' has a fairly compact, cone-shaped head, while the type species is rather open, especially when old and after having borne several heavy crops of fruit. *S. a.* 'Aspleniifolia' spreads out at a later stage, but often produces a quantity of epicormic growths on the more horizontal parts of the branch system. These cannot be seen unless the centre of the tree is studied and there is little point in cutting them out, indeed, the increased number which break out during the following and succeeding years will only add to the problem. *S.* 'Joseph Rock' (Rock 23657) has an upright habit. *S. commixta*, the Japanese Rowan, naturally wants to grow as a multi-stemmed tree and should be encouraged to do so in the nursery through to the final planting site.

S. reducta makes a small suckering shrub, up to 1 m. (3 ft.), and the only pruning needed is the removal of unwanted suckers from the ground.

Section 2. *Cormus*

S. domestica is in this group. It is a large grower living to a great age. The best type of tree to plant is a 1.8 to 2.4 m. (6 to 8 ft.) standard with a clear stem and a central leader. At maturity the lower and outer branches trail down near to ground level.

Section 3. Section *Sorbus* × Section *Aria*

S. ×*thuringiaca* is a small dense tree with an erect habit, but the central leader should be retained for as long as possible.

Section 4. *Aria* (Whitebeam)

S. torminalis forms a wide and spreading head often with little or no leader. It should be trained in the nursery with a 1.8 to 2.4 (6 to 8 ft.) clear trunk. This is a species that is only seen to full effect when able to develop its head unrestricted and without being hemmed in by neighbouring trees.

S. latifolia forms a tall tree and will retain a central leader quite easily with a clear trunk of 2.4 to 3.0 m. (8 to 10 ft.). *S. intermedia* will, unless encouraged to form and retain a leader both in the nursery and after planting, form a shrub, especially on the dryer and thinner soils. *S. aria* will form a shapely but close, often ovoid, head with an erect branching system; its selection 'Magnifica' produces magnificent foliage, which is only seen at its best when the branches come down unimpeded to at least eye level. The closely related species *S. vestita* has rather sparse branching, but the large leaves are its chief attraction. For this reason the lowest branches should be left to develop into the foreground, which should be kept clear to allow for their growth. This group will not withstand hard branch reduction.

Section 5. *Micromeles*

S. alnifolia is a fairly upright grower, but the lower branches should be encouraged, for the richly coloured autumn foliage and bunches of small red and yellow berries are very attractive. Some trees have a strong leader, which naturally makes a well-balanced specimen without much effort; others need regular training and encouragement. The trunk has attractive lenticelled bark that, if exposed by lifting the skirt slightly, will be another attraction. Other trees that fall into this section include *S. folgneri*, *S. meliosmifolia* and *S. caloneura*.

SPARTIUM

S. junceum, the Spanish Broom, benefits from annual pruning in the early spring as by this means the growth is more compact and rigid and is better suited to the border. Left unpruned, the main branches build up a mass of top growth, which eventually becomes so heavy that despite staking to prevent them bending over and exposing bare lengths and patches, the whole effect is one of neglect and untidiness.

In the nursery a bushy habit of growth is obtained by pruning hard back in the spring, just before the one-year-old plant breaks into growth. After this subject has been planted out into a sunny, well-drained position, the main branches are left to gain height, but are still pruned to at least half their length to encourage a bushy growth. Later, as the bush matures, the previous year's growths are cut back to within 25 mm. (1 in.) of the older wood just as growth is commencing in the spring. It is tedious work to prune each shoot individually and the growths should be gathered together in bundles, using a knife. The new shoots break out very quickly and the clipped effect is soon lost. A very straggly and neglected bush will regenerate even if it is cut down to ground level. This should be carried out in the spring.

This is a fine subject when grown with an informal stretch of Laurel hedging and the Spartium should be planted about 300 mm. (12 in.) inside the outer edge. No pruning is made in the initial years and thus the growths that are staked on the edge of the hedge to begin with tend to grow straight up, unbranched. Later, when the Spartium is well beyond the height for the hedge, the whole bush is pushed into the centre just leaving the flowering head to develop above the general line. This is pruned annually and the hedge kept within bounds informally using the secateurs.

SPHAERALCEA

S. fendleri is a small, semi-woody shrub that requires a sheltered position at the foot of a sunny wall. Thin but bushy growths are produced from a woody root-stock that develops 50 to 100 mm. (2 to 4 in.) above soil level. It is these growths, which have finished flowering, that are most likely to be killed back during the winter. Also at times, stronger and thicker growths are produced as extensions to the woody branch system. Pruning consists of cutting back to developing growths in the spring. In most cases this means a rather drastic cutback. This subject flowers on the current season's wood.

SPIRAEA

The shrubby members of this large genus fall broadly into two groups: (1) those which flower from wood made during the previous season and (2) those which flower on the current season's wood, that is, extensive shoot growth is produced which flowers in the same year.

It is important to relate pruning to the habit of growth and flowering and the two groups will therefore be dealt with individually.

Group 1. Those which flower from wood made during the previous season

Most of the species in this group produce short, leafy twigs from growths made during the previous season

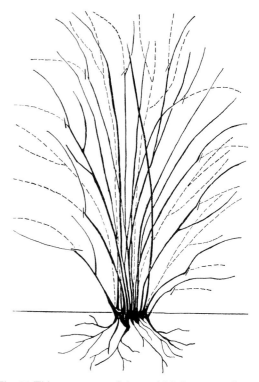

Fig. 46. This represents a *Spiraea* which flowers on the previous year's wood. The broken lines indicate growths which would be pruned out after flowering. Notice that a number of old growths are taken out entirely to ground level.

and these terminate in a flat head or cluster of flowers, usually by early summer. However, a number flower directly from last season's wood, examples being S. 'Arguta', S. gemmata, S. hypericifolia and S. thunbergii.

Despite this difference, the general pruning policy for the whole of this group consists of cutting out a proportion of the older wood after flowering to make way for the young growths which provide the next season's display. In some cases the cuts are made just above a suitable growth on the general framework, but occasionally an older branch may be cut out completely to ground level. With this policy in mind, the habit of growth of each individual species must also be taken into account. Some produce an arching growth and as an example we may choose S. thunbergii. A quantity of strong, upright growths are produced from the centre and crown of the shrub but, in addition, new wood is also formed on the older branch system. The extra weight, in addition to the flowers and fruits, causes these to arch over. After this occurs there is an increased tendency for the upright or horizontal portion of the bent branches to throw new growth. This is repeated over and over again, until a considerable amount of dead wood builds up under the bush as it is deprived of light. Thus some of the weaker as well as the older wood should be cut out after flowering, always ensuring a plentiful supply of new growths without leaving any snags or dead wood, see Fig. 46. If the bush is near the front of a border or grown as an isolated specimen, it should be left furnished down to ground level, but it may also be important to keep young growth to the centre of the bush to prevent undue spread. Other examples of this habit are S. canescens, S. gemmata, S. mollifolia, S. prunifolia, S. sargentiana and S. ×vanhouttei.

S. veitchii is a tall, graceful grower with strong, arching growths. Any pruning must retain this attractive habit. S. ×brachybotrys produces cascades of growth, the foliage remaining green until very late in the year. The bush is very dense and it is difficult to restrict the size without spoiling the effect. It flowers on long laterals of the previous season and some of the oldest wood may be pruned out after flowering.

As a contrast the following have a more erect habit, often with a very bushy top. They are S. japonica 'Nana', S. chamaedryfolia, S. longigemmis and S. media. S. henryi, however, has a very spreading habit.

Many species and hybrids in this group that also flower from the past season's wood have not been mentioned. The fact that many have a suckering habit must also be taken into account. Such growths that spread beyond the intended limits should be removed with care. These suckering species and hybrids are ideal for the wild garden or places where it is unnecessary to confine them.

S. nipponica needs very careful attention, it being advisable to prune after flowering to a few shoots, leaving only the strongest. At the same time vigour should be encouraged by liberal feeding.

S. chinensis may be killed down to ground level in winter as it is not fully hardy. Alternatively, it may be reduced to a few arching branches. This lack of hardiness is shared by S. cantoniensis and both species are better grown in the shelter of a wall.

Group 2. Those which flower on the current season's wood

As explained earlier, these put on extensive shoot growth during the summer, which produces flower in the same season. Often the growth originates at or a little above ground level. Most of the species and hybrids within this group are suckerous and spread to form a thicket of growths which, without attention, deteriorate in vigour and thus in flowering. By pruning this group hard in the spring, cutting out the weaker growths completely, vigour is concentrated into fewer shoots and therefore flowering and general appearance are improved. The extent of this pruning depends upon vigour, but much of the oldest wood, even though it may support young growth, is cut out completely to ground level, while the young canes which have flowered during the previous summer are shortened by one third or less. They are thinned out if spaced closer than 150 mm. (6 in.) or so apart, see Fig. 47. In addition, as the site becomes exhausted after a few years, perhaps with a heavy infestation of perennial weed, the whole clump may be dug up in

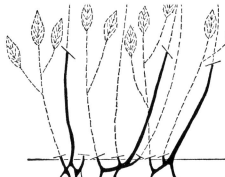

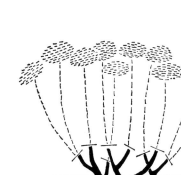

Fig. 47. *Spiraea douglasii* showing how the young growths are thinned and pruned in the spring, at which time the old flowering stems are also cut out.

Fig. 48. *Spiraea japonica* 'Anthony Waterer', showing the severe cutting back which is carried out before growth commences in the spring.

the spring. After cultivation and enrichment, selected young canes with roots and a piece of the old connecting growth attached are planted from 230 to 460 mm. (9 to 18 in.) apart, dependent upon the vigour of the subject. The young growths are cut down to 150 mm. (6 in.) immediately after planting. Some of the species and hybrids which respond to this method are *S. amoena*, *S. corymbosa*, *S. douglasii*, *S. japonica* and cultivars, *S.* 'Margaritae', *S. douglasii* subsp. *menziesii*, *S. salicifolia* and *S. ×sanssouciana*.

Some variation must be made in pruning dwarf species and forms that have this flowering habit. *S. japonica* 'Anthony Waterer' is pruned just before growth commences in the spring, cutting down to within 100 to 130 mm. (4 to 5 in.) of ground level. Thus a short length of the previous year's wood is left, though very old and dead wood should be cut right down to ground level. *S. japonica* 'Bullata' is a close compact grower. Pruning consists of cutting over the clump or shrub in the spring with a pair of shears taking care to avoid cutting into the old framework. Small compact growths spring up from ground level to flower later in the season, thus extending the display, see Fig. 48.

A number of those in this group give a succession of blooms if the old heads are removed as soon as they have faded.

STACHYURUS

The two species, *S. praecox* and *S. chinensis* have a natural arching habit, and nearby plantings and general cultivation should allow for free and unrestricted development. This includes furnishing right down to ground level. Both species have a stool-like habit and freely produce young, strong growths from the base. Thus some of the old and thin wood may be cut out low down, or at the base if necessary. This should be carried out after flowering in the spring, but regular annual pruning is not required.

Both species may be grown as wall subjects in colder districts, when they should be trained hard against the surface on the supporting wires. The branches are trained fanwise. The older branches are replaced by the young growths from the base after flowering, which means that they must be carefully tied in for the autumn and winter before they can be placed permanently after pruning. This cutting away, however, may not be needed annually, and in some cases it is even desirable to remove the young growths at a very early stage by rubbing them out, thus conserving the energy of the shrub.

STAPHYLEA

S. colchica is one of the most vigorous species. It is an upright grower and spreads by means of naturally layered branches and by suckerous growths which often appear at some distance from the plant. An over-grown bush may be cut back to suitable growths, or the old wood may be taken down to ground level. The young growths that spring up may be thinned and the best used for replacement purposes. Normally suckers are taken up clearly. While the main pruning may be carried out during the winter, the removal of an odd stray branch or light thinning of the old wood is better done immediately after flowering.

The slender branching and neat habit of *S. bumalda*, the compact, thick and upright growth of *S. pinnata* and the suckerous spread of *S. trifolia* are characteristics which should be taken into account when pruning. With the latter species, the strongest and most centrally placed suckers may be trained for renewal purposes, removing the remainder. *S. holo-carpa* has a permanent stem system and may develop into a large shrub or small tree.

STAUNTONIA

S. hexaphylla. A vigorous, twining shrub that is similar in many respects to the *Holboellia* spp. It is a tender subject and needs a wall in all but the most favoured localities. With horizontal wiring, vertical strands should be added to assist the young growths to cover the available space in the early years. Branching should be encouraged as close to ground level as possible.

Once the full height of the wall is reached, the growths may be allowed to hang down. Treatment after this should involve thinning out the weaker growths in the spring, wherever possible cutting out complete lengths rather than shortening, thus avoiding a congestion of poor material.

STEPHANANDRA

These shrubs are grown for their foliage and for the coloured stems, which are quite bright during the winter when the leaves have fallen. The flower display is not at all spectacular and pruning is aimed at main-taining vigour, thus ensuring healthy foliage and strong growth for winter colour. After flowering, the old growths are cut back annually, either to healthy side branches springing from lower down on this old wood, or to ground level. Enough old, flowered wood is cut out to leave the shrub well furnished. These shrubs have a stool-like habit and, with good culture and plenty of mulching, strong, young canes are thrown up from the base each year. Often, established clumps have a suckerous habit. The reason for pruning after flowering is to encourage the young growths while letting in sun and air for ripening, which in turn means good colouring. For this latter effect *S. tanakae* is the best species.

When pruning, the natural habit should be preserved. *S. incisa* is very graceful indeed with long arching branches and this habit should be retained as far as possible; its form 'Crispa' makes a good ground cover shrub, as it forms dense low mounds.

STEWARTIA

These grow best in a fairly sheltered position and a clearing among evergreen or small deciduous trees is ideal. A grass foreground is suggested, for the natural spread of their branch systems and mottled bark is attractive during the winter. There should be no attempt to restrict their size, for these are such choice subjects that it is better to prune back neighbouring trees and screening plants if more space is needed for good and free growth. A grass foreground also allows a natural spread on the lower branches, enabling the flowers and bark effects to be seen at close quarters without difficulty.

Some of the larger growers under ideal conditions often develop small trunks, but these form naturally as the strong, extending branches develop in the upper crown of the young tree. Thus the smaller branches springing from the trunk near ground level may be removed in order to show the bark to good effect. Never should the lower part of the main branches be cleared of twig growth at too early a stage. The timing for this becomes evident when lack of light causes dieback.

The species exhibit varied habits, some being stronger and more tree-like than others. *S. malacodendron*, for example, is a large shrub with a slender branching system. *S. pseudocamellia*, on the other hand, is a stout grower with upright branches.

The young plants should not be pruned in the nursery, rather it is important to encourage good growth and strong leaders then develop naturally. A young plant that is checked seldom makes good later and it is better to plant small than too large to reduce planting shock. It can then take several years for the newly planted shrub to settle down before it begins to grow away.

S. sinensis will begin to show its attractive flaking bark very early in life before the tree gets to 0.6 m. (2 ft.), but it is important not to remove the lower feathers too soon, or this will check the growth.

STYRAX

This genus of trees and shrubs contains a few choice species that are hardy enough to be grown in many climates. However, they do need care and shelter, especially when young. In the nursery, the larger growers, which are really small trees, need to be trained to form a single leader. *S. japonicus* forms an interesting, small tree with almost horizontal branching and fine, twiggy growth. Unless it is for the removal of dead wood or intensive competition for light with nearby subjects, pruning might quite easily spoil this natural beauty. *S. dasyanthus* is an example where training can produce a leader of 4.6 to 6.0 m. (15 to 20 ft.), resulting in the formation of a small tree. In such cases the lower branches up to a height of 0.9 to 1.2 m. (3 to 4 ft.) may eventually die back and need to be cut off. *S. hemsleyanus* often branches low at ground level and will form ascending branches with a more rigid, twig system. However, a leader can be trained up. *S. wilsonii* is also distinct, being a shrub with quite a dense habit.

Habit of growth must, therefore, be taken into account during training in the nursery. Many of the species break readily, even from older wood, if cuts need to be made. The young growths are prone to damage from late frosts.

SYCOPSIS

S. sinensis is an evergreen shrub or small tree of upright habit. It branches very freely from the base. A clear foreground encourages growth to develop on the lower branches, thus allowing the small flowers to be examined without difficulty. The thick, bushy habit is natural and no pruning is necessary, apart from the removal of dead twig growth that forms inside the bush.

Heavy snow may cause extensive damage and the growths should be freed at the first opportunity. If damage requiring some hard cutting back is suffered, regeneration occurs quite freely, even from the main branches.

SYMPHORICARPOS

These are strong-growing shrubs that quickly produce a thicket, even when they are growing in poor and shaded conditions. However, certain species have distinct habits and these need to be taken into consideration at planting time. By exercising care in the selection of position the need for pruning will be reduced, for these are plants which spread extensively and are difficult to control.

S. albus, the Snowberry, is an upright grower with slender lateral branches which droop heavily, especially when laden with fruit. Dead pieces should be cut out, but there is little need for regular pruning. It is a difficult shrub to control owing to the free production of suckers from the roots. As a hedge therefore it invades neighbouring ground and is thus difficult to confine. This suckering habit is restricted if a hard edge, for example a road, is alongside the length of the hedge. *S. occidentalis* has a similar habit, but *S. orbiculatus* produces arching growths when it gains height, and these overgrow shorter branches causing them to die. If this plant is grown on a large scale it is difficult to cut this dead wood out, and it is better to allow the plants to form a thicket.

SYRINGA

There are two distinct growing habits of this deciduous shrub or small tree. The varieties of *S. vulgaris* and a few other species build up a permanent framework of twiggy, compact growth, while the majority of the species throw strong shoots, often from low down in the bush, which eventually replace the older ones as they become weaker.

Subgenus *Syringa*
Series *Pinnatifoliae*

The only species in this series is *S. pinnatifolia*, a small shrub to 3 m. (10 ft.) with pinnate leaves, unlike any other lilac. This shrub needs no pruning, apart from the occasional removal of dead wood and some light pruning to restrict its growth.

Series *Pubescentes*

This series includes the species *S. pubescens*, *S. pubescens* subsp. *julianae*, *S. pubescens* subsp. *patula*, *S. pubescens* subsp. *microphylla* and *S. potaninii*. All make graceful medium-sized to large shrubs and will flower with minimal pruning.

S. meyeri and *S. m.* var. *spontanea* 'Palibin' are slow-growing compact shrubs, both making good hedges and can be clipped to maintain a dense growth. If left they will naturally form a compact plant.

Series *Syringa*

S. vulgaris and *S. ×hyacinthiflora* and the many cultivars flower from large buds that have formed on the previous season's wood. Generally, as the flowers open, the growth buds directly beneath them develop and extend rapidly, so that by the time the blossoms fade they are often several inches long. This habit can be directly related to the pruning. It is beneficial to remove the old flower heads to prevent wasted energy in seed production, but it is important in doing this to cut them off without injury to the developing growths. If these are injured, or if the growths are cut hard back, the plant will have to open up the season again with dormant buds. Valuable time will be lost and it is seldom that such late shoots are sufficiently mature to flower in the following season. However, the pruning of misshapen specimens may be necessary, in which case it should be carried out after flowering. Some of the height can be pruned off the shrub, to keep flowering stems at eye level. If the loss of bloom is unimportant, pruning or even a hard cutting back to renovate may be done during the winter.

It is a mistake to plant lilacs too closely. As an example, strongly growing varieties will meet after a few years even if they are planted at 4.5 m. (15 ft.) apart. Under crowded conditions most of the blossom is produced on the top of the bush where there is more light. With sufficient light even the low branches produce a few blossoms though the best flowering heads are in the crown. When used for hedging purposes, pruning should be carried out by cutting each shoot away individually, aiming to remove a portion each year back to a general line. A hard pruning over the entire surface will result in no flower the following year.

In former days Lilac varieties were frequently grafted onto *S. vulgaris*, but the practice is a bad one owing to the free production of suckers. These should be removed as they appear. The use of Privet as a stock may lead to difficulty, unless the shrubs are planted with the union well below the soil level to encourage scion rooting. Planting with the union above ground level leads to poor growth, and cutting back as a means of renovation will only aggravate the position.

It is best, if possible, to grow lilacs on their own roots and to encourage the production of suckers. These should then be thinned out to the strongest canes, creating multi-stemmed bushes that can eventually replace the older stems. In areas where the Lilac Borer (*Podosesia syringae*) is active, the encouragement of many stems allows for the opportunity to prune out stems that are infested with the larvae, without losing the whole plant.

In habits and vigour the varieties vary considerably and the ultimate height and form is as important when making a choice as flower colour.

The species in this section also include *S. ×persica*, which is a small shrub producing slender growths, which may even trail on the ground as they become longer and heavier over the years. Occasional shaping is therefore necessary, cutting back to upright growths or even down to ground level, provided that there are plenty of replacement shoots. *S. ×chinensis* can be treated in the same way.

S. oblata forms weak branches that bend over as they extend and branch. These should be cut back to upright growths after flowering.

Series *Villosae*

This group flowers on terminal buds, but the growth is often distinctive, and the free production of young shoots allows some of the older wood to be cut out as the blossoms fade.

S. emodi is grown for the stem effect as well as the flower, so some cleaning up of the main stems may be carried out to expose the bark. *S. josikaea*, *S. komarovii* subsp. *reflexa*, *S. tomentella*, *S. villosa*, *S. yunnanensis* and *S. wolfii* all fall into this series and should be grown to keep their natural habit with little pruning, apart from some stem renewal.

The many hybrids, like *S. ×prestoniae*, *S. ×henryi*, *S. ×josiflexa* and *S. ×swegiflexa*, make medium to large shrubs and must be given the space to develop or be pruned regularly to keep them to a reasonable size.

Care should be taken when pruning the cultivars of all Lilacs, as they are susceptible to Bacterial Blight (*Pseudomonas syringae*) which can be devastating. A means of preventing the spread of this disease is to sterilize the secateurs and saws with alcohol or strong bleach between pruning cuts and avoid pruning in wet humid conditions.

Subgenus *Ligustrina*

These are the tree lilacs, including *S. reticulata*, *S. r.* subsp. *amurensis* and *S. r.* subsp. *pekinensis*, and reach 9 m. (30 ft.). All have wonderful cherry-like bark, especially the latter. *S. reticulata* and *S. r.* subsp. *pekinensis* are definitely tree-like, having the form of a sizeable apple tree, but new shoots will break out readily from old wood if it needs to be cut back. They can be trained to a single stem in the nursery if a definite tree habit is desired. Apart from this, no pruning is needed.

S. r. subsp. *amurensis* is an upright grower, but crowded clusters of weak young wood in the centre should be thinned out.

TAIWANIA

T. cryptomerioides naturally forms a definite strong leader and, with a straight trunk running up through the centre of the tree, the outline is pyramidal, very similar in appearance to that of *Cryptomeria*. Allowing space for light and development should encourage the sparse lower slender branches. The spread of this tree is very fine and it makes an attractive specimen, particularly in a lawn setting. It will require some shelter in a warm location, but is hardier than most people believe. No pruning is needed for this tree, except for the removal of competing leaders following frost damage.

TAMARIX

These shrubs or small trees are often found growing naturally in coastal regions. Thus almost constant winds, poor soils and intensive sun produce a sturdy and often shortened habit. Under garden conditions, which are usually sheltered with a fairly rich soil, growth often tends to be longer and stronger, with the result that a straggly bush is produced. Extensive top growth, unless it is accompanied by an increase of the spread, results in the production of a dome-shaped bush and eventually leads to a loss of stability, when the shrub may be weighed down by snow or blown loose in the soil by the wind. It is worth noting that in nature extra stability may also be gained from the accumulation of wind-blown sand that often builds up round the shrubs to form a protective mound.

In the garden, pruning and if need be staking help to give stability. In the nursery, and for a year or so after planting, a bunched and sturdy framework should be built up by hard pruning. The species that flower in late summer or autumn do so on the young shoots that are produced during the spring and summer. Thus a sturdy growth may be maintained by pruning annually in the spring, before the new growth commences. These growths are then pruned back to within 50 to 80 mm. (2 to 3 in.) of the old wood. The species which flower late in the season make ideal subjects for an informal hedge, for trimming hard back may be carried out each year in the spring. However rigid and formal the outline after trimming, the effect as the growths are produced is quite the opposite and is very pleasing.

The spring-flowering species *T. tetrandra* and *T. parviflora* are pruned after the blossoms fade when long and straggly growths may be shortened. These species flower on growths made during the previous season. Very weak growths may be cut right back and an overgrown bush may be pruned hard, taking away much of the old wood. Flowering may, however, be missed for a year or two afterwards.

T. chinensis seldom flowers, but it has beautiful foliage. It needs a warm position. Pruning to keep the subject sturdy should be carried out in late spring, early summer, for flowering, should it occur, is during that period.

TAXODIUM

T. distichum, the Swamp Cypress, is the most common species. Its habit is to form a strong leading growth and to maintain this until a considerable height has been reached. Young trees for planting should be single-stemmed with a strong leader, and if the site is well prepared, a suitable height is very quickly gained, giving a typical 'church spire' effect.

At a later stage, often when a specimen is near to maximum height, strong, upright branches are thrown out, usually from the upper half of the trunk system. This is a natural habit of growth, for a mature tree has a flat-topped look and no attempt should be made to correct this.

Two other subjects, *T. distichum* var. *imbricatum* with a more narrow crown and *T. mucronatum*, the

Mexican Cypress, both much less common, are treated in the same way. The latter will need a mild climate to be successful.

TAXUS

T. baccata, the Common Yew, is better known in gardens as a hedge plant, but fine though it is when grown and trained for this purpose, it is also very good as a single specimen or for screening purposes on the edge of a garden or enclosed feature. In less formal settings a free lateral growth and spread is desirable, provided of course that there is sufficient space. Many of the varieties have distinctive habits, which will only develop to perfection if allowed to grow freely.

Should it become necessary to restrict spread by pruning and yet retain an informal effect, it must be carried out very carefully. The Yew responds so well to pruning that a flat, hedge-like surface is quickly built up if the cuts are all made on a definite line and in the one operation. An informal effect is only obtained by varying the position of the cut, taking some into the centre when whole branches are removed. It is emphasized that the process, which may be carried out in the early summer, should be a gradual one spread out over a period of three or four years. The alternative is a really drastic pruning, when the cuts are made right back into the main branches and over the whole bush or tree, but this is only necessary when the specimen is badly overgrown. Such drastic pruning should be made in late spring.

As the habits of growth among the varieties are so variable many form no distinct leader. Extreme cases are 'Horizontalis' and the other prostrate forms. With these it is often necessary to dig out bramble and other growth, which would otherwise swamp them or spoil their effect.

The nursery training of forms that naturally produce a leader is quite straightforward. For single-stemmed specimens, any rival leaders that appear are reduced to one and this is run up as far as possible through the centre, as the crown is formed. The stem is cleared of lateral growths to give a clean trunk if this is desired and the crown is formed by strong branch systems. When trained for hedging purposes the leaders are retained until the ultimate height intended for the particular feature is reached. A Yew hedge is trimmed during late summer to early autumn, but if overgrown and in need of a hard pruning this should be carried out during late spring.

The fastigiate forms are sometimes used and these, if desired, can be tied and trained to a very tight, columnar shape. The naturally erect branches may be held together by plastic-coated wiring which is bound tightly round the cylinder of growths at intervals. The subsequent growth quickly hides the binding but these should be pruned during late summer, otherwise the appearance will quickly become ragged. Being a fastigiate form, most of these growths are naturally upright and it is necessary to take these out individually with secateurs, as otherwise they will not be cut back cleanly. It may be desirable to tuck a proportion of these behind the wiring rather than remove them. In an exposed setting, staking of these tightly clipped fastigiate forms may also be necessary and tubular steel piping is most suitable for this purpose. It should run up the entire height and be hidden in the centre, as otherwise it may be unsightly.

TECOMA

T. capensis is a tender climber which will succeed only on sunny walls in the warmer regions. The rods should be trained to cover the available space and growths will be plentifully produced from these. The main pruning should be carried out in the spring, cutting the weaker and older growths back to the main rods. It may also be necessary to thin out some of the remaining growths if they are thickly placed, or have developed behind the wires. Some pruning of surplus wood may also be necessary during the summer. In time, a spur system builds up on the main rods, from which the young growths develop.

TERNSTROEMIA

T. japonica is an evergreen medium-sized shrub for the warm sheltered border. There is no need for

regular pruning, apart from the occasional shaping should that be needed.

TETRACENTRON

T. sinense. Under good conditions this subject will develop with little or no training into a small or medium-sized tree. An open foreground is desirable to allow for low branching. Late spring frosts may be damaging, especially to young growths on small trees.

TETRADIUM

These trees do not branch extensively. They should be trained with a definite leader in the nursery, which should be extended after planting in the permanent position. If vigour is maintained a clear trunk of 1.2 to 1.8 m. (4 to 6 ft.) can be formed, the leader extending up through the crown to a height of 4.6 to 6.0 m. (15 to 20 ft.). As the trees mature the outer branches are weighed down by extension growths, flowers and fruits, but this habit should be encouraged as it allows the head of blossom which appears in late summer to be seen to perfection. *T. daniellii* is one of the commonest species and with its horizontal branches it forms a wide-spreading tree. There is some evidence that *T. henryi* forms a leader and trunk more readily than others. *T. ruticarpum* makes a small shrubby tree.

Subjects in the genus as a whole require light and it proves difficult to grow a good, shapely tree when it is shaded on one side. For this reason also, encroaching branches from other trees should be kept well clear. They must have good drainage otherwise the wood deteriorates and cavities form.

TEUCRIUM

T. fruticans is normally grown against a sunny wall as it is not fully hardy. It is trained fanwise and usually bamboo canes are required to assist in this, first tying these to the wire system. Long growths that are not required for extension should be pruned back to suitable shoots in the spring, but not before the new growth commences, when it can be seen just how much wood has been killed during the winter.

T. chamaedrys is a low, procumbent subject which is used for ground cover. In time, it forms an untidy mass of growths with erect heads of flowers. It will, however, respond to cutting back in the spring. On a large scale a pair of shears may be used. If it needs to be cut back to prevent overlapping of an edge, this should be done carefully to leave an informal effect rather than a straight-clipped line.

THAMNOCALAMUS. *See* Bamboos

THUJA

Probably the most satisfactory species from the arboriculturist's point of view is *T. plicata*, as it is the strongest grower and produces a definite leader which runs up through the centre of the tree. Given sufficient space, the lower branches will spread extensively, providing adequate furnishing to ground level. Good, strong growths should be encouraged both in the nursery and after planting out. *T. standishii* is also a spreading tree in addition to forming a definite leader. *T. occidentalis*, on the other hand, has a columnar habit built up with a central leader and normally the lower branches do not spread extensively. *T. koraiensis* varies from being a shrub with an untidy habit to a small tree with a leader. Often among a batch of seedlings, a number show a tendency to produce a definite leader and, if a tree form is desired, these should be selected and encouraged.

Thuja is sometimes grown for hedging purposes and *T. plicata* in particular is ideal for this purpose. The leader should be retained and allowed to grow 150 to 300 mm. (6 to 12 in.) above the height intended for the hedge, before being pruned back to about 150 mm. (6 in.) below this height. The laterals are then pruned at the intended height, and as a result a much better top surface is procured than if the main stems were cut on this line. The lower branches quickly grow into each other to form a dense base as height is gained. *T. occidentalis* is also used for hedging.

THUJOPSIS

T. dolabrata, when raised from seed, shows a considerable variation in habit. While a number will eventually form a definite leader, others remain as rather untidy, spreading shrubs. Of those which grow out of this shrubby habit, a number produce rival leaders and the result is a small tree made up of slender upright trunks with their supporting branches. To be certain of a form with a strong central growth that will enable a leader to be trained, it is advisable to propagate by cuttings taken from growths at the top of strong leading shoots.

TILIA

The Common Lime, *T. ×europaea* is frequently found in tree collections and was quite often used as an avenue tree in former days. One of the reasons for this widespread planting may be connected with the fact that it is so easily propagated by layering. Limes generally do not like too dry a soil and given good conditions this hybrid will develop into a lofty tree. The leader should be retained up through the crown but, as the tree matures, the upper branches may rival the main leader. This appears to be a natural habit. The main lower branches are often nearly horizontal in character, but occasionally a strong upright growth develops along their length, often as a response to extra light on this part of the tree. A careful watch should be kept on any such growths and if need be, they should be checked or removed at an early stage. Old and mature trees having large, upright branches that have developed on a mature branch system also need regular inspection, and it may become necessary to remove such pieces in order to reduce excessive weight. Normally the tree should be raised as a standard with a 1.8 to 2.4 m. (6 to 8 ft.) leg, but it may be planted as a feathered tree, to be trained as the specimen develops. Large burrs often occur on the trunk and these develop masses of epicormic growths which should be pruned back hard each winter. These unsightly burrs and the extra work they involve, coupled with the fact that infestations of aphis frequently occur during the summer months and cause heavy deposits of honeydew, has made this hybrid an unpopular one to plant. Certainly there are better alternatives.

T. ×euchlora has a thick crown and the outer branches are semi-pendulous, forming a dense canopy. This may be allowed to develop down to ground level when planted as a lawn specimen. Often there is a considerable amount of wood to cut out from the underside of the crown, caused by dieback through lack of light. It is planted extensively as an avenue or street tree and with a good leader and a dense crown with well-spaced branches, it is rightly considered to be a safe tree.

Many other species and forms of Tilia have distinctive but characteristic habits of growth. *T. americana*, the Basswood, although it has fine, large leaves, often forms a stunted crown with dieback which needs attention. *T. cordata*, the Small-leaved Lime, is slow-growing and has a fine twig and branch system. There are several factory trees in the trade with upright forms, suitable for street planting and small spaces, for example *T. c.* 'Greenspire' from the United States and *T. c.* 'Swedish Upright' from Europe. *T. oliveri* forms a small tree with a branch system which is semi-pendulous and these branches should be allowed to develop to ground level.

The dense branching and habit of *T. platyphylla* 'Laciniata' is also very distinctive and produces an effect that is rare among Limes. But sometimes this variety has a tendency to form bark wounds and cavities. One of the most distinctive trees for the arboriculturist to plant and train is *T. tomentosa*, the Silver Lime. The crown is very thick, being formed of long, upright branches that are heavy and impressive. *T. t.* 'Petiolaris', the Weeping Silver Lime, has beautiful downward-sweeping branches that will spoil if pruned in any way, so it should be left to grow into a natural shape. Most trees are grafted onto *T. ×europaea* and any suckers from the rootstock should be removed as soon as possible.

In the nursery, young plants often grow rapidly and produce a heavy head of foliage. Thus the central leader should be caned and taped when necessary. Frequently, side growths which have been stopped produce sub-laterals very readily a week or so later. These should also be stopped at two leaves.

Of limes generally, many form cavities very readily and exposed wood must be inspected regularly and appropriate action carried out when necessary. Large pruning work should be carried out in mid to late summer in order to reduce the danger of bleeding and to promote rapid healing.

When limes are crown reduced heavily, they rapidly produce epicormic growth along the trunk and entire scaffold and sucker profusely from the stubs of the pruning cuts, creating the shaving-brush effect.

These trees seem to lose large quantities of small, dead twigs and branches during gales.

TOONA

T. sinensis at maturity is quite a large tree and is at its best with a long clean trunk. It is important therefore to attempt to train a central leader in the nursery and to encourage this by providing good growing conditions. Unfortunately, the tree wants to produce twin leaders and as one is removed, another will be produced naturally. As the tree develops, the lower branches may be removed to provide a clean trunk. The branching is heavy but sparse and often there is a good covering of smaller branches along their length. These should be left.

TORREYA

T. californica is better suited to the milder climates. It should form a definite leader, producing a straight trunk, and the branches, which occur in whorls, are often slightly pendulous at the extremities. It is important to train and nurse the leader from the seedling stage and a sheltered position should be selected for the young plants in the nursery, avoiding frost pockets. The leading growth, if it weakens or is killed, is quickly overtaken by the vigour of the laterals, and the shape is spoilt. *T. grandis* can be expected to form a definite leader. *T. nucifera* forms a large shrub in cultivation, for it usually branches strongly from ground level. Normally, very little pruning is needed.

TRACHELOSPERMUM

In all but the mildest parts of the country these need wall protection. *T. jasminoides* is an example. It produces twining extension growths and climbs in nature by this means, see Fig. 49. Once the space allotted is covered, the growths keep hard up against the wall and eventually this is furnished by a close mass of stem and foliage. Any growths that do extend out from the wall may be tucked behind the horizontal supporting wires. The flowers are produced on small laterals from the old wood.

Pruning in early spring consists of cutting back the small, dead pieces and the weaker growths as the stronger ones take their place. Any extension shoots which go beyond the wall or the space allocated, and which are surplus, may be cut back to a point just above a shorter, flowering growth. *T. asiaticum* also forms a close mat of growth. It is treated in the same way.

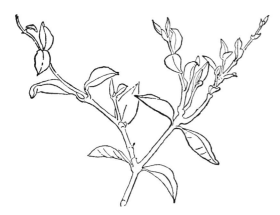

Fig. 49. A short compact branch taken from the masses of growth produced by a mature specimen of *Trachelospermum jasminoides*. Extension growths like the one on the left are produced on the outer edges.

TRACHYCARPUS

The only pruning of *T. fortunei*, the Chusan Palm, needed is the removal of dead leaves from the main trunk, mainly for cosmetic purposes or to prevent the risk of fire. These can be removed close to the trunk at any time of the year, leaving the fibrous material

covering the main stem. They can be grown as single- or multi-stemmed plants, depending on the required habit and space in the garden.

TRIPETALEIA

T. bracteata and *T. paniculata*. These rather rare, slow-growing Ericaceous shrubs require very little pruning and the only attention normally necessary is the removal of dead or weak wood.

TROCHODENDRON

T. aralioides forms a large shrub or even a small tree. Usually it branches freely from the base, but the main growths are upright, and it retains a leader quite readily. Even the laterals have an ascending habit, but the branchlets on the lower part of the tree are pendulous and may reach the ground giving a fully furnished effect.

There is no need for any pruning. In fact, the head of foliage that terminates each branchlet is quite large, making it very difficult to do so effectively, even if it is necessary to reduce size. The leading growths should never be pruned.

TSUGA

T. heterophylla, the Western Hemlock, is the most common species. It is a rapid grower on good soils, making a large tree with graceful branches drooping at the tips, and a typical tree has a sound and definite leader with a spire-like form. The young leader bends over and appears to have been lost, however it will straighten itself as it grows and caning as a form of encouragement is not required. It must have sufficient space and a clear foreground to be fully appreciated. As many of the lower branches as possible should be retained and kept in good health, in order that the shapely outline may be continued down to ground level. Should the leader be lost in the early stages, rival ones quickly develop. These should be reduced to one, certainly before their second season of growth. *T. canadensis*, the Eastern Hemlock, shows a tendency to produce a number of upright stems from near ground level and is often more irregular in outline than the former species. It also is only seen to advantage if the furnishing is complete to ground level.

Many of the other species are smaller growers and may be no more than large shrubs in cultivation. Included among these are *T. caroliniana*, *T. chinensis* and *T. diversifolia*. Although small, they should be given sufficient space to form a leader and spread out their branch systems which are often horizontal, with very adequate and attractive furnishing.

T. heterophylla may be used for hedging purposes, for which it will be found quite effective. The plants are set out at 0.9 m. (3 ft.) intervals and the leaders are retained until they are approximately 150 to 300 mm. (6 to 12 in.) above the desired height. The cut is then made to the first branches about 150 mm. (6 in.) below this line. The result is that rival leaders develop which in due course are also cut, thus forming a top surface at the required height. The sides are later formed by clipping along the line decided on, and it is surprising how the surface develops as the laterals extend after the leading growths have been cut on the branch systems. In turn these laterals are also pruned and thus a compact surface is built up. Clipping should take place in late summer although a young hedge may also require a mid to late spring pruning.

ULEX

The species are similar in their habit with the exception of *U. minor*, which is dwarf and compact. The young plants should be encouraged to bush out at an early stage, and, if necessary, pruning may be resorted to in the early spring before growth commences. As the shrubs develop they will also respond to cutting back. This should be done every two or three years after flowering in late spring. Provided the growth is reasonably compact and the bush shapely, there is no need to go hard back into the old wood. However, growths will break out freely from the older parts of the plant and there should be no hesitation in cutting straggly, bare-stemmed shrubs back really hard, almost down to ground level, including *U. europaeus*, which will soon become leggy if not clipped over regularly after flowering has finished. This is carried

out in the spring just as growth is about to commence and within a year or so the shrubs quickly make good.

ULMUS

Elms were found, with one or the other species predominating, over most of England, and it is for this reason that they frequently occurred as large specimens in our parks and gardens. Naturally these trees have been incorporated in development schemes, but concrete, tarmac and busy roads offered an entirely different and unkindly environment compared to the quiet country lane. No tree takes kindly to such treatment, but in addition, Elms have suffered badly from the aggressive form of Elm Disease (*Ophiostoma novo-ulmi*) spread by the Elm Bark Beetle (*Scolytus* spp.). As a result their numbers have been reduced to only a handful, with the exception of one or two cities, and the vigour of many of the remaining ones has suffered. There is another factor that has contributed to the unsafe condition of many Elms, particulary those in our towns and cities. Elms respond well to lopping or severe heading back and this practice has been indulged in, not only in cases of doubt about their safety, but because this was generally accepted as the correct thing to do. As explained in the section on lopping and topping, see page 73, trees that have been mauled in this way eventually become unsafe and further drastic action is necessary.

U. procera, the English Elm, has suffered most from the bad practice of lopping, mainly because it has a widespread distribution over much of southern England. Some of the blame for this may be due to the fact that this species has the reputation of suddenly dropping large limbs, which may snap when the tree is in full leaf, often in the evening after a hot, still day. From a height of 24 m. (80 ft.) or more this can be frightening and the possibility of this happening to a large tree over a public thoroughfare cannot be ignored. It is more likely to happen to a large English Elm than a Sycamore or Oak. However, trees that drop limbs in this manner cannot be healthy. Old age, root disturbance, or bad cultural conditions may be the cause of this, and all possible steps should be taken to keep the root system in a healthy condition, if necessary by aeration, drainage, feeding or watering. Thinning and a reduction in the crown may be all that is required to make the tree safe but a careful inspection is necessary before any decision is made. This species is a tall grower and, as the natural habit is to develop the leader to a considerable height, this should be encouraged. One feature which this species has, in common with a number of other species and hybrids, is the suckering habit. This can be so extensive that the whole area occupied by the root system of a large tree quickly becomes covered with a thicket, which changes the character of the site and in time impoverishes the specimen. It may, in certain circumstances, be an advantage to retain the thicket of Elm suckers. For example, as a hedge or a clump it may act as a windbreak in an otherwise exposed situation, perhaps with the parent tree already dead or in a bad condition. In a nature reserve also the thicket may give shelter to bird life and thus serve a useful purpose.

The varieties and forms vary; for example, *U. ×viminalis* is a smaller tree with pendulous branchlets. It appears to be prone to damage by gales and is therefore better in a sheltered position.

U. glabra, the Wych Elm, in its typical form has some very large branches. The leader should be retained for as long as possible in order to spread the branches and the weight evenly. This species is non-suckering and is therefore a contrast to *U. ×hollandica* and its forms and varieties, which are suckering but also form large trees. *U. ×h.* 'Major', the Dutch Elm, forms a very wide, spreading crown on a trunk which is often short and the arboriculturist can only retain the leader for so long. The ascending branches, as the tree reaches maturity, thicken to form a round head and almost appear to be rival leaders. At this stage the branching is rather open and even large old specimens withstand gale-force winds without damage, whereas with a failing specimen, a hot, still day is more likely to be disastrous because of the danger of falling limbs. It is often possible to keep people from such danger areas by the erection of neat 'shin' rails.

U. minor subsp. *sarniensis* forms a dense, conical head with a natural tendency to retain the leader to the complete height. In its typical form, *U. americana*, the White Elm, makes a large tree with a wide-spreading, graceful habit and pendulous branchlets.

U. villosa, the Marn Elm, has a most distinctive habit and the process of twig shedding is more deliberate than with most trees. Callused and healed scars are formed where the twigs have been shed as a definite habit of growth. The tree and its bark are best appreciated if a central leader is retained. This species is quite attractive in flower and it is worth allowing the branchlets to sweep down to the ground or at least eye level, so that they can be seen easily. The habit which this species has of producing large roots at or near the surface of the soil can be a nuisance, for as they enlarge they protrude well above ground level thus inhibiting the use of the mower. However, the way to overcome this is either to raise the level or to plant up the area beneath and around the tree with ground cover.

UGNI

The most commonly grown species in this evergreen genus is *U. molinae*, the Chilean Guava. There is no special need for pruning, except for the reduction of the long upright-growing shoots that may spoil the overall appearance of the small- to medium-sized specimens.

UMBELLULARIA

U. californica requires a sheltered spot, where it may be grown into quite a medium-sized tree. It should be trained to a single stem in the nursery, for if allowed it will break up into several rival leaders, which have a very upright habit. Thus the narrow angles between them at the point of junction may prove to be a weakness in later years, especially during periods of heavy snow. The slightest crack in the wood and outer bark lets in air and water and this will quickly set up rot, especially with a tree whose natural habitat is a sunnier climate.

With a single leader, the laterals are usually quite slender and well placed. The inside furnishing growths which are often found, even on the main leader, should be left.

The lower branches should be left to sweep down to eye level, for the buds are quite interesting, even during the winter, and the foliage has a strong pungent smell when crushed.

VACCINIUM

The members of this genus vary considerably in growth, but they have much in common. Normally they require very little pruning, apart from the removal of dead and weak growths. If cuts are to be made there is no difficulty in deciding just where they should be. There are often strong growths springing directly from the older wood, but a number of species such as *V. vitis-idaea* have creeping rhizomes and constantly send up renewing shoots from below ground. It is more likely that the larger, deciduous growers such as *V. corymbosum* will need pruning than, for example, *V. angusti-folium*, which is dwarf and compact. The larger shrubs eventually acquire a predominance of unproductive wood and benefit from some thinning.

If it is required, the pruning of the deciduous species may be carried out during the winter, but the evergreen species are better left until the spring. The main reason for this delay, apart from the general undesirability of pruning evergreens during the winter, is that much of the foliage may be lost during a severe spell and as a result there may be difficulty in distinguishing between the living and dead wood.

VIBURNUM

In general Viburnums have a very characteristic growth, being mostly stool-like in habit and often throwing young shoots freely from the base or from the lower and older branches. Thus there is an opportunity to cut out some of the older wood if it becomes necessary. Many species will regenerate freely if pruned hard, despite the fact that there may not be any young wood at the time of cutting.

The cutting out of the older wood may be often undertaken after flowering if it is needed, but the fruiting display of many species is quite attractive and should be left until the winter period. It is emphasized

however that, if the shrub is healthy, there is little need for frequent pruning.

Sometimes specimens become large and woody with bare branching near the base and with the flowers and foliage well above eye level, where they cannot be appreciated. This is often due to close planting and the desired effect is gained by shortening the branch systems to suitable points and thinning the neighbouring shrubs. This encourages the lower parts of the shrub to furnish up and develop.

Viburnums are divided into at least nine botanical groups or sections, but there is little difference between these where pruning is considered. It is important, however, to take into account the habit of growth of the individual species or variety before any pruning is attempted. *V. plicatum* is an example of this, for the horizontal growths from the main upright branches are tiered, and the effect is quite distinctive. Little pruning is required, although the strong canes, which often grow up through the centre of the bush from the base, may either be cut out at an early stage of their development or used for replacement. If the mature branch system is healthy, there seems to be little point in cutting such wood out just to use the younger growths. It is emphasized that the age and condition of the shrub must always be taken into account when deciding whether or not to retain these young central growths. They are essential to the young plant in order that it may gain height and stature. Fewer, if any, of such growths are produced by a mature shrub.

V. farreri has a growth habit which is characteristic of many viburnums. The branching is stool-like, with abundant young wood produced from ground level. They grow to a height of 1.2 to 1.8 m. (4 to 6 ft.) are erect and their general outline, especially with a young plant, is vase-shaped opening out to a rounded head. The oldest branches, if they become too old and weak for good flowering, may be cut out, often at ground level, to make way for younger growths. The lower and shorter branches near the base should be left for furnishing. Rooted branches that have layered naturally may be dug out, for the resultant growth from them produces an untidy, suckerous effect that may be considered out of place in the ornamental parts of the garden. Under more natural conditions this habit may be considered an advantage. When pruning does become necessary, whole branches should be taken, for a general 'tipping' of the bush would produce too formal an effect and might impede subsequent flowering. It should be undertaken immediately after flowering. The same methods may be adopted with many other species and varieties which are similar in growth, even though they may flower in the early to mid summer period. Thus, for pruning purposes, *V. rhytidophyllum* is much the same, for although it is a larger and coarser grower than *V. farreri* and is an evergreen, it will, under a good system of culture, send up plenty of renewal shoots from the base and respond in much the same way.

V. betulifolium is one of the better known fruiting forms. It should be allowed plenty of space and a clear foreground, in order that the heads of flower and the heavy bunches of fruit may be displayed to the full as they bend over under their own weight. When this shrub is really established, the long centrally placed branches may even grow through and onto neighbouring trees and shrubs for support.

V. tinus is a distinctive evergreen with quite a dense habit. This species responds vigorously to hard pruning and will break out freely, even when cut down to the oldest wood near ground level. This treatment is ideal for specimens which have grown too large for their position or which have become old and worn. It should be carried out in late spring. Shrubs that have been injured by a severe winter may be cut back hard in the same way.

V. odoratissimum and *V. o.* var. *awabuki* require the protection of a wall in many parts of the country. Each is better when grown as a standing bush with an odd tie if necessary to keep it close to the wall. *V. atrocyaneum* is also grown against a wall for protection. Pruning consists of cutting out the older wood after flowering, tying in the new growths hard against the surface.

VINCA

V. major is described as a semi-procumbent shrub. The stems are upright at first when they spring from the parent plant. Later they loop over and root at the tips, continually producing new vegetative growing points by this means. Growth quickly becomes matted and forms excellent cover against annual and perennial weeds. Some woody seedlings such as Ash or Elder may become established and an occasional hard cutting back, for example every other year, will enable a good general clean-up to be undertaken. This should be carried out in the spring before new growth commences. When restricting size along an edge, it is better to leave an informal rather than straight-clipped line.

V. minor is a smaller grower with a more prostrate habit which cannot be pruned in the same way. However, the whole area may be cut over to remove unwanted growth and weeds without extensive damage to the Vinca.

VITEX

V. agnus-castus. This shrub is tender and needs the protection of a wall in all but the warmest climates. The terminal inflorescence is produced in the late summer on wood of the current season. Thus it conforms well to annual pruning during early spring. The growths are pruned hard back to within 25 to 50 mm. (1 to 2 in.) of their bases once a general framework has been built up. This framework may be trained fanwise hard up against the surface of the wall

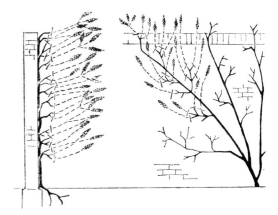

Fig. 50. *Vitex agnus-castus* trained to a wall. The previous year's growth with the old flower heads is pruned back to a spur system which is based on the main framework.

and a system of spurs gradually builds up along the entire length of the branches to give a complete furnishing, see Fig. 50. Occasionally, worn branches may be replaced by the plentiful growths that appear from the base.

Alternatively, the shrub may be trained as a free-growing bush within the shelter of a wall. To begin with, as the shrub builds up, very little pruning is necessary, but in maturity some reduction of the previous year's wood will help to maintain the quality of the growth and flowers. Regular pruning to definite levels and spurs may in time produce a rather unsightly habit. Care must therefore be taken to preserve the natural habit if it is grown as a bush. The free production of young growths from the base and on the branch system should be encouraged, so that older pieces or whole lengths may be cut out entirely on occasion.

V. negundo has a similar habit but is larger.

VITIS

Under the pergola system, some of the stronger vines produce growths that are at least 1.8 m. (6 ft.) in length. The species that are vigorous growers, such as *V. coignetiae*, are thus ideal for climbing over old stumps or even up large trees. In such a situation, after the first pruning that immediately follows planting, little attention is necessary. If pruning is attempted, it must be done very carefully in order to avoid cutting living stems that may appear dead. One mistake of this nature might sever a large portion of the crown.

Vines that are grown in a restricted space may be pruned back each winter to a framework, which is trained to cover a given area of wall or pergola. The pruning should be carried out in early to mid winter, for once they become active there is danger of bleeding from the cut surfaces, which is undesirable. The young wood which has just completed its growth is cut back to one or two buds. This results in the buildup of spurs which are twisted and gnarled and quite attractive. So is the bark which becomes flaked as the age of the rod increases.

Grown over a pergola, the stiffer growths do not hang down so freely as *Ampelopsis* or *Parthenocissus*, but are nevertheless, very attractive. However some stopping may be necessary when they are grown in a restricted space, as the strong shoots, which often grow out extensively become a nuisance. This stopping or summer pruning is carried out in July as the growths begin to ripen on the basal half. The cut is made just above a node at 5 to 6 leaves. Sub-laterals are often quickly produced, but these have a pleasing effect against the older foliage. As an example, the young growths of *V. coignetiae* are greyish-white and make a good contrast to the mature foliage. The shortened growths are cut back hard in the winter, see Fig. 50.

WEIGELA

This genus must not be confused with *Diervilla*, as the habits of growth and flowering and therefore the pruning needs, are quite different. The dozen or so species of *Weigela*, all from East Asia, flower on laterals from the previous year's wood, whereas *Diervilla*, consisting of three species from North America, flowers on the current season's wood.

Weigela species may be pruned, if necessary, after flowering in early to mid summer and in this way the shrub is spared from wasting energy in seed production. Mature bushes which are trained properly with a good balance of old and young wood may need thinning as growth extends and thickens and a proportion of the old wood is cut out often near or at ground level. The rule should be to leave the shrub well furnished and if this is applied, it will not be difficult to decide just where the cuts should be made. Often the branches arch over from the point of flowering and the new canes are produced on the more upright part of the growth below the portion which bends over.

Should a stool be overgrown and weak it may be cut hard back in the spring, for it will regenerate very readily. The crop of shoots that arise is often so thick that it must be thinned. This should be done in early to mid summer, for if it is done too early, secondary growth will develop which will be soft.

It is important to encourage good growth with the coloured forms. *W*. 'Looymansii Aurea' produces the best foliage and stem effects from young wood and therefore a considerable amount of the older wood should be cut out in the late summer. *W.* 'Florida Variegata' should be kept growing freely, although it is more compact in growth than many others. Occasionally a growth of pure green, without any variegation, will break out. This should be removed at an early stage, cutting away a portion of the older wood to which it is attached.

WISTERIA

Essentially all the species and forms have similar requirements and with their natural climbing habit they lend themselves to training over pillars or pergolas, up trees or against walls. They may also be trained in bush form to be grown as lawn specimens.

For pillar, pergola or wall training, the main growths are tied or placed to cover the allotted space. Initially these growths may be trained to approximately 230 mm. (9 in.) apart, but as compound spurs build up under a summer and winter pruning system on the laterals, some thinning may eventually be required. It is desirable to control the growths that are to form the framework in order to prevent them

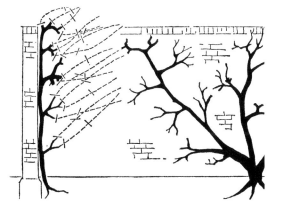

Fig. 51. *Wisteria* trained to a wall. The shrub consists mainly of large branches which are well furnished with a spur system. This is shown in the diagrams but on the left is a sectional drawing with the crop of extension growths which are produced annually. These are shown in broken outline with the positions of the summer and winter pruning.

becoming twisted together, as it is impossible to correct this later.

The lateral growths from the main stems are spur-pruned annually, but in order to promote freer and better flower bud formation, this should be carried out in two stages. First by summer pruning the laterals, which take the form of long, trailing growths, back to 150 mm. (6 in.) in midsummer; and secondly, during early winter or mid winter, to shorten these to two buds. The summer pruning may be carried out in one operation, or extended over a period of several weeks, taking back the growths as they begin to harden and ripen at the base, see Fig. 51.

It will be recognised that this system of pruning is similar to that carried out on cordon apples. In the same way, in addition to maintaining a satisfactory balance of growth and flowers, it does keep the climbers neat and enables one to restrict their size. At the same time it must be borne in mind that a considerable amount of ladder work is involved at least twice a year on a large specimen, which may well be 9 m. (30 ft.) high against the wall of a house.

The fact that it is possible to restrict size with a spur system of pruning without impairing flowering, enables these climbers to be grown as specimens in bush form, as already mentioned. However, the branches, although thickened, are not capable of supporting their own weight and thus, as they radiate out, they should be tied to upright stakes. Under this system they may reach a height of 1.8 to 2.4 m. (6 to 8 ft.). This can be done quite neatly with strong ties that allow for expansion. It should be pointed out that the branching will have a twisted or crooked and almost deformed appearance, but this is a natural habit and no attempt should be made to correct it, so long as the branches generally radiate from the centre. The summer and winter pruning is carried out on this framework in the way described above.

XANTHOCERAS

X. sorbifolium forms either a large shrub or a small tree. In the nursery stage it is encouraged to develop 4 to 6 main branches perhaps on a very short leg of 0.3 m. (1 ft.) or so. With older specimens the extending branches often bend down with their increasing weight, especially in an exposed position. This tendency may be checked if necessary by carefully reducing the weight on the branch ends and by bracing if required, using wire instead of cable, to make it less obvious.

This subject throws young growths very freely from old wood should there be any need for hard pruning. It is, however, a mistake to thin the central growths, as this is a natural habit. Sometimes this shrub is grown on walls where the main branches are secured and the extension wood is tied in each year. The growths coming away from the wall are pruned back in the autumn.

XANTHORHIZA

X. simplicissima, Yellow Root. Although to some extent this low-growing shrub to 1 m. (3 ft.) is an untidy grower, this is a natural habit that cannot be corrected by pruning. It spreads slowly by suckering, while as growth extends on the older branches they are weighed to the ground. No regular pruning is needed.

ZANTHOXYLUM

This is a genus of stoutly branched shrubs or small trees that retain very broad spines on even the oldest wood. Normally they require little pruning, but the crowns often develop considerable quantities of dead wood, as the buildup of extensive growths deprives others of light. This should be cut out in spring and it is worth noting that the dead wood often seems to be prone to Coral Spot (*Nectria cinnabarina*).

The main beauty of these interesting shrubs is in their habit of growth and heavy branching when they reach maturity and they should not be pruned to restrict their size if it can be avoided. The habit of growth does vary with the genus; for example, *Z. americanum* has an upright habit compared with *Z. armatum*, which is weaker in the branching and is inclined to spread along at ground level.

The members of this genus will often respond to hard cutting back by breaking out from the old wood, but it should if possible be avoided.

ZELKOVA

This genus is of great interest to the arboriculturist, as the few species have distinctive and yet contrasting habits of growth and outline. *Z. carpinifolia* forms a head with a large number of ascending branches that originate at one level as soon as laterals develop from the main leader. It is important to train a leader up to form a clear stem of 1.8 to 2.4 m. (6 to 8 ft.) as this enables the trunk and main branching to be seen to the best effect as the tree reaches maturity. Without training, this species will branch low, even at ground level. Should the removal of a limb be needed, it is often difficult to make a clean, final cut owing to the density and positioning of the branches.

Z. serrata forms heavy, spreading but semi-erect branches. The leader should be maintained for as long as possible and a clear trunk of 1.8 to 2.4 m. (6 to 8 ft.) is preferable. The outer branches sweep down nicely to produce graceful branching. *Z. sinica* also has an attractive trunk. *Z. ×verschaffeltii*, a very graceful tree, should have a clear 1.8 m. (6 ft.) trunk. *Z. abelicea* is a shrubby species that is difficult to train into a formal, straight specimen.

No regular pruning is desirable beyond that required for corrective training.

ZENOBIA

Z. pulverulenta. This shrub and the form *nitida* develop into bushy, vigorous shrubs. New extension growths are freely produced each season, both from the base and along the length of many of the branches. The energies may be directed into better and more vigorous growth and thus to give improved flowering during the following season, by pruning as the blossoms fade. The old flowered pieces and small weak branches are then cut off just above suitable growths. Occasionally a whole branch may be cut out completely from ground level. However, care should be taken not to cut away so much that the natural habit is spoilt. The rootstock has a suckering habit.

Should growth be very poor and weak the shrub will respond to most of the old wood being cut out, provided that the roots are encouraged by mulching and the growing conditions improved generally.

Appendix I.

Some Common Names with Their Botanical Equivalents

Acacia, False *Robinia pseudoacacia*

Alder *Alnus*

Alder, Caucasian *Alnus subcordata*

Alder, Common *Alnus glutinosa*

Alder, Green *Alnus viridis*

Alder, Japanese Green *Alnus firma*

Alder, Grey *Alnus incana*

Alder, Italian *Alnus cordata*

Alder, Red *Alnus rubra*

Almond, Common *Prunus amygdalus*

Almond, Dwarf Flowering *Prunus glandulosa*

Almond, Dwarf Russian *Prunus tenella*

Angelica Tree, Chinese *Aralia chinensis*

Apricot *Prunus armeniaca*

Arbor-vitae *Thuja* spp.

Ash, California *Fraxinus dipelta*

Ash, Common *Fraxinus excelsior*

Ash, Manchurian *Fraxinus mandshurica*

Ash, Manna *Fraxinus ornus*

Ash, Mountain *Sorbus aucuparia*

Ash, Red *Fraxinus pennsylvanica*

Ash, White *Fraxinus americana*

Aspen *Populus tremula*

Basswood *Tilia americana*

Beech, American *Fagus grandifolia*

Beech, Antarctic *Nothofagus antarctica*

Beech, Common European *Fagus sylvatica*

Beech, Dawyck *Fagus sylvatica* 'Dawyck'

Beech, Fern-leaf *Fagus sylvatica* Heterophylla Group

Beech, Oriental *Fagus orientalis*

Beech, Purple *Fagus sylvatica* Purpurea Group

Beech, Roble *Nothofagus obliqua*

Beech, Weeping *Fagus sylvatica* 'Pendula'

Big Tree *Sequoiadendron giganteum*

Birch *Betula* spp.

Birch, Himalayan *Betula utilis*

Birch, River *Betula nigra*

Birch, Silver *Betula pendula*

Bitternut *Carya cordiformis*

Blackthorn *Prunus spinosa*

Bladder Nut *Staphylea* spp.

Bladder Senna *Colutea* spp.

Bog Myrtle *Myrica gale*

Boston Ivy *Parthenocissus tricuspidata*

Bottle Brush *Callistemon* spp.

Box, Common *Buxus sempervirens*

Box, Elder *Acer negundo*

Broom, Common European *Cytisus scoparius*

Broom, Montpelier *Genista monspessulana*

Buckeye, Bottlebrush *Aesculus parviflora*

Buckeye, Red *Aesculus pavia*

Buckeye, Sweet *Aesculus flava*

Bullbay *Magnolia grandiflora*

Butterfly Bush *Buddleja davidii*

Butternut *Juglans cinerea*

Buttonbush *Cephalanthus occidentalis*

Buttonwood *Platanus occidentalis*

Californian Lilac *Ceanothus* spp.

California Nutmeg *Torreya californica*

Californian Poppy *Romneya coulteri*

Californian Redwood *Sequoia sempervirens*

Cape Figwort *Phygelius capensis*

Cedar, Atlas *Cedrus atlantica*

Cedar, Cyprian *Cedrus brevifolia*

Cedar, Deodar *Cedrus deodara*

Cedar, Incense *Calocedrus decurrens*

Cedar, Lebanon *Cedrus libani*

Cherry, Bird *Prunus padus*

Cherry, European Wild *Prunus avium*

Cherry, Manchurian *Prunus maackii*

Cherry, Tibetan *Prunus serrula*

Cherry, Japanese *Prunus* cultivars

Chestnut, Golden *Chrysolepis chrysophylla*

Chestnut, American *Castanea dentata*

Chestnut, Chinese *Castanea mollissima*

Chestnut, Spanish *Castanea sativa*

Chestnut, Sweet *Castanea sativa*

Chilean Fire-Bush *Embothrium coccineum*

Chinese Gooseberry *Actinidia deliciosa*

Chinese Persimmon *Diospyros kaki*

Chinquapin *Castanea pumila*

Christ-thorn *Paliurus spina-christi*

Cobnut *Corylus avellana*

Cottonwood *Populus trichocarpa*

Cowberry *Vaccinium vitis-idaea*

Crab, Flowering *Malus* spp.

Cranberry, American *Vaccinium macrocarpon*

Crowberry *Empetrum nigrum*

Currant, Flowering *Ribes sanguineum*

Currant, Buffalo *Ribes odoratum*

Cydonia *Chaenomeles speciosa*

Cypress, Italian *Cupressus sempervirens*

Cypress, Lawson *Chamaecyparis lawsoniana*

Cypress, Leyland ×*Cupressocyparis leylandii*

Cypress, Monterey *Cupressus macrocarpa*

Cypress, Swamp *Taxodium distichum*

Daisy Bush *Olearia phlogopappa*

Date Plum *Diospyros lotus*

Dawn Redwood *Metasequoia glyptostroboides*

Devil's Walking-stick *Aralia spinosa*

Dogwood, Cornelian *Cornus mas*

Dogwood, Mountain *Cornus nuttallii*

Dogwood, Pagoda *Cornus alternifolia*

Dogwood, Red-barked *Cornus alba*

Dogwood, Yellow-barked *Cornus sericea* 'Flaviramea'

Douglas Fir *Pseudotsuga menziesii*

Dove Tree *Davidia involucrata*

Elder *Sambucus* spp.

Elm, Dutch *Ulmus* ×*hollandica* 'Major'

Elm, English *Ulmus procera*

Elm, Smooth-leaved *Ulmus carpinifolia*

Elm, Wych *Ulmus glabra*

Fig *Ficus carica*

Filbert, Purple-leaf *Corylus maxima* 'Purpurea'

Firs, Silver *Abies* spp.

Firethorn *Pyracantha* spp.

Foxglove Tree *Paulownia tomentosa*

Fringe-tree, Chinese *Chionanthus retusus*

Fringe-tree, North American *Chionanthus virginicus*

Goldenrain-tree *Koelreuteria paniculata*

Golden Larch *Pseudolarix amabilis*

Gorse *Ulex* spp.

Hawthorn *Crataegus monogyna*

Hazel, Chinese *Corylus chinensis*

Hazel, Common *Corylus avellana*

Hazel, Turkish *Corylus colurna*

Heath, Besom *Erica scoparia*

Heath, Cornish *Erica vagans*

Heath, Corsican *Erica terminalis*

Heath, Cross-leaved *Erica tetralix*

Heath, Dorset *Erica ciliaris*

Heath, Irish *Daboecia cantabrica*

Heath, Spanish *Erica australis*

Heath, Tree *Erica arborea*

Heather *Calluna vulgaris*

Hemlock, Carolina *Tsuga caroliniana*

Hemlock, Eastern *Tsuga canadensis*

Hemlock, Northern Japanese *Tsuga diversifolia*

Hemlock, Western *Tsuga heterophylla*

Hercules Club *Aralia spinosa*

Hickory, Shagbark *Carya ovata*

Holly, European *Ilex aquifolium*

Honeysuckle *Lonicera periclymenum*

Hop Hornbeam *Ostrya carpinifolia*

Hop Hornbeam, Japanese *Ostrya japonica*

Hop-tree *Ptelea trifoliata*

American Hornbeam *Carpinus caroliniana*

Hornbeam, English *Carpinus betulus*

Horse-chestnut, Common *Aesculus hippocastanum*

Horse-chestnut, Indian *Aesculus indica*

Horse-chestnut, Japanese *Aesculus turbinata*

Horse-chestnut, Pink *Aesculus* ×*carnea*

Indian Bean-tree *Catalpa bignonioides*

Ironwood *Ostrya virginiana*

Ivy, Common *Hedera helix*

Japonica *Chaenomeles speciosa*

Judas-tree *Cercis siliquastrum*

Katsura *Cercidiphyllum japonicum*

Kaya Nut *Torreya nucifera*

Laburnum, Common *Laburnum anagyroides*

Larch, European *Larix decidua*

Larch, Japanese *Larix kaempferi*

Lemon Plant *Aloysia triphylla*

Laurel, Bay *Laurus nobilis*

Laurel, Californian *Umbellularia californica*

Laurel, Cherry *Prunus laurocerasus*

Laurel, Mountain *Kalmia latifolia*

Laurel, Portugal *Prunus lusitanica*

Laurel, Sheep *Kalmia angustifolia*

Laurustinus *Viburnum tinus*

Lavender, Old English *Lavandula angustifolia*

Lilac, Common *Syringa vulgaris*

Lilac, Himalayan *Syringa emodi*

Lime, American *Tilia americana*

Lime, Broad-leaved *Tilia platyphyllos*

Lime, Common *Tilia ×europaea*

Lime, Silver *Tilia tomentosa*

Lime, Small-leaved *Tilia cordata*

Ling *Calluna vulgaris*

Lobster Claw *Clianthus puniceus*

Locust, Caspian *Gleditsia caspica*

Locust, Honey *Gleditsia triacanthos*

Loquat *Eriobotrya japonica*

Maidenhair Tree *Ginkgo biloba*

Maple, Field *Acer campestre*

Maple, Cretan *Acer obtusifolium*

Maple, David's *Acer davidii*

Maple, Italian *Acer opalus*

Maple, Japanese *Acer palmatum*

Maple, Montpelier *Acer monspessulanum*

Maple, Niko *Acer maximowiczii*

Maple, Norway *Acer platanoides*

Maple, Oregon *Acer macrophyllum*

Maple, Paperbark *Acer griseum*

Maple, Silver *Acer saccharinum*

Maple, Sugar *Acer saccharum*

May *Crataegus monogyna*

Medlar *Mespilus germanica*

Mexican Orange Blossom *Choisya ternata*

Mock-Orange *Philadelphus* spp.

Monkey Puzzle *Araucaria araucana*

Moosewood *Acer pensylvanicum*

Mountain Ash *Sorbus aucuparia*

Myrtle, Common *Myrtus communis*

Mulberry, Black *Morus nigra*

Mulberry, White *Morus alba*

Nettle Tree *Celtis* spp.

Oak, Algerian *Quercus canariensis*

Oak, Armenium *Quercus pontica*

Oak, Chestnut-leaved *Quercus castaneifolia*

Oak, Coast Live *Quercus agrifolia*

Oak, Cork *Quercus suber*

Oak, Daimio *Quercus dentata*

Oak, English *Quercus robur*

Oak, Holm *Quercus ilex*

Oak, Hungarian *Quercus frainetto*

Oak, Kermes *Quercus coccifera*

Oak, Lucombe *Quercus ×hispanica* 'Lucombeana'

Oak, Pin *Quercus palustris*

Oak, Pyrenan *Quercus pyrenaica*

Oak, Red *Quercus rubra*

Oak, Sessile *Quercus petraea*

Oak, Turkey *Quercus cerris*

Oak, Willow *Quercus phellos*

Olive *Olea europaea*

Osage Orange *Maclura pomifera*

Osier, Purple *Salix purpurea*

Paper Mulberry *Broussonetia papyrifera*

Passion, Flower (Blue) *Passiflora caerulea*

Peach *Prunus persica*

Pear *Pyrus* spp.

Pecan *Carya illinoinensis*

Periwinkle *Vinca* spp.

Pine, Bhutan *Pinus wallichiana*

Pine, Bishop *Pinus muricata*

Pine, Lacebark *Pinus bungeana*

Pine, Monterey *Pinus radiata*

Pine, Mountain *Pinus mugo*

Pine, Northern Pitch *Pinus rigida*

Pine, Scots *Pinus sylvestris*

Pine, Stone *Pinus pinea*

Pine, Umbrella *Sciadopitys verticillata*

Pistachio, Chinese *Pistacia chinensis*

Plane, American *Platanus occidentalis*

Plane, London *Platanus ×hispanica*

Plane, Oriental *Platanus orientalis*

Plum, Cherry *Prunus cerasifera*

Plum, Garden *Prunus domestica*

Plum, Myrobalan *Prunus cerasifera*

Pomegranate *Punica granatum*

Pocket-handkerchief Tree *Davidia involucrata*

Poison Ivy *Rhus toxicodendron*

Poison Oak *Rhus toxicodendron*

Poplar, Balsam *Populus balsamifera*

Poplar, Black *Populus nigra*

Poplar, Grey *Populus ×canescens*

Poplar, Lombardy *Populus nigra* 'Italica'

Poplar, Ontario *Populus ×jackii*

Poplar, White *Populus alba*

Poplar, Yellow *Liriodendron tulipifera*

Poppy Bush *Dendromecon rigida*

Privet, Common *Ligustrum vulgare*

Privet, Oval-leaved *Ligustrum ovalifolium*

Quick *Crataegus monogyna*

Quince, Common *Cydonia oblonga*

Redbud, Western *Cercis occidentalis*

Redbud, North American *Cercis canadensis*

Rose, Austrian Briar *Rosa foetida*

Rose, Banks *Rosa banksiae*

Rose, Burr *Rosa roxburghii*

Rose, Burnett *Rosa pimpinellifolia*

Rose, Cherokee *Rosa laevigata*

Rose, China *Rosa chinensis*

Rose, Cabbage *Rosa ×centifolia*

Rose, Damask *Rosa ×damascena*

Rose, Dog *Rosa canina*

Rose, French *Rosa gallica*

Rose, Macartney *Rosa bracteata*

Rose, Musk *Rosa moschata*

Rose, Sweet Briar *Rosa rubiginosa*

Rose, Tea *Rosa ×odorata*

Rosemary *Rosmarinus officinalis*

Rowan *Sorbus aucuparia*

Rue *Ruta graveolens*

Sage *Salvia officinalis*

Sea Buckthorn *Hippophae rhamnoides*

Service-tree *Sorbus domestica*

Service-tree (Wild) *Sorbus torminalis*

Silk Vine *Periploca graeca*

Smoke-tree *Cotinus coggygria*

Snowberry *Symphoricarpos* spp.

Snowdrop-tree *Halesia carolina*

Snowy Mespilus *Amelanchier* **spp.**

Sorrel-tree *Oxydendrum arboreum*

Southernwood *Artemisia abrotanum*

Spanish Broom *Spartium junceum*

Spanish Gorse *Genista hispanica*

Spruce *Picea* spp.

Strawberry-tree *Arbutus unedo*

Sumach, Stag's Horn *Rhus typhina*

Sweet Fern *Comptonia peregrina*

Sweet Gale *Myrica gale*

Sweet Pepper Bush *Clethra alnifolia*

Sycamore, European *Acer pseudoplatanus*

Sycamore, American *Platanus occidentalis*

Tree of Heaven *Ailanthus altissima*

Tulepo *Nyssa sylvatica*

Tulip-tree *Liriodendron tulipifera*

Virginia Creeper *Parthenocissus quinquefolia*

Vine *Vitis* spp.

Walnut, Black *Juglans nigra*

Walnut, Common *Juglans regia*

Western Red Cedar *Thuja plicata*

Whitebeam *Sorbus aria*

Willow, Bay *Salix pentandra*

Willow, Crack *Salix fragilis*

Willow, Dragon's Claw *Salix babylonica* 'Tortuosa'

Willow, Goat *Salix caprea*

Willow, Golden *Salix alba* subsp. *vitellina*

Willow, Kilmarnock *Salix caprea* 'Kilmarnock'

Willow, Musk *Salix aegyptiaca*

Willow, Peking *Salix babylonica* var. *pekinensis*

Willow, Violet *Salix daphnoides*

Willow, Weeping *Salix babylonica*

Willow, White *Salix alba*

Wing-nut *Pterocarya* spp.

Winter Sweet *Chimonanthus praecox*

Winter's Bark *Drimys winteri*

Wire-netting Bush *Corokia cotoneaster*

Witch Hazel *Hamamelis* spp.

Witch Hazel, Ozark *Hamamelis vernalis*

Woodbine *Lonicera periclymenum*

Yellow Root *Xanthorhiza simplicissima*

Yellow Wood *Cladrastis* spp.

Yew, Common or English *Taxus baccata*

Appendix II

Tools and Equipment

As explained in the Preface, it is difficult to define the limits which must exist, for the purposes of this book at least, between the operations and work connected with the pruning of trees and shrubs and actual mature tree work, which is mainly concerned with heavier and more specialized equipment as used on large trees and often at considerable heights. The following list is intended to give the reader some idea of the different hand tools and equipment required for these two classes of work, without discussing motorized chainsaws or climbing equipment. No claim is made that it is a complete list, and most people would agree that the choice of tools and equipment is very much a matter of personal preference.

SAWS

Design

A saw should be comfortable to use with a well-shaped, securely fitted handle. These are often made of beech wood, but they are now being replaced, to some extent at least, by plastic with rubber grips that are similar in design or more ergonomic. The blade should be of high quality, hardened, rigid, carbon tool steel, and chrome-plated, so that it will retain an effective sharp cutting edge for a reasonable period without the need for re-sharpening.

Today in the arboricultural industry far too much use is made of the chainsaw for the removal of branches, probably due to commercial pressures and laziness. Untidy cuts tears and frayed ends are often the result of chainsaw misuse, and with the wealth of good quality handsaws specifically designed for tree pruning now readily available at an affordable price, there is no excuse for such shoddy work. It is often quicker to remove an average-sized limb with a sharp handsaw compared to using a weighty chainsaw.

Types of Saws

All the saws mentioned below are extremely sharp, and many accidents are caused by a loose handsaw or a blade cutting through a branch, especially a springy branch, faster than the arborist expects on the pull stroke, thereby catching and cutting the other hand, arm or thigh. Such cuts are often clean but deep, and in awkward places to treat. Care should be taken at all times, and a Kevlar glove should be worn on the free hand whenever these saws are being used. This will not completely prevent a cut but will reduce the amount of damage to tissue should there be a lapse in concentration on the final pull stroke.

Handsaws.   The principle of the saw is that a groove or kerf is made of sufficient width to allow the blade to pass through as the cut is being made. The earlier types of saw had a push cut action based on a flexible blade and teeth; the teeth, which were 'set' or bent alternately to one side or the other to form the groove, were essentially a series of cutting edges which tore at the fibres and other tissues. The broken pieces formed the dust that collected in the gaps between the teeth and was carried to the ends of the groove where it fell away. The width of the groove would vary according to the nature and condition of the wood. Green, soft or wet wood would need a comparatively wide groove, for the teeth would not cut through such material cleanly. Without sufficient width the blade would jam, and if it was then forced through there was a danger of the saw buckling. A good saw blade was tensioned during manufacture and it is for this reason that buckling would be corrected by an expert at an early stage before the tool became completely useless. Once jamming occurred, it was better to make a fresh start with a saw better suited for the purpose, than to push ahead with the risk of this happening again.

Large teeth, fewer in number, were sometimes set wider and they bit more deeply than the saws designed for use on hard and dry wood. With the latter type the teeth were smaller and more numerous but the set, and therefore the groove, was correspondingly smaller. As a guide, the number of teeth to the inch was taken as a measure of their size. Thus a saw with 10 points to 25 mm. (1 in.) had small teeth and produced a fine cut. With a decrease in the number of teeth to the inch they became progressively larger, the set wider, and the cut coarser. A rip saw may have had only 5 teeth to 25 mm. (1 in.). For tree work, the 650 mm. (26 in.) saw with 6 to 7 points to 25 mm. (1 in.) was preferred by many.

Tubular frame saw.   Next followed the popular 21-inch tubular frame saw with replaceable blades. It cut easily and quickly, but being coarse-toothed the finish was rough. There were many uses for this saw, for example cutting up fallen prunings. It had a limited use in actual tree pruning, if desired and where space allowed. The final cut on the main trunk or branch was difficult as the large frame prevented a close cut against the main stem or branch and often the final cut had to be made from below the branch in order to get a close enough cut, especially in tight crotches. After limited use, and usually due to abuse caused by breaking off dead wood with the back of the frame, the frame twisted and the blade tension was lost, which meant that the blade buckled and the cut often strayed, leaving an untidy wound.

Modern hand pruning saws. With this type of saw the blade, which usually varies from 240 to 330 mm. in length, has a pull cut action and can be straight or curved depending on the pruners' preference. Most of the good range saws on the market are very well built, durable, lightweight and very sharp, leaving a high quality finished cut, and the blade can access into most narrow-angled attachment points on the parent branch for the final cut.

The blades come in a variety of tooth patterns depending on the manufacturer. One of the most popular is the 'Fanno' pull cut tooth from the United States. It retains its edge for a good while and can be re-sharpened using a diamond shape file.

The 'Yardvark', manufactured by Oregon, has a blade with a unique tooth that can be re-sharpened easily with a chainsaw file. The cut is coarse, however, making it an ideal saw for larger-diameter work and not so good for diameters of 10 mm. or less.

The most recent introduction and sharpest of the saws is the Japanese tri-edge blade from ARS. This blade has teeth which have three razor-edged facets that cut so smooth, they leave the surface wound as though it were planed. The blades can be straight or curved with a variety of pitches (fine or coarse) suitable for different pruning operations. It is not possible to re-sharpen these, but replacement blades are available from most reputable dealerships.

Most professional makes of saw come with a scabbard or holster made from wood, plastic, leather or plastic-coated canvas, which makes the saw safer and easier to carry whilst working in the crown of a tree or moving between trees on the ground. A good scabbard protects the sharp blade and prevents accidental cuts from a loose flailing blade springing back after being caught on a small twig. Some scabbards come with a secateur pocket attached so that the arborist has quick access to two essential pruning tools by his side. This is an extremely useful accessory when carrying out formative pruning in the arboretum.

There are so many good quality handsaws available today for pruning trees and shrubs that the arborist must select the one that he or she feels most comfortable

Plate 49. A selection of modern pruning saws.

with and is most suited to the task in hand, see Plate 49. It is better to spend more money on a good saw, which if looked after will give many years good service and make light of hard work.

Folding pruning saws.   These are no longer a luxury item and must be a standard part of the pruner's general armory, see Plate 50. There are a variety of makes and models available from the same manufacturers of the modern handsaws, with the same blades and tooth patterns as above. The blades, which range from 16 to 24 cm. in length (the average length being 18 cm.), have a good locking mechanism by means of a locking button or lever on top of the saw which are easy and safe to use. The handles are made from moulded plastic with comfortable rubber grips and a good-sized hole at the back for a lanyard. The 18 cm. models will easily tackle most formative pruning jobs and if they are carried in the pocket can be made available conveniently should the need for branch removal arise.

The only disadvantage of these saws is that the blades are slightly thinner and can snap or buckle if placed under too much stress.

Pole saws.   The pole saw is designed for use on branches that are well out of reach of the ordinary saw and can be used from the ground, from a ladder or steps or whilst climbing in the tree. They can be used for removing hangers caught up as well as cutting living branches and dead wood.

The handle is usually made from lightweight aluminum or fibreglass, and either of a fixed length, added to by screw fixing extra sections, or telescopic. The blades, again made by the same manufacturers of the modern handsaws, are slightly curved between 250 and 350 mm. and should be kept protected by an adequate sheath to maintain the sharpness and prevent any unfortunate accidents. The sharpest and easiest to use are the Japanese tri-edge blades.

There are a number of disadvantages with this type of saw, despite the fact that it is a useful tool. It is important that the operator is aware of these:

Plate 50. An ideal pruning set used by the arborist for formative pruning.

(1) It is difficult to maintain full control of the blade because of the weight and length of the long handle. Care must be taken to make the cut accurate. If used from a ladder or a tree, careful positioning and the use of a safety harness are essential precautions to prevent over-balancing and perhaps a bad fall.

(2) It is not possible to undercut, and thus the branch may rip back from the parent stem if it falls away before the cut is completed. This will not of course happen with dead wood, and indeed this type of saw is often used for this purpose.

(3) Sawdust and the severed branch often fall straight down onto the operator, and in this case the use of a helmet and visor is advisable to prevent injury to the head and eyes.

The use of pole saws should be eliminated and care should be taken when working in close proximity to overhead power lines to avoid risk of electrocution, as the poles are likely to act as good conductors.

With the modern climbing techniques now practiced, most parts of the tree are accessible and the need to use this type of saw on large scale work has been greatly reduced.

Use of the Saw

Some knowledge and skill is required to use a saw properly. With a good saw it is possible to gain a strong but comfortable grip on the well-fashioned handle, whether it be a 'D' handle or pistol type. Most operators prefer to place the index finger so that it rests outside and in line with the blade, claiming that this ensures a stronger and more comfortable grip. The position of the cut is established by opening a small groove with a few pull strokes of the saw. It is also helpful to use the thumb of the free hand against the blade as a guide for accurate position.

When about to make a cut it is important to take up a good comfortable position, and it may be necessary to use a pair of steps or a ladder and safety harness for this. Also, when a large branch is being sawn it is often advisable to consider a means of retreat should the sawn end split and spring up suddenly toward the operator. This is important even when working on the ground, which should be clear of all obstacles. In all pruning one should always guard against the unexpected. Wind direction also needs consideration, for even a small piece of sawdust in the eye can be very painful and cause injury. Sometimes, especially when cutting wood of a toxic nature like *Rhus* spp., a pair of goggles is essential for protection.

Once the cut is under way, the strokes should settle into a rhythmic action, using the full length of the blade and working from the elbow without bending the wrist. Actual pressure is not needed, only the muscle speed to pull the saw through the cut. Let the saw do the work!

In tree work, it is wrong to change the angle of the blade frequently or to travel round the circumference of the stem or branch for ease of cutting. The temptation to do this is greater with a poor saw. A change of angle also presents an abrupt corner, and until this has worn down a greater strain is put on the edge to the teeth. There is also a danger of the cut closing, thus squeezing the blade, causing buckling. Conifer wood, for example Larch, is very resinous, and this may impede the free passage of the blade, thus making the work difficult. In these circumstances it is an advantage to oil the blade frequently with a solvent, at the same time using a cloth to produce a polished surface.

CUTTING TOOLS

Secateurs, or Hand Pruners

This tool has been developed quite extensively within recent years with the result that the more advanced types and patterns are precision-made, with bearings that enable the scientifically designed cutters to make a nearly perfect severance. With most of the modern ones, all parts are replaceable, see Plate 51.

Many of the older models were of the 'parrot' type, with two curved cutting blades of strong metal and, provided they were used properly without being strained, they lasted for a very long time. Two types of secateur are used today, the anvil type and the bypass type, the latter being by far the superior. Anvil secateurs work on the principle of a sharp cutting flat blade pressing onto an anvil or bed. The problem that occurs with this type is that the branch being cut is more often than not crushed between the two, bruising the live tissue left intact rather than leaving a clear cut; and with the greater need for force to completely sever the tissue, the handles are twisted out of alignment. With the bypass type a sharp curved blade bypasses a curved cutting plate and cleanly severs the branch without much cutting effort. The world's most popular bypass secateur today is the Swiss-made Felco No. 2. These are designed

Plate 51. A selection of long-handled pruners and secateurs.

for the right-handed operator; Felco No. 9 are for the lefthander.

It is important that the blade should be properly sharpened and the tool well maintained; when the blade is past resharpening a new replacement should be fitted. Regular cleaning with a solvent or WD-40 will remove the buildup of gums and resins following pruning and a light oiling will prevent rusting and sticking.

A good pair of secateurs is comfortable to hold and use. It is essential, therefore, that the handles should be well shaped, and controlled by a spring mechanism which is only sufficiently strong to open the secateurs once the cut has been completed. A spring which is stronger than necessary places a greater strain on the hands and may cause blistering. One pattern is produced with a cylindrical handle which turns with the fingers as the handles are opened and closed, thus reducing friction and the chance of blistering when carrying out lots of secateur work.

The need for good maintenance has already been mentioned. It is very necessary, for a blunt tool in poor condition will produce inferior cuts that may be jagged or split, often with torn or damaged bark. At best, the healing will be slow, while the danger of dead and diseased snags is increased. At the same time it must be remembered that the mechanism will be strained by forcing a blunt cutter through the wood and thus the performance will deteriorate still further.

Even a good sharp pair of secateurs can quite easily be misused and spoilt. For example, the blade, or blades, should be taken straight through the wood. By twisting the tool the blades are often strained. It is also wrong to cut through too large a piece, for the cut is likely to be a poor and jagged one with extensive bark injury, while the tool itself may be damaged, never to cut properly again. For safety, when the tool is not in use, the catch to hold the cutters in a closed position should be sound and trustworthy, otherwise an accident is likely to occur. A badly worn blade may not close properly and with a sharp exposed edge it may be dangerous even when not in use.

Pole Pruners

This tool is used for pruning smaller branches that are out of reach of the secateurs, either from the ground or from a pair of steps or a ladder.

The cutting unit consists of a swiveling blade that turns in a half circle onto the anvil or bypass through the operation of a lever at the lower end of the handle or arm. The lever and blade are connected by a stout wire or nylon cord that runs through eyeholes positioned at intervals along the arm. When closed, the blade is positioned between the two flat plates that form the hook-shaped anvil. A spring is often fitted to the lever so that the blade is pulled back into position for the next cut. This description applies to the standard tool, but from time to time various manufacturers produce modified versions. One pattern has a light alloy tubular handle that can be extended or even fitted with a saw blade instead of a pruner if required. The ARS telescopic pole pruner works on a trigger action and has a grip that holds the cut piece following severance to prevent it falling to the ground; it is ideal for collecting fruit or propagation material. The general principles of their use and movement, however, remain the same.

The tool is used quite simply by hooking the anvil over the branch, which is then cut off by operating the lever. Although the diameter of the branch that may be removed is limited by the size of the hook, some discretion is necessary in order to avoid making poor cuts and perhaps straining the tool. There is also the danger that if the blade jams in the cut an attempt to free this by reversing the lever may strain the wire.

It is important to position the tool carefully and hold it firmly each time a cut is made, but one of the greatest disadvantages of this tool is that the cut is made a considerable distance from the operator. Accuracy must therefore be sacrificed, and in this respect it is inferior to the secateurs. However, the disadvantages related to a poor cut and a possible snag are not so serious on a rapidly growing limb or trunk. One good use for this tool is on small dead twig growth which is often found at the extremities of a mass of dense branching, as for example on the Holm Oak.

Maintenance.   It is important to keep the tool in good condition, with the blade clean and well sharpened. The blade and lever should move freely and close properly, and be strongly and securely attached, while the gap in the anvil or the blade in bypass types should be kept clear of wood pieces, etc. The attachment wire and handle should also be inspected periodically to ensure that they are working correctly.

Parrot Bills, Long-handled Pruners, or Lopping Shears

There are various patterns, but in principle they are much stronger than hand secateurs and are thus suitable for tougher work and for cutting through large branches. The long handles ensure a good leverage or purchase but, in addition, the cut can be made well inside a bush at some distance from the operator. This is an advantage in cases of congested or thorny growth such as one gets with *Berberis* or *Rosa*. It is not a tool to use where accuracy and neatness are required, or where the cut is accessible and of a suitable size for secateurs. Many uses, however, can be found for it in clearing operations and for rough pruning prior to cleanly finishing off or felling. Unfortunately this type of pruning shear is often used to deliver the final cut to a branch too large in diameter to cut cleanly, where a saw would be the better tool to use. As a rule of thumb for final cuts, if the secateurs cannot cope with the branch diameter, then the handsaw should be used.

The cutting actions are the same as for the secateurs, with a longer pair of handles made from wood, steel or aluminum; the handles are of a fixed length, varying between 40 cm. and 90 cm., and sometimes telescopic.

Pruning Knife

There is considerable variation in the quality of knives, of which there are many types and patterns. Here are some of the more essential points.

The handle should be substantial and properly shaped to enable a good grip to be gained. This is most necessary when comparatively large pieces are to be cut, for example, when snagging (the removal of the snag end that is left above the union after budding).

Fig. 52. The 'Tina' 635 in use for snagging. This model has a strong curved blade and a comfortable handle that makes it an ideal tool for nursery work.

(Drawn from an illustration in the 'Tina' catalogue.)

The blade should be of hardened steel which is likely to retain a good edge, during use. Inferior blades can be sharpened up very speedily, but they will not retain a cutting edge for long. The shape of the blade is largely a matter of taste but the curved pattern is generally preferred for pruning for this facilitates a more extensive penetration as the cutting edge passes through the tissues. The point of attachment to the handle should be strong and secure, and without rock. The spring action must hold the blade securely in the open or closed position. A knife with a blade that turns back or closes too freely will be dangerous to use or to carry about.

One of the main uses is for paring the surface edges of saw cuts and other wounds in order to leave them smooth, thus facilitating healing. However, the knife is commonly used for pruning, especially on young trees under training, for in the hands of a skilled person the cut may often be positioned accurately with an absence of bruising. The operation of snagging has already been mentioned and this must be carried out neatly and accurately, otherwise an unsightly union may result which would be evident for many years, possibly for the life of the tree, see Fig. 52.

A comparison is often made between the cut made by a pair of secateurs and that made with a pruning knife; indeed, this is a point of great argument among gardeners of all classes. The case put forward for the secateurs is that the cut may be made easily even by an amateur and that the exposed surface is small. The knife cannot cut straight across the stem, but the increase in area that is exposed is negligible while in the hands of a skilled person no bruising occurs. Also a greater area of cambium is exposed for quick healing, see Fig. 53.

It is largely a matter of practice, for the efficient use of the knife requires considerable skill and unless care is taken serious injury from deep cuts may be caused to the hands and arms. On these grounds alone, it is advisable for the majority to use a good pair of secateurs. It should be noted, however, that the knife is one of the best tools to use for pruning *Cytisus* or *Spartium*, where the method is to cut a collection of growths which have been bundled together with the free hand. The severance of the shoots individually would be very time-consuming.

Fig. 53. This set of diagrams shows how a branch of
some thickness can if necessary be cut off flush with a
suitable and sharp knife.

(1) The main part of the branch is removed by making
wedge-shaped cuts that are enlarged until the portion
is severed, leaving a short stub as in (2).

(3) and (4) show how shavings are removed until only
a thin portion is left.

(5) Lastly, a downward cut is made in the direction of
the arrow.

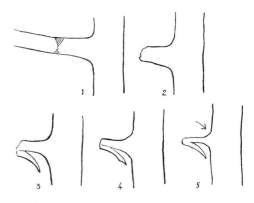

LADDERS AND STEPS

In the interests of efficiency and safety it is important to use only the best models.
A careful selection is also necessary for there are various patterns and lengths,
each being suited to a particular use and purpose.

A good ladder made by a reliable firm will have been manufactured according to
specifications laid down by the British Standard Institution. Two publications that
will be of interest to the arboriculturist are 'Portable Aluminum Ladders, Steps,
Trestles and Lightweight Staging' (B.S. 2037:1994) and 'Steps and Ladders'
(ANSI A14.1 and A14.2).

The arborist would do well to read through these publications so that they may
realize the amount of skill, thought and care which has been put into the subject,
and into the manufacture of the ladders and steps which they can purchase.

Three materials are in common use:

Timber

Wooden ladders are made from timber which is selected for weight and strength,
though these are not often used today by the arborist due to the heavy weight and
maintenance needed when not in use, as they weather and deteriorate if they are
not protected. One advantage with these is that the sag is less pronounced than
with most of the metal types, and there is less tendency for them to spring up and
down when in use. They should definitely be used in preference to metal ladders
if work is to be carried out near high-powered electrical installations.

Aluminum

Ladders made from this material are comparatively light in weight, do not deteriorate with age or rust and are corrosion resistant. As they are easy to position

Plate 52. An articulated ladder folded.

and move from tree to tree because of their light nature, they are the most used ladder material today in the industry.

Aluminum ladders are naturally good conductors of electricity and they should not be used in proximity to any electric cables.

Fibreglass

Fibreglass ladders are another alternative to aluminum as a non-conductor of electricity. They are harder to come by and therefore less used than aluminum in arboriculture.

The main types of ladders and steps may be classified as follows:

Extension Ladders

This is made up of two or three sections which, by a sliding action, may be adjusted to give varying heights. On the longer sectional ladders this action is operated by a rope and pulley system. With some patterns it is possible to use the sections individually as a single stage ladder.

Stepladders

These vary considerably in design but the back or legs are hinged and when opened out the steps are self-supporting. Patterns are also available with ladders on both sides and some which have a hinged platform at the top that rests in a horizontal position when the legs are open. Stepladders tend to be unstable on unlevel ground and their safe use is very limited.

Tripod Ladders

One set of steps with a single hinged leg as a support makes this type of ladder more stable in the field than stepladders; they are preferred by many to conventional ladders.

Articulated Ladders

These have about four sets of hinged steps that can be configured to any suitable combination for the task at hand, see Plates 52 and 53. There are about eight permutations from ordinary stepladders to a full-length ladder, but the convenience is that they fold up very small and can be easily transported to and from a job in the boot of a car and stored in a small shed.

Ladder Stabilizers

Ladder stabilizers are a useful means of converting an ordinary ladder into a form of freestanding stepladder and ensure a safe supporting system when working on slippery or uneven surfaces. They prevent ladders from slipping or toppling sideways and are extremely useful for trimming hedges.

Inspection and Maintenance of Ladders

Both ladders and steps must be kept in a perfect state of repair, and thus regular inspections are necessary to ensure that no fault has passed unnoticed. Accidents frequently occur through the use of ladders which are defective either from lack of maintenance or because they are beyond repair. Once a defect is discovered, even though it is a minor one, it

Plate 53. An articulated ladder in use.

should be repaired as soon as possible by an expert or scrapped. In a large establishment it is wise to have at least one spare of each pattern to allow for repairs without disruption of work.

The frequency of these inspections depends upon the amount of use the ladders are put to. If they are in use every day inspections should be on a weekly basis. The main points to look for are as follows:

(1) Check to see that the stiles are secure and cannot be pulled or pushed out of position. The wooden ladder of good quality is fitted with metal tie rods, or the rungs are arranged in such a way that the whole unit is rigid. (The stiles are the sides to which the rungs are attached).

(2) With timber ladders, the grain should run lengthways which makes a split less likely. A close inspection should be made to ensure that there are no cracks or splits present.

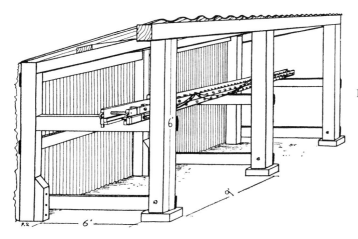

Fig. 54. The best method of ladder storage.

(3) Test the firmness of each rung in turn to ensure that there is no movement. It is important that there are no missing rungs and that with aluminum they are not bent or crushed.

(4) The ropes on extension ladders should be replaced at regular intervals.

(5) The working parts should move freely and they must, if necessary be oiled. The guide brackets and stops must be firmly secured.

(6) In the case of stepladders, the back should be securely fixed with hinges that function properly and are sufficiently strong. The extent to which the legs open should be limited to prevent them from spreading and causing the whole to collapse.

(7) Ladders or steps that have been accidentally dropped or hit in any way, perhaps by a falling limb, should be inspected immediately. Should there be any damage it must be repaired before they are used again, or scrapped.

In connection with safety, it should be remembered that regulations have been made under the Provision and Use of Work Equipment Regulations 1998 (PUWER 98). These regulations apply to all workplaces and situations where the Health and Safety at Work Act 1974 applies and are intended to ensure that work equipment does not result in an accident regardless of its age, condition or origin. Ladders are classed as workplace equipment and are covered by these regulations and both employers and workers have responsibilities. Faulty ladders must not be used.

Storage When Not in Use

The best method is to lay the ladders horizontally across bars 100 × 100 mm. (4 × 4 in.) placed at a true level and no more than 3 m. (10 ft.) apart. These should be under cover, see Fig. 54. It is better to use this method of storage than to hang them on pegs which are sometimes fixed to a wall for this purpose. With the latter method the stiles are strained and the rungs loosened. It is wrong to lean a ladder against a wall for storage, as other articles may in turn be laid or piled against it, and the extra weight may cause sagging which in time could cause weakening or straining of the stiles.

It is a good plan to secure ladders and steps with a padlock as a safeguard against use by unauthorized persons.

Safety Precautions

An erected ladder should not be left unattended unless precautions are taken to see that it is not interfered with in any way. A wide plank, at least 3.6 m. (12 ft.) in length, laid flat on the rungs is an effective and useful deterrent to the would-be unlawful climber. It should be chained and locked in position and the top of the ladder must always be tied to prevent dislodgment. However, it is much safer to take a ladder down completely, if it is to be left unattended for any length of time.

Glossary

Some of the less common botanical and technical terms.

ANSI

American National Standards Institute.

ARBORICULTURE

The selection, production, planting, maintenance and removal of all woody plants for amenity purposes.

ARBORIST

An individual engaged in the profession of arboriculture who, through experience, education and related training, possesses the competence to provide for or supervise the management of trees and other woody plants.

ARISINGS

The green waste material produced from a pruning operation.

AUXIN

Plant growth substance that regulates various aspects of root, shoot growth and other physiological processes.

BASAL TRUNK FLARE

The flare of the trunk at ground level, the beginnings of buttressing. Resulting from the perfect planting depth and the natural flexing and shaking of the stem.

BIGENERIC HYBRID

A sexual hybrid between two species of different genera. The name is preceded by the sign ×. For example, ×*Mahoberberis aquisargentii* is a hybrid between *Mahonia aquifolium* and *Berberis candidula*.

BOLE

Trunk of a tree.

BRANCH BARK RIDGE

Area of a tree's crotch where the growth and development of the two adjoining limbs pushes the bark into a ridge.

BRANCH COLLAR

Area where a branch joins another branch or the trunk. This is created by the respective overlapping of xylem cells.

BSI

British Standards Institute.

CALLUS TISSUE

Protective, undifferentiated growth of cells at the edges of wounded areas on trees.

CAVITY

A hole in the trunk or scaffold branches of a tree caused by the loss of a limb or some other form of structural damage.

CHIMAERA

A plant which is made up of two tissues growing together but remaining distinct. They may occur as graft hybrids or as the result of bud mutations.

CLONE

A plant that has been propagated vegetatively and not by normal sexual reproduction. This method is used for many cultivars in order to perpetuate some desirable characteristic.

CODIT

Compartmentalization of decay in trees. A model that shows the formation of the reaction zone proposed by Dr. Alex Shigo.

CODOMINANT STEMS

Forked branches of the same diameter.

CONSERVATION AREA (CA)

A protection order that allows a local planning authority 6 weeks to place a TPO on a tree.

CONSERVATION DEAD WOODING

The removal of loose pieces of dead wood, by kicking with the foot, or by cutting large pieces and breaking the rest off, leaving a peg of dead wood attached to the parent branch or trunk.

COPPICE

Certain trees such as *Castanea sativa*, Sweet Chestnut, and *Corylus avellana*, Hazel, are grown for the production of brushwood and stakes for various purposes. As the crop is collected they are cut down to within 0.3 m. (1 ft.) or so of ground level, a process which is repeated at intervals of 5 to 7 years. Such a planting is referred to as a coppice.

CROWN

The head of the tree that is made up of the main scaffold and branches.

CROWN CLEANING OUT

The removal of dead, diseased and dangerous wood from the crown of a tree.

CROWN REDUCTION

The overall reduction in the height and spread of a tree's crown by pruning branches back to a growing point.

CROWN RENOVATION, CROWN RENEWAL

The selective thinning of regrowth from pollards or cuts from hard crown reduction, retaining the dominant and stronger attachments to regenerate a new crown.

CROWN THINNING

The reduction in the density of foliage in the crown of a tree, by selective removal of unwanted branches inside the crown from the trunk to the dripline.

CULTIVAR

The term now officially recognised to distinguish a cultivated form from a botanical variety. Cultivars are distinguished in this book by using capitals for the initial letters of their distinctive names and by putting these names in single inverted commas, e.g. *Euonymus fortunei* 'Silver Queen'.

DEAD WOOD

Wood that no longer contains any living cells, serving no further purpose for the tree.

DECUMBENT

A prostrate or semi-prostrate growth, the ends of the shoots being turned up to a vertical position.

DECURRENT

Rounded growth habit of a tree.

DIOECIOUS

The male and female flowers occur on different plants.

DRIPLINE

The outer edge of the tree's canopy.

EPICORMIC SHOOT

A shoot system growing on a mature portion of the main stem, trunk or branch. Often these shoots are in clusters in the region of wounds or burrs, having originated from adventitious shoots or dormant buds.

EXCURRENT

Pyramidal growth habit of a tree, i.e. one with a central leading shoot.

FASTIGIATE

A variety or form with erect and often clustered growths.

FEATHERED MAIDEN

A one-year-old tree that has developed lateral shoots or feathers.

FLEECE

A fine geotextile material used as a form of protection from frost or winter cold on tender subjects.

FLUSH CUTTING

The complete removal of a limb to a parent branch or trunk, cutting as close to the origin as possible and removing the branch collar and branch bark ridge. Bad practice today.

FRUCTIFICATION

A fungal fruiting body.

GRAFT HYBRID

A plant made up of two distinct tissues. The plant must be propagated vegetatively, having originated in the first place from a graft union made up of stock and scion tissues, e.g. +*Laburnocytisus* 'Adamii' (*Laburnum anagyroides* + *Chamaecytisus purpureus*).

HANGERS

An arborist's term for cut branches left hanging in the tree after a pruning operation.

HONEYDEW

The sugary deposits from aphids after feeding on succulent foliage, e.g. *Tilia* spp.

HYBRID

Generally taken to refer to a sexual hybrid or cross between two species in the same genus, e.g. *Berberis* ×*stenophylla*, a hybrid between *B. darwinii* and *B. empetrifolia*.

INCLUDED BARK

Bark that is pushed inside a developing crotch, causing a weakened structure.

INFLORESCENCE

The flowering portion.

INTERNODES

The section of stem between two nodes.

KNUCKLES AND KNOBS

These are the swollen growths due to continued callus production following the annual removal of suckers from old pruning wounds on the ends of limbs. Usually associated with pollarding.

LACINIATE

A leaf that is fragmented or cut into narrow and often pointed lobes.

LATERALS

Distinct from the leading shoot, these are the side growths that develop at an angle from the main axis. As growth extends each lateral often produces a complex branch system, but the leading shoot(s) on these should not be as vigorous as the main leader.

LEADER, LEADING SHOOT

Generally the topmost growth on the framework of a young or mature tree. It should be the dominant growth and thus stronger than the remainder. One or more leading shoots may also be found on the laterals.

LEG

A clear length of main stem or trunk on a tree or a shrub before branching begins.

LIGNO-TUBER

A woody, swollen tuberous root from which growth emerges.

LION'S TAILING

Poor practice of thinning shoots along branches, leaving a clump of vegetation at the branch end.

LOCAL PLANNING AUTHORITY (LPA)

Department of local government with the statutory powers to protect trees.

LORETTE PRUNING

Method of summer pruning apples and pears to encourage fruiting growth and restrict vegetative growth.

MAX-TAPENER

A specialist tool used to fasten young stems securely to a cane in the nursery.

MERISTEMATIC CELLS

These make up a tissue that increases rapidly by cell division, provided that conditions are suitable. The cambium that develops as a healing tissue in the region of wounds is largely made up of meristematic cells.

MONOECIOUS

The flowers are either male or female with both types occurring on the same plant.

MONOLITH

A dead tree left standing and managed for the conservation of biodiversity.

MULCH

An organic or artificial material applied to the soil surface to suppress weeds and conserve moisture.

MULTI-STEMMED

Tree or shrub with several main stems arising from the ground or on a short stem.

NOTCHING

The removal of a wedge-shaped piece above a dormant bud in order to stimulate it to grow.

NICKING

The cutting of a small nick directly below a dormant bud to inhibit the bud development.

PETIOLE

A leaf stalk.

PHOTOTROPISM

Response in which the direction of light influences the angle of a tree's growth.

POLLARDING

A type of annual pruning carried out on trees from an early age to produce young stems from callused knuckles or knobs on an established framework of scaffolds for ornamental interest.

PROCUMBENT

Growth on or very close to the soil surface.

PROSTRATE

A plant with stems growing across the ground.

REACTION ZONE

Area of wood that reacts and actively resists the growth and spread of microorganisms.

SAPROXYLIC

Organisms that are dependent on dead or dying wood as part of their life cycle.

SCAFFOLD BRANCHES

The major framework branches growing from the trunk on a tree.

SCANDENT

A plant, generally woody, which gains height by the production of long growths that clamber over the host plants. Often they are held in position by recurved thorns.

SEISMOMORPHOGENESIS

Response in which the flexing and shaking of a tree's stem by the wind increases the speed of incremental growth of stem diameter.

SNAGGING

The removal of stubs or frayed ends left behind after bad pruning.

SPUR

A slow-growing and usually dwarf shoot system with rosettes of leaves. Frequently this type of growth is specialized for flowering and fruiting.

STAG-HEADED

The appearance of a tree following the dieback of the crown. Its name is derived from the similarity of the dead branches to a pair of deer's antlers.

STOLONIFEROUS

A plant with a creeping stem system developing at or just beneath ground level, from which vertical growths develop to give height.

STOOL

A plant with many shoots which originate at or just beneath the soil surface. Often new cane-like growths are produced annually.

STRATIFICATION

Certain seeds will not germinate immediately upon sowing and require a period of rest before germination. One method of ensuring that the seed is given ideal conditions during this period is to place the required number in single layers alternating with peat or sand. This practice is referred to as stratification.

SUBSHRUB

A plant that produces soft wood which is often lost completely during the winter. Such plants generally survive by the production of new growths from the older wood at the base.

TARGET PRUNING

The final pruning position to the outside of the branch collar and branch bark ridge. The opposite of flush cutting, and the correct form of pruning.

TOPPING

The indiscriminate cutting back of the major scaffold to stubs or lateral branches that are not large enough to assume the terminal role.

TREE PRESERVATION ORDER (TPO)

An order made by a local planning authority to protect amenity trees and woodland.

WOUND SEALANTS

A protective paint applied to pruning wounds.

Index